ADVANCES IN ECONOMETRICS

Volume 2 • 1983

EXACT DISTRIBUTION ANALYSIS IN LINEAR SIMULTANEOUS EQUATION MODELS

ADVANCES IN ECONOMETRICS

A Research Annual

EXACT DISTRIBUTION ANALYSIS IN LINEAR SIMULTANEOUS EQUATION MODELS

Editors: R. L. BASMANN
Department of Economics
Texas A & M University

GEORGE F. RHODES, JR.
Department of Economics
Colorado State University

VOLUME 2 • 1983

JAI PRESS INC.
Greenwich, Connecticut *London, England*

36 Sherwood Place
Greenwich, Connecticut 06830

JAI PRESS INC.
3 Henrietta Street
London WC2E 8LU
England

ISBN: 0-89232-183-0

Manufactured in the United States of America

CONTENTS

LIST OF CONTRIBUTORS

R. L. Basmann — Department of Economics, Texas A & M University

Anil K. Bhargava — Department of Economics, Northern Illinois University

Parthasaradhi Mallela — Department of Economics, Northern Illinois University

Roberto S. Mariano — Department of Economics, University of Pennsylvania

P. C. B. Phillips — Cowles Foundation, Yale University

John G. Ramage — Bell Laboratories, New Jersey

George F. Rhodes, Jr. — Department of Economics, Colorado State University

D. H. Richardson — Department of Economics, St. Lawrence University

R. J. Rohr — Department of Economics, Brown University

M. Daniel Westbrook — Department of Economics, Georgetown University

FOREWORD

Econometric statistics proper is a special branch of multivariate statistical analysis, cf Anderson (1958) p. 331. It deals with proposed solutions of a group of special problems, technical puzzles, and—unavoidably—with clarifications of conundrums, misunderstandings, and even superstitions, that arise in the use of the *multivariate general linear hypothesis* to represent an economic system in *general equilibrium,* (static or dynamic), cf Basmann (1963) pp. 949–952; (1965) pp. 1080–1083. More precisely econometric statistics deals with special consequences of representing equilibrium magnitudes of economic variables (such as quantities exchanged and market-clearing prices in multiple-market equilibrium) as the dependent variables in multivariate general linear hypotheses exemplified by the following:

$$Q = tr(Y - Z\Pi)\Sigma^{-1}(Y - Z\Pi)'$$

$$\phi(Y; Z\Pi, \Sigma) = (2\pi)^{-NG/2}|\Sigma^{-1}|^{N/2}e^{-1/2Q}$$

$$\langle y_{t1}, \ldots, y_{1G}\rangle \varepsilon R^{G}. \qquad (1a\text{–}c)$$

Y designates an $N \times G$ real sample matrix of explicitly characterized random variables y_{th}; Z designates an $N \times K$ real matrix of nonrandom variables, z_{tk}; Π is a $K \times G$ real matrix, and Σ is a $G \times G$ real positive definite matrix. Multivariate statistical analysis is concerned with the testing of null hypotheses about submatrices of Π and Σ and with the distributional properties of statistical estimators of those matrices. Econometric statistics is concerned with the special properties of such tests of hypotheses and estimators which are special consequences of the fact that matrices Π and Σ are not "permanent" or structural economic parameters, and cannot be treated as such as in multivariate analysis generally. Π and Σ are "temporary" economic parameters in the sense that they have existence only as long as the hypothetical general economic equilibrium represented by (1a–c) exists. For the representation of general economic equilibrium systems such as multiple markets, the general linear hypothesis takes the form

$$Q = tr(YB + Z\Gamma)\Omega^{-1}(YB + Z\Gamma)'$$
$$\phi(Y; Z\Pi, \Sigma) = (2\pi)^{-NG/2}|\Omega^{-1}|^{N/2}e^{-1/2Q}$$
$$\langle y_{t1}, \ldots , y_{tG}\rangle \varepsilon R^{G}. \qquad (2a\text{–}c)$$

When the general equilibrium hypothesis is adequately specified (a task for economists), the representations (2a–c) and (1a–c) are deductively equivalent. It is natural, however, for economists to be primarily concerned with estimates of the structural matrices B, Γ, Ω, and with tests of subject matter null hypotheses about submatrices of these structural matrices. The special field of econometric statistics evolved in response to that demand. But as we said at the outset it has evolved in several different directions. Those directions have their respective origins in different value judgments concerning the deductive implications of economic general equilibrium theory for elements of the structural matrix B. Reference to the B matrix implied by a simple two-commodity market equilibrium suffices to make this clear. There are four endogenous variables, namely, market exchange quantities y_{t1}, y_{t2} of two goods, and their respective market equilibrium prices y_{t3} and y_{t4}; there are two demand functions and two supply functions to form the four equations in (2a–c). General equilibrium theory calls for the following specification of the nonsingular B matrix:

$$B = \begin{bmatrix} -1 & 0 & \beta_{13} & \beta_{14} \\ -1 & 0 & \beta_{23} & \beta_{24} \\ 0 & -1 & \beta_{33} & \beta_{34} \\ 0 & -1 & \beta_{43} & \beta_{44} \end{bmatrix} \qquad (3)$$

The first and third rows of (3) contain parameters of the respective demand functions, the second and fourth rows contain parameters of the respective supply functions. The numerical values in the first two columns are consequences of definitions in economic theory. Referring to (3) we can describe the three main approaches to econometric statistics and their motivations very succinctly:

(A) The general approach of Theil, Basmann, Zellner, and many others since, has been to take the deductive implications of economic theory as given, and to extend the *classical methods of linear estimation* and hypothesis testing, satisfying consistence and meeting theoretical and practical criteria of classical statistical inference as far as possible.

(B) The economic structural definitions incorporated in the first two columns of the matrix B create some difficulties for application of the *maximum-likelihood principle* of estimation. A group of statisticians and econometricians associated with T. W. Anderson and L. R. Klein take the position that the deductive implications of *definitions in economic theory* can be ignored when maximum-likelihood estimates of structural coefficients turn out to be inconsistent with them *i.e.*, in a nutshell, "Normalization is arbitrary." H. Wold, long at odds with others in this group, goes much further in advocating a reformation of general equilibrium theory in economics in order to preserve the simplicity of maximum-likelihood methods of estimation. Wold calls for limitation of maintained economic hypotheses to those for which Ω is diagonal and B is recursive.

(C) Finally there is a rather heterogeneous group of econometricians who question the practical need for either the extensions of classical linear estimation or maximum-likelihood estimation. This group seeks to know just how much imprecision actually is suffered if *ordinary least squares* methods of estimation are applied to structural economic equations directly.

Each of the three approaches has its merits and demerits, of course. The papers in this Volume together include original and positive contributions to econometric statistics from each of the three approaches just described.

R. L. Basmann
George F. Rhodes, Jr.
Series Editors

REFERENCES

Anderson, T. W., *An Introduction to Multivariate Statistical Analysis*. New York: John Wiley and Sons, 1958.

Basmann, R. L., "Remarks Concerning the Application of Finite Sample Distributions of

GCL Estimators in Structural Economic Inference," *Journal of the American Statistical Association,* Vol. 58 (1963) pp. 943–976.

Basmann, R. L., "A Note on the Statistical Testability of 'Explicit Causal Chains' against the Class of 'Interdependent Models'," *Journal of the American Statistical Association,* Vol. 60 (1965) pp. 1080–1093.

MARGINAL DENSITIES OF INSTRUMENTAL VARIABLE ESTIMATORS IN THE GENERAL SINGLE EQUATION CASE

P. C. B. Phillips

ABSTRACT

A method of extracting marginal density approximations using the multivariate version of the Laplace formula is given and applied to instrumental variable estimators. Some leading exact distributions are derived for the general single equation case which lead to computable formulae and generalize all known results for marginal densities. These results are related to earlier work by Basmann (1963), Kabe (1964), and Phillips (1980b). Some general issues bearing on the current development of small-sample theory and its application in empirical work are discussed in the introduction to the article.

Advances in Econometrics, Volume 2, pages 1–24

ISBN: 0-89232-183-0

I. INTRODUCTION

The general problem of extracting finite sample distributions in econometrics has attracted attention since the early 1960s. One reason for the interest has been the widely acknowledged shortage of results in the area and the heavy reliance empirical investigators have, therefore, reluctantly had to place on asymptotic distribution theory in estimation and inference. That such a heavy reliance on asymptotic theory can lead to serious problems of bias and low levels of inferential accuracy in small sample situations is well understood, particularly by economists who have had to deal with short data series in empirical work. Moreover, some of the earliest results on small-sample distributions, particularly in time series models [for example, the work of Hurwicz (1950), which clearly illustrated the substantial small sample bias of the least squares estimator in the first order autoregression], must have made many investigators in the profession uneasy about setting the foundation for estimation and inferential procedures on asymptotic theory alone. Nevertheless, these procedures have out of necessity become firmly established, and the conventional coding of asymptotic statistics in computer regression outputs has helped to entrench the practice of a sole reliance on asymptotic theory in empirical work.

Since the early papers 20 years ago (Basmann, 1961; Bergstrom, 1962; Kabe, 1963, 1964), there has been a continuing and growing literature on small-sample distribution theory in econometrics. Three major schools of research emerged in the 1970s associated with the names of Professor T. W. Anderson at Stanford University, Professor R. L. Basmann at Texas A and M University, and Professor J. D. Sargan at the London School of Economics. The research work of these schools has very largely been complementary in extending the frontiers of knowledge in this field and in stimulating the interest of new research workers. Although the ultimate objective of this research has been to relieve the empirical worker from the heavy reliance he has had to place on asymptotic theory, as yet there has been no substantial payoff to this research in terms of applied econometric practice. This situation is most likely to change dramatically during the 1980s. In part, this is because the rather specialized results of the early research have recently given way to general theories and a powerful technical machinery that will make it easier to transmit results and methods to the applied econometrician in the precise setting of the model and the data set with which he is working. And, in part, this is because improvements in computing now make it feasible to incorporate into existing regression software subroutines that will provide the essential vehicle for this transmission.

Two parallel current developments in the subject are an integral part of this process. The first of these is concerned with the derivation of direct approximations to the sampling distributions of interest in an applied study. These approximations can then be utilized in the decisions that have to be made by an investigator concerning, for instance, the choice of an estimator or the specification of a critical region in a statistical test. Techniques that offer most promise in this regard are the Edgeworth approximation, whose use has been explored in general cases by Sargan (1976) and Phillips (1977, 1980a), and the modified Padé approximant introduced in Phillips (1982).

The second relevant development involves advancements in the mathematical task of extracting the form of exact sampling distributions in econometrics. In the context of simultaneous equations, the published literature has so far concentrated on the sampling distributions of estimators and test statistics in single structural equations involving only two, or at most three, endogenous variables. Recent theoretical work by Phillips and Rhodes has extended much of this work to the general case. In particular, Phillips (1980b) extracted the exact density function of the instrumental variable (IV) estimator in the most general case of a structural equation with $n + 1$ endogenous variables and an arbitrary number of degrees of overidentification. In the same setting, Rhodes (1981) found the exact density of the likelihood ration identifiability test statistic. Work that the author currently has underway should extend these general results to the k-class estimators and limited-information maximum likelihood (LIML). However, in spite of their generality, these results suffer a major handicap in computational work. The analytical methods used in these articles rely on the manipulation of matrix argument higher transcendental functions, and the final expressions for the density functions that have been obtained involve multiple infinite series in terms of zonal-type polynomials.

Zonal polynomials were introduced by James (1961) and can be represented as symmetric homogeneous polynomials in the latent roots of their matrix arguments. Extensions of these polynomials to include similar polynomials in two or more matrix arguments have been made by Davis (1979, 1980) and Chikuse (1981) and are also relevant in certain econometric applications (see Appendix B of Phillips, 1980b). These polynomials we will refer to under the generic name zonal-type polynomials. Although the series representations that involve these polynomials are very convenient mathematically, they present enormous difficulties in numerical work. This is, in part, due to the fact that no general formulae for the zonal-type polynomials are known. However, certain algorithms for the computation of the zonal polynomials themselves are available [see, in particular, James (1968) and McLaren (1976)],[1] and a complete computer program for the evaluation of the coefficients of these polynomials has been developed and made available by Nagel (1981). This is an important development and will in due course undoubtedly affect our present rather limited ability to numerically compute and readily interpret multiple series representations of probability density functions. Unfortunately, the availability of tabulations and algorithms for the zonal-type polynomials will cover only part of the computational difficulty. As noted by Muirhead (1978), the series that involves these polynomials often converge very slowly. This problem arises particularly when the polynomials have large arguments (large latent roots) and it becomes necessary to work deeply into the higher terms of the series in order to achieve convergence. This in turn raises additional problems of underflow and overflow in the computer evaluations of the coefficients in the series and the polynomials themselves. To take as a simple example the case of the exact density of the IV estimator in the two endogenous variable case, the author has found that in a crude summation of the doubly infinite series for the density a thousand or more terms seem to be necessary[2] to achieve adequate convergence when the true coefficient parameter is greater than 5 and the concentration parameter greater than 10. These are not in any way unrealistic values, and the problems increase with the size of the coefficient and concentration parameter. Expressed as a single series involving the ${}_1F_1$ function of a scalar argument, we find that computation of the series requires computation of the ${}_1F_1$ function for a scalar argument greater than 225. Use of the conventional asymptotic expansion of the ${}_1F_1$ function [which is normally recommended when the argument is greater than 10; see Slater (1965)] fails here because one of the parameters of the ${}_1F_1$ function grows as we enter more deeply into the series and the series itself no longer converges. Some special methods for dealing with these difficulties in this case have been developed in programming work for the author by Sidnie Feit and will be reported elsewhere. Undoubtedly, the additional problems we have encountered in this example quickly become much worse as the dimension of the argument matrices in the special functions and the zonal polynomials increases and as we need to make use of the more general zonal-type polynomials.

For direct computational work in the case of the IV estimator when there are more than two endogenous variables in the structural equation, the problems reported in the previous paragraph were overcome in Phillips (1980b) by extracting an asymptotic expansion of the exact joint density of the vector coefficient estimator. The leading term of this expansion has an error of $O(T^{-1})$ where T is the sample size, and in the univariate (two endogenous variable) case the resulting approximation is the saddlepoint approximation derived using other methods by Holly and Phillips (1979). As shown in this latter article, the approximation gives high accuracy for some plausible values of the parameters throughout a wide domain of the distribution, including the tails.

The rather specialized early research in small-sample theory naturally enough focused on problems that were essentially univariate in character in the sense that the statistics under analysis were scalar rather than vector random variates. Hence, in the context of a structural equation with two endogenous variables, attention concentrated on the sampling distributions of (1) estimators of the unknown coefficient of one of the endogenous variables, (2) structural variance estimators, and (3) t-ratio type test statistics. As the analytic theory has developed to encompass the more general cases discussed in previous paragraphs, the final problem has, at least in the important case (1) above, become multivariate[3] in character. For example, in the work by Phillips (1980b) on the IV estimator, the structural equation contains $n + 1$ endogenous variables, there are n unknown structural coefficients of these variables, and the final probability density function (pdf) of the estimator is a joint density in n dimensions.

In this multivariate setting, an important and outstanding problem is the characterization of the joint density in such a way that the final results can intelligently be used in practice. This problem bears an immediate resemblance to that of characterizing multidimensional Bayesian posterior distributions. Some of the current work in the latter area has taken the direction of numerical computation of posterior moments by Monte Carlo methods (see, for instance, Kloek and Van Dijk, 1978). Direct application of these techniques is hampered by the difficulties typically involved in the computation of the joint densities that have been described earlier (although approximations to the joint density functions could be used before applying this method). Moreover, Monte Carlo methods have concentrated on the computation of low order posterior moments. In many cases it will be preferable to work with the marginal density functions directly, since attention is often focused on individual parameters or coefficients rather than a group of parameters jointly.[4] In principle, the marginal densities can be obtained by analytic or numerical integration over the space of the auxiliary variables and for the domain of values for which the marginals are required. In practice, analytic integration currently presents severe technical difficulties for all but the simplest cases (and with the exception of the analysis of the leading terms in the density expansions); and numerical integration methods encounter dimensionality problems as well as/or computational difficulties in the joint density series representations described earlier. It is interesting to note that of the two significant parallel developments in small sample theory that were discussed earlier, the first of these yields marginal density approximations directly. This is an attractive feature of both the Edgeworth and the modified Padé approximants.

When the starting point in our analysis is the exact joint pdf of a group of parameters and we wish to sharpen our focus and characterize the sampling behavior of an individual parameter estimator, an alternative approach is required. This article presents a solution to this problem, a solution that involves the use of the multivariate version of Laplace's method [see, for example, Chapter 8 of Bleistein and Handelsman (1976)] to reduce the multidimensional integrals that define the marginals. This approach should be quite generally applicable in both sampling theoretic and Bayesian problems and seems to present no computational problems even in high-dimensional cases.

Section II of the paper will outline the essential features of the method, and an application to the marginal densities of the IV estimator in the general single equation case will be presented in Section III. This application enables us to assess, inter alia, the effect on the density of an individual coefficient estimator of an increase in the number of endogenous variables in the model, ceteris paribus. Some graphs that display this and other effects are given. Some leading exact results will be given in Section IV; these results lead to computable formulae and generalize all presently known results for exact marginal densities in single structural equations. Concluding remarks will be made in Section V.

II. ASYMPTOTIC EXPANSION OF THE MULTIPLE INTEGRAL DEFINING A MARGINAL DENSITY

To set up a general framework, we assume that a model is specified that uniquely determines the joint probability distribution of the system's endogenous variables $\{y_1, \ldots, y_T\}$ condition on certain fixed exogenous variables $\{x_1, \ldots, x_T\}$, where T is the sample size. If, as is usual, this distribution is absolutely continuous, it can be represented by its probability density function (pdf), which will depend in general on an unknown vector of parameters $\boldsymbol{\theta}$. Thus, we write $\mathrm{pdf}(\mathbf{y}|\mathbf{x};\ \boldsymbol{\theta})$ where $\mathbf{y}' = (y_1', \ldots, y_T')$ and $\mathbf{x}' = (x_1', \ldots, x_T')$. Estimation of $\boldsymbol{\theta}$ or a subvector of $\boldsymbol{\theta}$ leads to a function of the available data, which we will write as the n-vector $\boldsymbol{\theta}_T = \boldsymbol{\theta}_T(\mathbf{y}, \mathbf{x})$. Since most econometric estimators and test statistics are relatively simple functions of the sample moments of the data, which we will denote by m, we may also conveniently write $\boldsymbol{\theta}_T = \boldsymbol{\theta}_T^*(m)$. Frequently, these functions will just involve rational functions of the first and second sample moments of the data. In the more complicated cases, $\boldsymbol{\theta}_T$ will be determined by a system of estimating equations, such as $H_T(\boldsymbol{\theta}_T, m) = 0$, whose elements are usually rational functions of the sample moments. In any case, the representation $\boldsymbol{\theta}_T = \boldsymbol{\theta}_T^*(m)$ will be general enough for a large class of applications.

Our problem is to characterize the distribution of individual components of $\boldsymbol{\theta}_T$. In many of the relevant econometric cases, we can write down directly the pdf of the sample moments, namely, pdf(m), using established results from multivariate distribution theory. Otherwise, pdf(m) must be obtained by transformation and analytic integration of pdf($\mathbf{y}$). The next step is to find a suitable set of auxiliary variates $\mathbf{b}$ for which the transformation $m \rightarrow (\boldsymbol{\theta}_T, \mathbf{b})$ is 1:1 and then the density of $\boldsymbol{\theta}_T$ is given by the integral

$$\text{pdf}(\mathbf{r}) = \int_B \text{pdf}(m) \left| \frac{\partial m}{\partial(\mathbf{r}, \mathbf{b})} \right| d\mathbf{b} \tag{1}$$

where B is the space of definition of the $\mathbf{b}$ variates and we use $\mathbf{r}$ to denote $\boldsymbol{\theta}_T$ in the density. The marginal density of an individual component of $\boldsymbol{\theta}_T$—say, $\boldsymbol{\theta}_{Ti}$—follows by further integration

$$\text{pdf}(\mathbf{r}_i) = \int_{R_i} \int_B \text{pdf}(m) \left| \frac{\partial m}{\partial(\mathbf{r}, \mathbf{b})} \right| d\mathbf{b} d\mathbf{r}_{(i)} \tag{2}$$

where $\mathbf{r}_{(i)}$ is the vector of redundant variables in $\mathbf{r}$ and R_i is their space of definition. In (2) we use $\mathbf{r}_i$ to represent $\boldsymbol{\theta}_{Ti}$.

Although the integral defining (2) can be obtained analytically in some leading general cases for simultaneous equations estimators (we will give some examples in Section IV), the complexity of the representation of the joint density pdf($\mathbf{r}$) derived from (1) will normally present a severe obstacle to this step. Typically, pdf($\mathbf{r}$) has an analytic representation as a multiple infinite series involving zonal polynomials of argument matrices that are themselves rational functions of the elements of $\mathbf{r}$. In the absence of analytic formulae for these polynomials in terms of the elements of their argument matrices, the task of integrating out the surplus elements of $\mathbf{r}$ to extract the marginals pdf($\mathbf{r}_i$) will be possible only in the simplest cases.

An alternative approach, which simplifies the preceding task and which should lead to good asymptotic approximations in many cases, is based on the multivariate extension of Laplace's method applied to the multiple integrals (1) and (2). A full discussion of the method in the context of multidimensional integrals is given in Chapter 8 of Bleistein and Handelsman (1976). The method is applicable to integrals of the form

$$I(\lambda) = \int_D \exp\{\lambda\phi(\mathbf{x})\}g(\mathbf{x})d\mathbf{x}, \qquad \mathbf{x} = (x_1, \ldots, x_N) \tag{3}$$

where D is a simply connected domain in N-dimensional $\mathbf{x}$-space. If $\phi(\mathbf{x})$ and $g(\mathbf{x})$ are continuously differentiable to second order, if ϕ obtains an interior absolute maximum at $\mathbf{x}^*$ in D, and if the Hessian $\partial^2\phi(\mathbf{x}^*)/\partial\mathbf{x}\partial\mathbf{x}'$ is negative definite, then [equation (8.3.52) of Bleistein and Handelsman (1976)]

$$I(\lambda) \sim (2\pi/\lambda)^{N/2} \exp\{\lambda\phi(\mathbf{x}^*)\}g(\mathbf{x}^*)\{\det[-\partial^2\phi(\mathbf{x}^*)/\partial\mathbf{x}\partial\mathbf{x}']\}^{-1/2} \tag{4}$$

in the sense that $A \sim B$ if $A/B \to 1$ as $\lambda \to \infty$. The error on this approximation is of $O[\exp\{\lambda\phi(\mathbf{x}^*)\lambda^{-(N+2)/2}\}]$ as $\lambda \to \infty$. The right-hand side of (4) is, in fact, the leading term in an asymptotic expansion of $I(\lambda)$ as $\lambda \to \infty$ provided the functions $\phi(\mathbf{x})$ and $g(\mathbf{x})$ satisfy sufficient regularity conditions. Equation (8.3.50) of Bleistein and Handelsman (1976) gives this expansion explicitly. It is worth pointing out that (3) holds when $\mathbf{x}^*$ is an interior point of D and somewhat different formulas apply when the maximum of $\phi(\mathbf{x})$ is attained on the boundary of D. Intuitively, the asymptotic approximation (4) is based on the notion that as λ grows large the main contribution to the value of the integral comes from integrating in a small neighborhood of the point $\mathbf{x}^*$ where $\phi(\mathbf{x})$ attains its absolute maximum.

In applying (4) to the multiple integrals that define pdf($\mathbf{r}$) and pdf($\mathbf{r}_i$), we first need to represent the integrand in each case in a form that corresponds to that of (3). To fix ideas, we assume that (1) has the alternative representation

$$\text{pdf}(\mathbf{r}) = h(\mathbf{r}) \int_B \exp\{\lambda(T)\phi(\mathbf{r},\mathbf{b})\}g(\mathbf{r},\mathbf{b})d\mathbf{b} \tag{5}$$

for sufficiently smooth functions h, ϕ, and g and where $\lambda(T) \to \infty$ as $T \to \infty$.[5] If $\phi(\mathbf{r},\mathbf{b})$ attains an interior absolute maximum at $\mathbf{b}^* = \mathbf{b}^*(\mathbf{r})$ in the interior of B, we have directly the asymptotic representation

$$\text{pdf}(\mathbf{r}) = [2\pi/\lambda(T)]^{N/2}\, h(\mathbf{r})\exp\{\lambda(T)\phi^*(\mathbf{r})\}g^*(\mathbf{r})[\Delta(\mathbf{r})]^{-1/2} \tag{6}$$

where

$$\phi^*(\mathbf{r}) = \phi[\mathbf{r},\mathbf{b}^*(\mathbf{r})]$$
$$g^*(\mathbf{r}) = g[\mathbf{r},\mathbf{b}^*(\mathbf{r})]$$

and

$$\Delta(\mathbf{r}) = \det\{-\partial^2\phi[\mathbf{r},\mathbf{b}^*(\mathbf{r})]/\partial\mathbf{b}\partial\mathbf{b}'\}.$$

To approximate the marginal density (2), we apply the method again, this time to the integral (2) giving

$$\text{pdf}(\mathbf{r}_i) = [2\pi/\lambda(T)]^{(N+n-1)/2} h(\mathbf{r}_i, \mathbf{r}^*_{(i)}) \exp\{\lambda(T)\phi^*(\mathbf{r}_i, \mathbf{r}^*_{(i)})\} \cdot g^*(\mathbf{r}_i, \mathbf{r}^*_{(i)})[\Delta(\mathbf{r}_i, \mathbf{r}^*_{(i)})]^{-1/2}[\Delta_i(\mathbf{r}_i)]^{-1/2} \tag{7}$$

where

$$\Delta_i(\mathbf{r}_i) = \det\{-\partial^2\phi^*[\mathbf{r}_i, \mathbf{r}^*_{(i)}(\mathbf{r}_i)]/\partial\mathbf{r}_{(i)}\partial\mathbf{r}'_{(i)}\}$$

and where $\phi^*(\mathbf{r}) = \phi^*(\mathbf{r}_i, \mathbf{r}^*_{(i)})$ attains an absolute maximum in the interior of R_i, given $\mathbf{r}_i$, at $\mathbf{r}^*_{(i)} = \mathbf{r}^*_{(i)}(\mathbf{r}_i)$. The dimension of the vector $\mathbf{r}^*_{(i)}$ here is $n - 1$.

III. AN APPLICATION TO INSTRUMENTAL VARIABLE ESTIMATORS

As in Phillips (1980b), we work with the structural equation

$$\mathbf{y}_1 = \mathbf{Y}_2\boldsymbol{\beta} + \mathbf{Z}_1\boldsymbol{\gamma} + \mathbf{u} \tag{8}$$

where $\mathbf{y}_1$ ($T \times 1$) and $\mathbf{Y}_2$ ($T \times n$) are an observation vector and matrix, respectively, of $n + 1$ included endogenous variables; $\mathbf{Z}_1$ is a $T \times K_1$ matrix of included exogenous variables; and $\mathbf{u}$ is a random disturbance vector. The reduced form of (8) is given by

$$[\mathbf{y}_1 \vdots \mathbf{Y}_2] = [\mathbf{Z}_1 \vdots \mathbf{Z}_2]\begin{bmatrix} \boldsymbol{\pi}_{11} & \boldsymbol{\Pi}_{12} \\ \boldsymbol{\pi}_{21} & \boldsymbol{\Pi}_{22} \end{bmatrix} + [\mathbf{v}_1 \vdots \mathbf{V}_2] = \mathbf{z}\boldsymbol{\Pi} + \mathbf{V} \tag{9}$$

where $\mathbf{Z}_2$ is a $T \times K_2$ matrix of exogenous variables excluded from (8). The rows of the reduced form disturbance matrix $\mathbf{V}$ are assumed to be independent, identically distributed, normal random vectors. We assume that the usual standardizing transformations (Basmann, 1963, 1974) have been carried out, so that the covariance matrix of rows of $\mathbf{V}$ is the identity matrix and $T^{-1}\mathbf{Z}'\mathbf{Z} = \mathbf{I}_K$ where $K = K_1 + K_2$ and $\mathbf{Z} = [\mathbf{Z}_1 \vdots \mathbf{Z}_2]$. We also assume that $K_2 \geqslant n$ and the matrix $\boldsymbol{\Pi}_{22}$ ($K_2 \times n$) in (9) has full rank, so that (8) is identified, although this latter assumption will be relaxed in our discussion of some leading cases in Section IV. We let $H = [\mathbf{Z}_1 \vdots \mathbf{Z}_3]$, where $\mathbf{Z}_3$ ($T \times K_3$) is a submatrix of $\mathbf{Z}_2$ and $K_2 \geqslant n$, be a matrix of IVs to be used in the estimation of (8). The IV estimator of the parameter vector $\boldsymbol{\beta}$ in (8) is then

$$\boldsymbol{\beta}_{\text{IV}} = (\mathbf{Y}_2'\mathbf{M}_H\mathbf{Y}_2)^{-1}(\mathbf{Y}_2'\mathbf{M}_H\mathbf{y}_1)$$

where $\mathbf{M}_H = \mathbf{H}(\mathbf{H}'\mathbf{H})^{-1}\mathbf{H}' - \mathbf{Z}_1(\mathbf{Z}_1'\mathbf{Z}_1)^{-1}\mathbf{Z}_1'$, and under orthogonality this reduces to $\boldsymbol{\beta}_{\text{IV}} = (\mathbf{Y}_2'\mathbf{Z}_3\mathbf{Z}_3'\mathbf{Y}_2)^{-1}(\mathbf{Y}_2'\mathbf{Z}_3\mathbf{Z}_3'\mathbf{y}_1)$.

The exact joint probability density of $\boldsymbol{\beta}_{\text{IV}}$ obtained by Phillips (1980b) is given by

$$\mathrm{pdf}(\mathbf{r}) = \frac{\mathrm{etr}\{-(T/2)(\mathbf{I} + \boldsymbol{\beta}\boldsymbol{\beta}')\overline{\mathbf{\Pi}}_{22}'\overline{\mathbf{\Pi}}_{22}\}\Gamma_n[(L+n+1)/2]}{\pi^{n/2}[\det(\mathbf{I} + \mathbf{r}\mathbf{r}')]^{(L+n+1)/2}}$$

$$\cdot \sum_{j=0}^{\infty} \frac{(L/2)j}{j!\Gamma_n[(L+n)/2+j]} [\{(T/2)\boldsymbol{\beta}'\overline{\mathbf{\Pi}}_{22}'[\mathrm{adj}(\partial/\partial W)]$$

$$\overline{\mathbf{\Pi}}_{22}\boldsymbol{\beta}\}^j[\det(\mathbf{I} + \mathbf{W})]^{(L-1)/2+j} \tag{10}$$

$$\cdot\ {}_1F_1\{(L+n+1)/2, (L+n)/2+j; (T/2)(\mathbf{I} + \mathbf{W})$$

$$\overline{\mathbf{\Pi}}_{22}(\mathbf{I} + \boldsymbol{\beta}\mathbf{r}')(\mathbf{I} + \mathbf{r}\mathbf{r}')^{-1}(\mathbf{I} + \mathbf{r}\boldsymbol{\beta}')\overline{\mathbf{\Pi}}_{22}'\}]_{\mathbf{W}=\mathbf{0}}$$

where $L = K_3 - n$ (the number of surplus instruments used in the estimation of $\boldsymbol{\beta}$) and $\overline{\mathbf{\Pi}}_{22}$ is an $n \times n$ matrix [nonsingular when $\mathbf{\Pi}_{22}$ in (9) is of full rank] defined by the equation $\mathbf{\Pi}_{22}'\mathbf{\Pi}_{22} = \overline{\mathbf{\Pi}}_{22}'\overline{\mathbf{\Pi}}_{22}$. In (10) as in (1), we use $\mathbf{r}$ to represent the estimator (in this case $\boldsymbol{\beta}_{\mathrm{IV}}$), and $\mathbf{W}$ is a matrix of auxiliary variables.

The matrix argument in the ${}_1F_1$ function that appears in the preceding expression for the exact density (10) has elements that are rational functions in the components of $\mathbf{r}$. The multiple series representation of (10) will similarly involve zonal polynomials in the same matrix argument; and as discussed in the previous section, this feature of the problem combined with the absence of analytic formulae for the polynomials in terms of the elements of the argument matrix makes the analytic determination of marginal densities difficult except for specialized leading cases.

Using the asymptotic representation of the ${}_1F_1$ function, namely, as $T \to \infty$ and for a nonsingular matrix $\mathbf{R}$

$${}_1F_1(a, b; T\mathbf{R}) = [\Gamma_n(b)/\Gamma_n(a)]\mathrm{etr}(T\mathbf{R})(\det T\mathbf{R})^{a-b}[1 + O(T^{-1})]$$

(Constantine and Muirhead (1976), Theorem 3.2) in (10), we obtain the following asymptotic approximation of the joint density of $\boldsymbol{\beta}_{\mathrm{IV}}$

$$\mathrm{pdf}(\mathbf{r}) \sim \frac{T^{n/2}\mathrm{etr}\left(-\frac{T}{2}\left\{\frac{\mathbf{M}(\mathbf{r}-\boldsymbol{\beta})(\mathbf{r}-\boldsymbol{\beta})'}{1+\mathbf{r}'\mathbf{r}}\right\}\right)(\det \mathbf{M})^{1/2}}{2^{n/2}\pi^{n/2}(1+\mathbf{r}'\mathbf{r})^{(L+n+2)/2}} \cdot \frac{(1+\boldsymbol{\beta}'\mathbf{r})^{L+1}}{(1+2\boldsymbol{\beta}'\mathbf{r}-\boldsymbol{\beta}'\boldsymbol{\beta})^{L/2}} \tag{11}$$

[see Phillips (1980b) equation (15)] where $\mathbf{M} = \overline{\mathbf{\Pi}}_{22}'\overline{\mathbf{\Pi}}_{22}$ and which holds with a relative error of $O(T^{-1})$ as $T \to \infty$ for values of $\mathbf{r}$ in the domain defined by $1 + 2\boldsymbol{\beta}'\mathbf{r} - \boldsymbol{\beta}'\boldsymbol{\beta} > 0$. Alternatively, (11) can be extracted using an asymptotic expansion of a multiple integral similar to (5) but of the Fourier type (see Note 5).

We can now apply Laplace's method directly to extract marginal densities from (11). Without loss of generality, our attention will concentrate on pdf($\mathbf{r}_1$). We start by partitioning the matrix **M** and vectors $\boldsymbol{\beta}$ and **r** as

$$\mathbf{M} = \begin{bmatrix} m_{11} & \mathbf{m}_{21}' \\ \mathbf{m}_{21} & \mathbf{M}_{22} \end{bmatrix}, \ \boldsymbol{\beta} = \begin{bmatrix} \beta_1 \\ \boldsymbol{\beta}_2 \end{bmatrix}, \text{ and } \mathbf{r} = \begin{bmatrix} r_1 \\ \mathbf{r}_2 \end{bmatrix}$$

where m_{11}, β_1, and r_1 are scalars. We define

$$\overline{m}_{11} = m_{11} - \mathbf{m}_{21}'\mathbf{M}_{22}^{-1}\mathbf{m}_{21}$$

$$\overline{\mathbf{r}}_2 = \overline{\mathbf{r}}_2(r_1) = \boldsymbol{\beta}_2 - (r_1 - \beta_1)\mathbf{M}_{22}^{-1}\mathbf{m}_{21}$$

$$\phi(r_1, \mathbf{r}_2) = \frac{(r_1 - \beta_1)^2\overline{m}_{11} + (\mathbf{r}_2 - \overline{\mathbf{r}}_2)'\mathbf{M}_{22}(\mathbf{r}_2 - \overline{\mathbf{r}}_2)}{1 + r_1^2 + \mathbf{r}_2'\mathbf{r}_2}$$

$$g(r_1, \mathbf{r}_2) = \frac{(1 + \beta_1 r_1 + \boldsymbol{\beta}_2'\mathbf{r}_2)^{L+1}}{(1 + r_1^2 + \mathbf{r}_2'\mathbf{r}_2)^{(L+n+2)/2}\,(1 + 2\beta_1 r_1 + 2\boldsymbol{\beta}_2'\mathbf{r}_2 - \boldsymbol{\beta}'\boldsymbol{\beta})^{L/2}}.$$

By use of (4) in the $N = n - 1$ dimensional integral defining pdf(r_1), we obtain the following asymptotic approximation to the marginal density

$$\text{pdf}(r_1) \sim \left(\frac{T}{2\pi}\right)^{1/2} \frac{(\det \mathbf{M})^{1/2}}{[\det \mathbf{H}(r_1,\mathbf{r}_2^*(r_1))]^{1/2}}\, g[r_1,\mathbf{r}_2^*(r_1)]\exp\left\{-\frac{T}{2}\phi[r_1,\mathbf{r}_2^*(r_1)]\right\}$$

where

$$\begin{aligned}\mathbf{H}(r_1, \mathbf{r}_2) &= \partial^2[(1/2)\phi(r_1,\mathbf{r}_2)]/\partial\mathbf{r}_2\partial\mathbf{r}_2' \\ &= [\alpha_1(r_1,\mathbf{r}_2)\mathbf{I} + \alpha_2(r_1,\mathbf{r}_2)\mathbf{r}_2(\mathbf{r}_2 - \overline{\mathbf{r}}_2)']\mathbf{M}_{22} \\ &\quad + \alpha_3(r_1,\mathbf{r}_2)\mathbf{I} + \alpha_4(r_1,\mathbf{r}_2)\mathbf{r}_2\mathbf{r}_2'\end{aligned}$$

and the α_i are scalar functions given by

$$\alpha_1(r_1,\mathbf{r}_2) = (1 + r_1^2 + \mathbf{r}_2'\mathbf{r}_2)^{-1}$$

$$\alpha_2(r_1,\mathbf{r}_2) = -4(1 + r_1^2 + \mathbf{r}_2'\mathbf{r}_2)^{-2}$$

$$\alpha_3(r_1,\mathbf{r}_2) = -(1 + r_1^2 + \mathbf{r}_2'\mathbf{r}_2)^{-2}[(r_1 - \beta_1)^2\overline{m}_{11} + (\mathbf{r}_2 - \overline{\mathbf{r}}_2)'\mathbf{M}_{22}(\mathbf{r}_2 - \overline{\mathbf{r}}_2)]$$

$$\alpha_4(r_1,\mathbf{r}_2) = 4(1 + r_1^2 + \mathbf{r}_2'\mathbf{r}_2)^{-3}[(r_1 - \beta_1)^2\overline{m}_{11} + (\mathbf{r}_2 - \overline{\mathbf{r}}_2)'\mathbf{M}_{22}(\mathbf{r}_2 - \overline{\mathbf{r}}_2)]$$

In (12), $\mathbf{r}_2^* = \mathbf{r}_2^*(r_1)$ is the value of $\mathbf{r}_2$, given r_1, for which $\phi(r_1,\mathbf{r}_2)$ attains its minimum. The approximation (12) is valid for r_1 in the domain defined by $1 + 2\beta_1 r_1 + 2\boldsymbol{\beta}_2'\mathbf{r}_2^*(r_1) - \boldsymbol{\beta}'\boldsymbol{\beta} > 0$ and has a relative error of $O(T^{-1})$ in this domain.

To compute the marginal density approximant (12), we first evaluate $\mathbf{r}_2^*$ for the required values of r_1 by direct optimization of $\phi(r_1,\mathbf{r}_2)$. This is a simple and inexpensive computation in practice. It is most useful to commence calculations for $r_1 = \beta_1$ at which point $\mathbf{r}_2^* = \bar{\mathbf{r}}_2 = \boldsymbol{\beta}_2$ by inspection of $\phi(r_1,\mathbf{r}_2)$. The same point can be used as a starting value in the iteration to minimize $\phi(r_1,\mathbf{r}_2)$ as we move away from $r_1 = \beta_1$, and successive optima can similarly be used in later iterations. By continuity, we should always be close to the minimum at the start of each iteration, provided the grid of r_1 values is sufficiently fine. No problems of multiple minima were encountered in this particular application of the algorithm. Once $\mathbf{r}_2^* = \mathbf{r}_2^*(r_1)$ is found, the function (12) itself can be directly computed.

Marginal densities based on (12) were computed to explore the form of these densities for variations in the number of endogenous variables in the structural equation and to examine the sensitivity of these densities to various changes in the parameters on which they depend. Some graphs that illustrate these effects are shown in Figures 1–7. Each of these graphs refers to an equation with $n = 3$ (that is, an equation with $n + 1 = 4$ endogenous variables) except those in Figure 5, which show the densities for values of n ranging from 2 to 7. The case of $n = 2$ has not been considered in any detail here because results for that case were obtained by numerical integration and reported in Phillips (1980b). Monte Carlo results for the same model with $n = 2$ (the three endogenous variable case) have been obtained by Richardson and Rohr (Chapter 2, this volume).

Some features that emerge from the densities graphed in Figures 1 to 7 are as follows:

1. For comparable parameter values, the marginal distribution appears to concentrate as $T \to \infty$ more slowly when $n = 3$ than when $n = 2$ or $n = 1$. This can be seen by comparing the apparent rate of convergence in Figure 1 with that of Figures 1 and 5 of Phillips (1980b) (the latter two figures are not reproduced here). The differences seem to be more marked between $n = 2$ and $n = 1$ (and $n = 3$ and $n = 1$) than between $n = 3$ and $n = 2$.

2. The density is particularly sensitive to the degree of correlation (ρ) in the matrix of products of reduced form coefficients, $\mathbf{M} = \bar{\boldsymbol{\Pi}}_{22}'\bar{\boldsymbol{\Pi}}_{22}$ (see Figure 2). This confirms similar results noted in Phillips (1980b). The dispersion of the density also increases with $|\rho|$. Since $\mathbf{M}$ approaches singularity as $|\rho| \to 1$ and the equation becomes unidentifiable, this behavior accords with what we might expect from intuition. The central tendency of the distribution seems to be more sensitive to negative than positive values of ρ, a phenomena also noted in Phillips (1980b). The important factor in this phenomena is that the sensitivity occurs when

Figure 1. Densities of β_{1IV} for various values of T when

$$n = 1, \begin{matrix}\beta_1 = 0.6\\ \beta_2 = 0.6,\\ \beta_3 = 0.6\end{matrix} \mathbf{M} = \begin{bmatrix} 4.0 & 3.6 & 3.24 \\ 3.6 & 4.0 & 3.6 \\ 3.24 & 3.6 & 4.0 \end{bmatrix}, L = 3.$$

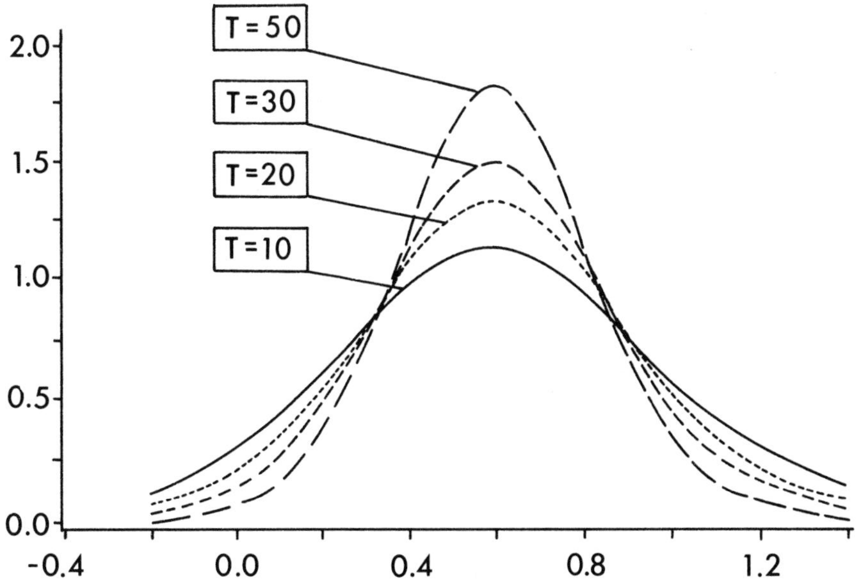

β_1 and ρ are of different signs. Thus, when the coefficients β_i and ρ all have the same sign, the common set of exogenous variables are compatible as instruments for $\mathbf{Y}_2$ in the regression and the marginal distributions appear to be adequately centered; but when β_i and ρ take opposite signs, the exogenous variables are less compatible as instruments for the columns of $\mathbf{Y}_2$ and the marginal distributions become less well centered about the true coefficients.

3. The dispersion and central tendency of the distribution can be very sensitive to the relative magnitude (μ) of the lengths of the reduced form coefficient vectors, as is clear from Figure 3. In other cases it is not, as in Figure 4. The rather dramatic difference between the two cases illustrated in Figures 3 (with μ varying) and 4 (with λ varying) can be directly explained from the analytic formula for the density given in (12). As λ increase in the matrix $\mathbf{M}$, it is clear that the parameter $\overline{m}_{11}$ increases, and from the form of $\phi(r_1,\mathbf{r}_2^*)$ in the exponential factor of (12) it follows that the density will display greater concentration about β_1. This is essentially equivalent to a direct increase in the size of what would be the

Figure 2. Densities of β_{1IV} for various values of correlation ρ in M when

$$n = 3, \begin{matrix} \beta_1 = 0.6 \\ \beta_2 = 0.6, \\ \beta_3 = 0.6 \end{matrix} \mathbf{M} = \begin{bmatrix} 4.0 & \rho 4.0 & 0 \\ \rho 4.0 & 4.0 & 0 \\ 0 & 0 & 4.0 \end{bmatrix}, L = 3, T = 20.$$

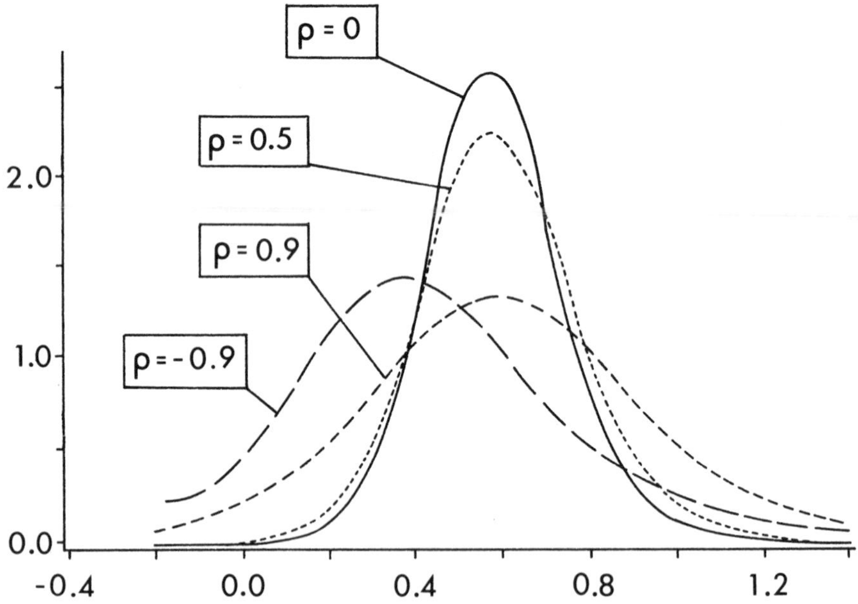

concentration parameter ($\mu^2 = T\overline{m}_{11}$) when $n = 1$ (the two endogenous variable case). As λ increases on the other hand, there is no such direct effect on the distribution of β_{1IV}. In fact, the graphs seem to suggest the contrary: that the increase in the concentration about β_3 in the distribution of β_{3IV}, which will result from the increase in λ (corresponding to the effect of an increase in μ on the distribution of β_{1IV} just discussed), may be achieved partially at the cost of a slight reduction in the concentration of the distribution of β_{1IV} (see, in particular, Figure 4). This is an effect that warrants some further investigation.

4. Figure 5 illustrates the effects of increasing the number of endogenous variables, ceteris paribus, on the marginal density of β_{1IV}. The effect is clear and monotonic in this case as a decrease in the precision of estimation. Further exploration of this case would also be of interest, for example, with the parameter values $\beta_1 = 0.6$, $\beta_i = 0$ ($i = 2,\ldots,n$), which would

Figure 3. Densities of β_{1IV} for various values of μ in M when

$$n = 3, \begin{matrix} \beta_1 = 0.6 \\ \beta_2 = 0.6, \\ \beta_3 = 0.6 \end{matrix} \mathbf{M} = \begin{bmatrix} \mu 4.0 & 0 & 0 \\ 0 & 4.0 & 0 \\ 0 & 0 & 4.0 \end{bmatrix}, L = 3, T = 20.$$

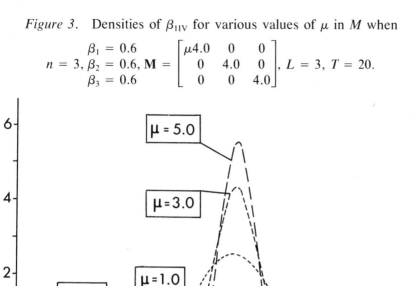

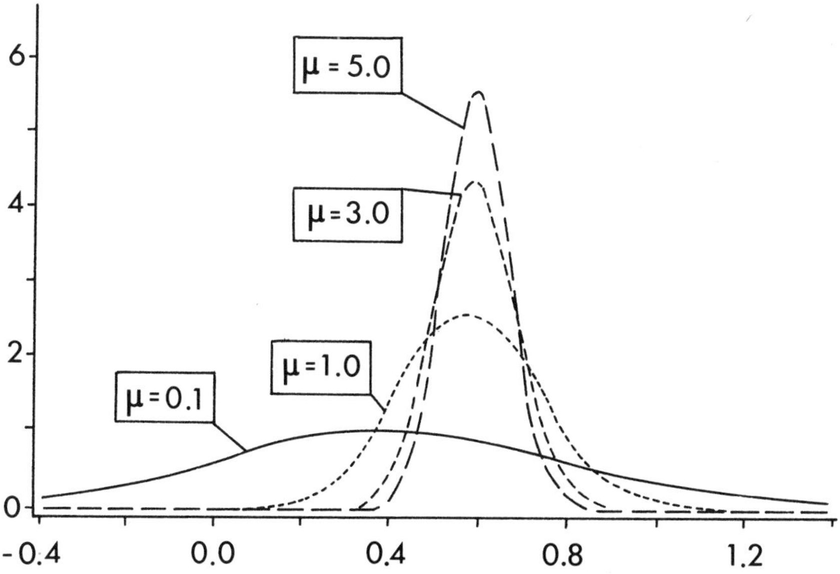

correspond to the erroneous inclusion of additional endogenous variables as regressors in the equation. Note that the recorded reduction in precision of estimation in this case accords with known results for the classical regression model.

5. The effects of variations in the coefficients of the other endogenous variables in the equation is explored in Figures 6 and 7. Once again we notice some rather interesting differences between the two cases. In both cases, as $\beta_2 - \beta_1$ increases and as $\beta_3 - \beta_1$ increases, the dispersion of the marginal distribution of β_{1IV} increases rapidly. However, as $\beta_2 - \beta_1$ increases, the bias becomes positive; when it decreases, the bias becomes negative. By contrast, there appear to be no major bias effects as $\beta_3 - \beta_1$ changes. The difference between the two cases arises from the difference between the correlation pattern in the matrix **M** of cross products of reduced form coefficients. This seems to confirm the point made earlier in (2) and noted first in Phillips (1980b) that the correlation pattern of this matrix has a very important influence on the form of the marginal densities.

Figure 4. Densities of β_{1IV} for various values of λ in M when

$$n = 3, \begin{matrix} \beta_1 = 0.6 \\ \beta_2 = 0.6, \\ \beta_3 = 0.6 \end{matrix} \mathbf{M} = \begin{bmatrix} 4.0 & 0 & 0 \\ 0 & 4.0 & 0 \\ 0 & 0 & \lambda 4.0 \end{bmatrix}, L = 3, T = 20.$$

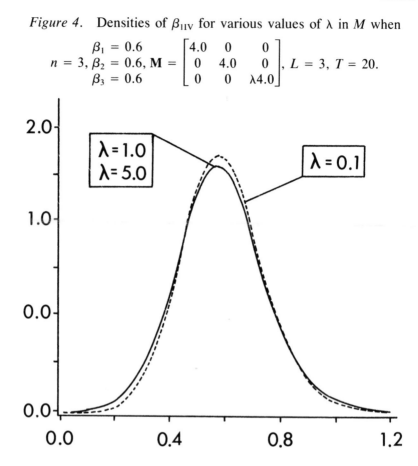

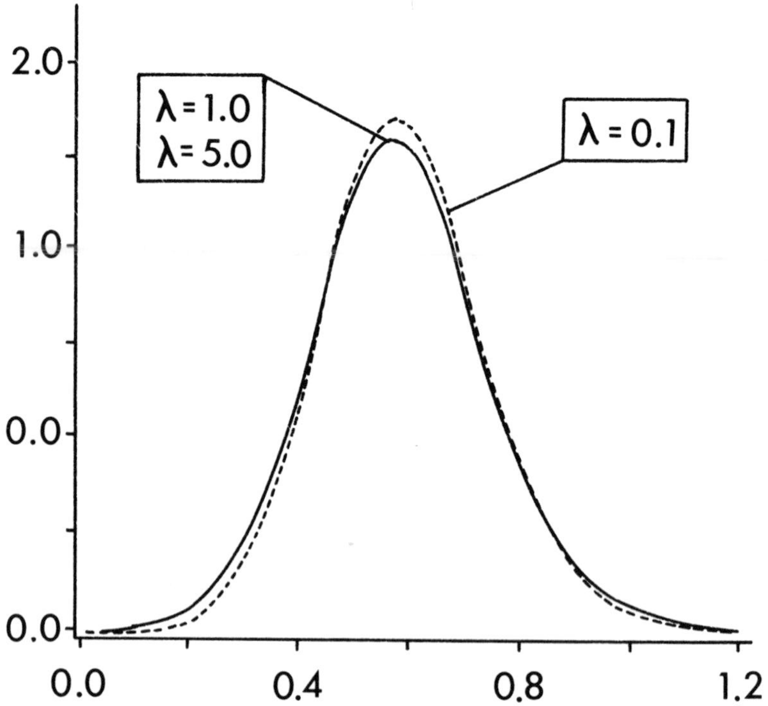

IV. EXACT DENSITIES IN SOME LEADING CASES

The exact joint density function given in (10) admits much simpler representations in certain leading cases. Some of these were already discussed in Section III of Phillips (1980b). Somewhat earlier, and before the general form of the exact density (10) was known, Basmann (1974) pointed out that the leading term in the multiple series could be obtained under a certain null hypothesis concerning the parameters. This built on the work by Basmann (1963) and Kabe (1964), which dealt with a specialized, leading three equation case.

In this section we shall give some further leading results for the general case of $n + 1$ equations.

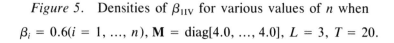

Figure 5. Densities of β_{IIV} for various values of n when $\beta_i = 0.6(i = 1, \ldots, n)$, $\mathbf{M} = \text{diag}[4.0, \ldots, 4.0]$, $L = 3$, $T = 20$.

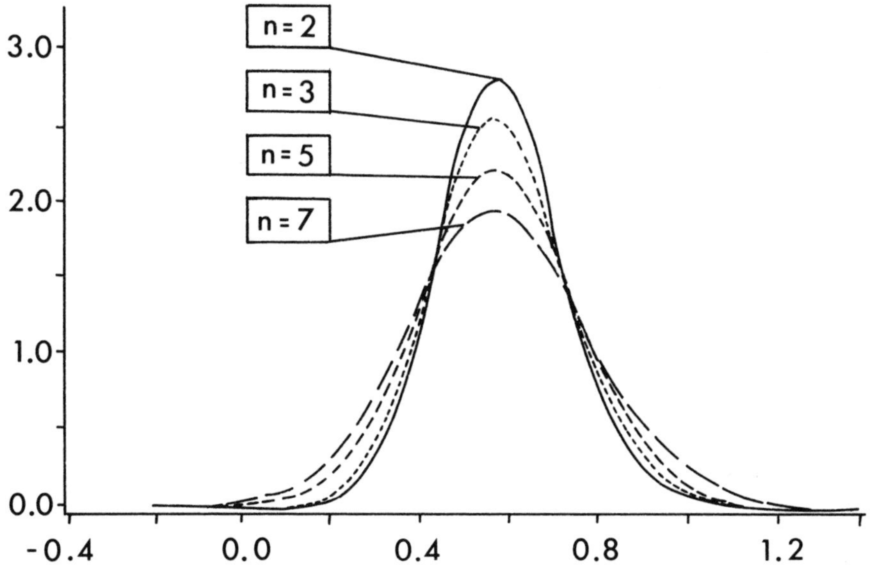

CASE 1: $\boldsymbol{\beta} = \mathbf{0}$
From (10) we deduce that

$$\text{pdf}(\mathbf{r}) = \frac{\text{etr}\{-(T/2)\bar{\boldsymbol{\Pi}}_{22}'\bar{\boldsymbol{\Pi}}_{22}\}\Gamma_n[(L+n+1)/2]}{\pi^{n/2}[\det(\mathbf{I}+\mathbf{rr}')]^{(L+n+1)/2}\Gamma_n[(L+n)/2]} \cdot {}_1F_1\{(L+n+1)/2, (L+n)/2; (T/2)\bar{\boldsymbol{\Pi}}_{22}(\mathbf{I}+\mathbf{rr}')^{-1}\bar{\boldsymbol{\Pi}}_{22}'\} \tag{13}$$

When, in addition, $\bar{\boldsymbol{\Pi}}_{22} = \mathbf{0}$, this reduces to the leading term in the complete multiple series for the exact density [that is, the leading term of (10)], namely,

$$\text{pdf}(\mathbf{r}) = \frac{\Gamma_n[(L+n+1)/2]/\Gamma_n[(L+n)/2]}{\pi^{n/2}(1+\mathbf{r}'\mathbf{r})^{(L+n+1)/2}} = \frac{\Gamma[(L+n+1)/2]}{\pi^{n/2}\Gamma[(L+1)/2](1+\mathbf{r}'\mathbf{r})^{(L+n+1)/2}} \tag{14}$$

The probability density function (14) was given for the two-stage least squares case by Basmann (1974), who also deduced the leading marginal densities, which follow directly from (14) by a simple integration, namely,

$$\text{pdf}(r_i) = \frac{\Gamma[(L+2)/2]}{\pi^{1/2}\Gamma[(L+1)/2](1+r_i^2)^{(L+2)/2}} \tag{15}$$

Figure 6. Densities of β_{1IV} for various values of β_2 when

$$n = 3, \begin{matrix} \beta_1 = 0.6 \\ \beta_2 = 0.6 \end{matrix}, \mathbf{M} = \begin{bmatrix} 4.0 & 3.6 & 3.24 \\ 3.6 & 4.0 & 3.6 \\ 3.24 & 3.6 & 4.0 \end{bmatrix}, L = 3, T = 20.$$

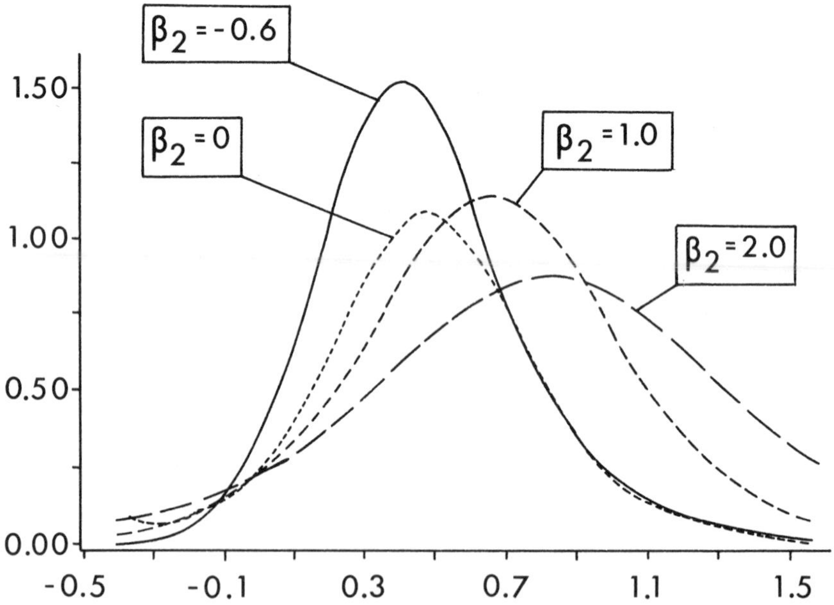

The leading marginal density function (15) has integer moments up to order $L = K_3 - n$ (the number of surplus instruments).

The matrix argument ${}_1F_1$ function in (13) is readily calculated for the three endogenous variable case ($n = 2$). Specifically, Herz (1955) and Muirhead (1975) give a series representation of the ${}_1F_1$ function in terms of the same function with a scalar argument. The form that (13) then takes is as follows:

$$\begin{aligned} \mathrm{pdf}(r_1, \mathbf{r}_2) = {} & \frac{\mathrm{etr}\{-(T/2)\overline{\mathbf{\Pi}}_{22}'\overline{\mathbf{\Pi}}_{22}\}\Gamma_2[(L+3)/2]}{\pi\Gamma_2[(L+2)/2](1+\mathbf{r}'\mathbf{r})^{(L+3)/2}} \\ & \cdot \sum_{j=0}^{\infty} \frac{[(L+3)/2]_j(1/2)_j}{[(L+1)/2]_j[(L+2)/2]_{2j}j!} \\ & \cdot {}_1F_1\{[(L+3)/2]+j, [(L+2)/2]+2j; \\ & \quad T/2[\mathrm{tr}(\overline{\mathbf{\Pi}}_{22}'\overline{\mathbf{\Pi}}_{22}) - (\mathbf{r}'\overline{\mathbf{\Pi}}_{22}'\overline{\mathbf{\Pi}}_{22}\mathbf{r})/(1+\mathbf{r}'\mathbf{r})]\} \\ & \cdot \{-(T/2)^2[\det(\overline{\mathbf{\Pi}}_{22}'\overline{\mathbf{\Pi}}_{22})]/(1+\mathbf{r}'\mathbf{r})\}^j \end{aligned} \tag{16}$$

Figure 7. Densities of β_{1IV} for various values of β_3 when

$$n = 3, \begin{matrix}\beta_1 = 0.6 \\ \beta_2 = 0.6\end{matrix}, \mathbf{M} = \begin{bmatrix} 4.0 & 3.6 & 3.24 \\ 3.6 & 4.0 & 3.6 \\ 3.24 & 3.6 & 4.0 \end{bmatrix}, L = 3,\ T = 20.$$

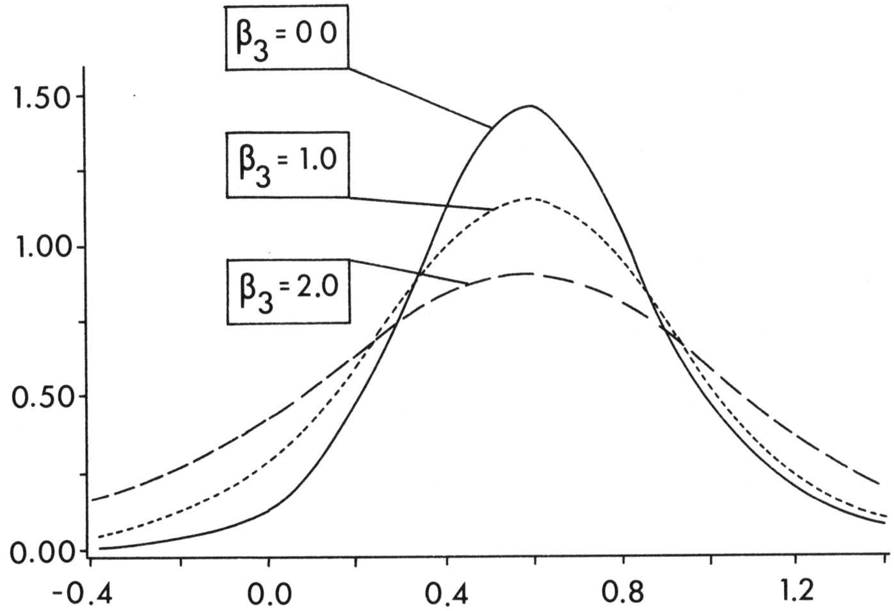

The marginal densities can now be extracted from (16) by integration. Since the derivations are lengthy, I only give the final formulae here. Specifically we obtain

$$\mathrm{pdf}(r_1) = \frac{[(L+1)/2]\exp\{-T/2)(m_{11}+m_{22})\}}{\pi(1+r_1^2)^{(L+2)/2}}$$

$$\cdot \sum_{j,k=0}^{\infty} \sum_{u+2v+w=k} \frac{[(L+3)/2]_j(1/2)_j[(L+3)/2+j]_k}{[(L+1)/2]_j[(L+2)/2]_{2j}[(L+2)/2+2j]_k}$$

$$\cdot \frac{\Gamma[(L+2)/2+j+k-v-w]\,\Gamma[v+w+(1/2)][-(T/2)^2(m_{11}m_{22}-m_{12}^2)]^j}{\Gamma[(L+3)/2+j+k]\,j!\,u!(2v)!w!}$$

$$\frac{[(T/2)\{m_{11}+m_{22}(1+r_1^2)\}]^u(Tr_1m_{12})^{2v}[(T/2)m_{11}]^w}{(1+r_1^2)^{j+k-u-w}} \tag{17}$$

where we use the notation $\mathbf{M} = (m_{ij}) = \bar{\mathbf{\Pi}}_{22}'\bar{\mathbf{\Pi}}_{22}$. This result generalizes all previous known formula for exact marginal densities in leading simultaneous equations cases. The following sections present special cases of (17) already in the literature.

CASE 2. $\boldsymbol{\beta} = \mathbf{0}$, $L = 1$, $m_{12} = 0$

This function was presented by Kabe (1964), equation (4.14), where the multiple series is in a somewhat different form).

$$\mathrm{pdf}(r_1) = \frac{\exp\{-(T/2)(m_{11} + m_{22})\}}{\pi(1 + r_1^2)^{3/2}}$$

$$\cdot \sum_{j,k=0}^{\infty} \sum_{u+w=k} \frac{(j+1)(1/2)_j(j+2)_k\Gamma[j+k-w+(3/2)]\Gamma[w+(1/2)]}{j!(3/2)_{2j}[2j+(3/2)]_k\Gamma[j+k+2)u!w!}$$

$$\cdot \frac{(-1)^j[(T/2)m_{11}]^{j+w}[(T/2)m_{22}]^j[(T/2)\{m_{11} + m_{22}(1 + r_1^2)\}]^u}{(1 + r_1^2)^{j+k-u-w}}$$

CASE 3. $\boldsymbol{\beta} = \mathbf{0}$, $L = 1$, $m_{22} = 0$, $m_{12} = 0$.

This function was presented by Basmann [1963, equation (4.18)].

$$\mathrm{pdf}(r_1) = \frac{\exp(-(T/2)m_{11})}{2(1 + r_1^2)^{3/2}} \sum_{k=0}^{\infty} \frac{1}{k!} {}_1F_1(1/2, 3/2 + k, (T/2)m_{11}) \left[\frac{Tm_{11}}{2(1 + r_1^2)}\right]^k$$

CASE 4. $\boldsymbol{\beta} = \mathbf{0}$, $L = 1$, $m_{11} = 0$, $m_{22} = 0$, $m_{12} = 0$.

This function was presented by Basmann [1963, equation (4.13)].

$$\mathrm{pdf}(r_1) = \frac{1}{2(1 + r_1^2)^{3/2}}$$

The general expression (17) for the marginal density may be used for numerical computations or, alternatively, the joint density (16) can be summed and the marginal densities extracted by a one dimensional quadrature. At present the author has no numerical experience to report with either of these approaches. However, the formulae suggest that numerical computations of the exact marginal densities are now possible for these leading cases when $n = 2$.

Working from the general leading case (Case 1), further analytic results can be obtained. We illustrate with the following final example without going into all the algebra.

CASE 5. $\boldsymbol{\beta} = \mathbf{0}$, $\overline{\boldsymbol{\Pi}}_{22} = \mathrm{diag}(0, \ldots, \Pi_{aa}, \ldots, 0)$.

We let r_a be the ath element of $\mathbf{r}$ and use $\mathbf{r}_b$ to denote the vector of the remaining elements. $\boldsymbol{\Pi}_{aa}^2$ is a concentration coefficient representing the squared length of the coefficients of $\mathbf{Z}_2$ in the reduced form equation for the ath endogenous variable. $T\boldsymbol{\Pi}_{aa}^2$ therefore corresponds to the usual concentration parameter in the two endogenous variable case (when $n = 1$). Then, from (13)

$$\mathrm{pdf}(r_a, \mathbf{r}_b) = \frac{\exp[-(T/2)\boldsymbol{\Pi}_{aa}^2]\Gamma_n[(L+n+1)/2]}{\pi^{n/2}(1+\mathbf{r}_b'\mathbf{r}_b + r_a^2)^{(L+n+1)/2}\Gamma_n[(L+n)/2]}$$
$$\cdot {}_1F_1\left[(L+n+1)/2, (L+n)/2; \frac{T\boldsymbol{\Pi}_{aa}^2(1+\mathbf{r}_b'\mathbf{r}_b)}{2(1+\mathbf{r}_b'\mathbf{r}_b + r_a^2)}\right]$$
$$= \frac{\exp[-(T/2)\boldsymbol{\Pi}_{aa}^2]\Gamma_n[(L+n+1)/2]}{\pi^{n/2}\Gamma_n[(L+n)/2]} \sum_{k=0}^{\infty} \frac{[(L+n+1)/2]_k}{[(L+n)/2]_k\, k!}$$
$$\cdot \left[\frac{T\boldsymbol{\Pi}_{aa}^2}{2}\right]^k \cdot \frac{(1+\mathbf{r}_b'\mathbf{r}_b)^k}{(1+\mathbf{r}_b'\mathbf{r}_b + r_a^2)^{k+(L+n+1)/2}}$$

We transform using $\mathbf{r}_b = (1 + r_a^2)^{1/2}\mathbf{z}$ where $\mathbf{z}$ has dimension $n - 1$. The Jacobian is $(1 + r_a^2)^{(n-1)/2}$ and the marginal density is given by

$$\mathrm{pdf}(r_a) = \frac{\exp[-(T/2)\boldsymbol{\Pi}_{aa}^2]\Gamma_n[(L+n+1)/2]}{\boldsymbol{\Pi}^{n/2}\Gamma_n[(L+n)/2](1+r_a^2)^{(L+2)/2}}$$
$$\cdot \sum_{k=0}^{\infty} \frac{[(L+n+1)/2]_k}{[(L+n)/2]_k\, k!}\left(\frac{T\boldsymbol{\Pi}_{aa}^2}{2}\right)^k \tag{18}$$
$$\sum_{l=0}^{k} \binom{k}{l} \frac{1}{(1+r_a^2)^l} \int \frac{(\mathbf{z}'\mathbf{z})^{k-l}\, d\mathbf{z}}{(1+\mathbf{z}'\mathbf{z})^{k+(L+n+1)/2}}$$

The integral in the final expression can be reduced analytically in the usual way by writing $\mathbf{z}' = (\mathbf{z}_c, z_d)$ where z_d is scalar and by changing the variable to x via the transformation $z_d = (1 + \mathbf{z}_c'\mathbf{z}_c)^{1/2}\tan x$. We can proceed in this way, taking each component of $\mathbf{z}$ separately, until the integral is evaluated.

V. FINAL COMMENTS

The method discussed in Section II should have fairly general applicability to the problem of extracting marginal densities and should be useful in the wider context of characterizing multidimensional distributions in both the sampling theoretic and Bayesian approaches. The numerical illustrations of the method as it is applied to the general single equation IV estimator in Section III show that the technique works well even for high dimensional cases and is successful in isolating the parameters that are most critical in determining the form of the marginal densities.

The exact density results for leading cases in Section IV extend the earlier work of Basmann and Kabe. The results are also amenable to computation, at least in the three endogenous variable case. Further work, which is currently in progress, will analyze the effects of misspecification within the same general single equation set up.

POSTSCRIPT

Since this article was written the author has developed some technical machinery which facilitates the analytic determination of marginal densities in full generality. Details of this research will be reported later.

ACKNOWLEDGMENTS

My thanks to Glena Ames for her skill and time in typing the manuscript. The research reported in this article was supported by the National Science Foundation under grant No. SES 8007571. The graphs in Section III were prepared and related programming work was conducted by Sidnie Feit, for whose help I am most grateful.

NOTES

1. It seems likely that a new algorithm for computation will soon become available based on the work of Towber (1979) on the irreducible polynomial representations of the general linear group.
2. Careful analysis of this problem has shown that series rearrangements prior to summation allow adequate convergence to be achieved using fewer terms in this case.
3. Of course, even in the two endogenous variable case, the usual analysis of case (1) starts off in a multidimensional framework. For example, Basmann (1961) initiates the derivations that lead ultimately to the density of the scalar coefficient estimator by considering the multivariate normal density of the least squares estimators of the reduced form coefficients. Bergstrom (1962) commenced his derivations with the joint density of the sample data vector in T dimensions. Kabe (1963) derived the same exact density as Basmann (1961) by working with the noncentral Wishart representation of the second moments of the data. His work formed the basis for the general two equation exact results obtained later by Richardson (1968) and Sawa (1969).
4. Kloek and Van Dijk (1978) do present some Monte Carlo estimates of marginal densities in their model in addition to moment estimates.
5. In certain cases, it will be more convenient to represent the density as a multiple integral of the Fourier type with an exponential kernel of the form $\exp\{i\lambda(T)\phi(\mathbf{r},\mathbf{b})\}$. In such cases, the major contribution to the value of the integral as $T \to \infty$ can come from points in the domain where the smoothness conditions on ϕ and g fail as well as stationary points of ϕ. An introduction to the asymptotic treatment of multiple integrals of this type is given by Bleistein and Handelsman (1976) in 8.4.

REFERENCES

Basmann, R. L. (1961). A note on the exact finite sample frequency functions of generalized classical linear estimators in two leading overidentified cases, *JASA 56*, 619–636.

Basmann, R. L. (1963). A note on the exact finite sample frequency functions of generalized classical linear estimators in a leading three equation case, *JASA 58*, 161–171.

Basmann, R. L. (1974). Exact finite sample distributions and test statistics: a survey and appraisal. In M. D. Intriligator and D. A. Kendrick (eds.), *Frontiers of Quantitative Economics,* Vol. II, Ch. 4, Amsterdam: North-Holland.

Bergstrom, A. R. (1962). The exact sampling distributions at least squares and maximum likelihood estimators of the marginal propensity to consume, *Econometrica 30,* 480–490.

Bleistein, N. and R. A. Handelsman (1976). *Asymptotic Expansions of Integrals,* New York: Holt, Rinehart & Winston.

Constantine, A. G. and R. J. Muirhead (1976). Asymptotic expansions for distributions of latent roots in multivariate analysis, *J. Multivar. Anal. 6,* 369–391.

Chikuse, Y. (1981). Distributions of some matrix variates and latent roots in multivariate Behrens-Fisher discriminant analysis, *Ann. Statist. 9,* 401–407.

Davis, A. W. (1979). Invariant polynomials with two matrix arguments extending the zonal polynomials: applications to multivariate distribution theory, *Ann. Inst. Stat. Math.,* 31, A, 465–485.

Davis, A. W. (1980). Invariant polynomials with two matrix arguments extending the zonal polynomials. In P. R. Krishnaiah (ed.), *Multivariate Analysis,* Amsterdam: North-Holland.

Herz, C. S. (1955). Bessel functions of matrix argument, *Ann. Math. 61,* 474–523.

Holly, A. and P. C. B. Phillips (1979). A saddlepoint approximation to the distribution of the *k*-class estimator in a coefficient in a simultaneous system, *Econometrica 47,* 1527–1547.

Hurwicz, L. (1950). Least squares bias in time series, In T. C. Koopmans (ed), *Statistical Inference in Dynamic Economic Models,* New York: Wiley.

James, A. T. (1961). Zonal polynomials of the real positive definite symmetric matrices, *Ann. Math. 74,* 456–469.

James, A. T. (1968). Calculation of zonal polynomial coefficients by use of the Laplace-Beltrami operator, *Ann. Math. Statist. 39,* 1711–1718.

Kabe, D. G. (1963). A note on the exact distributions of the GCL estimators in two leading overidentified cases, *JASA 58,* 535–537.

Kabe, D. G. (1964). On the exact distributions of the GCL estimators in a leading three equation case, *JASA 59,* 881–894.

Kloek, T. and H. K. Van Dijk (1978). Bayesian estimates of equation system parameters: An application of integration by Monte Carlo, *Econometrica 46,* 1–19.

McLaren, M. L. (1976). Coefficients of the zonal polynomials, *App. Stat. 25,* 82–87.

Muirhead, R. J. (1975). Expressions for some hypergeometric functions of matrix argument with applications, *J. Multivar. Anal. 5,* 283–293.

Muirhead, R. J. (1978). Latent roots and matrix variates: a review of some asymptotic results, *Ann. Stat. 6,* 5–33.

Nagel, P. J. A. (1981). Programs for the evaluation of zonal polynomials, *Am. Stat. 35,* 53.

Phillips, P. C. B. (1977). A general theorem in the theory of asymptotic expansions as approximations to the finite sample distributions of econometric estimators, *Econometrica 45,* 1517–1534.

Phillips, P. C. B. (1980a). Finite sample theory and the distributions of alternative estimators of the marginal propensity to consume, *Rev. Econ. Studies 47,* 183–224.

Phillips, P. C. B. (1980b). The exact finite sample density of instrumental variable estimators in an equation with $n + 1$ endogenous variables, *Econometrica 48,* 861–878.

Phillips, P. C. B. (1982). Best uniform and modified Padé approximants to probability densities in econometrics, presented to World Congress of Econometric Society, Aix-en-Provence, 1980 and published in W. Hildenbrand (Ed) "*Advances in Econometrics*," Cambridge University Press, pp 123–167.

Rhodes, G. F. (1981). Exact density functions and approximate critical regions for likelihood ratio identifiability test statistics, *Econometrica,* 49, pp. 1035–1056.

Richardson, D. H. (1968). The exact distribution of a structural coefficient estimator, *JASA 63,* 1214–1226.

Richardson, D. H. and R. J. Rohr (1983). "An experimental study of two stage least squares distributions in equations containing three endogenous variables" In R. Basmann and George F. Rhodes, Jr. (eds), Advances in Econometrics, vol. 2, Greenwich, Ct.: JAI Press, pp. 25–50.

Sargan, J. D. (1976). Econometric estimators and the Edgeworth approximation, *Econometrica 44,* 421–428; and Erratum, *Econometrica 15,* 272.

Sawa, T. (1969). The exact finite sampling distribution of ordinary least squares and two stage least squares estimator, *JASA 64,* 923–936.

Slater, L. J. (1965). Confluent hypergeometric functions, In M. Abramowitz and I. A. Stegun (eds), *Handbook of Mathematical Functions,* New York: Dover.

Towber, J. (1979). Young symmetry, the flag manifold and representations of $GL(n)$, *J. Algebra 61,* 414–462.

AN EXPERIMENTAL STUDY OF TWO-STAGE LEAST SQUARES DISTRIBUTIONS IN EQUATIONS CONTAINING THREE ENDOGENOUS VARIABLES

D. H. Richardson and R. J. Rohr

I. INTRODUCTION

This article presents the results of an experimental study of the exact finite-sample distribution functions of two-stage least squares estimators. The system of simultaneous equations under consideration is

$$\mathbf{Y}\mathbf{B} + \mathbf{X}\boldsymbol{\Gamma} = \mathbf{E} \tag{1}$$

where $\mathbf{Y}$ is an $N \times G$ matrix of observations on G endogenous variables; $\mathbf{X}$ is an $N \times K$ matrix of nonstochastic exogenous variables; and $\mathbf{E}$ is

Advances in Econometrics, Volume 2, pages 25–50

ISBN: 0-89232-183-0

an $N \times G$ matrix of unobservable disturbance terms. The rows of $\mathbf{E}$ are assumed to be independently and identically distributed according to the multivariate normal distribution with mean zero and covariance matrix $\mathbf{\Omega}$. The elements of $\mathbf{B}$ and $\mathbf{\Gamma}$ are real constants and $\mathbf{B}$ is nonsingular. The reduced form associated with (1) is

$$\mathbf{Y} = \mathbf{X\Pi} + \mathbf{V} \tag{2}$$

where $\mathbf{\Pi} = -\mathbf{\Gamma B}^{-1}$, $\mathbf{V} = \mathbf{EB}^{-1}$, and the covariance matrix of the rows of $\mathbf{V}$ is $\mathbf{\Sigma} = (\mathbf{B}')^{-1}\mathbf{\Omega B}^{-1}$.

The ith structural equation of (1) can be written as

$$\mathbf{y}_i = \mathbf{Y}_i\boldsymbol{\beta}_i + \mathbf{X}_i\boldsymbol{\gamma}_i + \boldsymbol{\varepsilon}_i \tag{3}$$

where $\mathbf{y}_i$ $(T \times 1)$ is a vector of observations on the normalized endogenous variable; $\mathbf{Y}_i$ $(T \times G_i - 1)$ is a matrix of observations on the $G_i - 1$ nonnormalized endogenous variables included in the equation; and $\mathbf{X}_i$ $(T \times K_i)$ is a matrix of included exogenous variables. Partitioning the reduced form conformably with (3) yields

$$\mathbf{y}_i = \mathbf{X}_i\boldsymbol{\pi}_1 + \mathbf{X}_i^*\boldsymbol{\pi}_2^* + \mathbf{v}_{1i} \tag{4a}$$

$$\mathbf{Y}_i = \mathbf{X}_i\mathbf{\Pi}_2 + \mathbf{X}_i^*\mathbf{\Pi}_2^* + \mathbf{V}_{2i} \tag{4b}$$

where $\mathbf{X} = (\mathbf{X}_i : \mathbf{X}_i^*)$.

The exact distribution functions of the two-stage least squares (2SLS) estimator of $\boldsymbol{\beta}_i$ in (3) has been fully explored for two included endogenous variables ($G_i = 2$) (cf. Anderson and Sawa, 1979, for references). This distribution function is characterized by three parameters: (1) the degree of overidentification $\nu_i = K - K_i - G_i + 1$; (2) a standardized coefficient $\bar{\boldsymbol{\beta}}$; and (3) a concentration parameter $\bar{\boldsymbol{\mu}}^2$. Anderson and Sawa (1979) have tabulated the distribution function for selected parameter values, and others have shown how the moments of the distribution depend on the three parameters [see Richardson and Wu (1971) for a summary of these properties]. The distributions of the estimators of $\boldsymbol{\gamma}_i$ in equation (3), as well as the ω_{ii} and the t-statistics associated with the coefficient estimators, and the identifiability test statistics, have also been studied for the $G_i = 2$ case (see Basmann, Richardson, and Rohr, 1974, for a list of references).

The distribution theory for three included endogenous variables ($G_i = 3$) is considerably more complicated and, consequently, not as well developed as for the $G_i = 2$ case (cf. Phillips, 1980). The distribution function of the 2SLS estimator of $\boldsymbol{\beta}_i$ in the general case depends on $G_i - 1$ standardized coefficients and a $(G_i - 1) \times (G_i - 1)$ concentration matrix as well as the overidentification parameter ν_i. The standardized coefficient vector $\bar{\boldsymbol{\beta}}_i$ is a subvector of the ith column of the matrix $\bar{\boldsymbol{\beta}}$

where[1]

$$\overline{\mathbf{B}} = \mathbf{P}^{-1}\mathbf{B}, \tag{5}$$

$\overline{\beta}_{ii} = -1$, and **P** is a lower triangular nonsingular matrix such that

$$\mathbf{P}' \, \Sigma \, \mathbf{P} = \mathbf{I}_G .$$

The concentration matrix for the *i*th equation is defined by

$$\overline{\mathbf{M}}_i = \Sigma_{22}^{-1} \, \mathbf{\Pi}_2^{*\prime} \, \mathbf{S}_i \mathbf{\Pi}_2^{*} \tag{6}$$

where

$$\mathbf{S}_i = \mathbf{X}_i^{*\prime}[\mathbf{I} - \mathbf{X}_i(\mathbf{X}_i'\mathbf{X}_i)^{-1}\mathbf{X}_i']\mathbf{X}_i^{*} \tag{7}$$

and Σ_{22} is the covariance matrix of nonnormalized endogenous variables included in the structural equation.

The major objective of the research reported here was to investigate how the distribution functions of estimators and test statistics in the $G_i = 3$ case are affected by values of the concentration matrix (6). For the $G_i = 2$ case, the distributions exhibit certain desirable properties when the concentration parameter is large. For example, the bias and concentration of the distributions of the estimators are both reduced when the concentration parameter increases in the $G_i = 2$ case. The extent to which these results carry over in the $G_i = 3$ case are presented here.

Of particular interest are the approximations to the distributions of estimators and test statistics. For the $G_i = 2$ case, the exact distributions can be approximated by simpler distributions (e.g., normal, chi-squared, t, F) for large values of the concentration parameter. Experimental distributions from sampling experiments were employed to examine the degree of approximation afforded by the limiting distributions in the $G_i = 3$ case.

The $G_i = 3$ experimental distributions were generated by two different sampling experiments. The generating population for each of the experiments was the same except for the concentration matrices. The elements of the concentration matrices of Experiment A were chosen to be 144 times larger than those of Experiment B. This design was purposely chosen to facilitate tests of hypotheses concerning the importance of the concentration matrix in the distribution theory.

Section II will present a brief outline of the design of the sampling experiments. Sections III, IV, V, and VI will present the experimental results for coefficient estimators, variance estimators, identifiability test statistics, and structural test statistics, respectively. Section VII will conclude the paper with a brief discussion of the results reported in the previous sections.

II. DESIGN OF THE EXPERIMENTS

The common generating population for the experiments consisted of three structural equations, three endogenous variables, and five exogenous variables. The structural equations were

$$y_{t1} = \beta_{21} y_{t2} + \beta_{31} y_{t3} + \gamma_{11} x_{t1} + \varepsilon_{t1} \tag{8}$$

$$y_{t1} = \beta_{22} y_{t2} + \beta_{32} y_{t3} + \gamma_{22} x_{t2} + \gamma_{32} x_{t3} + \varepsilon_{t2} \tag{9}$$

$$y_{t1} = \beta_{23} y_{t2} + \beta_{33} y_{t3} + \gamma_{43} x_{t4} + \gamma_{53} x_{t5} + \varepsilon_{t3} \tag{10}$$

The degrees of overidentification for equations (8), (9), and (10) are 2, 1, and 1, respectively. Thus, all of the 2SLS coefficient estimators possess finite means and the 2SLS estimators of the coefficients in equation (8) have finite variances (cf. Mariano, 1972).

The structural coefficient matrices for both experiments were

$$\mathbf{B} = \begin{bmatrix} -1.0 & -1.0 & -1.0 \\ 0.5 & -1.0 & 1.0 \\ 1.0 & 2.0 & 0 \end{bmatrix} \quad \mathbf{\Gamma} = \begin{bmatrix} 5.0 & 0 & 0 \\ 0 & 5.0 & 0 \\ 0 & 5.0 & 0 \\ 0 & 0 & 5.0 \\ 0 & 0 & 5.0 \end{bmatrix}$$

The structural disturbance covariance matrix $\mathbf{\Omega}$ was chosen so that the standardized coefficient matrix $\bar{\mathbf{B}}$ would equal $\mathbf{B}$. Because this result will hold for $\Sigma = \mathbf{I}$, we specified it as such and deduced

$$\mathbf{\Omega} = \begin{bmatrix} 2.25 & 2.50 & 1.50 \\ 2.50 & 6.00 & 0 \\ 1.50 & 0 & 2.00 \end{bmatrix}$$

Using previously selected values of $\mathbf{B}$ and $\mathbf{\Gamma}$, the reduced form coefficients were computed as

$$\mathbf{\Pi} = \begin{bmatrix} -10.0 & -10.0 & -10.0 \\ 5.0 & 5.0 & 2.5 \\ 5.0 & 5.0 & 2.5 \\ 10.0 & 5.0 & 7.5 \\ 10.0 & 5.0 & 7.5 \end{bmatrix}$$

A sample size of 15 was chosen for both experiments. The only difference between Experiments A and B was in the values assigned to the exogenous

Table 1. Concentration Matrices—Experiment A.

Equation	*M*	$|M|$	M
1	$\begin{bmatrix} 561.67 & 421.67 \\ \cdot & 424.17 \end{bmatrix}$	60,438	985.84
2	$\begin{bmatrix} 478.99 & 471.13 \\ \cdot & 517.70 \end{bmatrix}$	26,016	996.69
3	$\begin{bmatrix} 658.93 & 491.07 \\ \cdot & 408.93 \end{bmatrix}$	28,306	1067.86

variables. These values for Experiment A were 12 times those for Experiment B.

The sample endogenous variables were generated using fixed reduced-form coefficients and exogenous variables, with the disturbance vectors $\mathbf{V}_t$ obtained from a standard, normal, random-number generator. A set of 1000 independent samples were generated for each experiment.

The experiments were designed so that Experiment A and Experiment B would differ only in the size of the concentration matrices. The concentration matrices for Experiment A were chosen large enough to test leading conjectures concerning the 2SLS distributions. The concentration matrices for Experiment A are given in Table 1. All of the entries are at least 400, which was considered large enough to test conjectures. The corresponding concentration matrices for Experiment B are obtained by dividing the entries in Table 1 by 144.

III. COEFFICIENT ESTIMATORS

A. Analysis for Two Included Endogenous Variables

The coefficient of y_{t3} in structural equation (10) was equal to zero in the generating population ($\beta_{33} = 0$). Equation (10) was estimated twice; with β_{33} unrestricted and with the restriction that $\beta_{33} = 0$. When equation (10) is estimated under the restriction that $\beta_{33} = 0$, the estimators and test statistics follow the $G_i = 2$ distributions with $\nu_i = 2$. When β_{33} is not restricted in the estimation process, the appropriate distributions are for the $G_i = 3$ case with $\nu_i = 1$. The known properties of the exact distributions of the 2SLS estimators $\tilde{\beta}_{23}, \tilde{\gamma}_{43}$, and $\tilde{\gamma}_{53}$, obtained by restricting $\beta_{33} = 0$, serve two purposes for the experiments: (1) they provide a source of conjectures for equations containing three endogenous variables; (2) these empirical distribution functions serve as a reference point for checking the sampling variation and computation accuracy of other experimental distributions.

Table 2. Comparison of Exact Moments and Estimated Moments of $\tilde{\beta}_{23}$, $\tilde{\gamma}_{43}$, and $\tilde{\gamma}_{53}$

	Bias		*Mean-Square Error*	
Coefficient	*Exact*	*Estimate**	*Exact*	*Estimate*
EXPERIMENT A				
β_{23}	−0.0015	−0.0028 (0.0017)	0.0030	0.0030
γ_{43}	0.0046	−0.0234 (0.0236)	0.7062	0.5554
γ_{53}	−0.0033	−0.0105 (0.0122)	0.1719	0.1500
EXPERIMENT B				
β_{23}	−0.2811	−0.2797 (0.0205)	0.5622	0.4967
γ_{43}	0.8533	0.5081 (0.2710)	32.4762	73.7160
γ_{53}	−0.6274	−0.7374 (0.1467)	7.2418	7.7856

* Numbers in parentheses are standard errors of the estimates.

The exact biases and mean-square errors for the estimators $\tilde{\beta}_{23}$, $\tilde{\gamma}_{43}$, and $\tilde{\gamma}_{53}$ are given in Table 2. These calculations were made using formulas in Richardson and Wu (1971) and the experimentally selected values for $\bar{\beta}_{23}$ and $\bar{\mu}^2$. In both experiments, the parameter $\bar{\beta}_{23}$ was equal to 1. The concentration parameter $\bar{\mu}^2$ was equal to 658.93 in Experiment A and 4.58 in Experiment B. The moments for $\tilde{\gamma}_{43}$ and $\tilde{\gamma}_{53}$ were obtained from the moments of $\tilde{\beta}_{23}$ as follows:

$$E(\tilde{\gamma}_{43} - \gamma_{43}) = -3.03567E(\tilde{\beta}_{23} - \beta_{23})$$

$$E(\tilde{\gamma}_{53} - \gamma_{53}) = 2.23211E(\tilde{\beta}_{23} - \beta_{23})$$

$$E(\tilde{\gamma}_{43} - \gamma_{43})^2 = 57.0813E(\tilde{\beta}_{23} - \beta_{23})^2 + 0.53572E(\tilde{\beta}_{23})$$

$$E(\tilde{\gamma}_{53} - \gamma_{53})^2 = 12.7100E(\tilde{\beta}_{23} - \beta_{23})^2 + 0.13393E(\tilde{\beta}_{23}).$$

Biases and mean-square errors estimated from the experimental distribution functions are also given in Table 2. Notice that in several cases the estimated values differ considerably from the known exact values. For example, the estimated mean-square error of $\tilde{\gamma}_{43}$ in Experiment B is 2.3 times larger than the exact mean-square error. Considerable sampling variation in the bias and mean-square error estimates is apparent for both experiments. Many Monte Carlo studies compare estimated biases and mean-square errors as if there were no sampling variation. Our results demonstrate that this procedure can be misleading and, if followed, can produce erroneous conclusions.

An asymptotic expansion of the exact distribution function of

$$z = [\mu(\tilde{\beta}_{23} - \beta_{23})]/\sqrt{\omega_{33}} \tag{11}$$

for large $\bar{\mu}^2$ has been given by Sargan and Mikhail (1971) and Mariano (1973). The first term in the expansion is the standard normal distribution function and the remaining terms are of order $\bar{\mu}^{-1}$. The exact distribution of this standardized estimator can therefore be approximated by a standard normal distribution.

The Kolmogorov-Smirnov (K-S) test was used to test the hypothesis that the standardized estimator (11) was distributed according to the standard normal distribution. The K-S test statistic was 0.041 for Experiment A, which was not significant at the 5% level of significance, confirming the choice of $\mu^2 = 658.93$ as large enough for the normal approximation to be satisfactory. Moreover, the K-S test statistic computed from the empirical distribution in Experiment B was significant at a 0.1% level of significance. These tests indicate that $\bar{\mu}^2$ in Experiments A and B differed sufficiently to test conjectures about the distributions in the three-variable case.

The experimental distributions of (11) for Experiment A and Experiment B are plotted in Figure 1. The Experiment B distribution is skewed to the left and has more probability in the lower tail but considerably less in the upper tail than the Experiment A distribution.

B. Bias and Mean-Square Error

Analytic expressions for the exact bias and mean-square error for the estimators of $\boldsymbol{\beta}_i$ in the $G_i = 3$ case have been obtained by Ullah and Nagar (1974) and Bonan (1975). However, these expressions are very complicated functions of the parameters ν_i, $\bar{\boldsymbol{\beta}}_i$, and $\bar{\mathbf{M}}_i$, and it is difficult to determine analytically how changes in the parameters affect the bias and mean-square error using these formulas. Therefore, the following conjectures based on exact results for the $G_i = 2$ case were established:

CONJECTURE C.1. *The biases of the coefficient estimators decrease as the entries in the concentration matrix increase.*

CONJECTURE C.2. *The mean-square errors of the coefficient estimators (when defined) decrease as the entries in the concentration matrix increase.*

Figure 1. Empirical Distribution of (11).

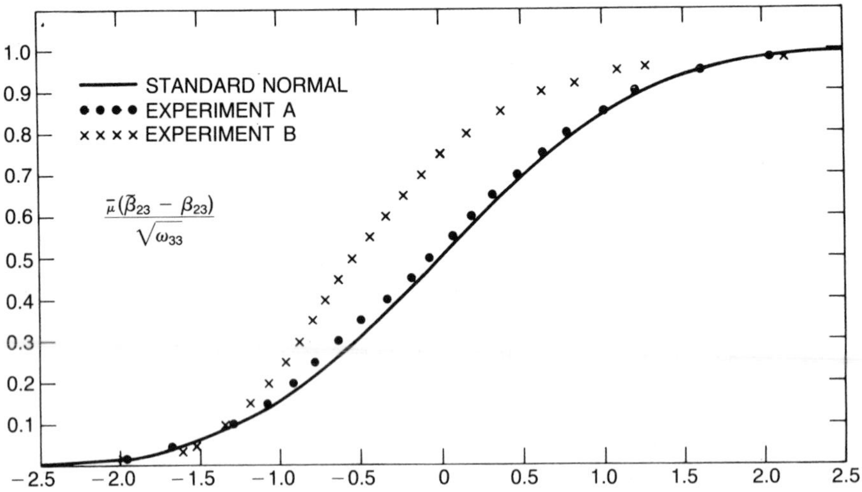

The bias and mean-square error of the coefficient estimators converge to zero as the sample size N grows indefinitely large. Since the sample size N affects the bias and mean-square error only through the concentration matrix and since $\overline{\mathbf{M}}_i = O(N)$, it follows that the bias and mean-square error vanish as the elements of $\overline{\mathbf{M}}_i$ increase without bound. Conjectures C.1 and C.2, relate not to this convergence property, but rather to the monotonicity of convergence as the elements of $\overline{\mathbf{M}}_i$ increase. If Conjectures C.1 and C.2 are valid, the estimated biases and mean-square errors will be larger for Experiment B than for Experiment A.

Data presented in Tables 3 and 4 support Conjectures C.1 and C.2. For all 11 coefficients, the bias is significantly smaller in Experiment A than it is in Experiment B. Also, the mean-square errors in equation (8) are significantly larger for Experiment B than for Experiment A.

Nagar (1959) and Bonan (1975) have obtained asymptotic expansions of the bias and mean-square error that are valid for large $\overline{\mathbf{M}}_i$. The following conjectures concern the accuracy of these approximations for our experimental design.

CONJECTURE C.3. *The exact biases of the estimators can be accurately approximated by the first term of the Nagar expansions.*

CONJECTURE C.4. *The exact mean-square errors of the estimators in equation (8) can be accurately estimated by the first term of the Nagar expansions.*

Table 3. Analysis of Biases.

	Estimated Bias (Standard Error)		*Nagar Bias*	
Coefficient	*Exp. A*	*Exp. B*	*Exp. A*	*Exp. B*
β_{21}	0.0042 (0.1273)	0.0559 (1.0205)	0.0035	0.4995*
β_{31}	−0.0087 (0.1479)	−0.4975 (1.0568)	−0.0058	−0.8361*
γ_{11}	−0.0098 (0.3688)	−1.4472 (4.8632)	−0.0091	−1.3154
β_{22}	−0.0154 (0.4029)	1.3561 (1.6493)	0	0*
β_{32}	0.0125 (0.3876)	−1.4490 (1.5405)	0	0*
γ_{22}	0.0608 (1.2196)	−3.2861 (7.5484)	0	0*
γ_{32}	0.0131 (0.6738)	−0.6270 (6.2507)	0	0*
β_{23}	−0.0045 (0.1727)	−0.4395 (1.4362)	0	0*
β_{33}	0.0043 (0.2207)	0.3187 (1.7937)	0	0*
γ_{43}	−0.0470 (1.2695)	−1.0086 (11.099)	0	0*
γ_{53}	−0.0049 (0.4600)	0.2776 (6.7902)	0	0*

* Indicates that the Nagar bias falls outside the 95% confidence interval.

Since $\overline{\mathbf{M}}_i$ is much larger in Experiment A than in Experiment B, one would expect Conjectures C.3 and C.4 to hold for Experiment A but not necessarily for Experiment B.

The Nagar approximations to the bias provide satisfactory approximations in Experiment A but not in Experiment B. Evidence supporting this conclusion is presented in Tables 3 and 4. For 10 out of 11 cases

Table 4. Mean-Square Errors for Equation (8).

	Experiment A		*Experiment B*	
Coefficient	*Estimated*	*Nagar*	*Estimated*	*Nagar*
β_{21}	0.0162	0.0160	1.0446	6.9290
β_{31}	0.0220	0.0212	1.3644	9.9127
γ_{11}	0.1361	0.1337	25.7450	57.1710

in Experiment B, the Nagar approximation to the bias does not fall in a 95% confidence interval based on the experimental distribution.[2] Table 4 shows that the Nagar approximation to the mean-square errors of the estimators in equation (8) are very accurate in Experiment A. However, in Experiment B the Nagar approximations consistently overstate the size of the mean-square errors. The experimental evidence thus confirms our expectation concerning the accuracy of the Nagar approximations as the elements of $\overline{\mathbf{M}}_i$ vary.

C. Median and Interquartile Range

Since the second moments of the estimators in equations (9) and (10) are not defined, it would be inappropriate to use sample variances as measures of dispersion for these distributions. This section will present the results of some tests of location and dispersion of the distributions that are based on the sample order statistics.

The following conjectures are considered:

CONJECTURE C.5. *The median of the coefficient estimator is equal to the true value of the parameter.*

CONJECTURE C.6. *The difference between the median of the coefficient estimator and its true value decreases as the elements of* $\overline{\mathbf{M}}_i$ *increase.*

CONJECTURE C.7. *The dispersion of the coefficient estimators, as measured by the interquartile range, decreases as the elements of* $\overline{\mathbf{M}}_i$ *increase.*

Conjecture C.5 is tested using the classical sign test for the median of the distribution (cf. Kendall and Stuart, 1961, pp. 513–515). The test is based on the number of sample estimates (K) exceeding the true value. The rejection region for the test at a 1% level of significance is $\{K < 459, K > 541\}$. Results of these tests are reported in Table 5. The hypothesis that the median is equal to the true value was rejected for 13 of the 22 distributions. The sample evidence clearly indicates that Conjecture C.5 is false; the medians of the coefficient estimators are not equal to the true values of the coefficients.

Sample medians and interquartile ranges are reported in Table 6. The experimental results clearly support Conjectures C.6 and C.7 For all 11 coefficients, the difference between the median and the true value of the parameters is greater in Experiment B than in Experiment A. Also, the

Table 5. Sign Test.

Coefficient	Number of Sample Observations Exceeding True Value of Parameter: Exp. A	Exp. B
β_{21}	518	521
β_{31}	471	228*
γ_{11}	482	337*
β_{22}	544*	888*
β_{32}	446*	78*
γ_{22}	467	317*
γ_{32}	493	361*
β_{23}	451*	769*
β_{33}	544*	664*
γ_{43}	458*	495
γ_{53}	522	486

* Indicates rejection of the two-sided test at a 1% level of significance.

interquartile ranges were significantly larger in Experiment A for all coefficients. The nonparametric measures indicate that the distributions of the coefficient estimators are highly skewed and more dispersed when the elements of the concentration matrix are small.

Table 6. Median and Interquartile Ranges.

	Experiment A		*Experiment B*	
	*Median Bias**	*IQR†*	*Median Bias**	*IQR†*
β_{21}	0.0050	0.1675	0.0423	0.9000
β_{31}	−0.0120	0.2040	−0.5252	0.8864
γ_{11}	−0.0160	0.5227	−1.8683	5.5109
β_{22}	0.0380	0.4821	1.3136	1.1215
β_{32}	−0.0553	0.4564	−1.4662	1.0797
γ_{22}	−0.0865	1.4465	−2.6289	7.6560
γ_{32}	−0.0132	0.9552	−1.7456	6.4810
β_{23}	−0.0205	0.2216	−0.4391	0.9955
β_{33}	0.0219	0.0115	0.3482	1.2077
γ_{43}	−0.1053	1.6694	−0.1210	15.1392
γ_{53}	0.0186	0.6347	−0.2272	7.6598

* Median bias = sample median − true value.
† Interquartile range.

D. Approximations to the Distribution Functions

One of the major conjectures to be examined concerns the limiting distributions of the standardized coefficient estimators

$$z = (\hat{\beta}_{ji} - \beta_{ji})/(\omega_{ii}\overline{M}_i^{jj})^{1/2} \qquad (12)$$

where $\overline{M}_i^{jj}$ is the jjth element of $\overline{\mathbf{M}}_i^{-1}$ (standardized estimator for the γ_{ji} are obtained by making an appropriate substitution for $\overline{\mathbf{M}}_i^{-1}$). Sargan and Mikhail (1971) have developed an asymptotic expansion for the distribution (12). The first term of the expansion, which is valid as the elements of $\overline{\mathbf{M}}_i$ approach infinity, is the standard normal distribution. We thus have

CONJECTURE C.8. *The standardized coefficient estimators (12) can be approximated by the standard normal distribution for large values of* $\overline{\mathbf{M}}_i$.

We expect Conjecture C.8 to be valid in Experiment A but not necessarily in Experiment B. This was found to be the case in the estimation of equation (10) under the specification $\beta_{33} = 0$, as discussed in Section III,A and illustrated in Figure 1.

The results of the K-S test for Experiment A are presented in Table 7. In general, these results are not supportive of Conjective C.8. Of the 11 estimators, all but two of the tests were significant at a 5% level of significance. We are thus led to conclude that the elements of the concentration parameters are not large enough to use the first term of the asymptotic expansion as an approximation.[3]

Table 7. Kolmogorov-Smirnov Test—Experiment A.

Equation	*Coefficient*	D_T^*	$P_r(D_T > D_T^*)$
(8)	β_{21}	0.029	0.360
	β_{31}	0.051	0.012
	γ_{11}	0.048	0.020
(9)	β_{22}	0.059	0.002
	β_{32}	—†	—†
	γ_{22}	0.046	0.031
	γ_{32}	0.024	0.637
(10)	β_{23}	0.060	0.001
	β_{33}	0.051	0.011
	γ_{43}	0.045	0.037
	γ_{53}	0.030	0.316

† Indicates a D_T^* which would be significant at 0.1%.

Table 8. Kolmogorov-Smirnov Test—Experiment B.

Equation	*Coefficient*	D_T^*	$P_r(D_T > D_T^*)$
(8)	β_{21}	0.065	0.000
	β_{31}	0.060	0.001
	γ_{11}	0.060	0.001
(9)	β_{22}	0.079	0.000
	β_{32}	0.081	0.000
	γ_{22}	0.063	0.001
	γ_{32}	0.061	0.001
(10)	β_{23}	0.064	0.001
	β_{33}	0.083	0.000
	γ_{43}	0.060	0.001
	γ_{53}	0.033	0.227

The results of the Kolmogorov-Smirnov test of Conjecture C.8 for Experiment B were as expected. For every coefficient estimator except $\hat{\gamma}_{53}$, the test was significant at a 0.1% level of significance. The actual values of the K-S test statistics are given in Table 8.

The empirical distribution of (12) for $\hat{\beta}_{32}$, from Experiment A, its 95% confidence band, and the standard normal distribution are plotted in Figure 2. The maximum deviation between the normal distribution and the nearest confidence band is less than 0.02. The maximum deviation occurs near the center of distribution, and the empirical distribution lies below the normal distribution in both the upper and lower tail. Thus,

Figure 2. Confidence Band (12) β_{32} Experiment A.

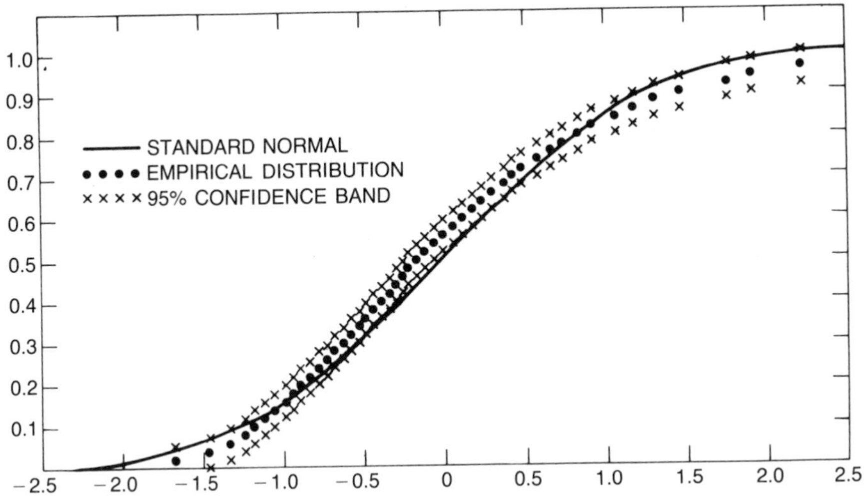

even though the goodness of fit test was rejected at a low level of significance, the normal approximation may be accurate enough for some purposes.

IV. VARIANCE ESTIMATORS

There are a number of estimators that have been defined for the structural variances ω_{ii}. These estimators are functions of the quadratic forms

$$G_{1i} = (\mathbf{y}_i - \mathbf{Y}_i\hat{\boldsymbol{\beta}}_{1i})'[\mathbf{I} - \mathbf{X}_{1i}(\mathbf{X}'_{1i}\mathbf{X}_{1i})^{-1}\mathbf{X}'_{1i}](\mathbf{y}_i - \mathbf{Y}_i\hat{\boldsymbol{\beta}}_{1i})$$

and

$$G_{2i} = (\mathbf{y}_i - \mathbf{Y}_i\hat{\boldsymbol{\beta}}_{1i})'[\mathbf{I} - \mathbf{X}(\mathbf{X}'\mathbf{X})^{-1}\mathbf{X}'](\mathbf{y}_i - \mathbf{Y}_i\hat{\boldsymbol{\beta}}_{1i}).$$

The quadratic form G_{1i} is obtained from estimated residuals when the exogenous variables $\mathbf{X}_i^*$ are excluded from the estimation process. The quadratic form G_{2i} is obtained from estimated residuals including all of the system exogenous variables. The three variance estimators are then

$$\hat{\omega}_{ii} = \frac{G_{1i}}{N - 2 - K_{1i}} \tag{13}$$

$$\tilde{\omega}_{ii} = \frac{G_{2i}}{N - K} \tag{14}$$

$$\bar{\omega}_{ii} = \frac{G_{1i} - G_{2i}}{\nu_i}, \qquad \nu_i > 0. \tag{15}$$

A. Tests of Conjectures

The exact distributions of the estimators (13)–(15) are not generally known, except for the case of two included endogenous variables (cf. Basmann and Richardson, 1973, and the references therein). The following conjectures are based on these results.

CONJECTURE V.1. *The bias of each of the estimators (13)–(15) is a decreasing function of elements of the concentration matrix.*

CONJECTURE V.2. *The distribution of G_{1i}/ω_{ii} can be approximated by the chi-squared distribution with $N - 2 - K_{1i}$ degrees of freedom for large values of the concentration matrix.*

CONJECTURE V.3. *The distribution of G_{2i}/ω_{ii} can be approximated by the chi-squared distribution with $N - K$ degrees of freedom for large values of the concentration matrix.*

CONJECTURE V.4. *The distribution of $(G_{1i} - G_{2i})/\omega_{ii}$ can be approximated by the chi-squared distributions with ν_i degrees of freedom for large values of the concentration matrix.*

The sample mean, variance, minimum, median, and maximum for each variance estimator are reported in Tables 9 and 10. For Experiment A, all the estimated biases are positive. For Experiment B, the estimated biases for $\hat{\omega}_i$ and $\tilde{\omega}_i$ are positive whereas those for $\bar{\omega}_{ii}$ are negative. The exact bias of $\bar{\omega}_{ii}$ is negative for the two equation case (cf. Basmann and Richardson, 1973, p. 51). Although the estimated biases for $\bar{\omega}_{ii}$ in Experiment A indicate that this result does not generalize to the three equation case, calculations employing the central limit theorem show that the estimated

Table 9. Summary Statistics—Variance Estimators. Experiment A

	EQUATION (8) $\omega^*_{11} = 2.25$	$\nu_1 = 2$	
	$\hat{\omega}_{11}$	$\tilde{\omega}_{11}$	$\bar{\omega}_{11}$
Mean	2.2821	2.2722	2.3315
Variance	0.8793	1.0166	5.6159
Minimum	0.4105	0.3978	0.0033
Median	2.1866	2.1739	1.6342
Maximum	9.0544	7.7754	18.3395
	EQUATION (9) $\omega^*_{22} = 6.0$	$\nu_2 = 1$	
	$\hat{\omega}_{22}$	$\tilde{\omega}_{22}$	$\bar{\omega}_{22}$
Mean	6.3098	6.3245	6.1626
Variance	14.9945	17.4322	72.1812
Minimum	0.6547	0.7201	0.0000
Median	5.3963	5.2824	2.7208
Maximum	40.4921	44.5310	69.7010
	EQUATION (10) $\omega^*_{33} = 2.0$	$\nu_3 = 1$	
	$\hat{\omega}_{33}$	$\tilde{\omega}_{33}$	$\bar{\omega}_{33}$
Mean	2.0720	2.0630	2.1625
Variance	0.9796	1.0845	9.2581
Minimum	0.2096	0.1785	0.0000
Median	1.9263	1.9097	1.0205
Maximum	8.1977	8.9816	20.2715

Table 10. Summary Statistics—Variance Estimators. Experiment B

	EQUATION (8) $\omega^*_{11} = 2.25$	$\nu_1 = 2$	
	$\hat{\omega}_{11}$	$\tilde{\omega}_{11}$	$\bar{\omega}_{11}$
Mean	3.3166	3.6347	1.7262
Variance	36.2703	52.0425	2.6789
Minimum	0.3929	0.2287	0.0014
Median	2.0321	2.0408	1.2417
Maximum	72.7707	86.9700	11.8447
	EQUATION (9) $\omega^*_{22} = 6.0$	$\nu_2 = 1$	
	$\hat{\omega}_{22}$	$\tilde{\omega}_{22}$	$\bar{\omega}_{22}$
Mean	17.9205	19.5307	1.8189
Variance	154,136	186,510	6.2424
Minimum	0.2043	0.1192	0.0000
Median	2.2315	2.2118	0.8009
Maximum	12,399	13,639	18.6594
	EQUATION (10) $\omega^*_{33} = 2.0$	$\nu_3 = 1$	
	$\hat{\omega}_{33}$	$\tilde{\omega}_{33}$	$\bar{\omega}_{33}$
Mean	6.0665	6.5220	1.5120
Variance	558.74	674.47	3.9251
Minimum	0.2812	0.2428	0.0000
Median	2.2067	2.2615	0.7754
Maximum	387.47	424.85	13.8550

biases are not significantly positive. Moreover, all three of the negative biases in Experiment B are significantly negative. Therefore, the experimental evidence does not refute the proposition that the bias of $\bar{\omega}_{ii}$ will be negative in the three equation case.

The estimated biases in Experiment A are significantly smaller than in Experiment B, thus supporting conjecture V.1.

Comparison of the estimated variances reveals an interesting pattern. In Experiment A, the estimated variance of $\bar{\omega}_{ii}$ is from 4 to 9 times larger than the estimated variance of $\hat{\omega}_{ii}$ and $\tilde{\omega}_{ii}$. But in Experiment B, the estimated variances of $\hat{\omega}_{ii}$ and $\tilde{\omega}_{ii}$ are from 10 to 170 times larger than those of $\bar{\omega}_{ii}$. It appears that $\hat{\omega}_{ii}$ and $\tilde{\omega}_{ii}$ are preferred to $\bar{\omega}_{ii}$ for large concentration matrices but that the reverse is true for small values of the concentration matrices. This relationship among the estimators may be explained by the nonexistence of moments of $\hat{\omega}_{ii}$ and $\tilde{\omega}_{ii}$. In the two equation case, all the moments of $\bar{\omega}_{ii}$ exist, but the hth moment of $\hat{\omega}_{ii}$ and $\tilde{\omega}_{ii}$ is defined only if $h < (\nu_i + 1)/2$ (cf. Basmann and Richardson, 1973, p. 44). If this moment existence theorem carries over to the three equation case, then the exact variances of $\hat{\omega}_{ii}$ or $\tilde{\omega}_{ii}$ would not exist.

Tests of Conjectures V.2, V.3, and V.4 were carried out using the empirical distribution functions from Experiment A. These results are reported in Table 11. Conjectures V.2 and V.3 for equation (9) were rejected at a 0.1% level of significance. All other tests were not significant at a 5% level of significance. Although the exact distribution of $\hat{\omega}_{ii}$ and $\tilde{\omega}_{ii}$ are not closely approximated by chi-squared distributions for concentration matrices as large as those in Experiment A, the distribution of $\bar{\omega}_{ii}$ was closely approximated by chi-square with ν_i degrees of freedom.

The Kologorov-Smirnov tests of Conjectures V.2, V.3, and V.4 for Experiment B were all significant at a 0.1% test size.

B. Confidence Intervals for the Variances

The chi-squared distributions of Conjectures V.2, V.3, and V.4 can be used to construct approximate confidence intervals for ω_{ii}. For example, if $\chi^2_n(\alpha)$ denotes the αth percentile of the chi-squared distribution with $n = N - K_{1i} - 2$ degrees of freedom, then

$$\frac{n\hat{\omega}_{ii}}{\chi^2_n(1 - \alpha/2)} \leqslant \omega_{ii} \leqslant \frac{n\hat{\omega}_{ii}}{\chi^2_n(\alpha/2)}$$

represents an approximate $100(1 - \alpha) > 0$ confidence interval for ω_{ii}.

Table 12 reports the number of samples (out of 1000) that actually fell within the approximate chi-squared intervals. For Experiment A, the approximate intervals based on $\bar{\omega}_{22}$ and $\bar{\omega}_{33}$ are much better than those for $\tilde{\omega}_{ii}$ and $\hat{\omega}_{ii}$. The $\tilde{\omega}_{22}$ and $\hat{\omega}_{33}$ intervals overestimate the nominal probability by 77 and 88%, respectively. In Experiment B, the approximations based on $\hat{\omega}_{ii}$ and $\tilde{\omega}_{ii}$ are also significantly worse than those based on $\bar{\omega}_{ii}$. In this

Table 11. Kolmogorov-Smirnov Test for the Variance Estimators in Experiment A.

Equation	*Estimate*	D^*_T	$P_r(D_T > D^*_T)$
(8)	$\hat{\omega}_{11}$	0.039	0.100
	$\tilde{\omega}_{11}$	0.032	0.274
	$\bar{\omega}_{11}$	0.024	0.604
(9)	$\hat{\omega}_{22}$	—*	—*
	$\tilde{\omega}_{22}$	—*	—*
	$\bar{\omega}_{22}$	0.021	0.820
(10)	$\hat{\omega}_{33}$	0.036	0.156
	$\tilde{\omega}_{33}$	0.032	0.264
	$\bar{\omega}_{33}$	0.040	0.077

* Indicates significant at a 0.1% level of significance.

Table 12. 90% Confidence Intervals for ω_{ii}.

	$\hat{\omega}_{ii}$			$\tilde{\omega}_{ii}$			$\overline{\omega}_{ii}$		
	(1)*	(2)†	(3)‡	(1)*	(2)†	(3)‡	(1)*	(2)†	(3)‡
EXPERIMENT A									
ω_{11}	47	48	95	46	48	94	56	58	114
ω_{22}	73	104	177	77	108	185	52	55	107
ω_{33}	55	75	130	61	72	133	53	62	115
EXPERIMENT B									
ω_{11}	97	188	285	104	200	304	63	12	75
ω_{22}	450	71	521	450	78	528	85	6	91
ω_{33}	76	282	358	75	299	374	55	19	74

* Number of samples for which upper confidence limit was less than ω_{ii}.
† Number of samples for which lower confidence limit was greater than ω_{ii}.
‡ Column 1 + column 2 or the number of samples in which ω_{ii} was within the confidence interval.

case $\hat{\omega}_{ii}$ and $\tilde{\omega}_{ii}$ severely overestimate the nominal probability whereas $\overline{\omega}_{ii}$ underestimates it slightly.

Based on these experimental results, if approximate confidence intervals are employed, then intervals using $\overline{\omega}_{ii}$ will introduce significantly less error than intervals based on the other methods. It should be mentioned, however, that intervals based on $\overline{\omega}_{ii}$ will be much wider because the degrees of freedom parameter ν_i is usually very small.

V. IDENTIFIABILITY TEST STATISTICS

The identifiability test statistic for the ith structural equation is

$$F_i = \frac{N - K}{\nu_i} \cdot \frac{G_{1i} - G_{2i}}{G_{2i}}$$

where G_{1i} and G_{2i} are defined in Section IV. This test statistic is designed to test the rank restrictions on the reduced form coefficients that are implied by the hypothetical exclusion of exogenous variables from the structural equation.

The exact distribution of F_i for the case of two included endogenous variables has been studied by Richardson (1968b) and Ebbeler (1970). In this case the exact distribution converges to the (central) F distribution with ν_i and $N - K$ degrees of freedom as the concentration parameter increases without bound. This result is the basis for the following conjecture:[4]

CONJECTURE F.1. *The distribution of the statistic F_i can be approximated by the F distribution with ν_i and $N - K$ degrees of freedom for large values of the concentration matrix.*

The experimental distributions of the F_i statistics in Experiment A were in good agreement with conjecture F.1. The Kolmogorov-Smirnov test statistics for equations (8)–(10) were 0.019, 0.030, and 0.029, respectively. The probabilities of larger values under the null hypothesis of Conjecture F.1 are 0.99, 0.32, and 0.37, respectively. Thus, we accept Conjecture F.1 at a level of significance as high as 30%.

The experimental distributions for Experiment B were not in agreement with Conjecture F.1. All of the Kolmogorov-Smirnov tests were significant at a 0.1% level. Based on these experimental results, the concentration parameters in Experiment B were not large enough to satisfy Conjecture F.1, whereas those in Experiment A were sufficiently large.

For hypothesis testing purposes, the relationship between the upper tails of the exact distribution of F_i and the F-distribution is important. Probability points from the upper tails of the empirical and hypothetical distributions are given in Table 13. For Experiment B, the experimental distribution lies above the hypothetical distribution. As a consequence, on the average, a valid identifiability hypothesis will be rejected more often using the F-distribution than it would be using the exact distribution of F_i when the elements of the concentration matrix are small.

Table 13. Upper Tail of F-Distribution.

Equation (8)			*Equation (9)*			*Equation (10)*		
x	P_o†	P^*‡	x	P_o†	P^*‡	x	P_o†	P^*‡
				EXPERIMENT A				
2.9245	0.900	0.902	3.2850	0.900	0.888	3.2850	0.900	0.894
4.1028	0.950	0.951	4.9646	0.950	0.942	4.9646	0.950	0.934
5.4564	0.975	0.974	6.9367	0.975	0.967	6.9367	0.975	0.966
7.5594	0.990	0.989	10.0440	0.990	0.987	10.0440	0.990	0.990
				EXPERIMENT B				
2.9245	0.900	0.919	3.2850	0.900	0.912	3.2850	0.900	0.945
4.1028	0.950	0.954	4.9646	0.950	0.957	4.9646	0.950	0.975
5.4564	0.975	0.979	6.9367	0.975	0.978	6.9267	0.975	0.986
7.5594	0.990	0.988	10.0440	0.990	0.992	10.0440	0.990	0.996

† P_o, Value of the (central) F-distribution with ν_i and $N - K$ degrees of freedom evaluated at x.
‡ P^*, Proportion of sample F statistics less than or equal to x.

VI. t-TEST STATISTICS

In this section the distributions of three alternative structural t-test statistics will be considered. The three test statistics differ only with respect to the variance estimator of ω_{ii}.

Letting δ_{ji} denote either β_{ji} or γ_{ji} and $\mathbf{Q}_i = \mathbf{Z}_i'\mathbf{X}(\mathbf{X}'\mathbf{X})^{-1}\mathbf{X}'\mathbf{Z}_i$ where $\mathbf{Z}_i = (\mathbf{Y}_i \vdots \mathbf{X}_{1i})$, the three test statistics are defined as

$$t_1 = \frac{\hat{\delta}_{ji} - \delta_{ji}}{(\hat{\omega}_{ii} q_i^{jj})^{1/2}} \tag{16}$$

$$t_2 = \frac{\hat{\delta}_{ji} - \delta_{ji}}{(\tilde{\omega}_{ii} q_i^{jj})^{1/2}} \tag{17}$$

$$t_3 = \frac{\hat{\delta}_{ji} - \delta_{ji}}{(\overline{\omega}_{ii} q_i^{jj})^{1/2}} \tag{18}$$

where q_i^{jj} is the jth diagonal element of $\mathbf{Q}_i^{-1}$.

A. Conjectures and Tests

The exact distribution of the test statistic t_3 has been obtained for the case of two included endogenous variables (cf. Richardson and Rohr, 1971). As the concentration parameter increases without bound, this distribution converges to Student's t-distribution with ν_i degrees of freedom. Similar results have been obtained for the test statistics t_1 and t_2 when the standardized β_{ji} coefficient is zero (cf. Rohr, 1976). These finite sample results for the $G_i = 2$ case constitute the basis of the following conjectures:

CONJECTURE T.1. *The distribution of the test statistics t_1 can be approximated by Student's t with $N - K + \nu_i$ degrees of freedom for large values of the concentration matrix.*

CONJECTURE T.2. *The distribution of the test statistic t_2 can be approximated by Student's t with $N - K$ degrees of freedom for large values of the concentration matrix.*

CONJECTURE T.3. *The distribution of the test statistic t_3 can be approximated by Student's t with ν_i degrees of freedom for large values of the concentration matrix.*

Table 14. Kolmogorov-Smirnov Tests.
t Test Statistics for Experiment A

		t_1		t_2		t_3	
Equation	*Coefficient*	D_T^*	P_r†	D_T^*	P_r†	D_T^*	P_r†
(8)	β_{21}	0.041	0.066	0.041	0.071	0.037	0.127
	β_{31}	0.060	0.002	0.059	0.002	0.051	0.011
	γ_{11}	0.036	0.153	0.035	0.179	0.032	0.267
(9)	β_{22}	—‡		—‡		0.060	0.002
	β_{32}	—‡		—‡		—‡	
	γ_{22}	—‡		—‡		0.050	0.015
	γ_{32}	0.045	0.035	0.043	0.054	0.032	0.258
(10)	β_{23}	—‡		—‡		—‡	
	β_{33}	0.052	0.009	0.054	0.006	0.051	0.011
	γ_{43}	0.050	0.012	0.051	0.011	0.051	0.010
	γ_{53}	0.036	0.152	0.038	0.118	0.026	0.517

† P_r, P_r $(D_t \geq D_T^*)$ under the null hypothesis.
‡ Indicates a D_T^* significant at 0.1%.

These conjectures were tested using the Kolmogorov-Smirnov test statistic. Results for Experiment A are reported in Table 14. Conjectures T.1 and T.2 were rejected at a 1% level of significance for 6 of the 11 coefficients. Results for Conjecture T.3 were slightly more favorable; it was rejected for 3 of the 11 coefficients. Good agreement was found for only three coefficients—γ_{11}, γ_{32}, and γ_{53}. Thus, the Student's t-distribution poorly approximates the exact distribution even when the concentration matrices are relatively large. The approximations using t_3 may be better, but only marginally so.

Tests of Conjectures T.1–T.3 for Experiment B were as expected. The null hypothesis was rejected at a 0.1% level of significance in 30 of the 33 separate tests. The three exceptions were all for Conjecture T.3. The coefficients were β_{21}, γ_{43}, and γ_{53}. The K-S values were 0.041, 0.031, and 0.039, respectively, and the corresponding probabilities were 0.067, 0.280, and 0.091.

B. Confidence Intervals and Inference

The preceding tests indicate that the structural t-test statistics are not distributed according to Student's t-distribution even for relatively large values of the concentration parameters. In this final section we shall consider the degree of accuracy afforded by using the Student's t-distributions as approximations for making statistical inference.

Approximate confidence intervals for the structural parameters δ_{ji} can be constructed using the distributions of Conjectures T.1–T.3. For example, a $100(1 - \alpha)\%$ confidence interval for δ_{ji} using t_1 is

$$\hat{\delta}_{ji} \pm (\hat{\omega}_{ii} q_i^{jj})^{1/2} t_{\alpha/2, N-K+\nu_i}$$

where $t_{\alpha/2,N-K+\nu_i}$ is the $\alpha/2$ percentile of Student's t-distribution with $N - K + \nu_i$ degrees of freedom.

The accuracy of these approximations was checked by computing the proportion of samples in which the confidence interval contained the true value of the parameter δ_{ji}. The results of these computations are presented in Table 15. For Experiment A the approximations were very good for all three test statistics. There was a tendency to underestimate the nominal probability in equation (9) and overestimate it in equation (10), but the degree of error was not large.

For Experiment B the approximations were not very good. The approximation errors seem to follow no particular pattern other than an overestimation for all of the γ coefficients for t_1 and t_2. One interesting outcome of the computations for Experiment B is the relative superiority of approximate intervals based on t_3. In every case the approximation error is less for t_3 than for either t_1 or t_2. It should be noted, however, that approximate confidence intervals using t_3 are much wider than those using t_1 or t_2. The approximations using t_3 may be more accurate, but

Table 15. Approximate Confidence Intervals.*

		Experiment A			*Experiment B*		
Equation	*Coefficient*	t_1	t_2	t_3	t_1	t_2	t_3
(8)	β_{21}	0.901	0.899	0.903	0.975	0.976	0.913
	β_{31}	0.903	0.893	0.900	0.842	0.835	0.853
	γ_{11}	0.914	0.905	0.902	0.914	0.911	0.885
(9)	β_{22}	0.888	0.878	0.894	0.606	0.620	0.790
	β_{32}	0.884	0.883	0.896	0.183	0.178	0.756
	γ_{22}	0.910	0.908	0.894	0.957	0.962	0.902
	γ_{32}	0.917	0.908	0.905	0.946	0.944	0.898
(10)	β_{23}	0.908	0.900	0.915	0.839	0.872	0.879
	β_{33}	0.902	0.904	0.919	0.960	0.961	0.895
	γ_{43}	0.914	0.909	0.916	0.970	0.971	0.915
	γ_{53}	0.913	0.900	0.917	0.960	0.959	0.900

* Entries are the proportion of samples for which the true coefficient was within the 90% confidence interval as calculated from the distributions in Conjectures T.1–T.3.

they may also be less useful in practice because of the wider intervals they produce.

Inspection of the third moments and empirical distribution functions indicates that the t-distributions are highly skewed. In general, the distributions are skewed to the right if the coefficient is positive and to the left if the coefficient is negative. This skewness will, of course, seriously impair the accuracy of approximate confidence intervals and approximate critical regions based on Student's t-distribution. This skewness property is consistent with the exact results derived for $G_i = 2$.

Finally, we consider the power of alternative tests of the hypothesis that the structural coefficient is 0. We assume that the critical region for testing this hypothesis is constructed using the Student's t-distributions as given in conjectures T.1–T.3. The test statistics in this case would be

$$t_1^* = \hat{\delta}_{ji}/(\hat{\omega}_{ii}q_i^{jj})^{1/2}, \qquad t_2^* = \hat{\delta}_{ji}/(\tilde{\omega}_{ii}q_i^{jj})^{1/2}, \qquad \text{and } t_3^* = \hat{\delta}_{ji}/(\overline{\omega}_{ii}q_i^{jj})^{1/2}.$$

Under the null hypothesis $\delta_{ji} = 0$, Conjectures T.1–T.3 state that these statistics are distributed as Student's t with $N - K + \nu_i$, $N - K$, and ν_i degrees of freedom, respectively. A test size of 10% is assumed for the alternative that $\delta_{ji} \neq 0$. The empirical distribution of t_1^*, t_2^*, and t_3^* were used to estimate the power function of the tests at the values of the coefficients δ_{ji} selected for the experiments. The results reported in Table 16 indicate that the t_3 tests have a very low power vis-à-vis t_1 and t_2. This is in agreement with results found by Maddala (1974). Although t_3 may be more accurate for estimating the level of significance, this advantage must be weighed against a considerable loss in the power of the test.

Table 16. Power of the t-Test Statistics.†
Experiment A

Equation	*Coefficient*	t_1^*	t_2^*	t_3^*
(8)	β_{21}	0.952	0.955	0.790
	β_{31}	1.000	1.000	0.987
(9)	β_{22}	0.958	0.939	0.342
	β_{32}	1.000	1.000	0.634
(10)	β_{23}	1.000	1.000	0.638
	β_{33}	0.094	0.100	0.075

† Entries are estimate of power of test that $\delta_{ji} = 0$ against $\delta_{ji} \neq 0$ using a 10% level of significance and the t-distribution of Conjectures T.1–T.3. NOTE: Since $\beta_{33} = 0$, estimate reported is an estimate of level of significance.

VII. SUMMARY AND CONCLUSIONS

There are many inherent difficulties in attempting to draw definite conclusions about exact distributions from experimental studies of the nature presented here. Some of the conclusions indicated here may be disproved by future experimental or analytical work. In the meantime, the above results are offered as a source of conjectures for future research on exact distribution theory and as an aid to empirical research.

The major results of the experimental results reported here can be summarized as follows.

1. The bias and mean-square error of the coefficient estimators decrease as the elements of the concentration matrix increase.
2. The biases of the variance estimators decrease as the elements of the concentration matrix increase.
3. The first term of Nagar approximations provide good measures of concentration for large $\overline{\mathbf{M}}_i$ but not for small $\overline{\mathbf{M}}_i$.
4. The variance estimators $\hat{\omega}_{ii}$ and $\tilde{\omega}_{ii}$ are less concentrated than $\overline{\omega}_{ii}$ for large concentration matrices, but the reverse is true for small concentration parameters.
5. Confidence intervals based on $\overline{\omega}_{ii}$ will provide better approximations to the nominal confidence level than approximations based on $\hat{\omega}_{ii}$ and $\tilde{\omega}_{ii}$; however, they produce wider confidence intervals.
6. The distribution of the identifiability test statistic can be closely approximated by the (central) F distribution, even for small values of the concentration matrices.
7. The structural t-statistics are *not* approximated accurately by to the Student's t-distribution. The actual distributions are highly skewed, and serious errors can result if Student's t-distribution approximations are used for statistical inference.
8. If the t-statistics are assumed to be distributed according to Student's t-distribution for purposes of constructing confidence intervals, the intervals for t_3 will be more accurate than those for t_1 or t_2. However, the width of the interval for t_3 is greater and the power of the test that the coefficient is zero is much lower using t_3 than for either t_1 or t_2.

In terms of immediate applications, these results are important in that they highlight the role of the concentration matrix in the exact distribution theory. This study indicates that the distributions of $\overline{\omega}_{ii}$ and F_i are fairly well behaved for large $\overline{\mathbf{M}}_i$ but that the distribution of the coefficient estimators, $\hat{\omega}_{ii}$, $\tilde{\omega}_{ii}$, and the t-statistics are not accurately approximated by the large sample distribution even for $\overline{\mathbf{M}}_i$ matrices as large as those of Experiment A. Moreover, for small $\overline{\mathbf{M}}_i$, as in Experiment B, the distributions are highly skewed and dispersed, and the approximations are clearly not good.

Anderson, Morimune, and Sawa (1978) have estimated the $\overline{\mathbf{M}}_i$ and $\overline{\beta}_i$ parameters for 11 ($G_i = 2$) structural equations that have appeared in the econometrics literature. For the cases examined, the estimated concentration parameters were small (8 of the 11 were less than 80). For the $G_i = 3$ case reported here, the experimental results indicate that the elements of $\overline{\mathbf{M}}_i$ must be larger than 400 to obtain a reasonable degree of approximation. Thus, for practical applications care should be exercised in using these approximations unless estimated concentration parameters are very large.

NOTES

1. This definition of $\overline{\boldsymbol{\beta}}_i$ is for $G_i = G$. If $G_i < G$, **B** and $\boldsymbol{\Sigma}$ should be replaced by appropriate submatrices. See Mariano (1972) for an explicit representation of **P**.

2. The standard errors for the estimated biases given in Table 3 were computed differently for equation (8) than for equation (9) or (10). For equation (8) the standard error of the estimated bias was $ST^{-1/2}$ where $T = 1000$, the number of replications, and S is the positive square root of

$$S^2 = \frac{1}{T-1}\sum_{i=1}^{1000}(\omega_i - \overline{\omega})^2$$

and ω_i is the coefficient estimate in the ith sample. This procedure is not appropriate for equations (9) and (10) because the second moments of the estimation in these equations are not defined. The standard error of the estimated bias in these cases was computed as

$$S^2 = \frac{1}{T-1}\sum_{\omega_i \in A}(\omega_i - \overline{\omega})^2$$

where A is the set of all ω_i such that $|\omega_i| \leqslant T^{1/2}$. This procedure was suggested in Gnedenko and Kolmogorov (1954, pp. 130–131) and Govindarajulu (1973).

3. In a separate paper, we compare the experimental distributions with higher order terms of the Sargan-Mikhail approximation (cf. Richardson and Rohr, 1982). The general conclusion of those comparisons is that the higher order terms of the Sargan-Mikhail approximations are not accurate, even for concentration matrices of the magnitude in Experiment A.

4. Basmann (1960) has also studied the experimental distribution of F_i for a three-variable equation. He found that the experimental distribution was closely approximated by the F-distribution given in Conjecture F.1 (cf. Basmann, 1960, pp. 657–658).

REFERENCES

Anderson, T. W. and T. Sawa (1973). Distribution of estimates of coefficients of a single equation in a simultaneous system and their asymptotic expansion, *Econometrica 41*, 683–714.

Anderson, T.W., K. Morimune and T. Sawa (1978). The numerical values of some key parameters in econometric models, *Institute of Mathematical Studies in the Social Sciences,* Technical Report No. 270, Stanford University.

Basmann, R. L. (1960). On finite simple distributions of generalized classical linear identifiability test statistics, *JASA 55,* 650–659.

Basmann, R. L. (1974). Exact finite sample distributions for some econometric estimators and test statistics: A survey and appraisal, *In* M. D. Intriligator and D. Kendrick (eds.), *Frontiers in Quantitative Economics,* Vol. II, Amsterdam: North-Holland pp. 209–288.

Basmann, R. L. and D. H. Richardson (1973). The exact finite sample distribution of a nonconsistent structural variance estimator, *Econometrica 41,* 41–58.

Basmann, R. L., D. H. Richardson and R. J. Rohr (1974). An experimental study of structural estimators and test statistics associated with dynamical econometric models,'' *Econometrica 42,* 717–730.

Bonan, D. J. (1975). Moments of least-squares estimates in the errors-in-variables model, University of California, Berkeley, Ph.D. thesis, unpublished.

Ebbeler, D. H. (1970). An investigation of the properties of the exact finite sample distributions of GCL statistics associated with the structural representation of an econometric model, Purdue University, Ph.D. thesis.

Gnedenko, B. V. and A. N. Kolmogorov (1954). *Limit Distributions for Sums of Independent Random Variables,* Reading, MA: Addison-Wesley.

Govindarajulu, Z. (1973). ''A central limit theorem for independent summands with infinite variances, *Proc. Indian Acad. Sci. 78,* 89–99.

Kendall, M. G. and A. Stuart (1961). *The Advanced Theory of Statistics,* Vol. 2, New York: Hafner.

Maddala, G. S. (1974). Some small sample evidence on tests of significance in simultaneous equations models, *Econometrica 42,* 841–885.

Mariano, R. S. (1972). The existence of moments of the ordinary least-squares and two-stage least-squares estimators, *Econometrica 40,* 643–652.

Mariano, R. S. (1973). Approximations to the distribution functions of Theil's *k*-class estimators, *Econometrica 41,* 715–721.

Nagar, A. L. (1959). The bias and moment-matrix of the general *k*-class estimators of the parameters in structural equations, *Econometrica 27,* 575–595.

Phillips, P. C. B. (1980). The exact distribution of instrumental variable estimators in an equation containing $n + 1$ endogenous variables, *Econometrica* 40, 861–878.

Richardson, D. H. (1968a). The exact distribution of a structural coefficient estimator, *JASA 63,* 1214–1226.

Richardson, D. H. (1968b). On the distribution of the identifiability test statistic, *In* J. P. Quirk and A. M. Zarley (eds.), *Papers in Quantitative Economics,* Lawrence, KA: University Press of Kansas.

Richardson, D. H. and R. J. Rohr (1971). The distribution of a structural t-statistic for the case of two included endogenous variables, *JASA 66,* 375–382.

Richardson, D. H. and R. J. Rohr (1982). Experimental evidence on approximations to two-stage least-squares distributions, *J. Statist. Comput. Simul. 15,* 221–232.

Richardson, D. H. and D. Wu (1971). A note on the comparison of ordinary and two-stage least-squares estimators, *Econometrica 39,* 973–981.

Rohr, R. J. (1976). On the distribution of two alternative structural *t*-statistics, *JASA 71,* 731–737.

Sargan, J. D. and W. M. Mikhail (1971). A general approximation to the distribution of instrumental variable estimates, *Econometrica 39,* 131–169.

Ullah, A. and A. L. Nagar (1974). ''The exact mean of the two-stage least-squares estimator of the structural parameters in an equation having three endogenous variables, *Econometrica 42,* 749–758.

SPECIFICATION ERROR ANALYSIS IN LINEAR SIMULTANEOUS SYSTEMS

Roberto S. Mariano and John G. Ramage

I. INTRODUCTION

Typically, in applied econometric work, economic theory provides some guidance but falls short of specifying the precise form of structural relationships. The possibilities for misspecification are numerous and, some claim, inevitable. The consequences can be serious, whether for estimation or testing or prediction. Even when the general structural form is reasonably well known, the practitioner must steer a narrow course between the dangers of under- and overspecification of a model. The omission of important variables leads to bias and inconsistency in estimation and bias in forecasting. Seriously misleading conclusions concerning basic relationships (e.g., spurious correlation) are possible as well. Overfitting a model introduces noise that can obscure basic relationships or cause

Advances in Econometrics, Volume 2, pages 51–95

ISBN: 0-89232-183-0

instabilities that result in inefficient estimates, lowered power for tests, and loss of forecast accuracy.

A great deal of methodology for dealing with model selection and specification has recently been developed in both the econometric and the statistical literatures. In spite of advances, the problems of potential misspecification are still formidable even in the linear regression context. These problems are compounded in the simultaneous-equations context because finite-sample statistical properties are much less well understood, even in correctly specified models. Methodology is largely extrapolated from the regression context and used for model selection, fit assessment, and inference without adequate knowledge of the consequences. In special cases where exact sampling results are available, commonly used procedures such as coefficient t tests have been shown to be seriously misleading. Often, little serious residual analysis is feasible or attempted in large-scale simultaneous-equations models.

Past contributions in the area of specification error analysis in simultaneous-equations models include those of Fisher (1961, 1966, 1967) and Ramage (1971). Fisher compared the large-sample, asymptotic behavior of the two-stage least squares (2SLS) and limited-information maximum likelihood (LIML) estimators in the presence of misspecification consisting of exclusion of relevant variables in a single equation. His principal result (1966, 1967) is that neither 2SLS nor LIML dominates the other for all possible values of the specification error according to his criterion, which amounts to a weighted sum of squares of the large-sample, asymptotic bias. No explicit distributional characteristics of the estimators under misspecification were derived.

Ramage (1971) made use of the small-disturbance, asymptotic method introduced by Kadane (1970, 1971) to compare various kinds of specification error in a single equation, including omission of relevant variables and misclassification of endogenous variables. He derived explicit expressions for the small-disturbance asymptotic bias and mean squared error (MSE) of the k-class estimators, including LIML, in the presence of misspecification and presented a number of comparison results among estimators and among types of misspecification.

Hale, Mariano, and Ramage (1980) (henceforth, HMR) examined the effects of misspecification on the exact sampling moments of the k-class estimators for k nonstochastic and between 0 and 1. Specification errors consisting of exclusion of relevant exogenous variables and inclusion of extraneous exogenous variables within the estimated equation and the equation system are examined. The misspecification can occur either in the estimated equation itself or in other equations of the system (or both simultaneously). Exact expressions and large concentration parameter asymptotic expansions are presented and analyzed for the bias and MSE of the k-class estimators in the case of two included endogenous variables. The basic results in the paper suggest that "ordinary least squares (OLS) will often be preferable to two-stage least squares when misspecification is a serious possibility. The relative insensitivity of OLS to specification error outweighs its disadvantage in terms of bias and MSE in the correctly specified case. Further, when relevant exogenous variables are omitted from the estimated equation but not from the system, the entire k-class, for nonstochastic k between 0 and 1, is dominated in terms of (large concentration parameter) asymptotic MSE by either OLS or 2SLS." Rhodes and Westbrook (1981) arrived at similar conclusions in their analysis of the exact sampling distributions of the OLS and 2SLS estimators under misspecification.

In this article we extend the results in HMR on exact moment expressions to the case of omitted endogenous variables. We also discuss the issues involved in the derivation of exact moments in cases where some endogenous variables are wrongly treated as exogenous. In the second part of this article, a large-sample, stochastic, approximation procedure is employed to extend the asymptotic analysis in HMR in various directions. This part of the article covers the general case of arbitrary number of included endogenous variables, applies not only to nonstochastic but also to stochastic values of k, and includes other types of misspecification such as the exclusion and the misclassification of endogenous variables. The asymptotic results presented here differ in two basic ways from the leading term results in HMR. First, the HMR results are derived by approximating the exact bias and MSE whereas the leading term analysis done in this article is based on exact moments of the stochastic approximation. Second, the HMR asymptotic results make use of the assumption that the sample size remains fixed or grows slowly relative to the concentration parameter. The additional asymptotic results presented in this article are based on the more natural assumption that the concentration parameter and the sample size grow at the same rate. This article extends Fisher's results (1961, 1966, 1967) in that inconsistent estimators like ordinary least squares (OLS) are considered as well and conditions are given under which OLS will be preferred among the estimators under study. The approach taken, though similar to Nagar's (1959) where large-sample, asymptotic expansions are developed for the estimators themselves, provides various refinements of the technique, thereby showing the usefulness and wider applicability of the approach for finite-sample analysis. The propriety of the approximations is rigorously shown: the deleted remainder in the expansion has the correct (small) order of magnitude in probability. Furthermore, a simple modification allows us to apply the technique to k-class estimators not only of the form $k = 1 + (a/T)$ as in Nagar, where T is sample size and a is a fixed constant, but also to other values of k, especially $0 \leq k < 1$ and k stochastic.

II. MODEL AND SPECIFICATION ERRORS TO BE CONSIDERED

In this article we are concerned with the estimation of a single equation—say, the first—in a static simultaneous equations model for G^* endogenous variables. The model can be written as:

$$\mathbf{Y}^* \mathbf{B}^* + \mathbf{Z}^* \mathbf{\Gamma}^* = \mathbf{U}^* \tag{1}$$

where $\mathbf{Y}^*$ is the $T \times G^*$ matrix of observations on the endogenous variables, $\mathbf{Z}^*$ is the $T \times K^*$ matrix of observations on the exogenous variables, and $\mathbf{U}^*$ is the $T \times G^*$ matrix of structural disturbances. The rows of $\mathbf{U}^*$ are assumed to be identically and independently distributed as G^*-variate normal random vectors with mean zero and covariance matrix $\mathbf{\Omega}^*$, that is, $\mathrm{N}(\mathbf{0}, \mathbf{\Omega}^*)$. We also assume that $\mathbf{B}^*$ is nonsingular, so that the reduced form of the system is

$$\mathbf{Y}^* = -\mathbf{Z}^* \mathbf{\Gamma}^* \mathbf{B}^{*-1} + \mathbf{U}^* \mathbf{B}^{*-1} = \mathbf{Z}^* \mathbf{\Pi}^* + \mathbf{V}^* \tag{2}$$

where the rows of $\mathbf{V}^*$ are identically and independently distributed

$$\mathrm{N}(\mathbf{0}, \mathbf{\Sigma}^*) \text{ for } \mathbf{\Omega}^* = \mathbf{B}^{*\prime}\mathbf{\Sigma}^*\mathbf{B}^*.$$

Consider the first equation in this system and distinguish the "true" and "apparent" versions as

$$\text{True} \qquad \mathbf{y}_1 = \mathbf{Y}_2\boldsymbol{\beta}^* + \mathbf{Y}_3\boldsymbol{\beta}_3^* + \mathbf{Z}_1\boldsymbol{\gamma}_1^* + \mathbf{Z}_2\boldsymbol{\gamma}_2^* + \mathbf{u}_1^* \tag{3}$$

$$\text{Apparent} \quad \mathbf{y}_1 = \mathbf{Y}_2\boldsymbol{\beta} + \mathbf{Z}_1\boldsymbol{\gamma} + \mathbf{u}_1 \tag{4}$$

We denote the sizes of the data matrices in (3) as follows:

$$\begin{aligned} &\mathbf{y}_1 : T \times 1 \\ &\mathbf{Y}_2 : T \times G_1 = T \times (g - 1) \\ &\mathbf{Y}_3 : T \times G_3 \\ &\mathbf{Z}_1 : T \times K_1 \\ &\mathbf{Z}_2 : T \times K_2 \end{aligned} \tag{5}$$

In the estimation of the apparent equation, some variables in $\mathbf{Z}_1$ may be treated as exogenous, whereas in fact they are endogenous. As specified, the apparent equation reflects the simultaneous occurrence of the two general types of misspecification that the paper focuses on: the omission of relevant variables (exogenous as well as endogenous) and the misclassification of endogenous variables. The omitted endogenous and exogenous variables are $\mathbf{Y}_3$ and $\mathbf{Z}_2$, respectively. If there are misclassified endogenous variables, then a submatrix of $\mathbf{Z}_1$ is endogenous. Throughout this article, we shall assume that the equation being estimated, as well as every other equation in the system, does not wrongly contain irrelevant variables.

The object of the analysis in this article is to assess the effects of misspecification by computing exact and asymptotic moment expressions for estimators of $\boldsymbol{\beta}$ based on the apparent equation when the true model actually obtains. We assume throughout that the apparent equation is identified. It is not necessary to assume that the rest of the equation system (1) is correctly specified. Furthermore, because of the specification errors in the equation as well as in the rest of the system, the apparent list of exogenous variables in the system may not coincide with the true one. We use $\mathbf{Z}$ $(T \times K)$ to denote the observation matrix for the variables treated as exogenous in the system.

The special cases of (3) and (4) that we shall consider in this article are summarized in Table 1. In this tabulation, we mean by $\mathbf{Z} \subset \mathbf{Z}^*$ that $\mathbf{Z}$ is a column submatrix of $\mathbf{Z}^*$. Note that if $\mathbf{Z} \subseteq \mathbf{Z}^*$, it necessarily follows that no endogenous variables in the system are misclassified as exogenous. This is so because we are assuming that every equation in the system does not contain irrelevant variables. Conversely, if some endogenous variables are wrongly treated as exogenous, then some of the columns of $\mathbf{Y}^*$ are in $\mathbf{Z}$ so that there is no nesting relationship between $\mathbf{Z}$ and $\mathbf{Z}^*$. Types 1 and 2 deal with the omission of relevant variables without any misclassification of endogenous variables. The difference between Types 1 and 2 lies in the fact that for the latter exogenous variables are wrongly excluded not only from the equation being estimated ($\boldsymbol{\gamma}_2^* \neq \mathbf{0}$)

Table 1. Specification Error Types.

Type	*Parameter Conditions*	*Description*
0	$\boldsymbol{\beta}_3^* = \mathbf{0}; \boldsymbol{\gamma}_2^* = \mathbf{0}; \mathbf{Z} = \mathbf{Z}^*$	Correct specification
1.A	$\boldsymbol{\beta}_3^* = \mathbf{0}; \boldsymbol{\gamma}_2^* \neq \mathbf{0}; \mathbf{Z} = \mathbf{Z}^*$	Omission of exogenous variables only
2.A	$\boldsymbol{\beta}_3^* = \mathbf{0}; \boldsymbol{\gamma}_2^* \neq \mathbf{0}; \mathbf{Z} \subset \mathbf{Z}^*$	
1.B	$\boldsymbol{\beta}_3^* \neq \mathbf{0}; \boldsymbol{\gamma}_2^* \neq \mathbf{0}: \mathbf{Z} = \mathbf{Z}^*$	Omission of exogenous and endogenous variables
2.B	$\boldsymbol{\beta}_3^* \neq \mathbf{0}; \boldsymbol{\gamma}_2^* \neq \mathbf{0}; \mathbf{Z} \subset \mathbf{Z}^*$	
5	$\mathbf{Z}$ endogenous	
5.A	$\boldsymbol{\beta}_3^* = \mathbf{0}; \boldsymbol{\gamma}_2^* = \mathbf{0}$	Misclassification of endogenous variables
5.B	$\boldsymbol{\beta}_3^* \neq 0$ or $\boldsymbol{\gamma}_2^* \neq 0$	Misclassification and omission of variables

but also from the whole system ($\mathbf{Z} \subset \mathbf{Z}^*$) as a consequence of specification errors in either the equation being estimated or the other equations in the system. Types 1.A and 2.A were studied extensively in HMR; Types 1.B and 2.B contain the additional complication that endogenous variables are omitted as well. Type 5 pertains to the misclassification of endogenous variables with Type 5.A excluding and Type 5.B including the omission of variables. (Types 3 and 4, studied and defined in HMR, pertain to the inclusion of irrelevant variables. These cases will not be considered in this article.)

III. CHARACTERIZATION OF *k*-CLASS ESTIMATORS UNDER MISSPECIFICATION

The k-class estimator of $\boldsymbol{\beta}$ based on the apparent equation (4) is

$$\hat{\boldsymbol{\beta}}_{(k)} = (\mathbf{Y}_2' \mathbf{P} \mathbf{Y}_2)^{-1} \mathbf{Y}_2' \mathbf{P} \mathbf{y}_1 \tag{6}$$

where

$$\begin{aligned} \mathbf{P} &= \mathbf{P}_1 + \bar{k}\mathbf{P}_2 \\ \mathbf{P}_1 &= \mathbf{P}_z - \mathbf{P}_{z_1} \\ \mathbf{P}_z &= \mathbf{Z}(\mathbf{Z}'\mathbf{Z})^{-1}\mathbf{Z}' \\ \mathbf{P}_{z_1} &= \mathbf{Z}_1(\mathbf{Z}_1'\mathbf{Z}_1)^{-1}\mathbf{Z}_1' \\ \mathbf{P}_2 &= \bar{\mathbf{P}}_z = \mathbf{I} - \mathbf{P}_z \\ \bar{k} &= 1 - k. \end{aligned} \tag{7}$$

Replacing $\mathbf{y}_1$ with its representation from the true equation, we get (since $\mathbf{PZ}_1 = \mathbf{0}$),

$$\hat{\boldsymbol{\beta}}_{(k)} = \boldsymbol{\beta}^* + (\mathbf{Y}_2'\mathbf{P}\mathbf{Y}_2)^{-1}\mathbf{Y}_2'\mathbf{P}\mathbf{w} = \boldsymbol{\beta}^* + \mathbf{H}_{22}^{-1}\mathbf{H}_{21} \tag{8}$$

where

$$\begin{aligned} \mathbf{w} &= \mathbf{Y}_3 \boldsymbol{\beta}_3^* + \mathbf{Z}_2\boldsymbol{\gamma}_2^* + \mathbf{u}_1^* \\ \mathbf{H} &= \mathbf{Y}'\mathbf{P}\mathbf{Y} = \mathbf{Y}'\mathbf{P}_1\mathbf{Y} + \bar{k}\mathbf{Y}'\mathbf{P}_2\mathbf{Y} = \begin{bmatrix} H_{11} & \mathbf{H}_{12} \\ \mathbf{H}_{21} & \mathbf{H}_{22} \end{bmatrix} \\ \mathbf{Y} &= (\mathbf{w}, \mathbf{Y}_2) \end{aligned} \tag{9}$$

In the partitioned form for $\mathbf{H}$, H_{11} is scalar. For the coefficient of $\mathbf{Z}_1$, we have

$$
\begin{aligned}
\hat{\gamma}_{(k)} &= \mathbf{C}[\mathbf{y}_1 - \mathbf{Y}_2\hat{\boldsymbol{\beta}}_{(k)}] \qquad \mathbf{C} = (\mathbf{Z}_1'\mathbf{Z}_1)^{-1}\mathbf{Z}_1' \\
&= \mathbf{C}(\mathbf{y}_1 - \mathbf{w}) - \mathbf{C}\mathbf{Y}_2(\hat{\boldsymbol{\beta}}_{(k)} - \boldsymbol{\beta}^*) + \mathbf{C}\mathbf{w} - \mathbf{C}\mathbf{Y}_2\boldsymbol{\beta}^* \qquad (10) \\
&= \boldsymbol{\gamma}_1^* - \mathbf{C}[\mathbf{Y}_2(\hat{\boldsymbol{\beta}}_{(k)} - \boldsymbol{\beta}^*) - \mathbf{w}].
\end{aligned}
$$

A. The Case of Omitted Variables (Types 1 and 2 Misspecification)

To facilitate our remaining discussion of the k-class estimators in this section, let us first consider the case where no endogenous variables are misclassified as exogenous and the only types of misspecification are in the form of omitted exogenous and/or endogenous variables (Types 1 and 2 in Table 1). In this case, $\mathbf{Z} \subseteq \mathbf{Z}^*$ so that the matrices $\mathbf{P}_1$ and $\mathbf{P}_2$ defined in (7) are nonstochastic and the k-class estimator $\hat{\boldsymbol{\beta}}_{(k)}$ can be characterized in terms of Wishart matrices as done in HMR.

More specifically, the two matrices $\mathbf{Y}'\mathbf{P}_1\mathbf{Y}$ and $\mathbf{Y}'\mathbf{P}_2\mathbf{Y}$, the linear combination of which forms $\mathbf{H}$ in (9), both have Wishart distributions. We can see from (2) and (9) that the rows of $\mathbf{Y}$ are independently distributed as multivariate normal with a common covariance matrix—say, $\tilde{\boldsymbol{\Sigma}}$—and means that are linear in the elements of corresponding rows in $\mathbf{Z}^*$. More specifically, if we follow the convention of using vec($\mathbf{Y}$) to denote the column vector obtained from stacking the columns of $\mathbf{Y}$, we have

$$\text{vec}(Y) \sim \text{N}[\text{vec}(\mathbf{Z}^*\tilde{\boldsymbol{\Pi}}), \tilde{\boldsymbol{\Sigma}} \otimes \text{I}] \qquad (11)$$

It follows from (11) then that the parameters in the Wishart distributions of $\mathbf{Y}'\mathbf{P}_1\mathbf{Y}$ and $\mathbf{Y}'\mathbf{P}_2\mathbf{Y}$ are as follows

$$
\begin{aligned}
\mathbf{Y}'\mathbf{P}_1\mathbf{Y} &\sim W_g[\text{tr}\mathbf{P}_1, \tilde{\boldsymbol{\Sigma}}; \tilde{\boldsymbol{\Pi}}'\mathbf{Z}^{*\prime}\mathbf{P}_1\mathbf{Z}^*\tilde{\boldsymbol{\Pi}}] \\
\mathbf{Y}'\mathbf{P}_2\mathbf{Y} &\sim W_g[\text{tr}\mathbf{P}_2, \tilde{\boldsymbol{\Sigma}}; \tilde{\boldsymbol{\Pi}}'\mathbf{Z}^{*\prime}\mathbf{P}_2\mathbf{Z}^*\tilde{\boldsymbol{\Pi}}]
\end{aligned} \qquad (12)
$$

We see that the means-sigma matrix in (12) for $\mathbf{Y}'\mathbf{P}_1\mathbf{Y}$ has full rank g under either $\mathbf{Z} = \mathbf{Z}^*$ or $\mathbf{Z} \subset \mathbf{Z}^*$; for $\mathbf{Y}'\mathbf{P}_2\mathbf{Y}$; the means-sigma matrix has rank zero for $\mathbf{Z} = \mathbf{Z}^*$ and nonzero when $\mathbf{Z} \subset \mathbf{Z}^*$. For the correctly specified case, we have exactly the same mathematical form for the k-class estimator as in (8) in terms of the regression function of a matrix that is a linear combination of Wishart matrices. For the analogue of $\mathbf{Y}'\mathbf{P}_1\mathbf{Y}$ in the correctly specified case, the means-sigma matrix has rank $(g - 1)$ and that of $\mathbf{Y}'\mathbf{P}_2\mathbf{Y}$ is central. We have summarized this discussion in Table 2.

As a consequence of the omission of relevant variables, there are, of course, other parameter changes in the Wishart distributions involved; for example, the degrees of freedom and the covariance matrix parameters.

Table 2. Ranks of Relevant Means-Sigma Matrices under Correct Specification and Omission of Relevant Variables.

Specification Status	*Means-Sigma Matrix for:* $\mathbf{Y'P_1Y}$	$\mathbf{Y'P_2Y}$
Correct	$g - 1$	0
Types 1.A and 1.B	g	0
Types 2.A and 2.B	g	$\neq 0$
Type 5	Not applicable	

These are discussed in more detail in HMR for Types 1 and 2. Such changes in the other parameters, however, are minor in the sense that they do not cause any additional complications beyond those already encountered in the correctly specified case. The increase in the rank of the means-sigma matrix for $\mathbf{Y'P_1Y}$ from $(g - 1)$ under correct specification to full rank g under Types 1 and 2 misspecification, on the other hand, is a major parameter change that nullifies the direct translation of existing finite-sample results to specification errors of these types. Under Type 2, the noncentrality of $\mathbf{Y'P_2Y}$ poses additional complications for $0 < k < 1$. No additional difficulties arise for $k = 0$ or $k = 1$ since for these values of k, $\mathbf{P}$ itself simplifies to a projection matrix so that $[\hat{\boldsymbol{\beta}}_{(k)} - \boldsymbol{\beta}^*]$ retains the same basic functional form as in Type 1.

The discussion in this subsection thus shows that the progression of generalization goes from the correctly specified case to Types 1.A and 1.B and then to Types 2.A and 2.B misspecification. Analytic finite sample results, such as exact moment expressions, for the first four cases follow as corollaries from results derived for Type 2. A misspecification such as those reported in HMR for the exact moment expressions for the k-class estimators. The translation of results from Type 2.A to Types 2.B, 1.A, 1.B, and correct specification is done through appropriate parameter changes in degrees of freedom, covariance matrix, and the means-sigma matrix.

B. The Case of Misclassified Endogenous Variables (Type 5 Misspecification)

Suppose now that in addition to the omission of relevant variables, some endogenous variables—say, $\mathbf{Y}_4 \subset \mathbf{Z}_1$—are mistakenly treated as exogenous in the estimation of $\boldsymbol{\beta}$. Because of specification errors in the other equations, there may be other endogenous variables in addition to $\mathbf{Y}_4$ that are misclassified in this manner. Let $\tilde{\mathbf{Y}}$ represent the data matrix on all the endogenous variables that are wrongly treated as exogenous so that $\mathbf{Y}_4 \subseteq \tilde{\mathbf{Y}} \subset \mathbf{Z}$. Although the misclassification of $\mathbf{Y}_4$ directly affects the estimation of β (additional simultaneity bias is introduced because of the failure to correct for the correlation between $\mathbf{Y}_4$ and $\mathbf{u}_1$), the misclassification of the other variables in $\tilde{\mathbf{Y}}$ has indirect effects to the extent that they are used as invalid instruments in the estimation of $\boldsymbol{\beta}$.

In this case, because $\tilde{\mathbf{Y}}$ is part of $\mathbf{Z}$, the matrix $\mathbf{P}$ in (6) is stochastic. Consequently, the characterization of $\hat{\boldsymbol{\beta}}_{(k)}$ discussed in the preceding subsection in terms of Wishart matrices does not apply anymore. Finite sample results pertaining to exact probability distributions and moments under this type of misspecification do not follow directly from those for the cases of omitted variables discussed earlier.

One possible approach toward exact moment expressions for this type of misspecification builds upon the analytical results that have already been obtained. Start with the conditional distribution of $\mathbf{Y} = (\mathbf{w}, \mathbf{Y}_2)$ given $\tilde{\mathbf{Y}}$. Under this conditional distribution of $\mathbf{Y}$, its rows would still be jointly independent multivariate normal with a common covariance matrix but with changing means that are linear in $\tilde{\mathbf{Y}}$. Thus, the conditional distributions of $\mathbf{Y}'\mathbf{P}_1\mathbf{Y}$ and $\mathbf{Y}'\mathbf{P}_2\mathbf{Y}$ given $\tilde{\mathbf{Y}}$ are also Wishart. This time, the parameters in these conditional distributions are determined by the conditional distribution and not the unconditional one. In particular the means-sigma matrices are quadratic functions of $\tilde{\mathbf{Y}}$ itself. Nevertheless, the ranks of the means-sigma matrices are as described in Table 1 for Type 2 misspecification.

From this perspective then, we can first obtain the conditional distributions and moments of $\hat{\boldsymbol{\beta}}_{(k)}$ given $\tilde{\mathbf{Y}}$. In its mathematical form, this problem is equivalent to the derivation of results for the *unconditional* distribution of $\hat{\boldsymbol{\beta}}_{(k)}$ in the case of omitted variables as discussed in the preceding section. The next step is what differentiates this present case from the case of omitted variables: the process of averaging these conditional results over the marginal distribution of $\tilde{\mathbf{Y}}$.

More specifically, suppose we are interested in obtaining the exact first moment expression for $\hat{\boldsymbol{\beta}}_{(k)} \cdot \mathrm{E}(\hat{\boldsymbol{\beta}}_{(k)})$ can be obtained in two steps:

1. First derive $\mathrm{E}(\hat{\boldsymbol{\beta}}_{(k)} \mid \tilde{\mathbf{Y}})$.
2. Then evaluate $\mathrm{E}(\hat{\boldsymbol{\beta}}_{(k)})$ through

$$\mathrm{E}(\hat{\boldsymbol{\beta}}_{(k)}) = \mathrm{E}(\mathrm{E}\hat{\boldsymbol{\beta}}_{(k)} \mid \tilde{\mathbf{Y}}) = \int \mathrm{E}(\hat{\boldsymbol{\beta}}_{(k)} \mid \tilde{\mathbf{y}}) \,\mathrm{pdf}(\tilde{\mathbf{y}})\, d\tilde{\mathbf{y}}.$$

Mathematically, under the standard assumptions we have made concerning the linear simultaneous equations model in (1), the first step reduces to exactly the same problem as deriving the *unconditional* mean of $\hat{\boldsymbol{\beta}}(k)$ under the Type 2 misspecification discussed in the preceding section. Thus, for example, the exact unconditional moment expressions developed in HMR under Type 2 misspecification would give the *conditional* moments of $\hat{\boldsymbol{\beta}}_{(k)}$ given $\tilde{\mathbf{Y}}$ provided that parameter values for degrees of freedom, variances–covariances, and means-sigma matrices are determined from the conditional distribution of $\mathbf{Y}$ given $\tilde{\mathbf{Y}}$. The second step—which requires the integration of the *conditional* moment relative to the multivariate normal distribution of $\tilde{\mathbf{Y}}$—is the additional complication that differentiates the mathematical problem involved in this case of misspecification from that considered in the preceding section.

The discussion in the preceding subsections has focused on a characterization of the k-class estimators that is suitable for the derivation of analytical small-sample results. Most current exact sampling results under misspecification deal with the limited special case of an apparent equation with two included endogenous variables (e.g., HMR; Rhodes and Westbrook, 1981). For the general case, recent results by Phillips (1980; Chapter 1, this volume) and Hillier and Srivastava (1981) can be used to derive exact expressions for distributions and moments under misspecification. Asymptotic expansions for the distribution functions of estimators can also be obtained in the manner of Fujikoshi et al. (1982).

IV. EXACT MOMENT EXPRESSIONS FOR THE k-CLASS ESTIMATORS UNDER TYPES 1 and 2 MISSPECIFICATION

In this section we consider exact bias and MSE expressions in the case of two included endogenous variables in the estimated equation. Exact results for Type 2.B misspecification are obtained directly from HMR; then, by appropriately specializing these expressions, we get the results for Types 1.A, 1.B, and 2.A. A detailed proof of these results, which proceeds from the reduction to canonical form described later, is provided in Appendix A. We will not discuss higher dimensional cases for exact moment results. We should note, however, that results for the case of three or more endogenous variables can also be obtained along the same lines as those in the recent article by Hillier and Srivastava (1981).

Following (3) and (4), for the special case we are considering here, we can now write the true and apparent versions of the equation being estimated as

$$\text{True:} \qquad \mathbf{y}_1 = \mathbf{y}_2\beta^* + \mathbf{Y}_3\beta_3^* + \mathbf{Z}_1\gamma_1^* + \mathbf{Z}_2\gamma_2^* + \mathbf{u}_1^* \tag{13}$$

$$\text{Apparent:} \qquad \mathbf{y}_1 = \mathbf{y}_2\beta + \mathbf{Z}_1\gamma + \mathbf{u}_1 \tag{14}$$

where $\mathbf{y}_2$ is $T \times 1$ and β and β^* are scalars. The sizes of the other vectors and matrices are as given in (5). With $\mathbf{P}_1$, $\mathbf{P}_2$, $\mathbf{P}$, and $\mathbf{w}$ as defined in (7) and (9), we now have

$$\hat{\beta}_{(k)} = \beta^* + (\mathbf{y}_2'\mathbf{P}\mathbf{w})/(\mathbf{y}_2'\mathbf{P}\mathbf{y}_2) \tag{15}$$

where

$$\mathbf{w} = \mathbf{Y}_3\boldsymbol{\beta}_3^* + \mathbf{Z}_2\boldsymbol{\gamma}_2^* + \mathbf{u}_1^* = \mathbf{y}_1 - \mathbf{y}_2\beta^* - \mathbf{Z}_1\boldsymbol{\gamma}_1^* \sim \mathrm{N}(\mu_w, \sigma_w^2\mathbf{I}). \tag{16}$$

From the reduced form equations, let

$$\begin{aligned} \mathbf{Y}_i &= \mathbf{M}_i + \mathbf{V}_i \\ \mathrm{vec}(\mathbf{V}_i) &\sim \mathrm{N}(\mathbf{0}, \boldsymbol{\Sigma}_{ii} \otimes \mathbf{I}) \\ \mathbf{M}_i &= \mathbf{Z}^*\boldsymbol{\Pi}_i. \end{aligned} \tag{17}$$

Then,

$$\begin{aligned} \mu_w &= \mathbf{M}_3\beta_3^* + \mathbf{Z}_2\boldsymbol{\gamma}_2^* \\ \sigma_w^2 &= \mathrm{var}(y_{t1} - y_{t2}\beta^*) \\ &= \sigma_{11} - 2\beta^*\sigma_{12} + \beta^{*2}\sigma_{22}. \end{aligned} \tag{18}$$

Furthermore,

$$\begin{aligned} \mathrm{cov}(w_t, y_{t2}) &= \mathrm{cov}(y_{t1} - y_{t2}\beta^*, y_{t2}) \\ &= \sigma_{12} - \beta^*\sigma_{22}. \end{aligned} \tag{19}$$

Before deriving moments, we utilize a reduction to canonical form through the following triangular transformation for $t = 1, 2, \ldots, T$

$$\begin{aligned} x_{t1} &= a_{11}w_t + a_{12}y_{t2} \\ x_{t2} &= a_{22}y_{t2} \end{aligned} \tag{20}$$

This reduction is chosen so as to transform the covariance matrix of (w_t, y_{t2}) to the identity so that for $\sigma_2 = (\sigma_{22})^{1/2}$,

$$\begin{aligned} a_{11} &= \sigma_2/(\sigma_{11}\sigma_{22} - \sigma_{12}^2)^{1/2} \\ a_{12} &= -(\sigma_{12} - \beta^*\sigma_{22})/[\sigma_2(\sigma_{11}\sigma_{22} - \sigma_{12}^2)^{1/2}] \\ a_{22} &= 1/\sigma_2. \end{aligned} \tag{21}$$

Using (15) and (20), we can express $\hat{\beta}_{(k)}$ in terms of $\mathbf{x}_1$ and $\mathbf{x}_2$ as follows:

$$\hat{\beta}_{(k)} = \beta^* + R + \mathrm{c}\hat{\beta}_{(k)}^* \tag{22}$$

where

$$\hat{\beta}_{(k)}^* = \mathbf{x}_2'\mathbf{P}\mathbf{x}_1/(\mathbf{x}_2'\mathbf{P}\mathbf{x}_2) \tag{23}$$

and

$$
\begin{aligned}
R &= -a_{12}/a_{11} = \operatorname{cov}(w_t, y_{t2})/\operatorname{var}(y_{t2}) = \rho\sigma_w/\sigma_2 \\
c &= a_{22}/a_{11} = (\sigma_w/\sigma_2)(1-\rho^2)^{1/2} \qquad (24) \\
\rho &= \operatorname{corr}(w_t, y_{t2}).
\end{aligned}
$$

By extending Sawa's (1972) use of moment-generating functions, we then obtain the moments of $\hat{\beta}^*_{(k)}$ and, through (22), also of $\hat{\beta}_{(k)}$. Details for this derivation are given in Appendix A. For the rest of this section, we shall summarize the moment expressions obtained. We utilize the following notation:

$$
\begin{aligned}
m &= \operatorname{tr}(\mathbf{P}_1 + \mathbf{P}_2)/2 = (T - K_1)/2 \\
n &= \operatorname{tr}\mathbf{P}_2/2 = (T - K)/2 \\
\delta_1 &= (\mathbf{E}\mathbf{y}_2)'\mathbf{P}_1(\mathbf{E}\mathbf{y}_2)/(2\sigma_{22}) \\
\delta_2 &= (\mathbf{E}\mathbf{y}_2)'\mathbf{P}_2(\mathbf{E}\mathbf{y}_2)/(2\sigma_{22}) \qquad (25) \\
\nu_1 &= (\mathbf{E}\mathbf{w})'\mathbf{P}_1(\mathbf{E}\mathbf{w})/(2\sigma_{22}) \\
\nu_2 &= (\mathbf{E}\mathbf{w})'\mathbf{P}_2(\mathbf{E}\mathbf{w})/(2\sigma_{22}) \\
\theta_1 &= (\mathbf{E}\mathbf{y}_2)'\mathbf{P}_1(\mathbf{E}\mathbf{w})/(2\sigma_{22}) \\
\theta_2 &= (\mathbf{E}\mathbf{y}_2)'\mathbf{P}_2(\mathbf{E}\mathbf{w})/(2\sigma_{22})
\end{aligned}
$$

We also make use of the following special function introduced in HMR in the extension of Sawa's (1972) results:

$$
G(k, \delta_1, \delta_2; m, n) = \sum_{r=0}^{\infty} p_r(\delta_2) G(k, \delta_1, 0; m + r, n + r) \qquad (26)
$$

where, for $\delta > 0$,

$$
p_r(\delta) = e^{-\delta}\delta^r/r!, \qquad (27)
$$

and $G(k, \delta, 0; m, n)$ is the function used by Sawa (1972) in his treatment of the correctly specified case:
(1) for $0 \leqslant k < 1$ and $m > 1$,

$$
G(k, \delta, 0; m, n) = e^{-\delta} \sum_{s=0}^{\infty} k^s[(n)_s/(m-1)_{s+1}]\,{}_1F_1(m-1, m+s; \delta) \qquad (28)
$$

(2) for $k = 1$ and $m - n > 1$,

$$
G(k,\delta,0; m,n) = [e^{-\delta}/(m-j-1)]\,{}_1F_1(m-n-1, m-n; \delta). \qquad (29)
$$

The function takes the value $+\infty$ outside the specified range of m and

n. The ${}_1F_1$ function is the standard hypergeometric function,

$$ {}_1F_1(a, b; \delta) = \sum_{i=0}^{\infty} (a)_i/[(b)_i i!]\delta^i, \tag{30} $$

for $b > 0$, $|\delta| < \infty$ and the quantity $(a)_i$ is defined for integer i by

$$ (a)_i = \Gamma(a + i)/\Gamma(a) \qquad a > 0 \text{ and } i \geqslant 0. \tag{31} $$

The parameters θ_1, θ_2, ν_1, ν_2, and δ_2 can be thought of as misspecification parameters. Relative to the correctly specified case, the effects of omission of variables on the probability distribution of $\hat{\beta}_{(k)}$ show directly through these five parameters. (Additionally, there are indirect effects through changes in m, n, and δ_1). Under Type 2 misspecification, θ_1, θ_2, ν_1, ν_2 and δ_2 are all different from zero. Under Type 1, however, $\mathbf{P}_2(\mathrm{E}\mathbf{y}_2) = \mathbf{P}_2(\mathrm{E}\mathbf{w}) = \mathbf{0}$ so that $\delta_2 = \theta_2 = \nu_2 = 0$. Under correct specification, all five misspecification parameters are equal to zero. Also, δ_1 is in the form of the usual concentration parameter (Basmann 1963, Richardson 1968; Sawa 1972, Mariano 1975 and 1982).

We can now state the main result for Types 2.A and 2.B misspecification as follows:

THEOREM 1: *Types 2.A and 2.B Misspecification.* Let k be nonstochastic, between zero and one. Then a necessary and sufficient condition for the bias in $\hat{\beta}_{(k)}$ to be finite is that

$$ T - K_1 \geqslant 2 \qquad \text{for } 0 \leqslant k < 1 $$

and

$$ K - K_1 \geqslant 2 \qquad \text{for } k = 1. $$

Furthermore, the MSE of $\hat{\beta}_{(k)}$ is finite if and only if

$$ T - K_1 \geqslant 3 \qquad \text{for } 0 \leqslant k < 1 $$

and

$$ K - K_1 \geqslant 3 \qquad \text{for } k = 1. $$

Whenever they exist, these moments are

$$ \begin{aligned} \mathrm{E}[\hat{\beta}_{(k)} - \beta^*] &= \mathrm{BIAS}_1 + \mathrm{BIAS}_2 \\ \mathrm{E}[\hat{\beta}_{(k)} - \beta^*]^2 &= \mathrm{MSE}_1 + \mathrm{MSE}_2 \end{aligned} \tag{32} $$

where

$$ \begin{aligned} \mathrm{BIAS}_1 &= R(1 - \delta_1)G(\delta_2; m + 1, n) \\ \mathrm{BIAS}_2 &= \theta_1 G(\delta_2; m + 1, n) - \bar{k}(R\delta_2 - \theta_2)G(\delta_2; m + 1, n + 1) \end{aligned} \tag{33} $$

$$\begin{aligned} \mathrm{MSE}_1 &= A_{11}H(\delta_2; m, n) + \bar{k}^2 A_{12} H(\delta_2; m, n+1) \\ &\quad + A_{13}H(\delta_2; m+1, n) + 2R(\mathrm{BIAS}_1) - R^2 \end{aligned} \tag{34}$$

$$\begin{aligned} \mathrm{MSE}_2 &= A_{21}H(\delta_2; m, n) + \bar{k}^2 A_{22} H(\delta_2; m, n+1) \\ &\quad + A_{23}H(\delta_2; m+1, n) \\ &\quad + \bar{k}A_4 H(\delta_2; m+1, n+1) \\ &\quad + \bar{k}^2 A_5 H(\delta_2; m+1, n+2) + 2R(\mathrm{BIAS}_2) \end{aligned}$$

$$\begin{aligned} A_{11} &= c^2(m-n) + R^2\delta_1 & A_{21} &= \nu_1 - 2R\theta_1 \\ A_{12} &= nc^2 & A_{22} &= R^2\delta_2 - 2R\theta_2 + \nu_2 \\ A_{13} &= (c^2 + 2R^2\delta_1)\delta_1 & A_{23} &= 2\theta_1(\theta_1 - 2R\delta_1) \\ A_4 &= 4a_1a_2 & a_1 &= R\delta_1 - \theta_1 \\ A_5 &= c^2\delta_2 + 4a_2^2 & a_2 &= R\delta_2 - \theta_2 \end{aligned} \tag{35}$$

$$\begin{aligned} H(\delta; m, n) &= [G(\delta; m, n) - G(\delta; m+1, n)]/2 \\ G(\delta; m, n) &\equiv G(k, \delta_1, \delta; m, n); \end{aligned}$$

and R, c, ρ are defined in (24) and δ_1, δ_2, θ_1, θ_2, ν_1, ν_2, m, and n in (25). The only difference between the results for Type 2.A and Type 2.B lies in the following alterations in the definitions for ρ and Ew:

$$\begin{aligned} &\text{Type 2.A} \qquad \rho = \mathrm{cov}(u_{t1}^*, y_{t2}) \\ &\qquad\qquad\quad\ \ \mathrm{E}w = Z_2\gamma_2^* \end{aligned} \tag{36}$$

$$\begin{aligned} &\text{Type 2.B} \qquad \rho = \mathrm{cov}(Y_{t3}\beta_3^* + u_{t1}^*, y_{t2}) \\ &\qquad\qquad\quad\ \ \mathrm{E}w = (\mathrm{E}Y_3)\beta_3^* + Z_2\gamma_2^*. \end{aligned} \tag{37}$$

The moment expressions in (32) are each decomposed into parts such that BIAS_1 and MSE_1 contain terms that remain after θ_1, θ_2, ν_1, ν_2, and δ_2 are set to zero. These are the bias and MSE expressions for the correctly specified case—they coincide with earlier results (e.g., Sawa, 1972).

Results for Types 1.A and 1.B misspecification are directly obtained from Theorem 1 by setting θ_2, ν_2, and δ_2 to zero. Thus,

THEOREM 2: *Types 1.A and 1.B Misspecification.* For nonstochastic k between 0 and 1, the necessary and sufficient conditions for the finiteness of the bias and MSE of $\hat{\beta}_{(k)}$ are as given in Theorem 1. The bias and MSE components in (32), furthermore, simplify to

$$\begin{aligned} \mathrm{BIAS}_1 &= R[1 - \delta_1 G(0; m+1, n)] \\ \mathrm{BIAS}_2 &= \theta_1 G(0; m+1, n) \end{aligned}$$

$$\text{MSE}_1 = A_{11}H(0; m, n) + \bar{k}^2 A_{12}H(0; m, n+1) + A_{13}H(0; m+1, n) + 2R(\text{BIAS}_1) - R^2$$

$$\text{MSE}_2 = A_{21}H(0; m, n) + A_{23}H(0; m+1, n) + 2R(\text{BIAS}_2)$$

where A_{11}, A_{12}, A_{13}, A_{21}, and A_{23} are as defined in (35).

V. ASYMPTOTIC EXPANSIONS FOR THE *k*-CLASS ESTIMATORS UNDER MISSPECIFICATION

In this section, we shall consider large-sample asymptotic expansions for the k-class estimators of $\boldsymbol{\beta}$ in the apparent version of the equation as written in (4):

$$\begin{aligned} &\text{True} & \mathbf{y}_1 &= \mathbf{Y}_2\boldsymbol{\beta}^* + \mathbf{Y}_3\boldsymbol{\beta}_3^* + \mathbf{Z}_1\boldsymbol{\gamma}_1^* + \mathbf{Z}_2\boldsymbol{\gamma}_2^* + \mathbf{u}_1^* \\ &\text{Apparent} & \mathbf{y}_1 &= \mathbf{Y}_2\boldsymbol{\beta} + \mathbf{Z}_1\boldsymbol{\gamma}_1 + \mathbf{u}_1. \end{aligned} \tag{38}$$

Here $\mathbf{Y}_2$ is $T \times G_1$, $G_1 \geqslant 1$. The apparent version contains three specification errors:

1. Omission of the exogenous variables $\mathbf{Z}_2$.
2. Omission of the endogenous variables $\mathbf{Y}_3$.
3. Treatment of endogenous components of $\mathbf{Z}_1$ as exogenous.

We use $\mathbf{Y}_4$ to denote the endogenous submatrix, if any, of $\mathbf{Z}_1$. As in the previous sections, we will use $\mathbf{Z}^*$ and $\mathbf{Z}$ to represent the data matrices for the true and apparent list of exogenous variables in the whole system.

Write the reduced-form equations for $\mathbf{Y}_2$, $\mathbf{Y}_3$, and $\mathbf{Y}_4$ as

$$\mathbf{Y}_i = \mathbf{Z}^*\boldsymbol{\Pi}_i + \mathbf{V}_i = \mathbf{M}_i + \mathbf{V}_i \qquad i = 2, 3, 4 \tag{39}$$

where

$$\text{vec}(\mathbf{V}_i) \sim \text{N}(\mathbf{0}, \boldsymbol{\Sigma}_{ii} \otimes \mathbf{I}). \tag{40}$$

Comparing (17) with (2), we see that $\boldsymbol{\Pi}_i$, $\mathbf{V}_i$, and $\boldsymbol{\Sigma}_{ii}$ are appropriate submatrices of $\boldsymbol{\Pi}^*$, $\mathbf{V}^*$, and $\boldsymbol{\Sigma}^*$, respectively.

From (6), the k-class estimator of $\boldsymbol{\beta}$ is

$$\begin{aligned} \hat{\boldsymbol{\beta}}_{(k)} &= (\mathbf{Y}_2'\mathbf{P}\mathbf{Y}_2)^{-1}\,\mathbf{Y}_2'\mathbf{P}\mathbf{y}_1 \\ &= \boldsymbol{\beta}^* + (\mathbf{Y}_2'\mathbf{P}\mathbf{Y}_2)^{-1}\mathbf{Y}_2'\mathbf{P}(\boldsymbol{\eta} + \mathbf{u}) \end{aligned} \tag{41}$$

where

$$\begin{aligned} \mathbf{P} &= (\mathbf{P}_z - \mathbf{P}_{z1}) + \bar{k}\,\bar{\mathbf{P}}_z = \mathbf{P}_1 + \bar{k}\mathbf{P}_2 \\ \boldsymbol{\eta} &= \mathbf{M}_3\boldsymbol{\beta}_3^* + \mathbf{Z}_2\boldsymbol{\gamma}_2^* \\ \mathbf{u} &= \mathbf{u}_1^* + \mathbf{V}_3\boldsymbol{\beta}_3^*. \end{aligned} \tag{42}$$

Note that if some of the system endogenous variables are misclassified as exogenous in the equation being estimated or elsewhere, then **P** would be stochastic. On the other hand, if there is no such specification error in the system, then both $\mathbf{P}_z$ and $\mathbf{P}_{z1}$ would be nonstochastic, and so also **P**, except for the possible randomness in k. Throughout this section, we will also assume that k is bounded in probability:

$$k = O_p(1). \tag{43}$$

A. Stochastic Approximation Lemma

To obtain our asymptotic expansions for $\hat{\boldsymbol{\beta}}_{(k)}$, we make use of the following

LEMMA 1: Let **X** be an $m \times m$ random matrix indexed by sample size T but with m independent of T. If

$$\mathbf{X} = O_p(T^{-1/2})$$

as $T \to \infty$, then, for any nonnegative integer r,

$$(\mathbf{I} - \mathbf{X})^{-1} = \sum_{i=0}^{r} \mathbf{X}^i + O_p[T^{-(r+1)/2}]. \tag{44}$$

PROOF: The proof of the lemma, from Ramage (1971), is given in Appendix B.

Suppose the observation matrix $\mathbf{Z}^*$ for the system exogenous variables is such that as $T \to \infty$,

(i) $\lim(\mathbf{Z}^{*\prime}\mathbf{Z}^*/T)$ is finite, positive-definite, and (45)
(ii) $\operatorname{vec}(\mathbf{Z}^{*\prime}\mathbf{V}^*/\sqrt{T})$ converges in distribution to $\mathrm{N}[\mathbf{0}, \boldsymbol{\Sigma}^* \otimes \lim(\mathbf{Z}^{*\prime}\mathbf{Z}^*/T)]$, where $\mathbf{V}^*$ is the matrix of reduced-form disturbances in the true system and $\operatorname{vec} \mathbf{V}^* \sim \mathrm{N}(\mathbf{0}, \boldsymbol{\Sigma}^* \otimes \mathrm{I})$

It follows from (45) that

$$\begin{aligned} \mathbf{Z}^{*\prime}\mathbf{Z}^*/T &= O(1) \\ \mathbf{Z}^{*\prime}\mathbf{V}^*/\sqrt{T} &= O_p(1). \end{aligned} \tag{46}$$

Let

$$\begin{aligned} \mathbf{A} &= \mathbf{Y}_2'\mathbf{P}\mathbf{Y}_2 \\ \mathbf{B} &= \mathbf{Y}_2'\mathbf{P}(\boldsymbol{\eta} + \mathbf{u}) \end{aligned} \tag{47}$$

so that, from (41),

$$\hat{\boldsymbol{\beta}}_{(k)} - \boldsymbol{\beta}^* = \mathbf{A}^{-1}\mathbf{B}. \tag{48}$$

Through (44) and (46), it would be possible for us to decompose **A** and **B** into terms of various orders of magnitude, say:

$$\begin{aligned}\mathbf{A} &= \mathbf{A}_2 + \mathbf{A}_1 + \mathbf{A}_0 \\ \mathbf{B} &= \mathbf{B}_2 + \mathbf{B}_1 + \mathbf{B}_0\end{aligned} \tag{49}$$

where the subscripts in the components indicates orders of magnitude in terms of powers of $(T^{1/2})$; for example, $\mathbf{A}_j = O_p(T^{j/2})$. Note that both **A** and **B** involve k and **P**. As we shall see later, $\mathbf{A}_0$ as well as $\mathbf{B}_0$ may contain terms that are $o_p(1)$. This generally occurs when either k or **P** is stochastic.

Using (48), (49), and Lemma 1, we then have

PROPOSITION 1: For any nonnegative integer r, if (49) holds, then

$$\begin{aligned}\hat{\boldsymbol{\beta}}_{(k)} - \boldsymbol{\beta}^* &= (\mathbf{I} + \boldsymbol{\Delta})^{-1}\boldsymbol{\alpha} \\ &= \sum_{i=0}^{r} (-\boldsymbol{\Delta})^i\boldsymbol{\alpha} + O_p[T^{-(r+1)/2}],\end{aligned} \tag{50}$$

where

$$\begin{aligned}\boldsymbol{\Delta} &= \mathbf{A}_2^{-1}(\mathbf{A}_1 + \mathbf{A}_0) \\ \boldsymbol{\alpha} &= \mathbf{A}_2^{-1}(\mathbf{B}_2 + \mathbf{B}_1 + \mathbf{B}_0).\end{aligned} \tag{51}$$

As an immediate consequence of this proposition, we get

COROLLARY 1:

$$\operatorname{plim}(\hat{\boldsymbol{\beta}}_{(k)} - \boldsymbol{\beta}^*) = \operatorname{plim} \mathbf{A}_2^{-1}\mathbf{B}_2 \qquad \text{as } T \to \infty. \tag{52}$$

The expansion for $\hat{\boldsymbol{\beta}}_{(k)}$ in Proposition 1 is analogous to Nagar's (1959). Here, however, a formal framework is provided within which the expansion can be interpreted as a stochastic approximation to the estimation error. Furthermore, the expansion as given in (50) and (51) is valid for any k, stochastic or nonstochastic, which is $O_p(1)$ and not just for values of k considered by Nagar, namely, k of the form $(1 + a/T)$ where a is nonstochastic.

B. Case $h = 1$: $\mathbf{Z}$, $\mathbf{Z}_1$, and k Nonstochastic

We now proceed to obtain explicit expressions for the components of **A** and **B**. First consider the case where **Z** and $\mathbf{Z}_1$ are nonstochastic (so that no endogenous variables are misclassified) and k is also nonstochastic but $O(1)$. In this case **P** itself is nonstochastic. The following decomposition follows readily from (46):

$$\mathbf{A} = \mathbf{A}_2^{(1)} + \mathbf{A}_1^{(1)} + \mathbf{A}_0^{(1)} \qquad \mathbf{B} = \mathbf{B}_2^{(1)} + \mathbf{B}_1^{(1)} + \mathbf{B}_0^{(1)} \tag{53}$$

where

$$\begin{aligned}
\mathbf{A}_2^{(1)} &= \mathbf{M}_2'\mathbf{P}\mathbf{M}_2 + \bar{k}(T - K)\boldsymbol{\Sigma}_{22} = O(T) \\
\mathbf{A}_1^{(1)} &= \mathbf{V}_2'\mathbf{P}\mathbf{M}_2 + \mathbf{M}_2'\mathbf{P}\mathbf{V}_2 + \bar{k}[\mathbf{V}_2'\mathbf{P}_2\mathbf{V}_2 - (T - K)\boldsymbol{\Sigma}_{22}] = O_p(T^{1/2}) \\
\mathbf{A}_0^{(1)} &= \mathbf{V}_2'\mathbf{P}_1\mathbf{V}_2 = O_p(1) \qquad (54) \\
\mathbf{B}_2^{(1)} &= \mathbf{M}_2'\mathbf{P}\boldsymbol{\eta} + \bar{k}(T - K)\boldsymbol{\rho} = O(T) \\
\mathbf{B}_1^{(1)} &= \mathbf{M}_2'\mathbf{P}\mathbf{u} + \mathbf{V}_2'\mathbf{P}\boldsymbol{\eta} + \bar{k}[\mathbf{V}_2'\mathbf{P}_2\mathbf{u} - (T - K)\boldsymbol{\rho}] = O_p(T^{1/2}) \\
\mathbf{B}_0^{(1)} &= \mathbf{V}_2'\mathbf{P}_1\mathbf{u} = O_p(1)
\end{aligned}$$

In the expressions for $\mathbf{B}_2^{(1)}$ and $\mathbf{B}_1^{(1)}$,

$$\begin{aligned}
\boldsymbol{\rho} &= \mathrm{E}(\mathbf{V}_2'\mathbf{u}/\mathrm{T}) \\
&= \text{covariance between the } t\text{th row of } \mathbf{V}_2 \text{ and the} \qquad (55) \\
&\quad\ t\text{th element of } \mathbf{u} \text{ as defined in (42).}
\end{aligned}$$

The above orders of magnitude hold for k nonstochastic with $\bar{k} = \mathrm{O}(1)$. If $\bar{k} = O(2\mathrm{SLS})$, then $\mathbf{A}_2^{(1)}$, $\mathbf{A}_1^{(1)}$, $\mathbf{B}_2^{(1)}$, and $\mathbf{B}_1^{(1)}$ undergo further obvious simplification. If $\bar{k} = O(1/T)$ as in Nagar's (1959) expansions, the above indicated orders of magnitude still hold; however, a cleaner decomposition can be obtained by combining, for example, $\bar{k}(T - K)\boldsymbol{\rho}$, which would be $O(1)$, with $\mathbf{A}_0$, etc.

C. Case $h = 2$: $\mathbf{Z}$ and $\mathbf{Z}_1$ Nonstochastic; k Stochastic

The second case we consider is when k is stochastic while $\mathbf{Z}$ and $\mathbf{Z}_1$ are nonstochastic. Since we are assuming that $k = O_p(1)$, the indicated orders of magnitude in (54) are still applicable.

However, $\mathbf{A}_1^{(1)}$, $\mathbf{A}_2^{(1)}$, $\mathbf{B}_1^{(1)}$, and $\mathbf{B}_2^{(1)}$ contain terms of higher orders of magnitude. Suppose the following expansion for k holds:

$$k = k_0 + k_{-1} + k_{-2} + k_r \qquad (56)$$

where $k_0 = O(1)$, $k_{-1} = O_p(T^{-1/2})$, $k_{-2} = O_p(T^{-1})$ and $k_r = O_p(T^{-3/2})$. Then terms of smaller order in the components of $\mathbf{A}$ and $\mathbf{B}$ in (53) would come from those having k_{-1} or k_{-2} as a factor.

The appropriate grouping of terms, with (56) holding, is for $\mathbf{A}$,

$$\mathbf{A} = \mathbf{A}_2^{(2)} + \mathbf{A}_1^{(2)} + \mathbf{A}_0^{(2)} + R_a \qquad (57)$$

where

$$\begin{aligned}
\mathbf{A}_2^{(2)} &= \mathbf{A}_2^{(1)}(k_0) \\
\mathbf{A}_1^{(2)} &= \mathbf{A}_1^{(1)}(k_0) - k_{-1}[\mathbf{M}_2'\mathbf{P}_2\mathbf{M}_2 + (T - K)\boldsymbol{\Sigma}_{22}]
\end{aligned}$$

$$\mathbf{A}_0^{(2)} = \mathbf{A}_0^{(1)} - k_{-2}[\mathbf{M}_2'\mathbf{P}_2\mathbf{M}_2 + (T - K)\boldsymbol{\Sigma}_{22}] \qquad (58)$$
$$-k_{-1}[\mathbf{V}_2'\mathbf{P}_2\mathbf{V}_2 - (T - K)\boldsymbol{\Sigma}_{22} + \mathbf{V}_2'\mathbf{P}_2\mathbf{M}_2 + \mathbf{M}_2'\mathbf{P}_2\mathbf{V}_2]$$
$$\mathbf{R}_a = O_p\ (T^{-1/2}),$$

where $\mathbf{A}_2^{(1)}(k_0)$ and $\mathbf{A}_1^{(1)}(k_0)$ are $\mathbf{A}_2^{(1)}$ and $\mathbf{A}_1^{(1)}$, defined in (54), evaluated at k_0. For $\mathbf{B}$, we have

$$\mathbf{B} = \mathbf{B}_2^{(2)} + \mathbf{B}_1^{(2)} + \mathbf{B}_0^{(2)} + \mathbf{R}_b \qquad (59)$$

where

$$\mathbf{B}_2^{(2)} = \mathbf{B}_2^{(1)}(k_0)$$
$$\mathbf{B}_1^{(2)} = \mathbf{B}_1^{(1)}(k_0) \quad - k_{-1}[\mathbf{M}_2'\mathbf{P}_2\boldsymbol{\eta} + (T - K)\boldsymbol{\rho}]$$
$$\mathbf{B}_0^{(2)} = \mathbf{B}_0^{(1)}(k_0) \quad - k_{-2}[\mathbf{M}_2'\mathbf{P}_2\boldsymbol{\eta} + (T - K)\boldsymbol{\rho}] \qquad (60)$$
$$- k_{-1}[\mathbf{M}_2'\mathbf{P}_2\mathbf{u} + \mathbf{V}_2'\mathbf{P}_2\mathbf{u} - (T - K)\boldsymbol{\rho} + \mathbf{V}_2'\mathbf{P}_2\boldsymbol{\eta}]$$
$$\mathbf{R}_b = O_p(T^{-1/2})$$

and $\mathbf{B}_2^{(1)}(k_0)$ and $\mathbf{B}_1^{(1)}(k_0)$ are $\mathbf{B}_2^{(1)}$ and $\mathbf{B}_1^{(1)}$, defined in (54), evaluated at k_0.

Note that in addition to the obvious difference between corresponding components $\mathbf{A}_j^{(1)}$ and $\mathbf{A}_j^{(2)}$ (as well as between $\mathbf{B}_j^{(1)}$ and $\mathbf{B}_j^{(2)}$), terms of order $T^{-3/2}$ and higher negative powers of T in the expansions under nonstochastic and stochastic k will also differ because of R_a and R_b.

D. Case $h = 3$: $\mathbf{Z}$, $\mathbf{Z}_1$, and k Stochastic

In this case, asymptotic expansions need to be developed for $\mathbf{A}$ and $\mathbf{B}$ separately through expansions for $(\mathbf{Z}'\mathbf{Z})^{-1}$ and $(\mathbf{Z}_1'\mathbf{Z}_1)^{-1}$. To develop these, we introduce some further notation, starting from (38) and (39):

$$\mathbf{Z} = \mathbf{M}_z + \mathbf{V}_z$$
$$\mathbf{Z}_1 = \mathbf{M}_x + \mathbf{V}_x. \qquad (61)$$

Note that under cases $h = 1$ and $h = 2$, $\mathbf{V}_x$ and $\mathbf{V}_z$ would be identically equal to zero. In this present case, however, there are nonzero columns in $\mathbf{V}_x$ and $\mathbf{V}_z$ corresponding to the misclassified endogenous variables (in the estimated equation for $\mathbf{V}_x$; and in the whole system, for $\mathbf{V}_z$). Consequently $\mathbf{V}_2'\mathbf{Z}$, which is $O_p(T^{1/2})$ under the first and second cases, is now $O_p(T)$. This introduces $O_p(T)$ terms into the components $\mathbf{A}_1^{(2)}$, $\mathbf{A}_0^{(2)}$, $\mathbf{B}_1^{(2)}$, and $\mathbf{B}_0^{(2)}$ defined in (58) and (60). As for $\mathbf{A}_2^{(2)}$ and $\mathbf{B}_2^{(2)}$, their orders of magnitude as indicated in (58) are still valid. However, because of the expansions for $(\mathbf{Z}'\mathbf{Z})^{-1}$ and $(\mathbf{Z}_1'\mathbf{Z}_1)^{-1}$, $\mathbf{A}_2^{(2)}$ and $\mathbf{B}_2^{(2)}$ will now contain higher order terms.

Using (61) and Lemma 1, we get

$$(\mathbf{Z}'\mathbf{Z})^{-1} = (\mathbf{M}_z'\mathbf{M}_z + T\boldsymbol{\Sigma}_{zz})^{-1} + O_p(T^{-3/2}) \tag{62}$$

$$(\mathbf{Z}_1'\mathbf{Z}_1)^{-1} = (\mathbf{M}_x'\mathbf{M}_x + T\boldsymbol{\Sigma}_{xx})^{-1} + O_p(T^{-3/2}) \tag{63}$$

where

$$\begin{aligned} \boldsymbol{\Sigma}_{zz} &= \mathrm{E}(\mathbf{V}_z'\mathbf{V}_z/T) \\ \boldsymbol{\Sigma}_{xx} &= \mathrm{E}(\mathbf{V}_x'\mathbf{V}_x/T). \end{aligned} \tag{64}$$

Now in (47), write **A** and **B** equivalently as

$$\begin{aligned} \mathbf{A} &= \mathbf{Y}_2'\mathbf{P}_1\mathbf{Y}_2 + \bar{k}\mathbf{Y}_2'\mathbf{P}_2\mathbf{Y}_2 \\ \mathbf{B} &= \mathbf{Y}_2'\mathbf{P}_1(\boldsymbol{\eta} + \mathbf{u}) + \bar{k}\mathbf{Y}_2'\mathbf{P}_2(\boldsymbol{\eta} + \mathbf{u}); \end{aligned} \tag{65}$$

and let

$$\begin{aligned} \boldsymbol{\Delta}_1 &= \mathbf{Y}_2'\mathbf{P}_1\mathbf{Y}_2 + O_p(T^{1/2}) \\ \boldsymbol{\Delta}_2 &= \mathbf{Y}_2'\mathbf{P}_2\mathbf{Y}_2 + O_p(T^{1/2}) \\ \tilde{\boldsymbol{\Theta}}_1 &= \mathbf{Y}_2'\mathbf{P}_1(\boldsymbol{\eta} + \mathbf{u}) + O_p(T^{1/2}) \\ \tilde{\boldsymbol{\Theta}}_2 &= \mathbf{Y}_2'\mathbf{P}_2(\boldsymbol{\eta} + \mathbf{u}) + O_p(T^{1/2}) \end{aligned} \tag{66}$$

so that for

$$\begin{aligned} \mathbf{A}_2^{(3)} &= \boldsymbol{\Delta}_1 + \bar{k}\boldsymbol{\Delta}_2 \\ B_2^{(3)} &\doteq \tilde{\boldsymbol{\Theta}}_1 + \bar{k}\tilde{\boldsymbol{\Theta}}_2 \end{aligned} \tag{67}$$

we have

$$\begin{aligned} \mathbf{A} &= \mathbf{A}_2^{(3)} + O_p(T^{1/2}) \\ \mathbf{B} &= \mathbf{B}_2^{(3)} + O_p(T^{1/2}) \end{aligned} \tag{68}$$

From (61) and (63), we can verify that

$$\begin{aligned} \boldsymbol{\Delta}_1 &= (\mathbf{M}_2'\mathbf{M}_z + T\boldsymbol{\Sigma}_{2z})(\mathbf{M}_z'\mathbf{M}_z + T\boldsymbol{\Sigma}_{zz})^{-1}(\mathbf{M}_z'\mathbf{M}_2 + T\boldsymbol{\Sigma}_{z2}) \\ &\quad - (\mathbf{M}_2'\mathbf{M}_x + T\boldsymbol{\Sigma}_{2x})(\mathbf{M}_x'\mathbf{M}_x + T\boldsymbol{\Sigma}_{xx})^{-1}(\mathbf{M}_x'\mathbf{M}_2 + T\boldsymbol{\Sigma}_{x2}) \\ \boldsymbol{\Delta}_2 &= (\mathbf{M}_2'\mathbf{M}_2 + T\boldsymbol{\Sigma}_{22}) \\ &\quad - (\mathbf{M}_2'\mathbf{M}_z + T\boldsymbol{\Sigma}_{2z})(\mathbf{M}_z'\mathbf{M}_z + T\boldsymbol{\Sigma}_{zz})^{-1}(\mathbf{M}_z'\mathbf{M}_2 + T\boldsymbol{\Sigma}_{z2}) \\ \tilde{\boldsymbol{\Theta}}_1 &= (\mathbf{M}_2'\mathbf{M}_z + T\boldsymbol{\Sigma}_{2z})(\mathbf{M}_z'\mathbf{M}_z + T\boldsymbol{\Sigma}_{zz})^{-1}(\mathbf{M}_z'\boldsymbol{\eta} + T\boldsymbol{\Sigma}_{zu}) \\ &\quad - (\mathbf{M}_2'\mathbf{M}_x + T\boldsymbol{\Sigma}_{2x})(\mathbf{M}_x'\mathbf{M}_x + T\boldsymbol{\Sigma}_{xx})^{-1}(\mathbf{M}_x'\boldsymbol{\eta} + T\boldsymbol{\Sigma}_{xu}) \\ \tilde{\boldsymbol{\Theta}}_2 &= (\mathbf{M}_{2\eta}' + T\rho) - (\mathbf{M}_2'\mathbf{M}_z + T\boldsymbol{\Sigma}_{2z})(\mathbf{M}_z'\mathbf{M}_z \\ &\quad + T\boldsymbol{\Sigma}_{zz})^{-1}(\mathbf{M}_z'\boldsymbol{\eta} + T\boldsymbol{\Sigma}_{zu}) \end{aligned} \tag{69a}$$

where

$$\begin{aligned}
\boldsymbol{\Sigma}_{2z} &= \text{plim}\mathbf{V}_2'\mathbf{V}_z/\mathrm{T} = \mathrm{E}(\mathbf{V}_2'\mathrm{V}_z/\mathrm{T}) \\
\boldsymbol{\Sigma}_{2x} &= \text{plim}\mathbf{V}_2'\mathbf{V}_x/\mathrm{T} = \mathrm{E}(\mathbf{V}_2'\mathbf{V}_x/\mathrm{T}) \\
\boldsymbol{\rho} &= \text{plim}\mathbf{V}_2'\mathbf{u}/\mathbf{T} = \mathbf{E}(\mathbf{V}_2'\mathbf{u}/\mathrm{T}) \\
\boldsymbol{\Sigma}_{zu} &= \text{plim}\mathbf{V}_z'\mathbf{u}/\mathrm{T} = \mathrm{E}(\mathbf{V}_z'\mathbf{u}/\mathrm{T}) \qquad (70) \\
\boldsymbol{\Sigma}_{xu} &= \text{plim}\mathbf{V}_x'\mathrm{y}/\mathrm{T} = \mathrm{E}(\mathbf{V}_x'\mathbf{u}/\mathrm{T}) \\
\mathbf{u} &= \mathbf{u}_1^* + \mathbf{V}_3\boldsymbol{\beta}_3^* \text{ [as defined in (42)]} \\
\boldsymbol{\Sigma}_{z2} &= \boldsymbol{\Sigma}_{2z}'; \boldsymbol{\Sigma}_{x2} = \boldsymbol{\Sigma}_{2x}'
\end{aligned}$$

Applying Lemma 1 once more, we infer from (68) that

$$\begin{aligned}
\hat{\boldsymbol{\beta}}_{(k)} - \boldsymbol{\beta}^* &= [\mathbf{A}_2^{(3)}]^{-1}\mathbf{B}_2^{(3)} + O_p(T^{-1/2}) \qquad (71) \\
&= (\boldsymbol{\Delta}_1 + \bar{k}\boldsymbol{\Delta}_2)^{-1}(\tilde{\boldsymbol{\Theta}}_1 + \bar{k}\tilde{\boldsymbol{\Theta}}_2) + O_p(T^{-1/2}).
\end{aligned}$$

As an immediate consequence of (71) we have the following more explicit statement of (52):

COROLLARY 2: Let k_0 = plim k as $T \to \infty$. Then

$$\text{plim}[\hat{\boldsymbol{\beta}}_{(k)} - \boldsymbol{\beta}^*] = \lim[(\boldsymbol{\Delta}_1 + \bar{k}_0\boldsymbol{\Delta}_2)^{-1}(\tilde{\boldsymbol{\Theta}}_1 + \bar{k}_0\tilde{\boldsymbol{\Theta}}_2)] \qquad (72)$$

Through straightforward algebra, finer expansions for (63) and (68) can be obtained—thus resulting in higher order terms for the expansion of $\hat{\boldsymbol{\beta}}_{(k)}$ itself in (71). We shall not report the details here since most of the remaining analysis in this section will focus on the leading term $[\mathbf{A}_2^{(3)}]^{-1}[\mathbf{B}_2^{(3)}]$ in (50).

Also, when $\mathbf{Z}$ and $\mathbf{Z}_1$ are nonstochastic (cases $h = 1$ and $h = 2$), $\mathbf{M}_z = \mathbf{Z}$, $\mathbf{M}_x = \mathbf{Z}_1$, and all covariance matrices in (69a) involving the subscript z or x are all equal to zero. Thus (69a), for cases $h = 1$ and $h = 2$, simplifies to

$$\begin{aligned}
\boldsymbol{\Delta}_1^{(1)} &= \mathbf{M}_2'\mathbf{P}_1\mathbf{M}_2 \\
\boldsymbol{\Delta}_2^{(1)} &= \mathbf{M}_2'\mathbf{P}_2\mathbf{M}_2 + T\boldsymbol{\Sigma}_{22} \qquad (69b) \\
\tilde{\boldsymbol{\Theta}}_1^{(1)} &= \mathbf{M}_2'\mathbf{P}_1\boldsymbol{\eta} \\
\tilde{\boldsymbol{\Theta}}_2^{(1)} &= \mathbf{M}_2'\mathbf{P}_2\boldsymbol{\eta} + T\rho
\end{aligned}$$

and (67) simplifies to the expressions given earlier for $\mathbf{A}_2^{(1)}$ and $\mathbf{B}_2^{(1)}$ in (54), except for the factor of T instead of $(T - K)$ multiplying $\boldsymbol{\Sigma}_{22}$ in $\mathbf{A}_2^{(1)}$ and $\boldsymbol{\rho}$ in $\mathbf{B}_2^{(1)}$.

We can also see from (69b) how the specification errors being analyzed in this section affect the k-class estimators. Note from (42) and (70) that

$$\begin{aligned}\boldsymbol{\Sigma}_{zu} &= \boldsymbol{\Sigma}_{z3}\boldsymbol{\beta}_3^* + \boldsymbol{\Sigma}_{zu}^*\\ \boldsymbol{\Sigma}_{xu} &= \boldsymbol{\Sigma}_{x3}\boldsymbol{\beta}_3^* + \boldsymbol{\Sigma}_{xu}^*\\ \boldsymbol{\Sigma}_{2u} &= \boldsymbol{\Sigma}_{23}\boldsymbol{\beta}_3^* + \boldsymbol{\Sigma}_{2u}^*\end{aligned}\tag{73}$$

for

$$\begin{aligned}\boldsymbol{\Sigma}_{z3} &= \mathrm{E}(\mathbf{V}_z'\mathbf{V}_3/T);\ \boldsymbol{\Sigma}_{x3} = \mathrm{E}(\mathbf{V}_x'\mathbf{V}_3/\mathrm{T})\\ \boldsymbol{\Sigma}_{zu}^* &= \mathrm{E}(\mathbf{V}_z'\mathbf{u}_1^*/T);\ \boldsymbol{\Sigma}_{xu}^* = \mathrm{E}(\mathbf{V}_x'\mathbf{u}_1^*/\mathrm{T})\\ \boldsymbol{\Sigma}_{23} &= \mathrm{E}(\mathbf{V}_2'\mathbf{V}_3/T);\ \boldsymbol{\Sigma}_{2u}^* = \mathrm{E}(\mathbf{V}_2'\mathbf{u}_1^*/\mathrm{T}).\end{aligned}\tag{74}$$

Also, recall that $\boldsymbol{\eta}$, containing the mean of the omitted variables, can be decomposed according to the endogenous and exogenous omitted components

$$\boldsymbol{\eta} = \mathbf{M}_3\boldsymbol{\beta}_3^* + \mathbf{Z}_2\boldsymbol{\gamma}_2^*.$$

In (69a) the effects of misclassifying endogenous variables are contained in the covariance matrices subscripted by either z or x: for example, $\boldsymbol{\Sigma}_{zz}$, $\boldsymbol{\Sigma}_{xu}$. The direct effects of omitting $\mathbf{Y}_3$ and $\mathbf{Z}_2$ show up in the two components of $\mathbf{M}_2'\boldsymbol{\eta}$, $\mathbf{M}_z'\boldsymbol{\eta}$, and $\mathbf{M}_x'\boldsymbol{\eta}$ in $\tilde{\boldsymbol{\Theta}}_1$ and $\tilde{\boldsymbol{\Theta}}_2$. The direct effect of simultaneity is reflected in the second component of $\boldsymbol{\Sigma}_{2u}$ in $\boldsymbol{\Theta}_2$, namely $\boldsymbol{\Sigma}_{2u}^*$. Interaction effects among these various sources of estimation error are reflected in $\boldsymbol{\Sigma}_{zu}$, $\boldsymbol{\Sigma}_{xu}$, $\boldsymbol{\Sigma}_{23}$ (in $\boldsymbol{\Sigma}_{2u}$), and $\boldsymbol{\Sigma}_{2z}$.

Also, Corollary 2 can be specialized to cases $h = 1$ and $h = 2$ (where variables are still omitted but none are misclassified) as well as to the correctly specified case.

Corollary 3: For misspecification cases $h = 1$ and $h = 2$,

$$\begin{aligned}\operatorname{plim}[\hat{\boldsymbol{\beta}}_{(k)} - \boldsymbol{\beta}^*] &= \lim[\mathbf{M}_2'\mathbf{P}_1\mathbf{M}_2 + \bar{k}_0(\mathbf{M}_2'\mathbf{P}_2\mathbf{M}_2 + T\boldsymbol{\Sigma}_{22})]^{-1}\\ &\quad\cdot [\mathbf{M}_2'\mathbf{P}_1\boldsymbol{\eta} + \bar{k}_0(\mathbf{M}_2'\mathbf{P}_2\boldsymbol{\eta} + T\boldsymbol{\rho})]\end{aligned}\tag{75}$$

This follows directly from (69b) and Corollary 2. The well-known result for the correctly specified case is recovered from (75) by setting $\boldsymbol{\eta} = \mathbf{0}$.

Corollary 4: For the correctly specified case,

$$\begin{aligned}\operatorname{plim}[\hat{\boldsymbol{\beta}}_{(k)} - \boldsymbol{\beta}^*] &= \lim[\mathbf{M}_2'\mathbf{P}_1\mathbf{M}_2 + \bar{k}_0(\mathbf{M}_2'\mathbf{P}_2\mathbf{M}_2 + T\boldsymbol{\Sigma}_{22})]^{-1}\\ &\quad\cdot [\bar{k}_0 T\boldsymbol{\rho}]\end{aligned}\tag{76}$$

E. Asymptotic Moments of $\hat{\boldsymbol{\beta}}_{(k)}$

Based on Proposition 1, asymptotic moments of $[\hat{\boldsymbol{\beta}}_{(k)} - \boldsymbol{\beta}^*]$ can now be defined in terms of the exact moments of retained leading terms in the expansion given in (50). Asymptotic moments defined in this manner will have to be interpreted with reference to the highest order of the terms retained in the expansion. In particular, for $r = 2$

$$\hat{\boldsymbol{\beta}}_{(k)} - \boldsymbol{\beta}^* = \mathbf{F}_0 + \mathbf{F}_{-1} + \mathbf{F}_{-2} + O_p(T^{-3/2}). \tag{77}$$

where

$$\begin{aligned} \mathbf{F}_0 &= \mathbf{A}_2^{-1}\mathbf{B}_2 \\ \mathbf{F}_{-1} &= \mathbf{A}_2^{-1}(\mathbf{B}_1 - \mathbf{A}_1\mathbf{A}_2^{-1}\mathbf{B}_2) \\ \mathbf{F}_{-2} &= \mathbf{A}_2^{-1}[\mathbf{B}_0 - \mathbf{A}_1\mathbf{A}_2^{-1}\mathbf{B}_1 - \mathbf{A}_0\mathbf{A}_2^{-1}\mathbf{B}_2 \\ &\quad + \mathbf{A}_1\mathbf{A}_2^{-1}\mathbf{A}_1\mathbf{A}_2^{-1}\mathbf{B}_2]. \end{aligned} \tag{78}$$

For

$$\mathbf{F} = \mathbf{F}_0 + \mathbf{F}_{-1} + \mathbf{F}_{-2} \tag{79}$$

the asymptotic bias and MSE of $\hat{\boldsymbol{\beta}}_{(k)}$ to order T^{-1} can be defined in terms of the first and second moments of **F**. For the three cases we have considered, $\mathbf{A}_2^{(h)}$ and $\mathbf{B}_2^{(h)}$ are all nonstochastic for $h = 1, 2, 3$ and we can easily verify the following.

PROPOSITION 2: For cases $h = 1, 2, 3$, the asymptotic bias and MSE of $\hat{\boldsymbol{\beta}}_{(k)}$ to order T^{-1} are, respectively,

$$\begin{aligned} \mathcal{B}^{(h)}(k) &= \mathcal{B}_0^{(h)}(k) + \mathcal{B}_1^{(h)}(k) + O(T^{-1}) \\ \mathcal{M}^{(h)}(k) &= \mathcal{M}_0^{(h)}(k) + \mathcal{M}_1^{(h)}(\mathrm{k}) + O(T^{-1}) \end{aligned} \tag{80}$$

where

$$\begin{aligned} \mathcal{B}_0^{(h)}(k) &= [\mathbf{A}_2^{(h)}]^{-1}\mathbf{B}_2^{(h)} \\ \mathcal{M}_0^{(h)}(k) &= [\mathcal{B}_0^{(h)}(k)]^2. \end{aligned} \tag{81}$$

In both asymptotic bias and MSE expressions, when **Z** and $k = O(1)$ are all nonstochastic ($h = 1$)

$$\mathrm{E}[\mathbf{A}_1^{(1)}] = \mathbf{0} \text{ and } \mathrm{E}[\mathbf{B}_1^{(1)}] = \mathbf{0} \tag{82}$$

so that the $O(T^{-1/2})$ term is zero and the remainder terms are $O(T^{-1})$. For cases $h = 2$ and $h = 3$, on the other hand, where P is stochastic, the $O(T^{-1/2})$ terms in (80) will in general differ from zero.

Although higher order terms in (80) can be obtained, we shall not pursue this direction further. Instead, we devote the remaining part of this section to a more detailed analysis of the $O(1)$ terms in the asymptotic bias and MSE expressions as functions of k (or of k_o).

The moments of F which we use in (80) to define the asymptotic moments of $[\hat{\boldsymbol{\beta}}_{(k)} - \boldsymbol{\beta}^*]$ are not necessarily good approximations to the exact moments of $[\hat{\boldsymbol{\beta}}_{(k)} - \boldsymbol{\beta}^*]$. Our concern here is with good approximations in probability and consequently in distribution. The moment results in Proposition 2 should be regarded as summary measures for the distribution of F that closely matches the distribution of $[\hat{\boldsymbol{\beta}}_{(k)} - \boldsymbol{\beta}^*]$ for large T. A good analogue from traditional large-sample theory is the use of moments of a limiting distribution; such asymptotic moments may be good approximations to exact moments for large sample sizes, though they need not be: exact moments may not even exist for any sample size.

An important distinction between the asymptotic expansions and moments presented here and many previous asymptotic results, including those of Kadane (1970, 1971), Sawa (1972), and Mariano (1975) in the correctly specified case and Ramage (1971) and HMR under misspecification, is that sample size and $\mathbf{M}_2'\mathbf{P}_1\mathbf{M}_2/\sigma_{22}$ (or the so-called concentration parameter in $G_1 = 1$) are here assumed to grow at the same rate. The distinction between the assumptions in this article and those in the references cited earlier, where T is assumed fixed as $\mathbf{M}_2'\mathbf{P}_1\mathbf{M}_2/\sigma_{22}$ increases, is exactly that made in Anderson and Sawa (1973) and Anderson (1977). That $\mathbf{M}_2'\mathbf{P}_1\mathbf{M}_2/\sigma_{22}$ and sample size grow at the same rate is an immediate consequence of the usual large-sample behavior of the exogenous variables that we have made in (45), namely that $\mathbf{Z}^{*\prime}\mathbf{Z}^*/T$ converges to a finite positive-definite limit as T increases indefinitely. This assumption is the same as that in Nagar (1959), and the method of analysis here is similar. As pointed out earlier, however, Nagar's approach applies only to k-class estimators with $k = 1 + a/T$ where a is constant, while the analysis presented here applies to the full k-class as well as to LIML. The only restriction on k is that k be $O_p(1)$, admitting an asymptotic expansion of the type (56).

Under these conditions, none of the references cited earlier gives good approximations in large samples except for estimators that are asymptotically equivalent to 2SLS. When T is taken to be fixed relative to $\mathbf{M}_2'\mathbf{P}_1\mathbf{M}_2/\sigma_{22}$ as the latter increases, as in the previous studies, the leading terms in the asymptotic moments in Proposition 2 are consistent with all these previous results, and in fact they match exactly with the appropriate special case of the misspecification results in Ramage (1971) and with the leading term results in HMR to the order of terms included.

F. The Case of One Right-Side Endogenous Variable ($G_1 = 1$)

Let us first consider the case where there is only one right-side variable treated as endogenous in the apparent equation—so that $G_1 = 1$ and $\hat{\beta}_{(k)}$ is scalar. The leading terms for asymptotic bias and MSE in (80) are of the form, where the superscript h is deleted for convenience:

$$\mathscr{B}_0(k) = (a_1 + b_1k)/(c_1 + d_1k) = a - b/(k - c) \tag{83}$$

$$\mathscr{M}_0(k) = [\mathscr{B}_0(k)]^2 \tag{84}$$

where

$$\begin{aligned} a_1 &= \tilde{\Theta}_1 + \tilde{\Theta}_2 \\ b_1 &= -\tilde{\Theta}_2 \\ c_1 &= \Delta_1 + \Delta_2 \\ d_1 &= -\Delta_2 \end{aligned} \tag{85}$$

and

$$\begin{aligned} a &= b_1/d_1 = \tilde{\Theta}_2/\Delta_2 \\ b &= (b_1c_1 - a_1d_1)/d_1^2 = (\tilde{\Theta}_1\Delta_2 - \tilde{\Theta}_2\Delta_1)/\Delta_2^2 \\ c &= -c_1/d_1 = 1 + \Delta_1/\Delta_2 \end{aligned} \tag{86}$$

where Δ_1, Δ_2, $\tilde{\Theta}_1$, $\tilde{\Theta}_2$ as defined in (69a) are specialized to the scalar case which we are considering now. Note that Δ_1 and Δ_2 are nonnegative while $\tilde{\Theta}_1$ and $\tilde{\Theta}$ are indefinite.

If higher order terms in asymptotic bias and MSE are to be neglected, the optimal choice of k to minimize asymptotic MSE is that which minimizes $|\mathscr{B}_0(k)|$.

From (83) we see that $\mathscr{B}_0(k)$ describes a rectangular hyperbolic relationship between $\mathscr{B}_0$ and k with horizontal axis at $\mathscr{B}_0 = a$ and vertical axis at $k = c > 1$. Furthermore, $\mathscr{B}_0(k)$ is increasing in k for $b > 0$ and decreasing in k for $b < 0$. The graphs for $B_0(k)$ are given for $b > 0$ in Figure 1 and for $b < 0$ in Figure 2.

Now, there is a unique root, k_*, for $\mathscr{B}_0(k)$ which is obtained directly by solving the equation $\mathscr{B}_0(k) = 0$:

$$k_* = c + b/a = 1 + \tilde{\Theta}_1/\tilde{\Theta}_2 \tag{87}$$

This value of k_*, which ranges over the whole real line, determines the relative asymptotic efficiencies of the various k-class estimators. Four cases are to be distinguished:

$$\begin{aligned} &\text{Case A. } c < k_* \\ &\text{Case B. } 1 < k_* < c \\ &\text{Case C. } 0 \leqslant k_* \leqslant 1 \\ &\text{Case D. } k_* < 0. \end{aligned} \tag{88}$$

Figure 1. $\mathscr{B}_0(k) = a - b/(k - c)$ when $b > 0$.

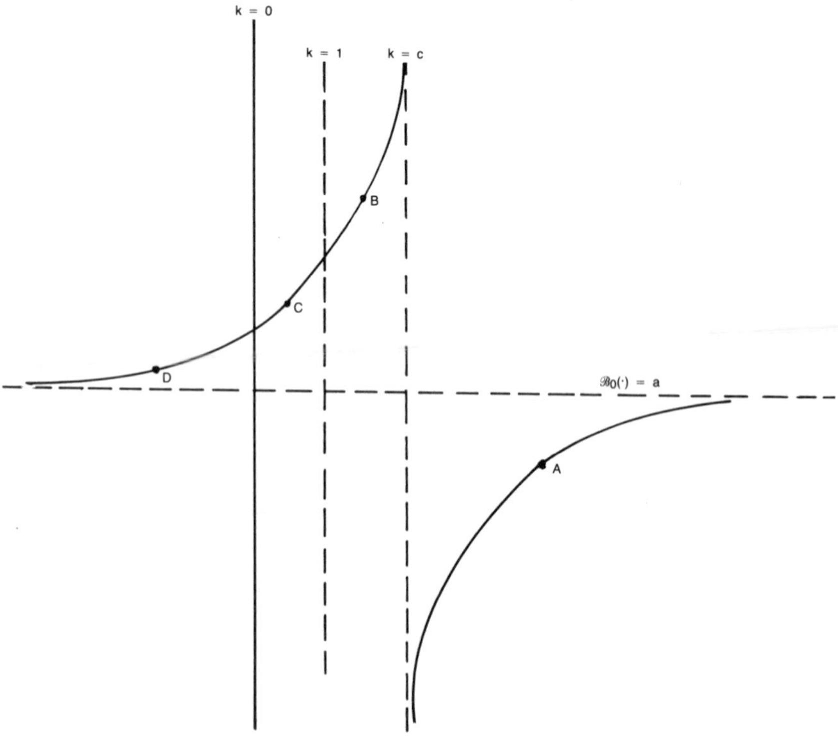

The value of k_* determines the location of the horizontal axis at which $\mathscr{B}_0(k) = 0$. Superimposing this horizontal axis on Figures 1 and 2 through the points marked A, B, C, and D, corresponding to the four cases delineated above) directly tells us the optimum value of nonstochastic k over the interval [0,1], in terms of minimizing $|\mathscr{B}_0(k)|$. Through this device we are also able to compare two-stage least squares with limited-information maximum likelihood. Table 3 summarizes the conclusions derived from this analysis. Note that

$$k_* = 1 + \tilde{\Theta}_1/\tilde{\Theta}_2$$

and that under correct specification $\tilde{\Theta}_1 = 0$. Thus, under Case C in Table 3, when there is no misspecification, the appropriate entries in the second and third columns are $k_* = 1$ and $k_{**} = 1$. That $k_{**} = 1$ bears out the result in the correctly specified case that absolute bias of the k-class (for nonstochastic k, $0 \leqslant k \leqslant 1$) is a decreasing function of k. That $k_* = 1$ simply reflects the result that 2SLS is consistent while the other estimators

Table 3. Optimum Values of k under Misspecification (in the Case of One RHS Endogenous Variable).†

Cases	k_*	k_{**}	*LIML vs* k_{**}	*LIML vs 2SLS*
A	$c < k_*$	0	Better if $l_0 > c + \varepsilon_1$ Worse, otherwise $(0 < \varepsilon_1 < \infty)$.	Better if $l_0 > c + \varepsilon_2$ Worse, otherwise $(0 < \varepsilon_2 < \infty)$.
B	$1 < k_* < c$	1	Better if $l_0 < c - \varepsilon_3$ Worse, otherwise $(0 < \varepsilon_3 < \infty)$	As in Column 4
C	$0 \leqslant k_* \leqslant 1$	k_*	Always worse	Worse unless $l_0 > c + \varepsilon_4$ $(0 < \varepsilon_4 \leqslant \infty)$
D	$k_* < 0$	0	Worse unless $l_0 > c + \varepsilon_5$ $(0 < \varepsilon_5 \leqslant \infty)$	Worse unless $l_0 > c + \varepsilon_6$ $(0 < \varepsilon_6 \leqslant \infty)$

† k_* = Value of k such that $\mathscr{B}_0(k_*) = 0$; $k_* = 1 + \bar{\Theta}_1/\bar{\Theta}_2$.

k_{**} = value of k such that $\mathscr{B}_0(k_{**}) = \min|\mathscr{B}_0(k)|$ for k [0,1].

c = $1 + \Delta_1/\Delta_2$.

l_0 = plim l; for $k = l$, $\hat{\beta}_{(k)} = \hat{\beta}_{\text{LIML}}$.

$\mathscr{B}_0(k) = (\bar{\Theta}_1 + \bar{k}\bar{\Theta}_2)/(\Delta_1 + \bar{k}\,\Delta_2)$ for $\bar{k} = 1 - k$.

Figure 2. Graph of $\mathscr{B}_0(k) = a - b/(k - c)$ when $b < 0$.

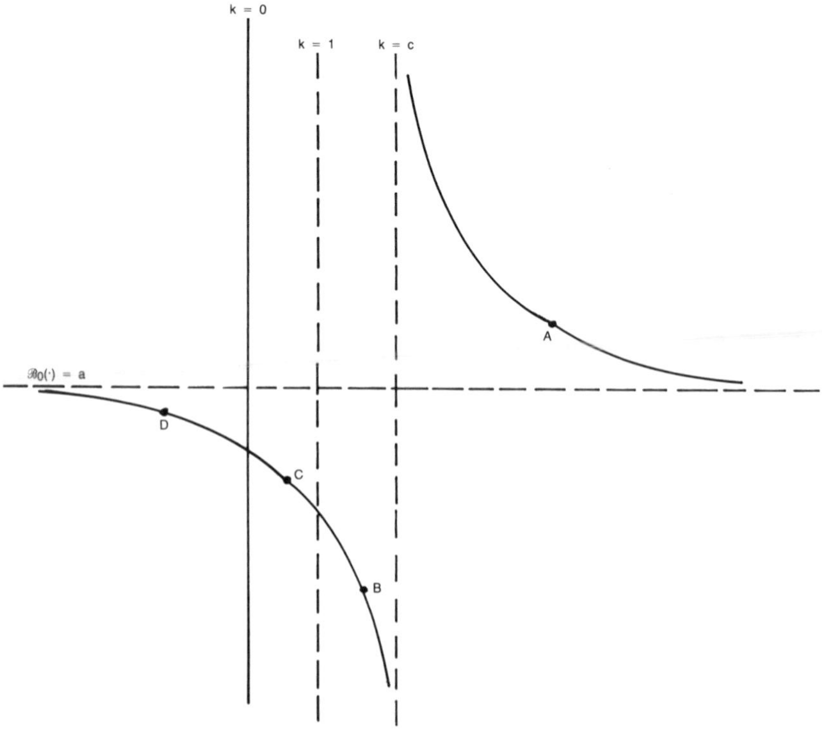

for nonstochastic $k \epsilon [0,1)$ are inconsistent. Also, recall that we are focusing only on the dominant $O(1)$ term in the asymptotic MSE expression which, under misspecification, is squared bias and is dependent upon k. Thus, the optimality of 2SLS in the correctly specified case should be interpreted accordingly. In particular, it does not contradict the earlier result in Sawa (1972), which gives an optimal k strictly between zero and one based on higher order terms in the MSE expression. By the same token, the analysis presented here cannot be used to compare LIML and 2SLS in the correctly specified case where the $O(1)$ term is zero for both estimators. Such a comparison requires higher order terms beyond the $O(1)$ term.

Under misspecification, however, a partial comparison can be made based on the leading terms alone. For LIML, the lowest order term is $\mathscr{B}_0(l_0)$, where l_0 is the leading term in the expansion for the root generating the LIML estimator. In the correctly specified case, $l_0 = 1$, which is consistent with Mariano (1975). Looking at the last column in Table 3, we see that the only situation where LIML is inadmissible under our stated criterion is Case C, where the optimal k_* lies between zero and one. For the other three cases, the performance of LIML relative to $k \epsilon [0,1]$ depends on the size of l_0 and its distance from k_* and c. More details given in the last column of Table 3 follow directly from Figures 1 and 2.

With regard to nonstochastic k in the closed interval [0,1], Table 3 shows that OLS is preferred within this class under Cases A and D. These two cases, especially when considered, as we do later, within the context of Type 1 misspecification, correspond to situations when misspecification is a more substantial problem than simultaneity. Preference for 2SLS within this class occurs in Case B; 2SLS may also dominate in Case C, but only when $\Theta_1 = 0$. These conclusions, when specialized to Type 1 misspecification, agree with those reported in HMR, based on large concentration parameter-fixed sample size asymptotics.

Note also that the indeterminacy of $\mathcal{B}_0(k)$ at

$$k = c = 1 + \Delta_1/\Delta_2$$

is indicative of the fact that, as in the correctly specified case, LIML does not have exact moments of positive integral order. This instability in the asymptotic moments of $\hat{\beta}_{(k)}$ under misspecification also reflects the behavior of the k-class estimators in the correctly specified case for $k > 1$ (see Theil, 1971, p. 530, and Sawa, 1972).

The results presented here are also consistent with the conclusions reached by Fisher in two of his papers dealing with the effects of misspecification on single-equation estimators (1961, 1966). In a third paper (1967), which compares 2SLS and LIML on the basis of their large sample probability limits, however, Fisher makes the following assertion:

> It is shown that for any parameter and small enough specification error, the probability limits of two-stage least squares and limited-information maximum-likelihood, while different, lie on the same side of the true parameter value, the difference between them being of the second order of smalls relative to the effects of the specification error on either one of them.

It is clear from our analysis here that the probability limits of the 2SLS and LIML estimates of β under misspecification are given by the limits of $[\beta^* + \mathcal{B}_0(1)]$ and $[\beta^* + \mathcal{B}_0(l_0)]$, respectively, as T approaches infinity. In this notation, Fisher's assertions are that lim $\mathcal{B}_0(1)$ and lim $\mathcal{B}_0(l_0)$ have the same sign for small enough specification error and that the difference between these two limits is small compared to either. One can see from Figures 1 and 2 the extent to which these claims hold. They turn on the facts that the limit of l_0 is 1 as specification error tends to zero and that $\mathcal{B}_0(\cdot)$ is continuous in k over the interval $O < k < 1 + \Delta_1/\Delta_2$ where $\Delta_1/\Delta_2 = O(1)$ as $T \rightarrow \infty$. Thus, $\mathcal{B}_0(1)$ and $\mathcal{B}_0(l_0)$ can be made to be of the same sign by suitably choosing a small enough specification error leading to a value of l_0 close enough to one. However, apart from such limiting considerations under which Fisher's claims hold, it is possible to construct examples of sign differences in $\mathscr{B}_0(1)$ and $\mathscr{B}_0(l_0)$. For example, one can easily see from Figure 2 that under case $\mathscr{B}$, if $k_* < l_0 < c$, then $\mathscr{B}_0(1) > 0$ while $\mathscr{B}_0(l_0) < 0$.

To get a better understanding of the cases A, B, C, and D that we have distinguished in (88), consider the situation (cases $h = 1$ and $h = 2$) where $\mathbf{Z}$ and $\mathbf{Z}_1$ are both nonstochastic. Here, we get the following simplification [as in (69b)]:

$$\begin{aligned} \Delta_1 &= 2\sigma_{22}\delta_1 \\ \Delta_2 &= \sigma_{22}(2\delta_2 + T) \\ \tilde{\Theta}_1 &= 2\sigma_{22}\theta_1 \\ \tilde{\Theta}_2 &= \sigma_{22}(2\theta_2 + T\zeta) \end{aligned} \tag{89}$$

where

$$\begin{aligned} \delta_1 &= \mathbf{M}_2'\mathbf{P}_1\mathbf{M}_2/(2\sigma_{22}) \\ \delta_2 &= \mathbf{M}_2'\mathbf{P}_2\mathbf{M}_2/(2\sigma_{22}) \\ \theta_1 &= \mathbf{M}_2'\mathbf{P}_1\boldsymbol{\eta}/(2\sigma_{22}) \\ \theta_2 &= \mathbf{M}_2'\mathbf{P}_2\boldsymbol{\eta}/(2\sigma_{22}) \\ \sigma_{22} &= \text{variance of the RHS endogenous variable} \\ \sigma_{22}\zeta &= \text{covariance between the RHS endogenous variable and the} \\ &\quad\ \text{disturbance term in the apparent equation} \end{aligned} \tag{90}$$

The parameters θ_1, δ_2, and θ_2 contain the effects of misspecification, with θ_1 and θ_2 being decomposable further according to the omitted exogenous and endogenous components of η. They are as defined in (25) of the preceding section. The effects of the endogeneity of the right-side variable $\mathbf{Y}_2$ is contained in ζ which measures the combined covariance of $\mathbf{Y}_2$ with the structural disturbance term as well as the omitted endogenous variables $\mathbf{Y}_3$. If no exogenous variables are omitted from the system so that $\mathbf{Z} = \mathbf{Z}^*$ (Type 1 misspecification defined in Section II), then $\theta_2 = 0$ and $\delta_2 = 0$. The conditions identifying the four cases in Table 3 can also be stated in terms of $(\delta_1, \delta_2, \theta_1, \theta_2, \zeta)$. The details for all this specialization to Type 1 and Type 2 misspecification are summarized in Table 4.

If there are no specification errors at all, θ_1 as well as θ_2 and δ_2 is equal to zero and we get

$$\mathscr{B}_0(k) = \bar{k}T\zeta/(2\delta_1 + \bar{k}T)$$

Table 4. Conditions on k_* under Various Types of Misspecification.†

Cases	Types of Misspecification: General	Type 2	Type 1
A: $c < k_*$	$\operatorname{sgn} \tilde{\Theta}_1 = \operatorname{sgn} \tilde{\Theta}_2$ $\tilde{\Theta}_2/\tilde{\Theta}_1 < \Delta_2/\Delta_1$	$\operatorname{sgn}(2\theta_2 + T\zeta) = \operatorname{sgn} \theta_1$ $\lvert 2\theta_2 + T\zeta \rvert < \lvert \theta_1 \rvert (2\delta_2 + T)/\delta_1$	$\operatorname{sgn} \zeta = \operatorname{sgn} \theta_1$ $\lvert \zeta \rvert < \lvert \theta_1 \rvert / \delta_1$
B: $1 < k_* < c$	$\operatorname{sgn} \tilde{\Theta}_1 = \operatorname{sgn} \tilde{\Theta}_2$ $\tilde{\Theta}_2/\tilde{\Theta}_1 > \Delta_2/\Delta_1$	$\operatorname{sgn}(2\theta_2 + T\zeta) = \operatorname{sgn} \theta_1$ $\lvert 2\theta_2 + T\zeta \rvert > \lvert \theta_1 \rvert (2\delta_2 + T)/\delta_1$	$\operatorname{sgn} \zeta = \operatorname{sgn} \theta_1$ $\lvert \zeta \rvert > \lvert \theta_1 \rvert / \delta_1$
C: $0 \leqslant k_* \leqslant 1$	$\operatorname{sgn} \tilde{\Theta}_1 \neq \operatorname{sgn} \tilde{\Theta}_2$ $\lvert \tilde{\Theta}_2 \rvert \geqslant \lvert \tilde{\Theta}_1 \rvert$	$\operatorname{sgn}(2\theta_2 + T\zeta) \neq \operatorname{sgn} \theta_1$ $\lvert 2\theta_2 + T\zeta \rvert \geqslant \lvert 2\theta_1 \rvert$	$\operatorname{sgn} \zeta \neq \operatorname{sgn} \theta_1$ $\lvert \zeta \rvert \geqslant \lvert 2\theta_1/T \rvert$
D: $0 > k_*$	$\operatorname{sgn} \tilde{\Theta}_1 \neq \operatorname{sgn} \tilde{\Theta}_2$ $\lvert \tilde{\Theta}_2 \rvert < \lvert \tilde{\Theta}_1 \rvert$	$\operatorname{sgn}(2\theta_2 + T\zeta) \neq \operatorname{sgn} \theta_1$ $\lvert 2\theta_2 + T\zeta \rvert < \lvert 2\theta_1 \rvert$	$\operatorname{sgn} \zeta \neq \operatorname{sgn} \theta_1$ $\lvert \zeta \rvert < \lvert 2\theta_1/T \rvert$
c	$1 + \Delta_1/\Delta_2$	$1 + 2\delta_1/(2\delta_2 + T)$	$1 + 2\delta_1/T$
k_*	$1 + \tilde{\Theta}_1/\tilde{\Theta}_2$	$1 + 2\theta_1/(2\theta_2 + T\zeta)$	$1 + 2\theta_1/T\zeta$
$\mathscr{B}_0(k)$	$\dfrac{(\tilde{\Theta}_1 + \bar{k}\tilde{\Theta}_2)}{(\Delta_1 + \bar{k}\Delta_2)}$	$\dfrac{[2\theta_1 + \bar{k}(2\theta_2 + T\zeta)]}{[2\delta_1 + \bar{k}(2\delta_2 + T)]}$	$\dfrac{(2\theta_1 + \bar{k}T\zeta)}{(2\delta_1 + \bar{k}T)}$

† Δ_1, Δ_2, $\tilde{\Theta}_1$, $\tilde{\Theta}_2$: see (69a); δ_1, δ_2, θ_1, θ_2, ζ: see (90).

for the correctly specified case. Note that under Types 1 and 2 misspecification (as well as correct specification), ζ is the covariance between the right-side endogenous variable $\mathbf{Y}_2$ and $\mathbf{w}\,(=\mathbf{Y}_3\boldsymbol{\beta}_3^* + \mathbf{Z}_2\boldsymbol{\gamma}_2^* + \mathbf{u}_1^*)$ divided by the variance of $\mathbf{Y}_2$. Thus, ζ can be considered as a measure of the extent of simultaneity in the equation being estimated. On the other hand, θ_1 and θ_2 are misspecification parameters which measure two kinds of partial correlation between the means of the included endogenous variable and the wrongly omitted component $(\mathbf{Y}_3\boldsymbol{\beta}_3^* + \mathbf{Z}_2\boldsymbol{\gamma}_2^*)$. θ_1 deals with the partial correlation explained by $\mathbf{Z}$ given $\mathbf{Z}_1$; θ_2 deals with the partial correlation conditional on $\mathbf{Z}$. From Table 4, especially the last column, we see that Cases A and D correspond to situations where the incidence of misspecification is more serious than simultaneity. These are precisely the situations, see Table 3, when OLS would be preferred to 2SLS or any other k-class estimators for $k\epsilon(0,1)$.

G. The Case of Two or More Right-Side Endogenous Variables ($G_1 \geq 2$)

Recall from (71) and Proposition 2 that the leading term in the asymptotic bias of $\hat{\boldsymbol{\beta}}_{(k)}$ in the general case is

$$\mathscr{B}_0(k) = \mathbf{a} + (\boldsymbol{\Delta}_1 + \bar{k}\boldsymbol{\Delta}_2)^{-1}\boldsymbol{\tau} \tag{91}$$

where

$$\mathbf{a} = \boldsymbol{\Delta}_2^{-1}\bar{\boldsymbol{\Theta}}_2$$
$$\boldsymbol{\tau} = \bar{\boldsymbol{\Theta}}_1 - \boldsymbol{\Delta}_1\boldsymbol{\Delta}_2^{-1}\bar{\boldsymbol{\Theta}}_2. \tag{92}$$

From (91), we see that any component of $\mathscr{B}_0(k)$, say the first, can be written as

$$\mathrm{B}_{01}(k) = a_1 + \psi_1(k)/\phi(k) \tag{93}$$

where a_1 is the first component of $\mathbf{a}$ defined in (92) and $\phi(\cdot)$ and $\psi_1(\cdot)$ are polynomials in k of degree G_1 and $G_1 - 1$, respectively:

$$\phi(k) = \det(\boldsymbol{\Delta}_1 + \bar{k}\Delta_2)$$
$$\psi_1(k) = \text{first element of [adjoint } (\boldsymbol{\Delta}_1 + \bar{k}\boldsymbol{\Delta}_2)]\boldsymbol{\tau}. \tag{94}$$

Note that the denominator $\phi(k)$ in (93) remains the same for each component of $\mathscr{B}_0(k)$. $\mathrm{B}_{01}(k)$ is indeterminate and has vertical asymptotes at the zeros of $\phi(k)$, or equivalently, the eigenvalues of $(\boldsymbol{\Delta}_1 + \boldsymbol{\Delta}_2)$ relative to $\boldsymbol{\Delta}_2$. These eigenvalues are all strictly greater than one.

Now, consider the case $G_1 = 2$. We have, in this case

$$B_{01}(k) = a_1 + [b_1(k - \alpha_1)]/[(k - c_1)(k - c_2)] \tag{95}$$

where c_1 and c_2 are the eigenvalues of $\mathbf{\Delta}_2^{-1}(\mathbf{\Delta}_1 + \mathbf{\Delta}_2)$:

$$(\mathbf{\Delta}_1 + \mathbf{\Delta}_2 - c_i\mathbf{\Delta}_2) = \mathbf{0} \qquad i = 1, 2; \tag{96}$$

and

$$\begin{aligned} b_1 &= -(\Delta_{22}^{(2)}\tau_1 - \Delta_{12}^{(2)}\tau_2)/\det(\mathbf{\Delta}_2) \\ \alpha_1 &= [(\Delta_{12}^{(1)} + \Delta_{12}^{(2)})\tau_2 - (\Delta_{22}^{(1)} + \Delta_{22}^{(2)})\tau_1]/[b_1 \det(\mathbf{\Delta}_2)]. \end{aligned} \tag{97}$$

Here, we take

$$\begin{aligned} \mathbf{\Delta}_i &= \begin{bmatrix} \Delta_{11}^{(i)} & \Delta_{12}^{(i)} \\ \Delta_{21}^{(i)} & \Delta_{22}^{(i)} \end{bmatrix} \qquad \text{for } i = 1, 2. \\ \boldsymbol{\tau}' &= (\tau_1\ \tau_2) \end{aligned} \tag{98}$$

As given in (95), $B_{01}(k)$ is equal to a_1 at $k = \alpha_1$; has a horizontal asymptote at $B_{01} = a_1$ and vertical asymptotes at $k = c_1$ (as long as $\alpha_1 \neq c_1$) and $k = c_2$ (as long as $\alpha_2 \neq c_2$); and has first derivative equal to zero (if $\alpha_1 < c_1$ or $\alpha_1 > c_2$) at

$$\begin{aligned} k_1 &= \alpha_1 - [(\alpha_1 - c_1)(\alpha_1 - c_2)]^{1/2} \\ k_2 &= \alpha_1 + [(\alpha_1 - c_1)(\alpha_1 - c_2)]^{1/2}. \end{aligned} \tag{99}$$

The behavior of $B_{01}(k)$ as k changes depends on the sign of b_1 and the location of a_1 relative to c_1 and c_2. Table 5 contains a summary of the signs of $dB_{01}(k)/dK$ for different cases. These provide the basis for the graphs of $B_{01}(k)$ in Figure 3.

Table 5. Sign of $dB_{01}(k)/dk$ for Different Values of b_1 and α_1.†

b_1 / α_1	$b_1 > 0$	$b_1 < 0$
$\alpha_1 < c_1$ or $\alpha_1 > c_2$	< 0 for $k < k_1$ > 0 for $k_1 < k < k_2$ < 0 for $k_2 < k$	> 0 for $k < k_1$ < 0 for $k_1 < k < k_2$ > 0 for $k_2 < k$
$c_1 < \alpha_1 < c_2$	< 0 for all k	> 0 for all k

† $B_{01}(k) = a_1 + b_1(k - \alpha_1)/[(k - c_1)(k - c_2)]$.
c_1, c_2 = eigenvalues of $\Delta_2^{-1}(\Delta_1 + \Delta_2)$.
$k_1 = \alpha_1 - [(\alpha_1 - c_1)(\alpha_1 - c_2)]^{1/2}$.
$k_2 = \alpha_1 + [(\alpha_1 - c_1)(\alpha_1 - c_2)]^{1/2}$.
α_1: $B_{01}(k) = a_1$ at $k = \alpha_1$.
b_1: see (97).

Figure 3. Graphs of $B_{01}(k) = a_1 + b_1(k - \alpha_1)/[(k - c_1)(k - c_2)]$

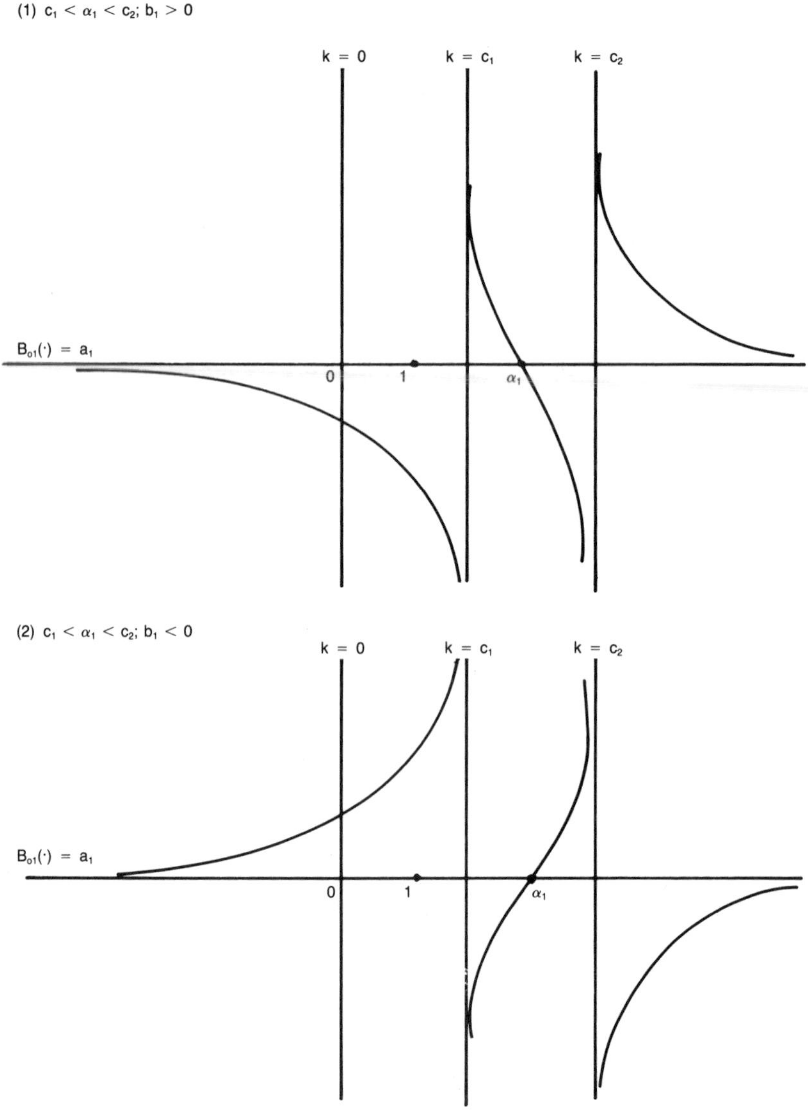

Figure 3. (continued)

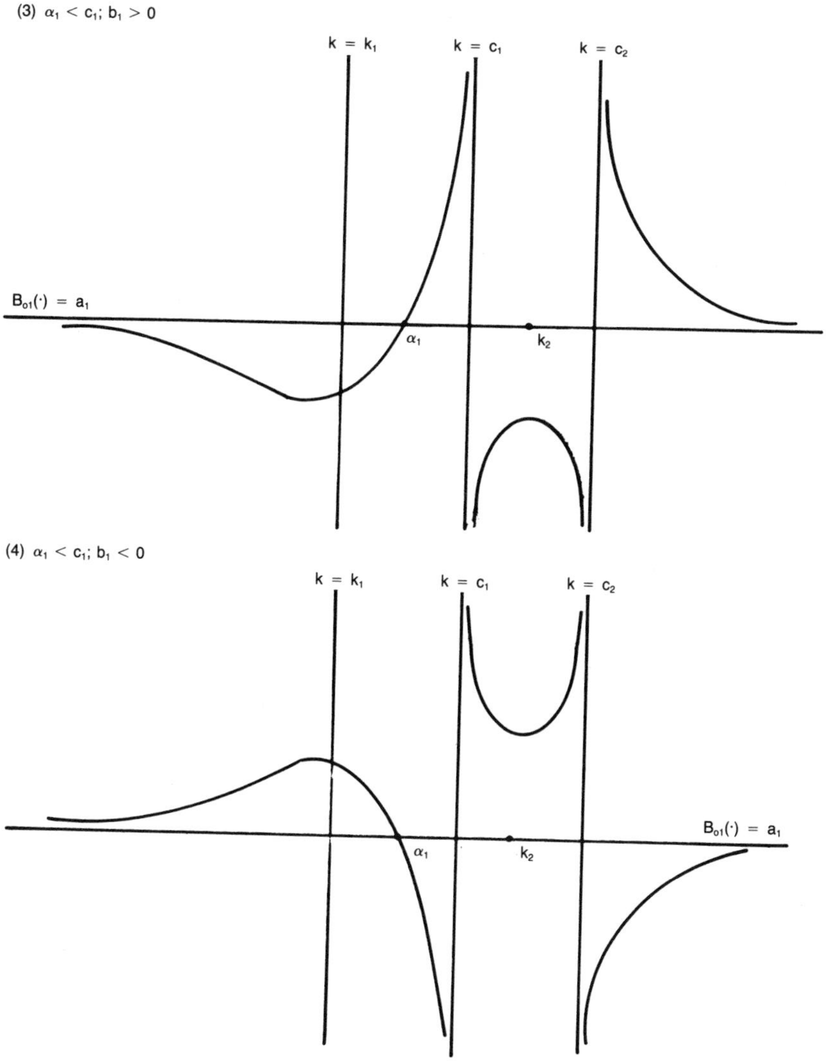

Figure 3. (continued)

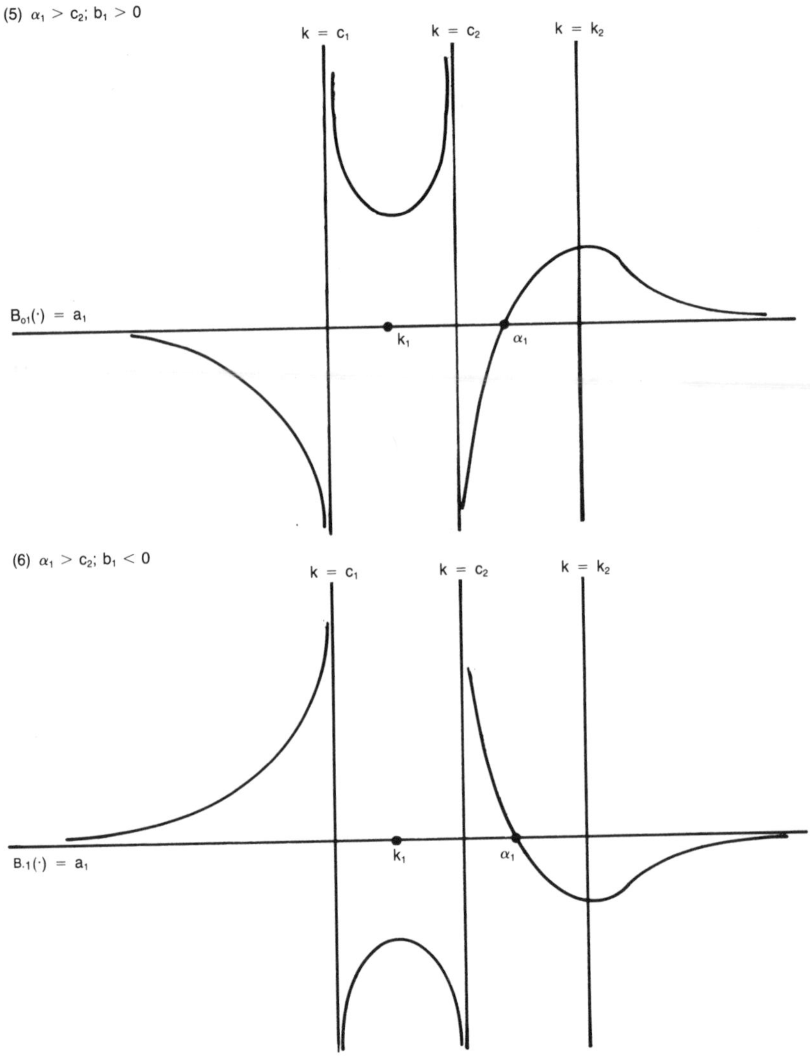

APPENDIX A

Derivation of Exact Moment Expressions (Proof of Theorem 1)

Let $\mathbf{x}_1$ and $\mathbf{x}_2$ be the $T \times 1$ vectors whose tth elements are defined in (20) so that $\mathbf{x}_1$ and $\mathbf{x}_2$ are independent and

$$\mathbf{x}_i \sim \mathrm{N}(\boldsymbol{\mu}_i, \mathbf{I}) \qquad i = 1, 2 \tag{A1}$$

where, in terms of the quantities in (21), (23) and (24)

$$\begin{aligned}\boldsymbol{\mu}_i &= a_{11}\mathrm{E}w + a_{12}\mathrm{E}\mathbf{y}_2 \\ &= (\mathrm{E}w - R\mathrm{E}y_2)/\sigma_2 c = (\boldsymbol{\eta} - R\boldsymbol{\mu})/c \qquad \text{(A2)} \\ \boldsymbol{\mu}_2 &= \mathrm{E}y_2/\sigma_2 = \boldsymbol{\mu}.\end{aligned}$$

Our primary objective here is to derive moment expressions for $\mathbf{x}_2'\mathbf{P}\mathbf{x}_1/\mathbf{x}_2'\mathbf{P}\mathbf{x}_2$ where $\mathbf{P}$ is defined as in (7).

LEMMA A1. Joint moment generating function (mgf) of bilinear forms of normal variables: Let $\mathbf{x}_1$ and $\mathbf{x}_2$ be distributed as in (A1) and let $\mathbf{P}$ be a $T \times T$ matrix. Then the joint mgf of $\mathbf{x}_2'\mathbf{P}\mathbf{x}_1$ and $\mathbf{x}_2'\mathbf{P}\mathbf{x}_1$ is

$$\begin{aligned}\phi(\mathbf{x}, t) &= \mathrm{E}[\exp\{s(\mathbf{x}_2'\mathbf{P}\mathbf{x}_2) + t(\mathbf{x}_2'\mathbf{P}\mathbf{x}_1)\}] \\ &= |\mathbf{Q}|^{-1/2}\exp\{-(\boldsymbol{\mu}_2'\boldsymbol{\mu}_2 - \boldsymbol{\nu}_2'\mathbf{Q}\boldsymbol{\nu}_2)/2\}, \qquad \text{(A3)}\end{aligned}$$

where

$$\begin{aligned}\mathbf{Q} &= (\mathbf{I} - 2s\mathbf{P} - t^2\mathbf{P}^2) \\ \boldsymbol{\nu}_2 &= \mathbf{Q}^{-1}(\boldsymbol{\mu}_2 + t\mathbf{P}\boldsymbol{\mu}_1). \qquad \text{(A4)}\end{aligned}$$

The joint mgf exists as long as $\mathbf{P}$ is symmetric with eigenvalues between 0 and 1, inclusive, and $(t^2 + 2s) < 1$.

PROOF: The proof is implicit in Sawa's discussion [1972, p. 663]. Define

$$\begin{aligned}\mathbf{C} &= \begin{bmatrix}\mathbf{I} & -t\mathbf{P} \\ -t\mathbf{P} & (\mathbf{I} - 2s\mathbf{P})\end{bmatrix} \\ \boldsymbol{\nu}_1 &= \boldsymbol{\mu}_1 + t\mathbf{P}\boldsymbol{\nu}_2 \\ \boldsymbol{\nu} &= (\boldsymbol{\nu}_1', \boldsymbol{\nu}_2')' \\ \mathbf{x} &= (\mathbf{x}_1', \mathbf{x}_2')'.\end{aligned}$$

The result follows from the following identity:

$$\begin{aligned}&\exp\{s\mathbf{x}_2'\mathbf{P}\mathbf{x}_2 + t\mathbf{x}_2'\mathbf{P}\mathbf{x}_1\}n(\mathbf{x}_1|\boldsymbol{\mu}_1, \mathbf{I})n(\mathbf{x}_2|\boldsymbol{\mu}_2, \mathbf{I}) \\ &\quad = |\mathbf{C}|^{-1/2}\exp\{-(1/2)[\boldsymbol{\mu}_1'\boldsymbol{\mu}_1 + \boldsymbol{\mu}_2'\boldsymbol{\mu}_2 - \boldsymbol{\nu}'\mathbf{C}\boldsymbol{\nu}]\}n(\mathbf{x} \mid \boldsymbol{\nu}, \mathbf{C}^{-1}),\end{aligned}$$

where $n(\cdot \mid \cdot)$ is a multivariate normal density. Note that

1) Under the stated assumptions, $\mathbf{Q} > 0$.
2) $\mathbf{C} > \mathrm{o} \Leftrightarrow \mathbf{Q} > 0$.
3) $|\mathbf{C}| = |\mathbf{Q}|$.
4) $\boldsymbol{\nu}'\mathbf{C}\boldsymbol{\nu} = \boldsymbol{\mu}_1\boldsymbol{\mu}_1 + \boldsymbol{\nu}_2'\mathbf{Q}\boldsymbol{\nu}_2$.

LEMMA A2: For $\mathbf{P} = (\mathbf{P}_z - \mathbf{P}_{z_1}) + \bar{k}\,\overline{\mathbf{P}}_z$, the joint mgf of ($\mathbf{x}_2'\mathbf{P}\mathbf{x}_2$, $\mathbf{x}_2'\mathbf{P}\mathbf{x}_1$) has the form

$$\phi(s,t) = \exp\{f(s, t; m - n, \delta_1, \theta_1, \boldsymbol{\nu}_1) + f(\bar{k}s, \bar{k}t; n, \delta_2, \theta_2, \boldsymbol{\nu}_2)\},$$

where

$$\begin{aligned} f(s, t; a, \delta, \theta, \boldsymbol{\nu}) &= -\delta + a\log b(s, t) + b(s, t)c(t; \delta, \theta, \boldsymbol{\nu}) \\ b(\mathbf{x}, t) &= [1 - 2s - t^2]^{-1} \\ c(t; \delta, \theta, \boldsymbol{\nu}) &= d^2(t)\delta + 2(t/c)d(t)\theta + (t/c)^2\boldsymbol{\nu} \\ d(t) &= [1 - (R/c)t]. \end{aligned} \tag{A5}$$

PROOF: Define

$$\begin{aligned} \dot{\boldsymbol{\mu}} &= \mathbf{P}_z\boldsymbol{\mu} & \ddot{\boldsymbol{\mu}} &= \overline{\mathbf{P}}_z\boldsymbol{\mu} \\ \dot{\boldsymbol{\eta}} &= \mathbf{P}_z\boldsymbol{\eta} & \ddot{\boldsymbol{\eta}} &= \overline{\mathbf{P}}_z\boldsymbol{\eta} \\ \mathbf{S} &= [\mathbf{I} - (R/c)t\mathbf{P}]. \end{aligned} \tag{A6}$$

Note that the vectors with single dots are orthogonal to those with double dots. Upon applying Lemma A2 to ($\mathbf{x}_2'\mathbf{P}\mathbf{x}_2$, $\mathbf{x}_2'\,\mathbf{P}\mathbf{x}_1$) and replacing $\boldsymbol{\mu}_1$ from (A2), it is immediate that

$$\begin{aligned} \phi(s,t) &= \mathrm{E}[\exp\{s(\mathbf{x}_2'\mathbf{P}\mathbf{x}_2) + t(\mathbf{x}_2'\mathbf{P}\mathbf{x}_1)\} \\ &= |\mathbf{Q}|^{-1/2}\exp\{-(1/2)\boldsymbol{\mu}'\boldsymbol{\mu} + (1/2)[\mathbf{S}\boldsymbol{\mu} + \\ &\qquad (t/c)\mathbf{P}\boldsymbol{\eta}]'\,\mathbf{Q}^{-1}[\mathbf{S}\boldsymbol{\mu} + (t/c)\mathbf{P}\boldsymbol{\eta}]\}. \end{aligned} \tag{A7}$$

Note the following eigenvalue/eigenvector relations:

$$\begin{aligned} \mathbf{P}\dot{\boldsymbol{\mu}} &= \dot{\boldsymbol{\mu}} & \mathbf{P}\ddot{\boldsymbol{\mu}} &= \bar{k}\ddot{\boldsymbol{\eta}} \\ \mathbf{P}\dot{\boldsymbol{\eta}} &= \dot{\boldsymbol{\eta}} & \mathbf{P}\ddot{\boldsymbol{\eta}} &= \bar{k}\ddot{\boldsymbol{\eta}} \\ \mathbf{S}\dot{\boldsymbol{\mu}} &= d(t)\dot{\boldsymbol{\mu}} & \mathbf{S}\ddot{\boldsymbol{\mu}} &= d(\bar{k}t)\ddot{\boldsymbol{\mu}} \\ \mathbf{S}\dot{\boldsymbol{\eta}} &= d(t)\dot{\boldsymbol{\eta}} & \mathbf{S}\ddot{\boldsymbol{\eta}} &= d(\bar{k}t)\ddot{\boldsymbol{\eta}} \\ \mathbf{Q}^{-1}\dot{\boldsymbol{\mu}} &= b(s, t)\dot{\boldsymbol{\mu}} & \mathbf{Q}^{-1}\ddot{\boldsymbol{\mu}} &= b(\bar{k}s, \bar{k}t)\ddot{\boldsymbol{\mu}} \\ \mathbf{Q}^{-1}\mathbf{P}_z\boldsymbol{\eta} = \mathbf{Q}^{-1}\dot{\boldsymbol{\eta}} &= b(s, t)\dot{\boldsymbol{\eta}} & \mathbf{Q}^{-1}\ddot{\boldsymbol{\eta}} &= b(\bar{k}s, \bar{k}t)\ddot{\boldsymbol{\eta}}. \end{aligned} \tag{A8}$$

It is then easy to see from (A5) and (A8) that

$$\begin{aligned} &(1/2)[\mathbf{S}\boldsymbol{\mu} + (t/c)\mathbf{P}\boldsymbol{\eta}]'\mathbf{Q}^{-1}[\mathbf{S}\boldsymbol{\mu} + (t/c)\mathbf{P}\boldsymbol{\eta}] \\ &\quad = b(s,t)c(t; \delta_1, \theta_1; \boldsymbol{\nu}_1) + b(\bar{k}s, \bar{k}t)c(\bar{k}t; \delta_2, \theta_2, \boldsymbol{\nu}_2). \end{aligned} \tag{A9}$$

From the definition of $\mathbf{P}$ in (7), it is clear that $\mathbf{P}$ has the eigenvalues 0, 1, and $\bar{k}$, with multiplicities K_1, $K - K_1$, and $T - K$, respectively. It follows that $\mathbf{Q}^{-1}$ has eigenvalues 1, $b(s, t)$ and $b(\bar{k}s, \bar{k}t)$, with the same multiplicities K_1, $K - K_1$, and $T - K$ (see A4). Then

$$|\mathbf{Q}|^{-1/2} = [b(s, t)]^{m-n}[b(\bar{k}s, \bar{k}t)]^n. \tag{A10}$$

The result of the lemma follows from (A7), (A9) and (A10).

To compute the first two moments of the standardized estimator $\beta^*_{(k)}$, we make use of Sawa's Lemma 1 (1972, p. 658), which states that for $\mathbf{X}_1$ positive and $\mathbf{X}_2$ arbitrary, for positive integer r,

$$\mathrm{E}(\mathbf{X}_2/\mathbf{X}_1)^r = 1/\Gamma(r)\int_{-\infty}^{0}(-s)^{r-1}[(\partial^r/\partial t^r)\phi(s,t)]_{t=0}\,\mathrm{ds}, \tag{A11}$$

where $\phi(s,t)$ is the joint mgf of $(\mathbf{X}_1, \mathbf{X}_2)$ which should exist for $s < \varepsilon$, $|t| < \varepsilon$, for some $\varepsilon > 0$.

By analogy to Sawa (1972) we define

$$\begin{aligned} g(s; m, n) &= 2\phi(s, 0) \\ h(s, m, n) &= -sg(s; m+1, n) \\ &= -1/2[g(s; m+1, n) - g(s; m, n)], \end{aligned} \tag{A12}$$

where $\phi(s, t)$ is given in Lemma A2. The integrands in (A11) for $r = 0, 1$ are expressed in terms of the functions g and h in the following lemma.

Lemma A3:

$$\begin{aligned} \partial\phi(s, t)\partial t\,|_{t=0} &= -c^{-1}[a_1 g(s; m+1, n) \\ &\quad + \bar{k}a_2 g(s; m+1, n+1)] \\ -s\partial^2\delta(s, t)\partial t^2\,|_{t=0} &= c^{-2}[A_1 h(s; m, n) \\ &\quad + \bar{k}^2 A_2 h(s; m, n+1) \\ &\quad + A_3 h(s; m+1, n) + \bar{k}A_4 h(s; m+1, n+1) \\ &\quad + \bar{k}^2 A_5 h(s; m+1, n+2) \end{aligned} \tag{A13}$$

where $\{a_i\}$ and $\{A_i\}$ are defined in (35).

Proof: From Lemma A2,

$$\begin{aligned} \partial\phi(s, t)\partial t &= \phi(s, t)[\partial f(s, t; \cdot)/\partial t + \partial f(\bar{k}s, \bar{k}t; \cdot)/\partial t] \\ \partial^2\phi(s, t)\partial t^2 &= \phi(s, t)\{[\partial f(s, t; \cdot)/\partial t + \partial f(\bar{k}s, \bar{k}t; \cdot)/\partial t]^2 \\ &\quad + [\partial^2 f(x, t; \cdot)/\partial t^2 + \partial^2 f(\bar{k}s, \bar{k}t; \cdot)/\partial t^2]\}. \end{aligned}$$

Using

$$\begin{aligned} \partial b(s, t)/\partial t &= 2tb^2(s, t) \\ \partial^2 b(s, t)/\partial t^2 &= 2[1 + 4t^2 b(s, t)]b^2(s, t) \\ \partial c(t; \cdot)/\partial t &= (2/c\{-Rd(t)\delta + [d(t) \\ &\quad - (R/c)t]\theta + (t/c)\nu\} \\ \partial^2 c(t; \cdot)/\partial t^2 &= (2/c^2)(R^2\delta - 2R\theta + \nu), \\ \partial f(s, t; \cdot)/\partial t \,\Big|_{t=0} &= -(2/c)(R\delta - \theta)b(s, 0) \\ \partial^2 f(s, t; \cdot)/\partial t^2 \,\Big|_{t=0} &= (2/c^2)[c^2 a + (R^2\delta - 2R\theta + \nu) \\ &\quad + c^2\delta b(s, 0)]b(s, 0). \end{aligned} \tag{A14, A15}$$

Then from (A13) and (A15),

$$\begin{aligned} \partial\phi(s, t)/\partial t \,\Big|_{t=0} &= -(2/c)[a_1 b(s, 0) + \bar{k}a_2 b(\bar{k}s, 0)]\phi(s, 0) \\ \partial^2\phi(s, t)/\partial t^2 \,\Big|_{t=0} &= (2/c^2)\{2[a_1 b(s, 0) + \bar{k}a_2 b(\bar{k}s, 0)]\}^2 \\ &\quad + [A_1 + c^2\delta_1 b(s, 0)]b(s, 0) \\ &\quad + \bar{k}^2[A_2 + c^2\delta_2 b(\bar{k}s, 0)]\phi(s, 0). \end{aligned} \tag{A16}$$

The result of the lemma follows upon observing that

$$\begin{aligned} 2b^r(s, 0)\phi(s, 0) &= g(s; m + r, n) \\ 2b^r(\bar{k}s, 0)\phi(s, 0) &= g(s; m + r, n + r) \\ 2b(s, 0)b(\bar{k}s, 0)\phi(s, 0) &= g(s; m + 2, n + 1). \end{aligned} \tag{A17}$$

LEMMA A4. Representation of $G(k, \delta_1, \delta_2; m, n)$: Let

$$G(k, \delta_1, \delta_2; m, n) = \int_{-\infty}^{0} g(s; m, n)\, \mathrm{ds}.$$

Then G has the representation given in (26)

PROOF: We extend Lemma 3 in Sawa (1972, p. 659). From (A12) and Lemma A2,

$$\begin{aligned} g(s; m, n) &= 2[b(s, 0)]^{m-n}[b(\bar{k}s, 0)]^n \exp\{-(\delta_1 + \delta_2)\} \\ &\quad \cdot \exp\{\delta_1 b(s, 0)\} \exp\{\delta_2 b(\bar{k}s, 0)\}. \end{aligned} \tag{A18}$$

The integrand has a more general form than that in Sawa's Lemma 3 [1972, (4.8) on p. 659]. We expand the last factor in (A18) and integrate term by term using Sawa's result to get the representation of (26). Theorem 1 follows directly from (A11) and Lemma A4 and upon using the relation (22) between $\beta_{(k)}$ and $\beta^*_{(k)}$. Note that

$$(\hat{\beta}_{(k)} - \beta^*)^2 = c^2[\hat{\beta}^*_{(k)}]^2 + 2R(\hat{\beta}_{(k)} - \beta^*) - R^2. \tag{A19}$$

APPENDIX B

Proof of Lemma 1

The main reference is Ramage (1971). $\mathbf{X}$ is an $m \times m$ random matrix indexed by sample size T but with m independent of T. The crucial result needed for the proof is

$$\mathbf{X} = o_p(1) \Rightarrow (\mathbf{I} - \mathbf{X})^{-1} = O_p(1) \tag{A20}$$

Given this result, the lemma follows immediately from the following computation:

$$\begin{aligned} \sum_{i=0}^{r} \mathbf{X}^i &= (\mathbf{I} - \mathbf{X})^{-1}(\mathbf{I} - \mathbf{X})\left(\sum_{i=0}^{r} \mathbf{X}^i\right) \\ &= (\mathbf{I} - \mathbf{X})^{-1}\left[\sum_{i=0}^{r} \mathbf{X}^i - \sum_{i=0}^{r} \mathbf{X}^{i+1}\right] \\ &= (\mathbf{I} - \mathbf{X})^{-1}[\mathbf{I} - \mathbf{X}^{r+1}] \\ &= (\mathbf{I} - \mathbf{X})^{-1} - (\mathbf{I} - \mathbf{X})^{-1}\mathbf{X}^{r+1}. \end{aligned} \tag{A21}$$

To establish (A20), we introduce the matrix norm $[\cdot]$, defined in terms of the vector space norm $\|\cdot\|$ as follows:

$$[\mathbf{X}] \stackrel{def}{=} \sup_{\nu} \|\mathbf{X}\boldsymbol{\nu}\| \,/\, \|\boldsymbol{\nu}\|. \tag{A22}$$

We first establish the following intermediate results:

(i) $\mathbf{X} = O_p(1) \Leftrightarrow [\mathbf{X}] = O_p(1)$ (A23)

(ii) $[\mathbf{X}] < 1 \Leftrightarrow (\mathbf{I} - \mathbf{X})^{-1}$ exists and $[(\mathbf{I} - \mathbf{X})]^{-1} \leqslant 1/(1 - [\mathbf{X}])$. (A24)

Because all norms are equivalent in terms of large-sample order for finite-dimensional vector spaces, any representative norm can be chosen for

$\|\cdot\|$. The sup norm is convenient here:

$$\|\boldsymbol{\nu}\|_\infty = \sup_i |\nu_i|.$$

Then, as is well known,

$$[\mathbf{X}]_\infty = \sup_i \sum_j |X_{ij}|. \tag{A25}$$

We include a proof of (A25) for completeness.

$$\begin{aligned}\|\mathbf{X}\boldsymbol{\nu}\|_\infty &= \sup_i \left|\sum_j X_{ij}\nu_j\right| \\ &\leqslant \sup_i \sum_j |X_{ij}||\nu_j| \\ &\leqslant (\sup_i \sum_j |X_{ij}|)\|\nu\|_\infty.\end{aligned}$$

Then

$$[\mathbf{X}]_\infty \leqslant \sup_i \sum_j |X_{ij}|.$$

To establish the inequality in the other direction, define i^* by

$$\sum_j |X_{i^*j}| = \sup_i \sum_j |X_{ij}|$$

and $\boldsymbol{\nu}^*$ by

$$\nu_j^* = \operatorname{sgn} X_{i^*j}.$$

Then $\|\boldsymbol{\nu}^*\|_\infty = 1$ for an $\mathbf{X} \neq \mathbf{0}$, and

$$\begin{aligned}[\mathbf{X}]_\infty &= \sup_{\boldsymbol{\nu}} \|\mathbf{X}\boldsymbol{\nu}\|_\infty / \|\boldsymbol{\nu}\|_\infty \\ &\geqslant \|\mathbf{X}\boldsymbol{\nu}^*\|_\infty = \sup_i \left|\sum_j X_{ij}\nu_j^*\right| \\ &\geqslant \left|\sum_j X_{i^*j}\nu_j^*\right| = \sum_j |X_{i^*j}| = \sup_i \sum_j |X_{ij}|.\end{aligned}$$

The first intermediate result (A23) follows from (A25)

$$\max |X_{ij}| \leqslant [X]_\infty \leqslant m \max |X_{ij}|. \tag{A26}$$

To establish the second intermediate result (A24), define

$$\boldsymbol{\omega} = (\mathbf{I} - \mathbf{X})\boldsymbol{\nu} \tag{A27}$$

Then

$$\begin{aligned} \|\boldsymbol{\omega}\| &= \|(\mathbf{I} - \mathbf{X})\boldsymbol{\nu}\| = \|\boldsymbol{\nu} - \mathbf{X}\boldsymbol{\nu}\| \\ &\geqslant \|\boldsymbol{\nu}\| - \|\mathbf{X}\boldsymbol{\nu}\| \\ &\geqslant \|\boldsymbol{\nu}\| - [\mathbf{X}]\|\boldsymbol{\nu}\| = (1 - [\mathbf{X}])\|\boldsymbol{\nu}\| \end{aligned} \tag{A28}$$

It follows that $(\mathbf{I} - \mathbf{X})$ is a 1:1 transformation when $[\mathbf{X}] < 1$, since if there exist $\boldsymbol{\nu}_1$ and $\boldsymbol{\nu}_2$ such that

$$(\mathbf{I} - \mathbf{X})\boldsymbol{\nu}_1 = \boldsymbol{\omega} = (\mathbf{I} - \mathbf{X})\boldsymbol{\nu}_2,$$

then

$$\begin{aligned} (\mathbf{I} - \mathbf{X})(\boldsymbol{\nu}_1 - \boldsymbol{\nu}_2) &= \mathbf{0} \\ &\Rightarrow 0 = \|(\mathbf{I} - \mathbf{X})(\boldsymbol{\nu}_1 - \boldsymbol{\nu}_2)\| \\ &\geqslant (1 - [\mathbf{X}])\|\boldsymbol{\nu}_1 - \boldsymbol{\nu}_2\| > 0, \end{aligned}$$

a contradiction. Hence $(\mathbf{I} - \mathbf{X})^{-1}$ exists when $[\mathbf{X}] < 1$. The rest of (A24) follows immediately:

$$\begin{aligned} &\|(\mathbf{I} - \mathbf{X})^{-1}\boldsymbol{\omega}\| = \|\boldsymbol{\nu}\| \leqslant \|\boldsymbol{\omega}\|/(1 - [\mathbf{X}]) \\ &\Rightarrow [(\mathbf{I} - \mathbf{X})^{-1}] = \sup_{\boldsymbol{\omega}} \|(\mathbf{I} - \mathbf{X})^{-1}\boldsymbol{\Omega}\|/\|\boldsymbol{\omega}\| \leqslant 1/(1 - [\mathbf{X}]) \end{aligned}$$

Finally, we establish (A20). For constant $B > 1$,

$$\begin{aligned} P_r[[(\mathbf{I} - \mathbf{X})^{-1}] > B] &= P_r[[(\mathbf{I} - \mathbf{X})^{-1}] > B \text{ and } [\mathbf{X}] < 1] \\ &\quad + P_r[[(\mathbf{I} - \mathbf{X})^{-1}] > B \text{ and } [\mathbf{X}] \geqslant 1] \\ &\leqslant P_r[1/(1 - [\mathbf{X}]) > B \text{ and } [\mathbf{X}] < 1] \\ &\quad + P_r[[\mathbf{X}] \geqslant 1] \\ &= P_r[[\mathbf{X}] > 1 - B^{-1} \text{ and } [\mathbf{X}] < 1] + \\ &\quad P_r[[\mathbf{X}] \geqslant 1] \\ &\leqslant 2P_r[[\mathbf{X}] > 1 - B^{-1}]. \end{aligned} \tag{A29}$$

For any $\varepsilon > 0$, since $[\mathbf{X}] = O_p(1)$, B_ε can be chosen so large that

$$P_r[[\mathbf{X}] > 1 - B_\varepsilon^{-1}] < \varepsilon/2.$$

Then

$$P_r[[(\mathbf{I} - \mathbf{X})^{-1}] > B_\varepsilon] < \varepsilon \tag{A30}$$

and (A20) is established.

ACKNOWLEDGMENT

Partial support from the following projects at the University of Pennsylvania is gratefully acknowledged: National Science Foundation grant SOC 79-07964 at the Department of Economics and the Oak Ridge National Laboratory Contract 7954 at the Wharton Analysis Center for Energy Studies.

REFERENCES

Anderson, T. W. (1977). Asymptotic expansions of the distributions of estimates in simultaneous equations for alternative parameter sequences, *Econometrica 45,* 509–518.

Anderson, T. W. and T. Sawa (1973). Distributions of estimates of coefficients of a single equation in a simultaneous system and their asymptotic expansions, *Econometrica 41,* 683–714.

Basmann, R. L. (1963). Remarks concerning the application of exact finite sample distribution functions of GCL estimators in econometric statistical inference, *JASA 58,* 943–976.

Fisher, F. (1961). On the cost of approximate specification in simultaneous equation estimation, *Econometrica 29,* 139–170.

Fisher, F. (1966). The relative sensitivity to specification error of different *k*-class estimators, *JASA 61,* 345–356.

Fisher, F. (1967). Approximate specification and the choice of a *k*-class estimator, *JASA 62,* 1265–1276.

Fujikoshi, Y., K. Morimune, N. Kunitomo and M. Taniguchi (1982). Asymptotic expansions of the distributions of the estimates of coefficients in a simultaneous equation system, *J. Econometrics* 18, 191–205.

Hale, C., R. S. Mariano and J. G. Ramage (1980). Finite sample analysis of misspecification in simultaneous equation models, *JASA 75,* 418–417.

Hillier, G. and V. K. Srivastava (1981). The exact bias and mean square error of the *k*-class estimators for the coefficient of an endogenous variable in a general structural equation. Monash University Discussion Paper.

Kadane, J. B. (1970). Testing overidentifying restrictions when the disturbances are small, *JASA 65,* 182–185.

Kadane, J. B. (1971). Comparison of *k*-class estimators when the disturbances are small, *Econometrica 39,* 723–737.

Mariano, R. S. (1975). Some large-concentration-parameter asymptotics for the *k*-class estimators, *J. Econometrics 3,* 171–177.

Mariano, R. S. (1982). Analytical small-sample distribution theory in econometrics: The simultaneous-equations case, *Int. Econ. Rev.*, 23, 503–533.

Nagar, A. L. (1959). The bias and moment matrix of the general *k*-class estimators of the parameters in structural equations, *Econometrica 27,* 575–595.

Phillips, P. C. B. (1980). The exact distribution of instrumental variable estimators in an equation containing $n + 1$ endogenous variables, *Econometrica 48,* 861–878.

Phillips, P. C. B. (1982). Marginal densities of instrumental variable estimators in the general single equation case, *Adv. Econometrics,* this issue.

Ramage, J. G. (1971). A perturbation study of the *k*-class estimators in the presence of specification error, Yale University, Ph.D. Thesis, unpublished.

Rhodes, G. and D. Westbrook (1981). A study of estimator densities and performance under misspecification, *J. Econometrics,* 16, 311–337.

Richardson, D. H. (1968). The exact distribution of a structural coefficient estimator, *JASA 63,* 1214–1226.

Sawa, T. (1972). Finite-sample properties of the *k*-class estimators, *Econometrica 40,* 653–680.

Theil, H. (1971). *Principles of Econometrics,* New York: John Wiley & Sons.

TESTING SINGLE EQUATION IDENTIFYING RESTRICTIONS WITH GENERATED REGRESSORS

George F. Rhodes, Jr.

I. INTRODUCTION

Testing for functional form in economic models, including identification and specification, has been urged more frequently and forcibly in recent literature on economic theory and method and on econometric practice. Malinvaud, in a Ragnar Frisch Lecture to the Econometric Society, acknowledges this need and calls for further development of techniques for testing model form (see Malinvaud, 1981). This need is recognized by Dent and Geweke (1980) and by others in the volume edited by Kmenta and Ramsey (1980), *Evaluation of Econometric Models*. Of course, this recognition is not new. Some of the most fundamental and challenging work during the early days of the Cowles Commission dealt with the problems of testing model form as one method of testing and implementing

Advances in Econometrics, Volume 2, pages 97–128

ISBN: 0-89232-183-0

economic theory. Rather considerable progress has been made based upon that early foundation. But the knowledge has not been collected into one source nor given a common framework.

Efficient use of shrinking research resources shows the need for the current state of knowledge to be presented in a single source with a common notation and framework. This article attempts such a presentation for a modest part of the literature, namely, that part dealing with testing identifiability restrictions in single equations embedded within a linear simultaneous equation system. Whereas treatments of the algebraic conditions for identifiability are ubiquitous, and rather uniform, such is not the case with methods for empirical tests of the conditions. Rather, the latter are found in diverse (and sometimes obscure) sources, using sundry (and sometimes confusing) notations. It is the aim of this article to present a unified and comprehensive introduction to the literature on testing identifiability in single equations.

Presentation here is not limited to survey of known results. It extends the literature in two ways. First, there are some new results presented for the first time in this article. These include derivation of statistical properties of exact test statistics, such as the property of invariance for the likelihood ratio, GCL, and Wald tests. There is proposal of an alternative to the double root test for rank conditions and presentation of new experimental evidence regarding approximations to that exact distribution function. Second, there is evaluation and comparison of sampling experiment results and their implications for selection of tests and for judging reliability of the tests and their approximations. To this are added some corrections and extensions to previous interpretations.

II. MATHEMATICAL FORMULATIONS OF LINEAR MODELS

The primary focus of this article is the multivariate linear model. The model components are $\mathbf{y}$, a $G \times 1$ vector of endogenous variables; $\mathbf{z}$, a $K \times 1$ vector of exogenous variables; $\mathbf{\Pi}$, a $G \times K$ matrix of fixed coefficients; and $\mathbf{v}$, a $G \times 1$ vector of random elements. These elements are combined to form the reduced form equation system representing the *maintained hypothesis:*

$$\mathbf{y} = \mathbf{\Pi z} + \mathbf{v}. \tag{1}$$

The maintained hypothesis conveys significant information regarding economic behavior. Linear models imply that a limited scope of economic behavior patterns will be observed in the population. They are testable against other classes of models as well as against actual observations.

Among the classes of potential models for a population, the linear equation system is one of the most elegant. Its testability against observations and other models is enhanced by its implied constraints on observed behavior.

The cognitive content, and hence the testability, of the maintained hypothesis may be increased by adding other hypotheses implied by the theory. Additional hypotheses are expressed as linear constraints in the $(G \times G)$ coefficient matrix $\mathbf{B}$. The *structural form* hypothesis is created by these additional constraints. To obtain the structural form, the reduced form is premultiplied by $\mathbf{B}$:

$$\mathbf{By} = \mathbf{B\Pi z} + \mathbf{Bv}. \tag{2}$$

For notational convenience, let $-\mathbf{\Gamma} = \mathbf{B\Pi}$ and $\mathbf{u} = \mathbf{Bv}$. Then the typical structural form is expressed as

$$\mathbf{By} + \mathbf{\Gamma z} = \mathbf{u}. \tag{3}$$

Two different kinds of hypotheses are expressed by the reduced form. One type of hypothesis deals with basic propositions regarding economic behavior. It includes the assertion that $\mathbf{y}$ and $\mathbf{z}$ are linearly related in the population, that elements of $\mathbf{y}$ are jointly determined whereas elements of $\mathbf{z}$ are predetermined, that the set of jointly determined variables is exactly $\mathbf{y}$, and that the relation $\mathbf{y} = \mathbf{\Pi z} + \mathbf{v}$ holds for the entire population. Basic economic propositions inherent in the reduced form may be augmented by economic propositions contained in the structural form. Additional propositions from the structural form include indicating which elements of $\mathbf{y}$ are contained in a specific structural equation; that certain linear combinations of $\mathbf{y}$ must appear in certain equations; and that specific constraints must be effective in the population. Even very simple linear models imply definite restrictions on economic behavior patterns in the population. These are expressed in the reduced and structural forms.

The second type of information specified when creating reduced form and structural models concerns sampling properties of observations drawn from the population. Here are specified such characteristics as the distribution functions and moments of the vectors $\mathbf{v}$ and $\mathbf{u}$. Further, relationships among various sample values of $\mathbf{u}$ and $\mathbf{v}$ are specified, such as serial correlation, constant covariance matrices, and zero mean vectors. This second group may also include observation attributes that follow from experimental design, experimental method, and measurement error, rather than from economic behavior inherent in the population. Perhaps the most ubiquitous of these assumptions is the assertion that $\mathbf{v}$ is a random vector with multivariate distribution function $N(\mathbf{0}, \mathbf{\Sigma})$. This proposition is not supported as a deductive conclusion nor as an empirical regularity. Rather, its use leads to tractable theorems in estimation and inference. Indeed, it seems to be the only proposition that leads to reasonably tractable inference formulae for simultaneous equations. All of the distribution theory presented in this article is derived using this assumption.

Where issues of economic modeling are faced in logical sequence, the question of distinguishing among alternative structural form models will appear very early. The identifiability of structural form models is one of the issues in the first type of hypotheses expressed by the reduced and structural forms. Essentially the question is this: Can the proffered structural form be distinguished from alternative structural forms using observational information? Parameters of the reduced form model are always identified, meaning that there is a unique solution to the least squares and maximum likelihood formulae mapping the sample space into the estimates. But structural form parameters may not be identified under this conception of identification. This is clear from a glance at equations (2) and (3).

What is seen is this: There are in principle infinitely many combinations of matrices $\mathbf{B}$ and $\mathbf{\Gamma}$ that satisfy the mapping

$$-\mathbf{\Gamma} = \mathbf{B\Pi} \tag{4}$$

for a given matrix $\mathbf{\Pi}$. Equations in (4) represent a system of inhomogeneous linear equations. There are $G \times K$ equations and $(G \times K) + (G \times G)$ unknown elements. Additional equations will be required if there is to be a solution for $\mathbf{B}$ and $\mathbf{\Gamma}$ in terms of $\mathbf{\Pi}$.

Behavior patterns expressed by identifying hypotheses for each of the equations in the maintained hypotheses must be mutually consistent. Taken together they will specify domains for $\mathbf{\Pi}$ and for $\mathbf{B}$ and $\mathbf{\Gamma}$ that correspond to the expected observations. Thus, it may also be useful to test for system identifiability as well as equation-by-equation identifiability. System testing is based on the recognition that observations organized according to the full collection of restrictions should provide a model for the theory. Tests of system identifiability are not discussed in this article. A more complete treatment of system identifiability is found in Rhodes and Westbrook (1981).

Notice also that the equations in (4) may be examined one at a time. For any of the G equations—say, the jth—the mapping from the reduced form to the structure is

$$-\boldsymbol{\gamma}_j = \boldsymbol{\beta}_j\mathbf{\Pi} \tag{5}$$

where $\boldsymbol{\gamma}_j$ and $\boldsymbol{\beta}_j$ are the jth row vectors of $\mathbf{\Gamma}$ and $\mathbf{B}$. Each of these matrix equations is a system of inhomogeneous linear equations. The basic issue of identifiability for a single equation is whether there is a unique solution to (5). Assurance of a unique solution to (5) will often require additional equations to be supplied as part of model creation. These are known as identifying restrictions, because they are added to assure that there exists the required mapping from $\mathbf{\Pi}$ to the structural parameters.

Adding equations to either (4) or (5) raises two primary issues in economic modeling. The first issue is an analytical one: Are the restrictions sufficient to identify the structural parameters? This is basically an issue in linear algebra. The second issue is the primary concern of this article: Are the identifying restrictions consistent with the sample drawn from the population the model is supposed to represent? There are a great many possible forms for the restrictions to take. In this article the scope is limited to restrictions of the form

$$\boldsymbol{\beta}_j = (\beta_{j1}, \ldots, \beta_{j,g+1}, 0, \ldots, 0) \tag{6}$$

$$\boldsymbol{\gamma}_j = (\gamma_{j1}, \ldots, \gamma_{jk}, 0, \ldots, 0) \tag{7}$$

It is assumed that $K - k \geqslant g$.

Fairness to the subject and to the profession requires taking note here of the vast reduction in subject matter scope of this article. The basic issue of identifiability in linear models is quite comprehensive. It asks how many structural models are consistent with a given collection of observations. This article considers only a small subset of that issue, namely, are the zero restrictions imposed to identify a single equation in a structural system consistent with the data? Even in this narrow realm there are some clarifications to be made. First, the restrictions can always be thought of as applying to the reduced form. The issue can be restated as, "Is the reduced form domain implied by the identifying restrictions consistent with the observations?" Second, the identifiability issue does not affect the basic testability of the linear reduced form against alternative maintained hypotheses. Third, the basic restrictions expressed in the identifiability relations have to do with the economic behavior of the population. That is, they are economic rather than statistical in nature. In this they contrast with questions that are basically statistical in origin, such as properties of disturbance terms. Viewed in this way, identifiability testing usually results in testing propositions about economic behavior.

The formulation of the test statistics studied here is based on the fact that identifiability conditions can always be stated in terms of the maintained as opposed to the structural hypothesis. Applying the test statistics amounts to testing hypotheses specifying ranks for matrices of reduced form parameters.

The restrictions in (7) can be written in vector notation. They also can lead to several testable hypotheses. Drop the subscript j and write

$$\begin{aligned} \boldsymbol{\beta} &= (\boldsymbol{\beta}_\Delta, \mathbf{0}) = (\beta_1, \ldots, \beta_{g+1}, 0, \ldots, 0) \\ \boldsymbol{\gamma} &= (\boldsymbol{\gamma}_*, \mathbf{0}) = (\gamma_1, \ldots, \gamma_k, 0, \ldots, 0). \end{aligned} \tag{8}$$

Using this notation the mapping from $\mathbf{\Pi}$ to $\boldsymbol{\beta}$, $\boldsymbol{\gamma}$ is expressed as

$$(\boldsymbol{\beta}_\Delta, \mathbf{0})\mathbf{\Pi} = -(\boldsymbol{\gamma}_*, \mathbf{0}) \tag{9}$$

Partition $\mathbf{\Pi}$ to conform with the partitioning of $\boldsymbol{\beta}$ and $\boldsymbol{\gamma}$:

$$\mathbf{\Pi} = \begin{bmatrix} \mathbf{\Pi}_{11} & \mathbf{\Pi}_{12} \\ \mathbf{\Pi}_{21} & \mathbf{\Pi}_{22} \end{bmatrix} \begin{matrix} g+1 \\ G-g-1 \end{matrix} \quad \text{columns: } k, \; K-k \tag{10}$$

Then the relations among maintained and structural parameters are written as

$$\begin{aligned} \boldsymbol{\beta}_\Delta \mathbf{\Pi}_{11} &= -\boldsymbol{\gamma}_* \\ \boldsymbol{\beta}_\Delta \mathbf{\Pi}_{12} &= \mathbf{0}. \end{aligned} \tag{11}$$

Solution sets available for these equations indicate whether the behavioral patterns they characterize are consistent with observations drawn from the subject population. A unique solution for (11) implies that the equation is identified, that it can be distinguished from other structures using at most a countable collection of observations. Where there is not a unique solution, it is said that the structure is not identified. Testing for identifiability amounts to testing whether the data are consistent with the conditions required for existence of a unique solution.

A glance at (11) shows that the entire system of equations will have a unique solution if, and only if, there is a unique solution to $\boldsymbol{\beta}_\Delta \mathbf{\Pi}_{12} = \mathbf{0}$.

There are test statistics based on conditions required for unique solution of $\boldsymbol{\beta}_\Delta \mathbf{\Pi}_{12} = \mathbf{0}$. Test statistics are classified according to the solution condition to be tested. The necessary and sufficient condition for existence of a (nontrivial) solution to $\boldsymbol{\beta}_\Delta \mathbf{\Pi}_{12} = \mathbf{0}$ is $\rho(\mathbf{\Pi}_{12}) = g$. There are two classes of test statistics based on this condition. They test these null hypotheses

$$\begin{aligned} &\text{(i) } H_0\text{:} \quad \rho(\mathbf{\Pi}_{12}) = g + 1 \\ &\text{(ii) } H_0\text{:} \quad \rho(\mathbf{\Pi}_{12}) \leq g - 1. \end{aligned}$$

A third class of tests is based on the need for a normalization rule. Solution of $\boldsymbol{\beta}_\Delta \mathbf{\Pi}_{12} = \mathbf{0}$ will require specification of one value of $\boldsymbol{\beta}_\Delta$. The normalization rule represents the decision as to which element of $\boldsymbol{\beta}_\Delta$ is associated with the "dependent" endogenous variable. The null hypothesis is

$$\text{(iii)} \quad H_0\text{: } \beta_{\Delta i} = -1 \qquad \text{for any one of } i = 1, \ldots, g + 1.$$

Procedures have been developed to test each of the three identifiability hypotheses. Names associated with the three hypotheses are

(i) "Zero restrictions test" $\rho(\mathbf{\Pi}_{12}) = g + 1$
(ii) "Rank condition test" $\rho(\mathbf{\Pi}_{12}) \leq g - 1$
(iii) "Normalization rule test" $\beta_{\Delta i} = -1$.

Discussion of the various test statistics and their properties will be easier if a common notation is used. That notation is presented in the next section. Following that presentation, discussion of the test statistics resumes.

A. Functional Components, Including Nuisance Parameters, for Testing Formulas

This section is used to introduce a common notation that will be used throughout the presentation. Against the background of that notation the nuisance parameter problem is presented and discussed with specific reference to testing identifiability of parameters in linear structural equations. That discussion will set the stage for presentation of known results, some new results, and some conjectures regarding methods of identifiability testing. For convenience and without loss of generality the discussion centers on the first equation in a simultaneous system. Subscripts indicating the equation have been dropped.

1. *Notation*

$\mathbf{y}$ is the $(T \times 1)$ vector of observations on the normalized endogenous variable

$\mathbf{Y}$ is the $(T \times g)$ matrix of observations on the other included endogenous variables

$\boldsymbol{\gamma}$ is partitioned as $(\boldsymbol{\gamma}_*, \mathbf{0}_2, \mathbf{0}_3) = (\boldsymbol{\gamma}_*, \gamma_2, \gamma_3)$ where $\boldsymbol{\gamma}_*$ are the structural coefficients on the included exogenous variables; $\boldsymbol{\gamma}$ is $(K \times 1)$; $K = K_1 + K_2 + K_3$.

$\mathbf{Z} = (\mathbf{Z}_1 \vdots\ \mathbf{Z}_2 \vdots\ \mathbf{Z}_3)$ is the $(T \times K)$ matrix of observations on the exogenous variables, partitioned to conform with $(\boldsymbol{\gamma}_*, \mathbf{0}_2, \mathbf{0}_3)$.

$\boldsymbol{\beta}$ is partitioned as $(-\mathbf{1} \vdots \boldsymbol{\beta}_\Delta)$ and is the vector of coefficients for $[\mathbf{y} \vdots \mathbf{Y}]$, the included endogenous variables; $\boldsymbol{\beta}$ is $[(g + 1) \times 1]$.

$\mathbf{u}$ is the $(T \times 1)$ vector of unobservable structural form disturbances for $\mathbf{y}$.

$\mathbf{U}_1$ is the $(T \times g)$ matrix of unobservable structural form disturbances for $\mathbf{Y}$.

$\mathbf{U} = (\mathbf{u} \vdots \mathbf{U}_1)$

$\mathbf{v}$ is the $(T \times 1)$ vector of reduced form disturbances corresponding to $\mathbf{y}$.
$\mathbf{V}_1$ is the $T \times g$ matrix of reduced form disturbances corresponding to $\mathbf{Y}$.
$\mathbf{V} = (\mathbf{v} \vdots \mathbf{V}_1)$

Observations are organized in the first structural equation as

$$[\mathbf{y} \vdots \mathbf{Y}]\,\boldsymbol{\beta} = \mathbf{Z}\boldsymbol{\gamma} + \mathbf{U}. \tag{12}$$

The corresponding portion of the reduced form is

$$[\mathbf{y} \vdots \mathbf{Y}] = \mathbf{Z}\boldsymbol{\Pi}' + \mathbf{V}.$$

$\hat{\beta}_\Delta$ are the GCL estimates of $\boldsymbol{\beta}_\Delta$.

$\tilde{\beta}_\Delta$ are the LIML estimates of $\boldsymbol{\beta}_\Delta$. (13)

$\hat{\gamma}_*$ are the GCL estimates of $\boldsymbol{\gamma}_*$.

$\tilde{\gamma}_*$ are the LIML estimates of $\boldsymbol{\gamma}_*$.

The following functions are formulated for later use:

$$G_1(\boldsymbol{\beta}_\Delta) = (\mathbf{y} - \mathbf{Y}\boldsymbol{\beta}_\Delta)'(\mathbf{I} - \mathbf{Z}_1(\mathbf{Z}_1'\mathbf{Z}_1)^{-1}\mathbf{Z}_1')(\mathbf{y} - \mathbf{Y}\boldsymbol{\beta}_\Delta)$$
$$G_2(\boldsymbol{\beta}_\Delta) = (\mathbf{y} - \mathbf{Y}\boldsymbol{\beta}_\Delta)'(\mathbf{I} - \mathbf{Z}(\mathbf{Z}'\mathbf{Z})^{-1}\mathbf{Z}')(\mathbf{y} - \mathbf{Y}\boldsymbol{\beta}_\Delta)$$
$$Q(\boldsymbol{\beta}_\Delta) = G_1(\boldsymbol{\beta}_\Delta) - G_2(\boldsymbol{\beta}_\Delta)$$
$$\phi = \frac{G_1(\boldsymbol{\beta}_\Delta) - G_2(\boldsymbol{\beta}_\Delta)}{G_2(\boldsymbol{\beta}_\Delta)}$$
$$\mathbf{A}_1 = \mathbf{I} - \mathbf{Z}_1(\mathbf{Z}_1'\mathbf{Z}_1)^{-1}\mathbf{Z}_1'$$
$$\mathbf{A}_3 = \mathbf{I} - \mathbf{Z}(\mathbf{Z}'\mathbf{Z})^{-1}\mathbf{Z}'$$
$$\mathbf{A}_2 = \mathbf{A}_1 - \mathbf{A}_3$$
$$\mathbf{M}_2 = \mathbf{A}_2 - \mathbf{A}_2\mathbf{Y}(\mathbf{Y}'\mathbf{A}_2\mathbf{Y})^{-1}\mathbf{Y}'\mathbf{A}_2'$$
$$\tilde{\sigma}^2 = \text{2SLS estimate of structural variance}$$
$$\mathbf{Y}_\Delta = [\mathbf{y} \vdots \mathbf{Y}]$$
$$\mathbf{W}_{\Delta\Delta} = \mathbf{Y}_\Delta'\mathbf{A}_3\mathbf{Y}_\Delta$$
$$\mathbf{W}^*_{\Delta\Delta} = \mathbf{Y}_\Delta'\mathbf{A}_1\mathbf{Y}_\Delta$$
$$\mathbf{W}_d = \mathbf{Y}_\Delta'\mathbf{A}_2\mathbf{Y}_\Delta$$

$\lambda_1 \geqslant \lambda_2 \geqslant \dots \geqslant \lambda_{g+1} \geqslant 0$ are the ordered roots of $|\mathbf{W}_d - \lambda\mathbf{W}_{\Delta\Delta}| = 0$

$$\mathbf{S}_{\Delta\Delta} = \mathbf{Y}'\,\mathbf{A}_3\mathbf{Y}$$
$$\mathbf{S}^*_{\Delta\Delta} = \mathbf{Y}'\,\mathbf{A}_1\mathbf{Y}$$
$$\mathbf{S}_d = \mathbf{Y}'\,\mathbf{A}_2\mathbf{Y}$$

$\xi_1 \geqslant \xi_2 \geqslant \dots \geqslant \xi_g \geqslant 0$ are the ordered roots of $|\mathbf{S}_d - \xi\,\mathbf{S}_{\Delta\Delta}| = 0$.

Formulas presented in this section are used in composing test statistics for the various identifiability hypotheses.

2. *Nuisance Parameters in Linear Models*

Various single equation and full system estimators and test statistics have a common basis in a single pair of matrix quadratic forms. These quadratic forms were presented previously as

$$\mathbf{W}_{\Delta\Delta} = \mathbf{Y}_\Delta'\mathbf{A}_3\mathbf{Y}_\Delta = \begin{bmatrix} \mathbf{y}'\mathbf{A}_3\mathbf{y} & \mathbf{y}'\mathbf{A}_3\mathbf{Y} \\ \mathbf{Y}'\mathbf{A}_3\mathbf{y} & \mathbf{S}_{\Delta\Delta} \end{bmatrix}$$

$$\mathbf{W}_{\Delta\Delta}^* = \mathbf{Y}_\Delta'\mathbf{A}_1\mathbf{Y}_\Delta = \begin{bmatrix} \mathbf{y}'\mathbf{A}_1\mathbf{y} & \mathbf{y}'\mathbf{A}_1\mathbf{Y} \\ \mathbf{Y}'\mathbf{A}_1\mathbf{y} & \mathbf{S}_{\Delta\Delta}^* \end{bmatrix}$$

For example, k-class estimators of endogenous variable coefficients are all defined through the normal equations:

$$(\mathbf{S}_{\Delta\Delta}^* - k\mathbf{S}_{\Delta\Delta})\hat{\beta}_\Delta = (\mathbf{Y}'\mathbf{A}_1\mathbf{y} - k\mathbf{Y}'\mathbf{A}_3\mathbf{y})$$

so that the entire k-class of estimators are based on $\mathbf{W}_{\Delta\Delta}$ and $\mathbf{W}_{\Delta\Delta}^*$. Further, the k-class identifiability test statistics can all be defined as the percentage increase in the sum of square errors due to imposing the identifying restrictions. Let $\hat{\beta}_k$ be the k-class estimates of $\boldsymbol{\beta}_\Delta$. Then the k-class identifiability test statistic is

$$\hat{\phi}_k = \frac{G_1(\hat{\beta}_k) - G_2(\hat{\beta}_k)}{G_2(\hat{\beta}_k)}.$$

Thus, k-class identifiability test statistics are also functions of $\mathbf{W}_{\Delta\Delta}^*$ and $\mathbf{W}_{\Delta\Delta}$. These two matrices are matrix variate random variables. Where their density functions contain nuisance parameters, density functions of $\hat{\boldsymbol{\beta}}_k$ and $\hat{\boldsymbol{\phi}}_k$ may contain those same nuisance parameters.

Here is repeated the assumption that the row vectors of

$$[\mathbf{v} : \mathbf{V}_1]$$

are distributed independently and identically as $N(\mathbf{0}, \boldsymbol{\Sigma})$. This assumption implies that

$\mathbf{W}_{\Delta\Delta}$ is distributed as central Wishart with $T - K$ degrees of freedom and covariance matrix $\boldsymbol{\Sigma}$

$\mathbf{W}_{\Delta\Delta}^*$ is distributed independently of $\mathbf{W}_{\Delta\Delta}$ as noncentral Wishart with $K_2 + K_3$ degrees of freedom, covariance matrix $\boldsymbol{\Sigma}$, and means-sigma matrix $\boldsymbol{\Omega} = \boldsymbol{\Sigma}^{-1}\mathrm{E}(\mathbf{Y}_\Delta')\mathbf{A}_1\mathrm{E}(\mathbf{Y}_\Delta)$.

Let $\omega_1 \geq \omega_2, \ldots, \geq \omega_{g+1}$ be the ordered roots of $\mathbf{\Omega}$, $n = T - K$, and $m = K_2 + K_3$. Thus, any parameter in the densities of $\mathbf{W}_{\Delta\Delta}$ or $\mathbf{W}^*_{\Delta\Delta}$ not specified by the null hypothesis will be a nuisance parameter. This fact is, of course, independent of the probability function assigned to $\mathbf{V}$. Thus, in the example at hand, distribution functions of $\mathbf{W}_{\Delta\Delta}$ and $\mathbf{W}^*_{\Delta\Delta}$ depend on $\mathbf{\Sigma}$ and $\mathbf{\Pi}$; that is, on $\mathbf{\Sigma}$ and $\mathbf{\Omega}$. In certain cases $\mathbf{\Sigma}$ is replaced by $\mathbf{\Sigma}_1$, the covariance matrix of $\mathbf{V}_1$, and $\mathbf{\Omega}$ is replaced by $\mathbf{\Omega}_1 = \mathbf{\Sigma}_1^{-1}\mathrm{E}(\mathbf{Y}')\mathbf{A}_1\mathrm{E}(\mathbf{Y})$.

The role of these nuisance parameters is explored in greater detail later in this article; however, it is useful to see their role and place in the density functions of $\mathbf{W}_{\Delta\Delta}$ and $\mathbf{W}^*_{\Delta\Delta}$. I begin by reviewing matrix argument hypergeometric functions and zonal polynomials. These functions are required foundation for studying the sampling distributions of identifiability test statistics.

The density functions of $\mathbf{W}_{\Delta\Delta}$ and $\mathbf{W}^*_{\Delta\Delta}$ are special cases of the noncentral Wishart density. Let $\mathbf{S}$ be a positive definite symmetric (PDS) matrix; then $\mathbf{S}$ has a noncentral Wishart density function

$$\text{(i) } F(S) = \frac{\mathrm{etr}(-\Omega)\,\mathrm{etr}(-\tfrac{1}{2}\mathbf{\Sigma}^{-1}\mathbf{S})|\mathbf{S}|^{(n-m-1)/2}}{2^{mn/2}\Gamma_m(n/2)|\mathbf{\Sigma}|^{n/2}}\,{}_0F_1(n/2; \mathbf{\Sigma}^{-1}\mathbf{\Omega}\mathbf{S}/2) \qquad \mathbf{S} > 0$$

$$\text{(ii) } = 0 \qquad \text{elsewhere.}$$

B. Zero Restriction Tests

Zero restriction tests focus on the null hypothesis

$$H_0\colon\ \rho(\mathbf{\Pi}_{12}) = g + 1$$

against the alternative hypothesis

$$H_a\colon\ \rho(\mathbf{\Pi}_{12}) \leq g.$$

Where H_0 is accepted in favor of H_a, the equation is not identified, indicating that the structural form is not consistent with observed behavior. Three test statistics have been proposed for deciding between H_0 and H_a: (1) the likelihood ratio test; (2) Basmann's GCL test; and (3) a Wald test.

1. *Likelihood Ratio Test*

Of the three tests proposed, the likelihood ratio (LR) test is the most general. It is also the test about which most statistical properties are known. Apparently, Anderson and Rubin (1949) first developed the likelihood ratio test for zero restrictions. They show that the likelihood ratio is

$$l = (1 + \lambda_{g+1})^{-T/2}. \qquad (14)$$

The statistic λ_{g+1} can be derived either as the minimum root of $|\mathbf{W}_d - \lambda \mathbf{W}_{\Delta\Delta}| = 0$ or as the minimum of $[G_1(\boldsymbol{\beta}_\Delta) - G_2(\boldsymbol{\beta}_\Delta)]/G_2(\boldsymbol{\beta}_\Delta)$. The former is the derivation through the maintained hypotheses; the latter is derived through the structural hypothesis.

Rhodes (1981) has derived the exact finite sample density function of λ_{g+1} [see p. 1038, Eq. (2.4) and let $\lambda_{g+1} = g_P$.] The basic form of that pdf is shown here without the constant. [Density functions are, for the most part, presented herein without the normalizing constant term. This being the case, the symbol of proportionality, $\propto$, is used in place of $=$.] Notice the role of $\boldsymbol{\Omega}$. In this special case, as is well known, $\boldsymbol{\Sigma} = \mathbf{I}$ without loss of generality.

$$h(\lambda_{g+1}) \propto \sum_{k=0}^{\infty} \sum_{\kappa} \frac{[(m+n)/2]_\kappa \, C_\kappa(\boldsymbol{\Omega})}{k!(n/2)_\kappa \, C_\kappa(\mathbf{I})} \sum_{s=0}^{\infty} \sum_{\sigma} \sum_{\theta} [(g+1)(n/2) + k + s] \times \frac{[(g+2-m)/2]_\sigma}{s![(n+g+2)/2]_\theta} \, b_{\kappa\sigma}^{\theta} \, (n/2)_\theta \, C_\theta(\mathbf{I}) \, (1+\lambda_{g+1})^{-[(g+1)n/2+k+s+1]} \quad 0 < \lambda_{g+1} < \infty \tag{15}$$

where $n = T - K_1$; and κ, σ, θ, and $b_{\kappa\sigma}^{\theta}$ are constants associated with the partition of $\boldsymbol{\Omega}$. Refer to Rhodes (1981) for details.

Kadane (1970, 1974) showed that the test stastistic is consistent, but Rhodes (1981) showed that the test is not sufficient and that it is not unbiased. The lack of sufficiency and the bias both follow primarily from the central role of the nuisance parameter $\boldsymbol{\Omega}$. The roots $\lambda_1, \lambda_2, \ldots, \lambda_{g+1}$ are jointly sufficient for $\omega_1, \ldots, \omega_{g+1}$, but no strict subset of the sample roots is jointly sufficient for the corresponding subset of the population roots.

The bias of the test rests upon a property that was not discussed in Rhodes (1981) but is introduced here. This is the property of monotonicity. A monotonic test is one whose power function is monotonic in the nuisance parameters. *The likelihood ratio identifiability test is monotonic in the roots of* $\boldsymbol{\Omega}$, $\omega_1, \ldots, \omega_{g+1}$. An unbiased test is one where the power is never less than the significance level. Thus, the bias of the test depends on specification of $\omega_1, \ldots, \omega_{g+1}$ under the alternative hypothesis. That there are combinations of the nuisance parameters that make the test biased is shown by the power function of the normalization test presented in Figures 1 and 2. The power functions of the zero restriction test and the normalization test have identical forms.

It is well known that this test statistic is invariant with respect to the normalization rule. Its derivation as the minimum of a ratio of quadratic

Figure 1. Exact Power Function of Likelihood Ratio Test of Normalizing Restrictions ($g = 3$).*

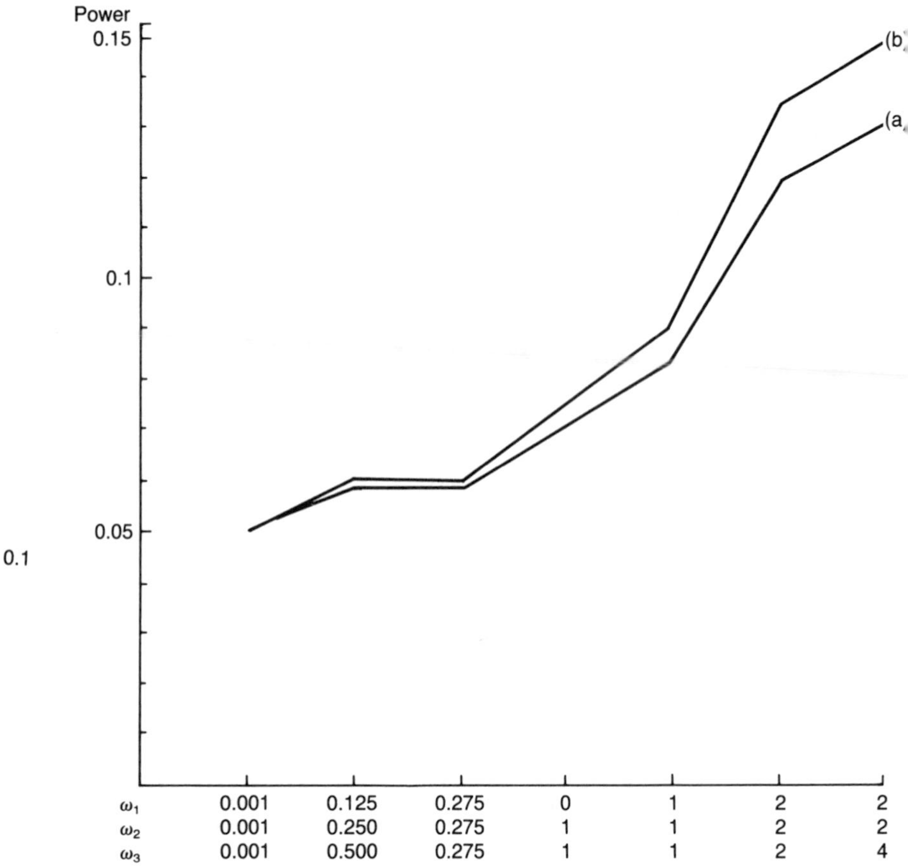

* See Pillai and Dotson (1969), Table 8, p. 63. Values shown are (a) $\Pr\{\xi_3 > 0.1740 | m = 8, n = 34\}$ and (b) $\Pr\{\xi_3 > 0.0694 | m = 8, n = 84\}$.

forms gives this property. What this invariance means is that the test strictly applies only to the zero restriction hypothesis.

That the test statistic and test are invariant with respect to the normalization rule is a special case of the following theorem.

THEOREM 1: *The likelihood ratio rest of zero restrictions is invariant under the class of nonsingular transformations on the maintained hypothesis induced by*

$$\mathbf{Y}_\Delta \mathbf{P}'$$

where $\mathbf{P}'$ *is any* $(g + 1) \times (g + 1)$ *real nonsingular matrix.*

Figure 2. Exact Power Function of Likelihood Ratio Test of Normalizing Restrictions ($g = 2$).

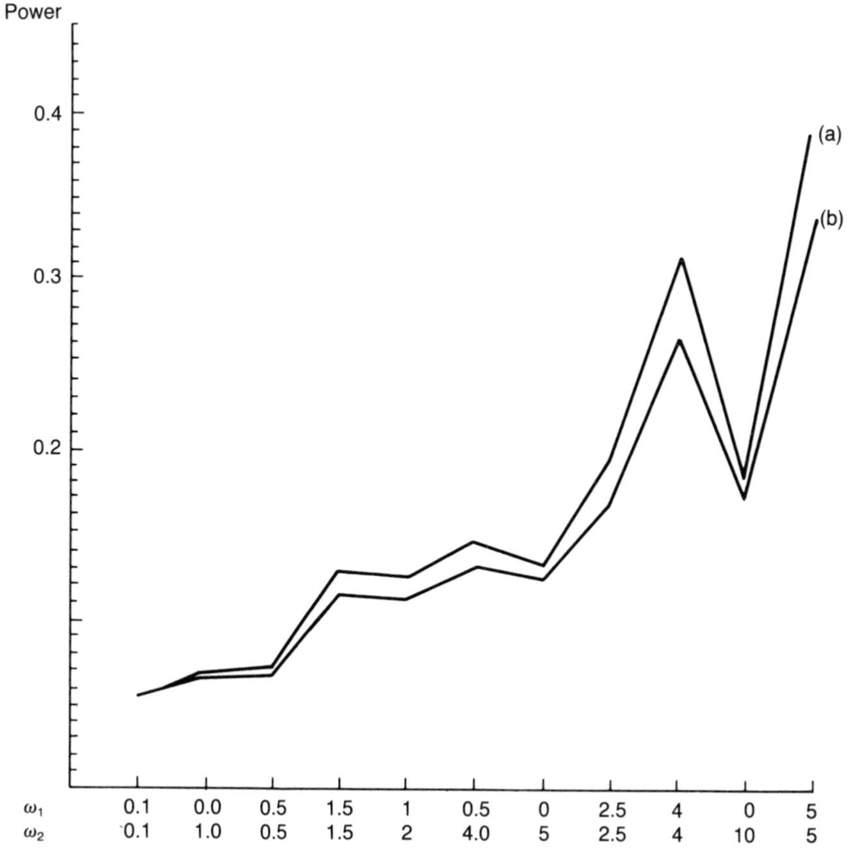

* See Pillai and Dotson (1969), Table 10, p. 65. Values shown are (a) Pr $\{\xi_2 > 0.4761 | m = 5, n = 13\}$ and (b) Pr $\{\xi_2 > 0.0667 | m = 5, n = 83\}$.

PROOF: The roots of $|\mathbf{PY}'_\Delta \mathbf{M}_d \mathbf{Y}_\Delta \mathbf{P}' - \lambda \mathbf{PY}'_\Delta \mathbf{M}_{\Delta\Delta} \mathbf{Y}_\Delta \mathbf{P}'| = 0$ are identical with those of $|\mathbf{Y}'_\Delta \mathbf{M}_d \mathbf{Y}_\Delta - \lambda \mathbf{Y}'_\Delta \mathbf{W}_{\Delta\Delta} \mathbf{Y}_\Delta| = 0$. Consequently, the nonsingular transformations induced by every square nonsingular $\mathbf{P}$ will leave λ unchanged. This meets the definition of *invariance* applied to statistical tests [cf. Lehmann (1959), Chapter 6; or Cox and Hinkley (1979), Section 5.3].

Alternative normalization rules form a subclass of the general linear group specifying $\mathbf{P}$. Thus, the likelihood ratio test for zero restrictions is invariant for all scale changes, including those induced by alternative normalizing choices.

The last sample property to be discussed is the existence of moments. For the likelihood ratio statistic, moments exist up to the greatest integer strictly smaller than $(g + 1)(T - K)/2$, that is,

$$E(\lambda_{g+1}^{h}) < \infty$$

so long as

$$h < (g + 1)(T - K)/2.$$

Rhodes (1981) presents a proof of this condition, along with formulas for $E(\lambda_{g+1}^{h})$. This result is significant primarily in assessing accuracies of critical region approximations. I will refer to it later in that context.

The asymptotic property of consistency for this test has already been mentioned. There are two other asymptotic properties worth mentioning in this connection. The liklihood ratio derived here has the classical asymptotic chi-squared property. That is

$$T \ln (1 + \lambda_{g+1}) \overset{A}{\sim} \chi^2(K_2 + K_3 - g) \tag{16}$$

This property is the basis for one method of constructing approximate critical regions for testing the zero restriction hypothesis. The second property has served the same function. It is this: the moments of

$$[(T - K)/(K_2 + K_3 - g)]\lambda_{g+1} \tag{16$'$}$$

converge to those of the $F(K_2 + K_3 - g, T - K)$ distribution as $T \to \infty$, or as the structural variance goes to zero. Consequently, a second approximate critical region based on (16′) has been proposed.

2. *GCL Test*

The GCL test was introduced by Basmann (1960, 1965, 1966). Its exact finite sample density for $g = 1$ (two endogenous variables) was derived by Basmann (1965, 1966) and by Richardson (1967). The test statistic is the percentage increase in sum of squares for the regression of $\mathbf{y} - \mathbf{Y}\boldsymbol{\beta}_\Delta$ on $\mathbf{Z}_1$ against the regression on $\mathbf{Z}$. That is, the test statistic equals

$$\hat{\phi}_{\text{GCL}} = \frac{G_1(\hat{\boldsymbol{\beta}}_\Delta) - G_2(\hat{\boldsymbol{\beta}}_\Delta)}{G_2(\hat{\boldsymbol{\beta}}_\Delta)}. \tag{17}$$

The general form of the finite-sample density function for arbitrary g remains unknown.

Enough is known about the test statistic to compare its properties with those of the likelihood ratio test. Like the LR test, the GCL test is consistent. Also, its moments converge to the moments of the $F(K_2 + K_3 - g, T - K)$. It is not known whether the test is sufficient or whether it is unbiased. Investigation of these properties can proceed along with derivation of sampling distributions for the test statistic.

One important contrast between LR and GCL statistics is that they differ in the number of moments defined. The GCL test has moments up to the integer smaller than $(T - K)/2$. The LR test has moments up to $(g + 1)(T - K)/2$, or more moments by a factor of $g + 1$. This fact suggests that they will not be equally well approximated by $\chi^2(K_2 + K_3 - g)$ or $F(K_2 + K_3 - g, T - K)$.

A second difference between LR and GCL tests is that the GCL test statistic is *not invariant* for testing the zero restriction hypothesis. There is a GCL test statistic for each of the $g + 1$ normalization rules associated with a single equation. What this lack of invariance means is that great care must be taken in interpreting test results based on the GCL identifiability test. The zero restriction hypothesis is actually tested *subject to* the normalization conditions. The GCL test reduces the null hypothesis space to its intersection with the normalization rule. That is, the GCL test augments the null hypothesis to include both the zero restrictions *and* the normalization rule. Because the GCL estimate $\hat{\boldsymbol{\beta}}_\Delta$ must depend on the normalization rule, it is not possible to test the entire null hypothesis of zero restrictions using a single GCL test.

The advantage of the GCL test is that it may be used to test simultaneously the zero restrictions and a specific normalization rule. This may be a desirable state of affairs if 2SLS is the estimation method chosen.

3. *Wald Tests*

Byron (1972, 1974), Wegge (1978), and Hwang (1980) have explored the use of Wald tests for overidentifying zero restrictions. The general formulation of the Wald tests is direct and intuitively appealing. The primary reference is Wald (1943). Let $h(\theta) = 0$ be a collection of restrictions on parameters θ from a distribution function $F(\cdot;\theta)$ and let $\hat{\theta}$ be the maximum likelihood estimates of θ. Then Wald (1943) derives some general conditions under which quadratic forms in $h(\hat{\theta})$ are asymptotically distributed as chi-squared statistics.

Wald tests for zero restrictions proposed by Byron and by Wegge require designation of a specific subcollection of the restrictions as *overidentifying restrictions*. The test statistics are formulated based on the designated taxonomy of zero restrictions. Thus, we say that

$$\boldsymbol{\gamma}_3 = \mathbf{0}_3$$

are the required identifying restrictions. Then

$$h(\theta) = \boldsymbol{\gamma}_2 = \mathbf{0}_2$$

are the overidentifying restrictions to be tested using the Wald test. Byron formulated the test in the maintained hypothesis. Wegge (1978) formulated it in the structural form space. Hwang (1980) showed their equivalence. The formula for the structural form test statistic is

$$\hat{W} = (\hat{\gamma}_2 - \gamma_2)'(\mathbf{Z}_2'\mathbf{M}_2\mathbf{Z}_2)(\hat{\gamma}_2 - \gamma_2)/\hat{\sigma}_2. \tag{18}$$

By Wald's theorem, $\hat{W}$ is asymptotically distributed as χ^2 with K_2 degrees of freedom.

Apart from this asymptotic chi-squared property, only a few other properties are known for the Wald test statistic. The main result previously given is that the Wald test is asymptotically equivalent to both the likelihood ratio and GCL tests; see Hwang (1980). Consequently, this test is also consistent. This asymptotic equivalence immediately focuses attention on the small-sample performance of the test statistics. This topic is taken up in Section IV.

Finally, we consider one additional property presented here for the first time. It appears that the Wald test, like the GCL test, lacks the property of invariance for testing zero restrictions. The GCL test lacks symmetry (invariance) because each normalization gives a different test. The Wald test lacks symmetry because each alternative choice of the overidentifying restrictions gives a different test statistic. Because there are $K_2 + K_3$ restrictions and K_3 of these are required for exact identification, there are

$$\binom{K_2 + K_3}{K_2}$$

different sets of hypothetical overidentifying restrictions. Each of these will present a different test statistic. Hence, the Wald test is *not invariant* for the test of zero restrictions.

Of the three tests proposed, the least is known about the Wald test. It is consistent, asymptotically χ^2, and not invariant. At this time, there does not appear to be any knowledge of its finite sample distribution or of other asymptotic or small-sample properties. Like the LR and GCL tests, it has been the subject of some sampling experiments. These are discussed in Section III.

The properties of the three tests of zero restrictions are summarized and compared in Table 1.

C. Rank Condition Tests

Rank condition tests are designed to test the null hypothesis

$$H_0: \quad \rho(\mathbf{\Pi}_{12}) \leq g - 1$$

against the alternative

$$H_a: \quad \rho(\mathbf{\Pi}_{12}) = g.$$

These hypotheses are based on the fact that $\rho(\mathbf{\Pi}_{12}) = g$ is the necessary and sufficient condition for identification because it is the necessary and sufficient condition for $\mathbf{\Pi}_{12}\boldsymbol{\beta}_\Delta = \mathbf{0}$ to have a unique solution. If $\rho(\mathbf{\Pi}_{12}) = g + 1$, the only solution is the trivial one and the structural parameters are not identified. This condition is the subject of the zero restriction test. If $\rho(\mathbf{\Pi}_{12}) \leqslant g - 1$, there are infinitely many solutions and the parameters are still not identified. The zero restriction test does not apply if an equation is exactly identified. On the other hand, the rank condition test is available for exactly, as well as for overidentified, equations.

Only one test has been proposed specifically for testing the rank condition. It is based on the fact that the rank of $\mathbf{\Pi}_{12}$ is equal to the number of positive roots of the equation

$$|\mathbf{W}_d - \lambda \mathbf{W}_{\Delta\Delta}| = 0.$$

The zero restriction test focused on the smallest of these, λ_{g+1}. Where one concludes that $\lambda_{g+1} = 0$, the zero restriction test is satisfactory and attention turns to whether $\lambda_g = 0$. If $\lambda_{g+1} = 0$ and $\lambda_g > 0$, the equation is identified. If $\lambda_g = 0$ also, identification fails. Thus, the zero restriction test is a test of necessary conditions. Where the necessary conditions hold, the test of sufficient conditions is then performed.

For testing the null hypothesis $\lambda_{g+1} = \lambda_g = 0$ against the complementary alternative, the likelihood ratio statistic is

$$l = (1 + \lambda_{g+1})^{-T/2}(1 + \lambda_g)^{-T/2}.$$

Conditions are met for $-2\ln(l)$ to be asymptotically distributed as a

Table 1. Statistical Properties of Zero Restriction Identifiability Test Statistics.

Property	*Likelihood Ratio*	*GCL*	*Wald*
Moment existence	$(g + 1)(T - K)/2$	$(T - K)/2$	NK
Sufficient	No	NK	NK
Unbiased	No	NK	NK
Invariance	Yes	No	No
Monotonicity	Yes	NK	NK
Similarity	NK*	NK	NK
Exact density	Yes	No	No
Consistency	Yes	Yes	Yes
Asymptotic d.f.	Yes	Yes	Yes
Asymptotic moments	$F(K_2 + K_3 - g, T - K)$	$F(K_2 + K_3 - g, T - K)$	NK

* NK, Not known.

chi-squared statistic with $(K - K_1 - g + 1)$ degrees of freedom. Thus, the critical region proposed for testing the rank condition is

$$T \ln\{(1 + \lambda_{g+1})(1 + \lambda_g)\} \geqslant \chi^2(K - K_1 - g + 1). \tag{19}$$

This test is known as the Koopmans and Hood (1953) double root test. It is discussed in some detail by Dent and Geweke (1980).

There is a problem, however, with interpreting the outcome of this test as formulated. Where the null hypothesis is not rejected, there is the clear implication of underidentification. But a problem of interpretation arises when the null hypothesis is rejected. This is because the complement includes both underidentification $[(\lambda_{g+1} > 0) \cap (\lambda_g > 0)]$ and identification $[(\lambda_{g+1} = 0) \cap (\lambda_g > 0)]$. Thus, although the test is logically valid, it is somewhat awkward to interpret. Nevertheless, its performance has been studied in sampling experiments; the results are reported in Section III.

The problem with this form of the double root test prevails whether or not the necessary condition has already been tested. Where it has not been tested, the problem is as described in the previous paragraph. Where it has been tested, there is information available that is not included in the double root test. Of course, it is not expected that the double root test would be performed if the necessary condition is already rejected. Where it is known that the zero restriction test has not rejected the necessary condition, the double root test would be improved by taking account of this extra information.

What is proposed here is a modification of the double root test to include the outcome of the zero restriction test. The proposed test has its critical region boundary ζ based on the conditional probability

$$\Pr\{\lambda_g > \zeta | \lambda_{g+1} = 0\} = \alpha. \tag{20}$$

ζ is a boundary value of the critical region determined by the conditional distribution of λ_g given λ_{g+1}, $F(\lambda_g | \lambda_{g+1})$. This will be called the conditional root test.

The double root and conditional root tests share several properties with the LR test for zero restrictions. For example, none of the tests is sufficient; that is, none is based on a sufficient statistic. The roots λ_1, ..., λ_{g+1} are jointly sufficient for the population roots. However, no strict subset of the sample roots is sufficient for the corresponding subset of population roots. Thus, these tests do not use all available sample information.

The zero restriction and double root tests are not generally unbiased. Recall that a test is unbiased if the critical region size does not exceed the power under any alternative parameter configuration in the domain. The distribution functions for the tests are monotonic in the nuisance parameters ω_1, ..., ω_{g-1}, the population values of λ_1, ..., λ_{g-1}. Thus, there are parameter spaces under the alternative hypothesis that make the power smaller than the significance level. This problem is illustrated by the graphs of the power function shown in Figures 1 and 2. Therefore, zero restriction and double root tests are not unbiased. It is not known at this time whether the conditional root test is unbiased or not. However, the *conjecture* is adduced: The conditional root test is not unbiased.

Zero restriction and double root tests are both monotonic and invariant (symmetric). The invariance property for the double root test is proved exactly the same way as it was for the zero restriction test. The monotonicity property is a property of likelihood ratio tests (see Lehmann, 1959). The distribution function of the roots $\lambda_1, \ldots, \lambda_{g+1}$ is monotonic in the population roots, $\omega_1, \ldots, \omega_{g+1}$. It is expected that the conditional root test will also retain monotonicity and invariance.

At this time it is not known whether the double root test or the conditional root test is consistent. I *conjecture* that both tests are consistent, but this remains to be proved. It seems reasonable to believe that the conditions leading to the asymptotic chi-squared distribution will also give consistent tests.

D. Normalization Restriction Tests

Normalization restriction tests have an essential role in simultaneous equation economic models. This importance comes from two considerations: one based on economic behavior, another based on statistical properties of estimators. There are cases where the normalization restriction is dictated by the theory being modeled. Basmann (Chapter 6, this volume) gives one example in the case of a consumption function. In such cases, tests of normalizing restrictions may be interpreted as partial tests of theoretical propositions. Thus, in the first instance, the test of normalizing restrictions is important because it actually tests behavioral propositions.

In the second case, the normalization rule may help select the appropriate statistical estimators. Basmann (1957) points out that the GCL estimators are best among consistent estimators. On the other hand, they are not invariant against the imposed normalization. It follows that the test of normalization restrictions may aid the selection of an optimal estimator. It seems important to separate the issues of estimation technique from those of economic theory so far as possible. This point is made clearly by Basmann (Chapter 6, this volume). What remains is the conclusion that tests of normalization are essential in simultaneous equations estimation and inference. They have an especially important role where they constitute tests of economic theories.

1. *GCL Tests*

I have already pointed out that the normalization rule is an implicit part of the null hypothesis tested by the GCL version of the test for zero restrictions. Thus, it constitutes one test for normalization. Here the problem is that rejection of the null hypothesis does not tell whether the zero restriction failed or the normalization restriction failed. Either one of these conditions may fail, but they cannot both fail together.

2. *Likelihood Ratio Test*

A likelihood ratio test for normalization has been proposed. It is identical in form to the likelihood ratio test for zero restrictions. The likelihood ratio is

$$l = (1 + \xi_g)^{-T/2} \tag{21}$$

where ξ is the minimum root of

$$|\mathbf{Y}'\mathbf{A}_2\mathbf{Y} - \xi\mathbf{Y}'\mathbf{A}_3\mathbf{Y}| = 0. \tag{22}$$

There are g roots for (22). Each of them must be positive for the normalization rule to hold. This follows from the restriction

$$\boldsymbol{\beta}\boldsymbol{\Pi}_{12} = \mathbf{0}.$$

Assume a normalization making the first element of $\boldsymbol{\beta}$ equal to -1 and partition $\boldsymbol{\Pi}_{12}$ conformably to obtain

$$(-\mathbf{1} \vdots \boldsymbol{\beta}_\Delta)\begin{pmatrix} \overline{\boldsymbol{\pi}}_{12} \\ \cdots \\ \overline{\boldsymbol{\Pi}}_{12} \end{pmatrix} = \mathbf{0},$$

or

$$-\overline{\boldsymbol{\pi}}_{12} + \boldsymbol{\beta}_\Delta \overline{\boldsymbol{\Pi}}_{12} = \mathbf{0}. \tag{11$'$}$$

Then a unique solution to (11′) requires that $\overline{\boldsymbol{\Pi}}_{12}$ is nonsingular. A necessary and sufficient condition for $\rho(\overline{\boldsymbol{\Pi}}_{12}) = g$ is that ξ_g is strictly positive. Thus, the likelihood ratio test statistic (21) tests the null hypothesis

$$H_0\colon\ \rho(\overline{\boldsymbol{\Pi}}_{12}) \leqslant g - 1$$

against the alternative hypothesis

$$H_{\mathrm{a}}\colon\ \rho(\overline{\boldsymbol{\Pi}}_{12}) = g.$$

Rejection of H_0 in favor of H_{a} supports the normalization imposed.

Of course, there is a test statistic $(1 + \xi_g)^{-T/2}$ for each of the g possible normalization restrictions imposed. It is entirely possible that H_{a} will be accepted for several or all of these using the LR test.

I derived the exact finite sample density function of ξ_g for arbitrary numbers of included endogenous and excluded exogenous variables (see Rhodes, 1982). The exact density of ξ_g is identical in form with that of the zero restriction test statistic in equation (15). Only the parameters are different. To obtain the normalization test statistic, the following substitutions are made:

Zero restriction test	*Normalization test*
$n = T - K$	$n = T - K$
$m = K_2 + K_3$	$m = K_2 + K_3$
$k = T - K_2 - K_3$	$k = T - K_2 - K_3$
$\mathbf{\Omega} = \mathbf{\Sigma}^{-1}\mathrm{E}(\mathbf{Y}'_\Delta)\mathbf{A}_2\mathrm{E}(\mathbf{Y}_\Delta)$	$\mathbf{\Omega}_1 = \mathbf{\Sigma}_{22}^{-1}\mathrm{E}(\mathbf{Y}')\mathbf{A}_2\mathrm{E}(\mathbf{Y})$
$p = g + 1$	$p = g$

The exact density is not reproduced here, but its properties are recounted. Also, graphs of its power function are given to illustrate the nuisance parameter and bias problems associated with this class of tests.

As a likelihood ratio test, this test is consistent. Its power will increase to unity as the sample size grows indefinitely large. This seems to be an essential property for a test to possess.

The test is not sufficient or unbiased. Like its zero restriction test counterpart, it is not based on a sufficient statistic. The g roots of (22) are jointly sufficient for their population counterparts, but subsets of them are not jointly sufficient for matching subsets of population roots. A proof of this is found in the appendix of Rhodes (1981). The failure to be unbiased comes from the presence of the nuisance parameters, the roots of $\mathbf{\Omega}_1$. To any particular null hypothesis, there may correspond at least one power function smaller than the significance level for some configuration of population roots specified by the alternative hypothesis. It should be noted, however, that the test statistic is unbiased against any alternative where the nuisance parameters are identical between the null and alternative hypotheses. This is a sufficient, but not a necessary condition for the test to be unbiased. The property of bias is based on the *monotonicity* of the distribution. This property is simply that the power function is monotonic in any subset of the population roots that are all varied in the same direction. These properties are illustrated in Figures 1 and 2.

Discussion of the invariance property for this test must be approached with caution. As a test of a specific normalization restriction, this test is invariant against the class of transformations $\mathbf{P}'\mathbf{Y}$ where $\mathbf{P}$ is one class of nonsingular square matrices of order g. It is thus invariant in the same sense as the likelihood ratio test of zero restrictions is invariant. However, it is important to keep in mind that there will be a different set of these invariant tests for each normalization restriction. Each exact finite sample distribution function associated with a specific normalizing transformation will have the same functional form as each of the others. However, the nuisance parameter configuration for each one will be unique to that normalizing transformation. Thus, even though test statistics for two transformations have identical values, they will give different significance levels from their exact distributions. In this more general sense, these tests are not invariant.

Approximations to critical regions of this test statistic have been proposed, for example, by Farebrother and Savin (1974) and Dent and Geweke (1980). These are based on the fact that

$$T \ln (1 + \xi_g)$$

is distributed asymptotically as a χ^2 with $K_2 + K_3 - g + 1$ degrees of freedom. Approximate critical regions based on

$$[(T - K)/(K_2 + K_3)]\xi_g$$

being approximately distributed as $F(K_2 + K_3, T - K)$ have also been proposed. I have not been able to find any sampling experiment studies showing the accuracy of the proposed approximations. However, several studies have used these approximations for the test statistic for zero restrictions. These have strongly rejected both the χ^2 and F approximations. Construction of the normalization rule test suggests smaller values of population roots and degrees of freedom than in the corresponding test of sufficient conditions. What this means is that the approximations are not likely to do better in the test of normalizing transformations than they do in the tests of zero restrictions. Hence, I conclude that they are not likely to provide reliable approximations for the exact distributions of the test statistics.

Two additional methods of approximating exact critical regions have been proposed for this case. One attributable to Basmann (ch 6, this volume) has been explored in some detail. He proposed the critical region

$$\frac{T - K}{m - g + 1}\xi_g \geqslant F(m - g + 1, T - K).$$

Where this condition is fulfilled, the null hypothesis is rejected in favor of the normalizing restrictions. This approximation has dominated the $\chi^2(m - g + 1)$ and $F(m, T - K)$ approximations where the standardized concentration parameter is large.

I have proposed an alternative approximation for the critical region based on the exact distribution of the LR statistic. That approximation is based on the asymptotic conditional distribution of ξ_g given $\xi_1, \ldots, \xi_{g-1}$ as the population roots of $\mathbf{\Omega}_1$, say, $\phi_1, \ldots, \phi_g$, increase without bound. The asymptotic conditional density function is based on transformed values $\eta_i = \xi_i/(1 + \xi_i)$. The actual asymptotic conditional density function employed is

$$\text{(i) } g(\eta_g|\eta_1, \ldots, \eta_{g-1}) \propto \prod_{i=1}^{g-1}(\eta_i - \eta_g)^{1/2} \exp(-\phi_g)\eta_g^{(m-g-1)/2}$$
$$\times (1 - \eta_g)^{(n-g-1)/2} \, {}_1F_1[(n + m - g + 1)/2; \quad (23)$$
$$(m - p + 1)/2; \phi_g \eta_g) \qquad 0 < \eta_g < \eta_{g-1}$$
$$\text{(ii) } \qquad \propto 0 \qquad \text{elsewhere}$$

as $\phi_1, \ldots, \phi_{g-1}$ increase without bound. The power function associated with (23) can be accurately approximated by numerical integration. Consequently, it is possible to apply this decision rule:

$$\textit{If} \int_0^{\eta_g} g(\eta_g|\eta_1, \ldots, \eta_{g-1})d\eta_g > 1 - \alpha, \textit{ then} \qquad (24)$$

reject the null hypothesis. Under the null hypothesis $\phi_g = 0$, so that no nuisance parameters are involved in approximating the critical region.

The test implied by (24) has several properties to recommend it. It includes the information from the sample regarding the entire parameter space. This follows from inclusion of $\eta_1, \ldots, \eta_{g-1}$ in the density. It is therefore asymptotically sufficient. On the other hand, it does not contain any nuisance parameters. Further study will show whether (24) is superior to the $F(m - g + 1, T - K)$ approximation. It did provide better accuracy using data from Basmann's Hanford experiment (cf. Rhodes, 1981a).

III. EXPERIMENTAL EVIDENCE

Several sampling experiments have augmented the analytical studies of identifiability test statistics and their properties. These sampling experiments have helped to deal with three major types of problems associated with direct analytical studies. The first major problem encountered is the sheer difficulty of deriving the density functions for the test statistics. While the derivations are surmountable, one could wish they were considerably more tractable than they appear at present. Properly designed sampling experiments can suggest clues to strategies and tactics for deriving the distributions as well as suggesting whether the results of the derivations will be worth the effort. Basmann's (1958, chapter 6 this volume) early sampling experiment provides direction of this kind. Indeed, it was designed partly with this aim in mind (see Basmann, 1960).

Assessing accuracy of approximations to critical regions is a second feature use of sampling experiments. Several approximations based on asymptotic distributions and other properties have been proposed. Sampling experiments have been used to appraise the accuracy of proposed approximations and to compare their performances under alternative circumstances.

The third use of sampling experiments is in studying the role and effect of nuisance parameters on exact distribution functions and on accuracy of approximations. Nuisance parameters appear as integral components of the exact distribution functions. But their effects are hidden by the complicated forms of the functions. Sampling experiments can be used to isolate and study the effects of the nuisance parameters.

Use of sampling experiments to study distributions associated with identifiability testing has been limited relative to what could have been achieved. This fact is remarkable considering the central role of identifiability hypotheses in simultaneous equation models and comprehensive economic theories. Nonetheless, experiments conducted so far have laid extensive foundation for further work along with answering some difficult problems raised in early analytical studies. I shall review those experimental results in this section.

A. Sampling Experiments for Zero Restriction Tests

Sampling experiments for zero restriction tests have followed natural stages of development. They have focused primarily on evaluating the accuracy of various proposed critical region approximations. To a lesser extent they have also explored the role of nuisance parameters and guided analytical studies of exact density functions.

Basmann's experiment at Hanford Laboratories begins the first stage of sampling experiments; the basic references are Basmann (1960), Basmann (1958), and Basmann (Chapter 6, this volume). Indeed, this sampling experiment laid the foundation for further study in all three basic areas of sampling experiment use. Here I shall focus primarily on Basmann's results regarding asymptotic approximations to exact critical regions.

Approximations to likelihood ratio and GCL test statistics are justified primarily on one of two grounds. The first is the result that (-2)ln (likelihood ratio) is asymptotically distributed as a chi-squared random variable under conditions met by the likelihood functions relevant to identifiability testing. The second result is that the limiting moments of the test statistics are those of a certain F distribution. Both of these results are tied up with the expectation that they will provide accurate approximations as $\bar{\mu}^2$, the concentration parameter, increases without bound. Basmann's experimental results were used to provide baseline tests of six conjectures founded on these asymptotic considerations.

To be consistent with previous notation in this paper, I shall use

$\hat{\phi}_1$ as the GCL identifiability test statistic,

$\hat{l}$ as the likelihood ratio for the zero restriction test

$\hat{\phi}_{\hat{l}}$ as the likelihood ratio identifiability test statistic

noting that $\hat{\phi}_{\hat{l}} = \lambda_{g+1}$.

Basmann's results were used to test these conjectures:

$$T \ln (1 + \hat{\phi}_{\hat{l}}) \overset{A}{\sim} \chi^2(m - g) \tag{25}$$

$$[(T - K)/m]\, \hat{\phi}_{\hat{l}} \overset{A}{\sim} F(m, T - K) \tag{26}$$

$$[(T - K)/(m - g)]\hat{\phi}_{\hat{l}} \overset{A}{\sim} F(m - g, T - K) \tag{27}$$

$$T \ln (1 + \hat{\phi}_1) \overset{A}{\sim} \chi^2(m - g) \tag{28}$$

$$[(T - K)/m]\, \hat{\phi}_1 \overset{A}{\sim} F(m, T - K) \tag{29}$$

$$[(T - K)/(m - g)]\hat{\phi}_1 \overset{A}{\sim} F(m - g, T - K) \tag{30}$$

where $\overset{A}{\sim}$ denotes "is approximately distributed as."

Design parameters for the experiment are shown in Table 2. Also included there are design parameters for other sampling experiments used to study identifiability test statistics. The values of $\overline{\mu}^2$, ω_1, and ω_2 are certainly large enough to meet the requirements of the conjectures. The results of testing (25)–(30) are as follows. Conjectures (27) and (30) are *not rejected* by the experimental data. The other four conjectures were strongly rejected (see Basmann, 1960 and Chapter 6, this volume). The evidence in this case is sufficient to eliminate (25), (26), (28), and (29) from further consideration. It suggests that (27) and (30) may be reliable in small equation systems with large values of $\overline{\mu}^2$.

In providing this baseline experiment, Basmann also focused attention on a second collection of issues: What constellations of parameters assure that the F distribution will reliably approximate the exact critical region? In so doing, he effectively set the stage for the second phase of sampling experiments.

A second phase of sampling experiments has built upon Basmann's foundation by extending the experimental designs. R. P. Byron (1972, 1974) has used sampling experiments to study Wald tests of zero restrictions. He used both two-equation and three-equation models. Both Wald and GCL tests were included in his experiments; he also studied the power functions. [Byron also included system tests. Discussion of these will appear in Rhodes and Westbrook (1981).] Richardson and Rohr (Chapter 2, this volume) studied the GCL test in a three equation model. They built upon Basmann's foundation by using a full three-equation model

Table 2. Reduced Form Design Parameters for Sampling Experiments.

			Equation 1				Equation 2				Equation 3				Gen Variance		
Experiments	G†	$N-K$‡	ω_1§	ω_2	ω_3	$\bar{\mu}^2$	ω_1	ω_2	ω_3	$\bar{\mu}^2$	ω_1	ω_2	ω_3	$\bar{\mu}^2$	$\lvert\Sigma\rvert$‖	$t_r\Sigma$	*Tests Studied*
Basmann (1960 and ch. 6, this vol.)	3	10	300.17	10.89	0	1,119.02	—	—	—	—					1,480,906.57	772.52	GCL and LR
Richardson-Rohr (ch. 2, this vol.)									0	26,016.00	1693.36	33.43	0	28,306.00	1	3	GCL
									0	1.25	11.76	0.23	0	1.36	1	3	
System A	3	20	1900.53	71.55	0	60,438.00	1562.08	99.93	—	5.64					3.38	16	Wald
System B	3	20	13.20	0.50	0	2.91	10.85	0.69									
Byron (1972)	2	′	1.86	0	—	1.83	99.64	0									GCL and Wald
Byron (1974)									—	6.36					8	7	
Model 1	2	*	19.97	0		6.66	9.536	0	—	4.57					146	61	
Model 2	2	*	2.46	0		2.32	9.857	0	—	3.35	14.57	0	—	11.91	124.68	25	
Model 3	3	*	29.04	0	—	4.25	3.349	0									
Model 1									—	28.82					8	7	
misspecified	2	*	19.97	0		6.66	43.2329	0									
Model 2									—	4.67					146	61	
misspecified	2	*	2.46	0		2.32	10.07	0									
Model 3									—	3.36	15.37	0	—	12.56	124.68	25	
misspecified	3	*	29.77	0		4.36	3.359	0									
Rhodes-Westbrook (this vol.)																	
System A	2	20	18.56	0	—	18.56	14.08	0		0.8125					0.75	2	GCL and LR
System A misspecified	2	20	279.70	0.19		258.56	14.08	0		0.8125					0.75	2	LR
System B	2	20	2.56	0		2.56	291.42	0		16.8125					0.75	2	
System B misspecified	2	20	2.56	0		2.56	29.50	0.59		4.8125					0.75	2	

† G, Number of endogenous variables in system.
‡ $N-K$, Number of observations minus number of exogenous variables.
§ ω_i, Roots of $\mathbf{\Omega}$.
‖ Σ, Reduced form covariance matrix.
* $K = 6$; $T = 30, 60, 100$.
′ $K = 5$; $T = 30, 60$.

(whereas Byron's three-equation system has a maximum g equal to 1) and by using one system with small values for ω_1, ω_2, and $\bar{\mu}^2$. The Rhodes and Westbrook (Chapter 5, this volume) experiment extended Basmann's foundation by including equation systems with both large and small values of $\bar{\mu}^2$ and ω_1 in the same model. Like Byron, we also studied empirical power functions. Like Basmann, we focused on GCL and likelihood ratio tests. The main features of the five experimental designs are included in Table 2.

Study of results from the second phase of experiments solves some open questions. It also raises new issues in concepts and applications of identifiability tests. Results are considered first.

Byron's work on Lagrange multiplier and Wald tests warrants some important conclusions. Wald tests are *not superior* to GCL tests in power or in the accuracy of χ^2 and F tests to the exact distribution functions. Neither are they useful in isolating specific restrictions that lead to failure of identification hypotheses. They are less general, in that they require designation of some parameter relations as just-identifying and some as overidentifying restrictions. On this basis, I conclude that GCL tests dominate Wald tests under the criterion that GCL tests are easier to apply and more general. This conclusion is reversed if the researcher has some good reason to test a specific subset of overidentifying restrictions. Byron's results and the corresponding conclusions hold for two- and three-equation systems.

A second issue is the size of $\bar{\mu}^2$ (and the roots ω_i, $i = 1, \ldots, g$) that justify use of the $F(m - g, T - K)$ approximation for the GCL test statistic. The Richardson-Rohr and Rhodes-Westbrook experimental results strongly reject this approximation for small values of $\bar{\mu}^2$. (Refer to Table 2 to see the magnitudes of $\bar{\mu}^2$ used in these studies.) Byron (1974) uses values of $\bar{\mu}^2$, ω_1, and ω_2 that are approximately intermediate to the small values in Richardson-Rohr and Rhodes-Westbrook, where the approximation is rejected, and to the larger values in Rhodes-Westbrook, where the approximation appears to be acceptable. Empirical power functions in Byron's (1974) report are usually about 1 percent smaller or larger than the corresponding significance levels. On this basis I conjecture that the parameter values in Byron (1974) constitute minimum values where the F approximation to GCL critical regions will be reliable within the bounds of observational accuracy. At the least, these values provide a firm starting point for further study. This information should be considered carefully when designing further sampling experiments.

Investigation of power of the tests was initiated in the second phase of experiments. This is a very difficult issue to treat within current levels of knowledge. It is desirable, of course, to study power functions of exact tests. However, it is not feasible to calculate extensively exact power functions. Some limited power function calculations for the likelihood ratio test are available in Pillai and Dotson (1969). As an alternative, study of power functions would be enhanced by availability of accurate approximations to exact distribution functions. But the reliability of available approximations is still very much in doubt. These facts limit the range of studies available to assess powers of alternative tests.

Two experiments have included studies of power functions, those of Byron (1974) and of Rhodes and Westbrook (Chapter 5, this volume). Each of these studies is limited to study of powers of the approximate tests. That is, they calculate the proportion of sample points in rejection regions defined by asymptotic approximations. The limited accuracy of the asymptotic approximations belies the interpretation of these as studies of exact power. Rather, they are properly understood as testing the accuracy of the approximations as approximations of exact power functions. Data in Rhodes and Westbrook (Chapter 5, this volume) strongly reject the claim that the F statistic closely approximates the power function.

What I conclude about experimental studies of power functions is that very little is known about exact power functions. Certainly we cannot claim superiority for one test based on power function comparisons. Moreover, sampling experiment studies of power functions are not going to provide useful information until more analytical formulas associated with exact power functions are available.

Sampling experiments so far have focused on zero restriction tests. Although considerable progress has been made, it has largely acted to reduce the field of viable alternative tests and properties. The major questions as to which test statistics are best and which approximations are reliable remain open. I am convinced that solutions will come more efficiently through further analytical studies than through sampling experiments.

B. Sampling Experiments for Double Root Tests of Rank Conditions

Basmann has provided results of his Hanford experiment along with permission to use them. Here I have used them to assess the accuracy of the $\chi^2(m - g + 1)$ and $F(m - g + 1, T - K)$ approximations for the double root test. Specifically, data from Basmann's Hanford experiment have been applied to test two empirical conjectures.

$$T \ln(1 + \lambda_{g+1})(1 + \lambda_g) \overset{A}{\sim} \chi^2(m - g + 1) \tag{31}$$

$$[(T - K)/(m - g + 1)]\lambda_g \overset{A}{\sim} F(m - g + 1, T - K) \tag{32}$$

Conjecture (32) was tested both with and without conditioning upon the

Table 3. Comparison of $\chi^2(m - g + 1)$ and $F(m - g + 1, T - K)$ Approximations for Double Root Test with Data from Basmann's Hanford Experiment.*

	Significance Level		
Test Statistic	*10%*	*5%*	*1%*
$\chi^2(2)$	0.975	0.940	0.825
$F(2, 10)$	0.895	0.770	0.480
$F(2, 10)$†	0.887	0.766	0.477

* Refer to Basmann (1960) and Dent and Geweke (1980). Values in the table are proportions of sample test statistics falling within critical regions specified by the approximate tests.

† Proportion of rejections conditioned upon outcome of zero restriction test approximated by $F(1, 10)$.

outcome of the zero restriction test. Results of the calculations are summarized in Table 3.

Data in Table 3 imply strong rejection of both (31) and (32). The rejections hold whether the approximation is conditioned upon outcome of the zero restriction test or not. One must conclude that further research is necessary in order to find reliable methods for testing rank conditions.

C. Sampling Experiments for Normalization Rule Tests

Rhodes (1982) conducted sampling experiments to assess the accuracies of the F and chi-squared approximations for the likelihood ratio test of normalization restrictions. Results reported there indicate that the F approximation is more accurate than the chi-squared approximation. They also indicate that the F approximation will be acceptable for large values of nuisance parameters but not acceptable for smaller values. Details are found in that article.

IV. OPPORTUNITIES FOR FURTHER RESEARCH AND CONTRIBUTIONS

Foundations of research laid by Anderson and Rubin at Cowles and by Basmann at Hanford have served well. What has been built upon those foundations is significant and extensive, as the preceding review shows. However, there is considerable room for both further building as well as for extending the foundations. In this brief section I shall mention some of the opportunities for extending and building that will improve our potential for investigating model form by comparing models with actual observations.

Work has barely begun on deriving exact sampling distribution functions for the test statistics. We do not yet have the exact distributions for the general cases of the GCL or Wald tests of necessary conditions. We do not have the distribution functions for the double root or conditional test statistics for testing the sufficient conditions. One consequence of this lacuna is inability to derive the various important statistical properties of these tests. Nor are we able to choose among the various tests, using their properties as criteria. Although some progress has been made and we are able to see some of the relevant exact distributions, there is much more to be done.

Enough is known about the forms of the exact distributions to say that much work remains to be done in finding accurate approximations for them. It is clear that the F and chi-squared approximations are serviceable for only limited parameter constellations. Phillips' work on Pade and other approximations has not been extended into the arena of test statistics. So far it has been confined to studying distributions of coefficient estimators. The asymptotic conditional approximations proposed and developed by Rhodes are promising. However, there is yet much development and study before these fulfill the promise that appears at the present. The problems of finding approximations that account for sample information, prior information, and nuisance parameters are challenging and essential. Finding such approximations will bring considerable economies in allocating research resources in empirical investigations relying on linear models fit to observations.

All of the extant tests seem to share the lack of sufficiency as a general property. This signals need for extending the foundations of testing model form. How will we design tests that take account of prior information? How will we design tests that allow testing among multiple alternatives? The class of conditional tests proposed by Rhodes, both the conditional root test for sufficient conditions and the asymptotic conditional tests, seems to promise opportunity to explore new methods. These should not be viewed as final answers to the problems that they address. They represent steps in new directions. They may lead to methods for solving the "nuisance parameter problem." What they signal most definitely is the need for more extension of the foundations of statistical testing in multiple variable models. I believe that this represents one of the most significant opportunities for research into economic method available.

All of this development will be enhanced by focus on the basic problems of economics, those of testing economic theories against observations. Indeed, the original draft of this article began with a brief treatment of relations among theories, models, and structures and their implications for testing economic propositions. What became clear was that that topic is so basic, so unexplored, and so large that it must be left for a treatment of its own. But it should be recognized that our understanding of it is minute compared to what is necessary for major steps in economics.

REFERENCES

Anderson, T. W. and H. Rubin (1949). Estimation of the parameters of a single equation in a complete system of stochastic equations, *Ann. Math. Statist. 20,* 46–63.

Anderson, T. W. and H. Rubin (1950). The asymptotic properties of estimates of the parameters in a single equation in a complete system of stochastic equations, *Ann. Math. Statist. 21,* 570–582.

Basmann, R. L. (1957). A generalized classical method of linear estimation of coefficients in a structural equation. *Econometrica 25,* 77–83.

Basmann, R. L. (1958). An experimental investigation of some small-sample properties of (GCL) estimators of structural equations: some preliminary results. Richland, Washington: General Electric Company (mimeo).

Basmann, R. L. (1960). On finite sample distributions of generalized classical linear identifiability test statistics, *JASA 55,* 650–659.

Basmann, R. L. (1965). On the application of the identifiability test statistic in predictive testing of explanatory economic models: Part 1, *Econometric Annual of the Indian Economic Journal 13,* 387–423.

Basmann, R. L. (1966). On the application of the identifiability test statistic in predictive testing of explanatory economic models: Part 2, *Econometric Annual of the Indian Economic Journal 14,* 233–252.

Basmann, R. L. (1968). Hypothesis formulation in quantitative economics: A contribution to demand analysis, *In* J. Quirk and A. Zarley (eds.), *Papers in Quantitative Economics,* Lawrence, KA: University Press of Kansas, p. 338.

Basmann, R. L. (1974). Exact finite sample distributions for some econometric estimators and test statistics: A survey and appraisal, *Frontiers Quant. Econ. 2,* 209–288.

Byron, R. P. (1972). Testing for misspecification in econometric systems using full information, *Int. Econ. Rev. 13,* 745–756.

Byron, R. P. (1974). Testing structural specification using the unrestricted reduced form, *Econometrica 42,* 869–883.

Cox, D. R. and D. V. Hinkley (1979). *Theoretical Statistics,* London: Chapman and Hall.

Dent, W. and J. Geweke (1980). On specification in simultaneous equation models, *In* J. Kmenta and J. B. Ramsey (eds.), *Evaluation of Econometric Models,* New York: Academic Press, pp. 169–196.

Farebrother, R. W. (1974). The graph of a *k*-class estimator, *Rev. Econ. Studies 41,* 533–538.

Farebrother, R. W. and N. E. Savin (1974). The graph of the *k*-class estimator, *J. Econometrics 2,* 373–388.

Hwang, H-S. (1980). A comparison of tests of overidentifying restrictions, *Econometrica 48,* 1821–1825.

Kadane, J. B. (1970). Testing overidentifying restrictions when the disturbances are small, *JASA 65,* 182–185.

Kadane, J. B. (1974). Testing a subset of the overidentifying restrictions, *Econometrica 42,* 853–868.

Kadane, J. B. and T. W. Anderson (1977). A comment on the test of overidentifying restrictions, *Econometrica 45,* 1027–1032.

Kitchen, J. O. (1968). *Extended Tables of Zonal Polynomials,* Institute of Statistics, UNC at Chapel Hill, Mimeo Series No. 565.

Kmenta, J. and J. B. Ramsey (1980). *Evaluation of Econometric Models.* New York: Academic Press.

Koopmans, T. C. and W. C. Hood (1953). The estimation of simultaneous linear economic relationship, *In* W. C. Hood and T. C. Koopmans (eds.), *Studies in Econometric Method,* New York: John Wiley & Sons, pp. 112–199.

Lehmann, E. L. (1959). *Testing Statistical Hypotheses,* New York: John Wiley & Sons.

Malinvaud, E. (1981). Econometrics faced with the needs of macroeconomic policy, *Econometrica 49,* 1363–1375.

Pillai, K. C. S. and C. O. Dotson (1969). Power comparisons of tests of two multivariate hypotheses based on individual characteristic roots, *Ann. Inst. Stat. Math. 21,* 49–66.

Rhodes, G. F., Jr. (1981). Exact density functions and approximate critical regions for likelihood ratio identifiability test statistics, *Econometrica 49,* 1035–1055.

Rhodes, G. F. (1982). A study of the likelihood ratio test for normalizing restrictions. Colorado State University (mimeo).

Rhodes, G. F. and M. D. Westbrook (1981). An experimental investigation of identification and misspecification. Colorado State University Experiment Station, Scientific Series Paper No. 2682.

Richardson, D. H. (1967). On the distribution of the identifiability test statistic, *Research Papers in Theoretical and Applied Economics,* University of Kansas, Paper No. 8. Reprinted in J. P. Quirk and A. M. Zarley (eds.), *Papers in Quantitative Economics,* Lawrence, KA: University Press of Kansas (1968).

Wald, A. (1943). Tests of statistical hypotheses concerning several parameters when the number of observations is large, *Trans. Am. Math. Soc. 54,* 426–482. Reprinted in A. Wald (ed.), *Selected Papers in Statistics and Probability,* Stanford, CA: Stanford University Press (1957), pp. 323–379.

Wegge, L. L. (1978). Constrained indirect least squares estimators, *Econometrica 46,* 435–449.

SIMULTANEOUS EQUATIONS ESTIMATORS, IDENTIFIABILITY TEST STATISTICS, AND STRUCTURAL FORMS

M. Daniel Westbrook and George F. Rhodes, Jr.

I. INTRODUCTION

Economists are favored to face problems in statistical measurement and inference of exceptional interest and challenge. Issues in economic theory and policy are no less challenging or portentous today than they were when Petty, Cournot, Turgot, and other early political economists initiated the use of mathematical and statistical tools in economics.[1] We study systems that, at least apparently, are complex, ever-changing, and delicate. Development of theories and models to explain and predict observed patterns in such systems provides a continual source of intricate conceptual and practical problems in logic, mathematics, and statistics. One especially

Advances in Econometrics, Volume 2, pages 129–196

ISBN: 0-89232-183-0

fruitful source of interesting statistical problems is found in the use of systems of interdependent equations to model economic systems. In the more than three decades since Trygve Haavelmo (1947) demonstrated the application of the indirect least squares (ILS) procedure for estimating the marginal propensity to consume in a simultaneous equations model, increasingly complex models have been constructed in an effort to capture and reveal the relationships embodied in the structures of actual economic systems. Increasingly complex statistical techniques for estimating the parameters of such systems have evolved concurrently.

Among the statistical problems that arise in implementing simultaneous equations models, two of particular interest are selection of functional form and choice of estimation technique. These issues are symbiotic, at least by current knowledge. Often the choice of estimator is conditional upon model form; and although tests of functional form are logically prior to estimation, test statistics are based on estimates of the model to be tested. Statistical treatment of these problems presents formidable conceptual and technical puzzles. As the problems themselves are multifaceted, so are the solutions: there are many research approaches to illuminating these puzzles and to discovering their solutions.

One such approach is the *sampling experiment*. The sampling experiment reported in this article is intended as a baseline sampling experiment that provides a foundation for continuing research into issues of functional form and estimator selection in systems of linear simultaneous equations. Since testing functional form is logically prior to problems of choosing estimation techniques, those issues are treated first in our exposition. Our attention is restricted to tests of hypotheses that exclude specified variables from particular equations in systems of linear structural equations, thus contributing to the *identification* of those equations.

Following treatment of identifiability tests, results regarding four prominent estimation techniques are presented. The four estimation techniques treated are two-stage least squares (2SLS), three-stage least squares (3SLS), limited-information maximum likelihood (LIML), and full-information maximum likelihood (FIML).

A. Model Selection and Misspecification

Does a proffered model adequately represent the economic system to be explained and economic events to be adequately predicted?

We focus on a particular aspect of this question by considering the relationship between structural and reduced form simultaneous equations models. Explication of that relationship reveals the relevance of testing the exclusion restrictions that are imposed upon any structural economic model.

Given the maintained hypothesis that a specified set of exogenous variables determines a specified set of jointly determined endogenous variables, a system of simultaneous linear equations in those variables may be proffered as a mathematical representation of the structure of an economic system. The whole collection of variables, the endogenous/exogenous dichotomy, and the selection of variables appearing in each individual equation are each conjectured by economic theory. The mathematical representation thus constructed constitutes a structural economic hypothesis, and it is, in principle, empirically testable. The particular tests that interest us in this article are tests of exclusion restrictions imposed a priori for the purpose of identifying individual equations and the system as a whole. These exclusion restrictions constitute the identifiability hypothesis, and testing the identifiability hypothesis is logically prior to any estimation or predictive use of a model.

The identifiability hypothesis is not often tested in practice, despite admonitions delivered by R. L. Basmann (1965), Dent and Geweke (1980), Farebrother and Savin (1974), T. C. Liu (1960), and Christopher Sims (1980). Rather, the validity of the exclusion restrictions is averred by appeals to "reasonableness," or they are introduced as "assumptions." Apparently, this neglect is partly occasioned by the fact that statistical procedures for testing identifiability are not sufficiently well developed for general application. We hope that the results reported here and in the article by George Rhodes (this volume, page 97) will help to remedy that situation. In Section V of this article, we examine the exact finite-sample properties and relative performances of three alternative identifiability test statistics: two apply to single equations; one tests the identification of the entire structure. Each test statistic was exposed to a variety of true identifiability configurations and to identifiability configurations that were deliberately misspecified.

Having now introduced the term *misspecification,* we would like to explain the manner in which that term and its companion, *correct specification,* are used in this article. In standard economic parlance *specification* and *misspecification* are *existential* terms and the notions that they represent are not open to empirical falsification under the usual rules of scientific inquiry. In the context of a properly designed sampling experiment, however, the terms do represent specific features of the experimental design. In this experiment the question of proper specification refers *only* to the propriety of the exclusion restrictions employed when the models are estimated. The question is whether or not the same exclusion restrictions are imposed for estimation as were employed in the generation of the data.

As Arnold Zellner (1979) has noted, "Not much analysis is available on the sensitivity of alternative asymptotically justified estimates to various kinds of specification error.'' It is difficult to interpret the effects of specification error in previously reported sampling experiments because it is rarely clear whether a particular kind of misspecification has actually been isolated. For our examination of identifiability test statistics, we have isolated one particular kind of misspecification, and we have studied the effects of that kind of misspecification on the exact finite-sample properties of alternative simultaneous equations estimators as well.

The particular misspecification that we have included in our experiment is the specification error that arises in a simultaneous equations model when, as part of the identifiability hypothesis, some of the exogenous variables are incorrectly excluded from an equation in the model. Hale, Mariano, and Ramage (1980) have studied the effects of this type of misspecification on the exact sampling distributions of the *k*-class estimators for a single equation in a simultaneous equations model, including in their studies the LIML and instrumental variable (IV) estimators. Their analysis proceeds from a statement of asymptotic expressions for the bias and mean-square errors (MSE) of the estimators, where the appropriate moments are defined. Their results suggest that in respect of asymptotic MSE the entire *k*-class (including LIML and IV) is dominated by either OLS or 2SLS when misspecification is a serious possibility. They further conjecture that OLS may be preferable to 2SLS under some circumstances.

Rhodes and Westbrook (1981) derived the exact density functions of the OLS and 2SLS estimators when exogenous variables are wrongly excluded from the equation being estimated, where two endogenous variables appear in the equation of interest. Our primary result was that under misspecification OLS may indeed be the superior estimation technique. In addition, we found that misspecification can actually improve estimator performance by reducing both bias and variance. In the present article, we extend the investigation of the effects of misspecification to include LIML, FIML, and 3SLS. Our investigation is also distinct from the analytical investigation of Hale, Mariano, and Ramage (1980) in that we examine the location and dispersion of the estimators' exact finite-sample distribution functions where the measures of ''bias'' and ''variance'' are not defined. This includes all applications of LIML and FIML.

B. The Choice among Estimators

Which of the alternative estimators is best under any particular set of circumstances?

Answers to this question must be based on what is known about the sampling distributions of the alternative estimators; in particular, we compare them with respect to criteria such as bias, dispersion, and mean squared error. Computational complexity and expense has received diminished attention in the selection process because of the extensive availability of computing capability.

So far the evidence bearing on the sampling behavior of the estimators has been primarily a reflection of a pair of dichotomies by which the estimators may be classified. First, we note that the four estimators mentioned may be classified as either general classical linear (GCL) estimators or maximum-likelihood (ML) estimators. Maximum-likelihood estimators are often recommended since in many situations, and under fairly common assumptions, the ML estimators possess optimal asymptotic properties. An alternative classification scheme divides the four estimators into two classes according to whether they estimate separately the parameters of each individual equation or estimate simultaneously all parameters of all equations. The single-equation techniques are 2SLS and LIML; the full-system techniques are 3SLS and FIML. The full-system techniques are often recommended because they employ more of the information imposed upon the equation system than do the single-equation techniques and because they are asymptotically more efficient.

Examination of the asymptotic distributions of the alternative estimators was a natural first step in cataloging their properties and in assigning their relative rankings. In practice, however, econometricians are constrained to use finite (usually small) samples, and asymptotic properties may not constitute evidence relevant to the behavior of the exact sampling distributions of the estimators. As a consequence, asymptotic properties may be weak or misleading choice criteria. Definitive comparison of the estimators requires characterization of the properties of the relevant exact distribution functions themselves. Unfortunately, the exact finite-sample distribution functions of the simultaneous equations estimators are not as readily accessible as their asymptotic distributions were. (The exact finite-sample distribution literature is reviewed in the next section.)

Indeed, the difficulties involved in deriving exact finite-sample distribution functions have encouraged reliance on the properties of the asymptotic distributions in ranking the competing estimators, tacitly conferring the asymptotic properties upon the finite-sample distributions. But the extent to which the small-sample behavior of the estimators is reflected in their asymptotic properties is almost entirely unknown. Indeed, among the earlier finite-sample results was the assessment by Basmann (1960) that the asymptotic properties are not always maintained by the exact finite-sample distributions of the GCL estimators. It is also true that for finite samples, asymptotically equivalent estimators can yield quite different point estimates. Arnold Zellner (1979) suggests that "this may be interpreted as indicating that the asymptotic properties of different estimates take hold at different sample sizes, or, more likely, that specification errors are present and affect alternative estimates differently." This is a crucial distinction, and it is not clear that previous sampling experiments have accounted for it. In this article we focus specifically on the exact finite-sample properties of the estimators in the absence of misspecification of any kind. We then extend the results by introducing misspecification of a specific well-defined nature that is, as our good fortune would have it, intimately associated with the question of model selection.

C. Sampling Experiment Methodology

In light of the formidable difficulties encountered in the analytical characterization of the small-sample properties of the alternative estimators, considerations of research economy have redirected our efforts—from an analytical approach to an experimental approach. The essence of sampling experimentation is that each estimation technique is applied in turn to a completely specified model for a number of replications. Information about the relative performances of the competing estimators is contained in the empirical sampling distributions of the estimates and test statistics thus generated. Taking the empirical distributions as approximations to the exact finite-sample distributions, we may judge (for example) how well they may be approximated by some well-known function, and we may formulate answers to questions concerning some aspects of estimator performance: e.g., which estimator is most frequently close to the "true" parameter value or which test statistics provide the best performances. Of course, our evidence is conditional upon the particular model used in the investigation.

Literally hundreds of sampling experiments have been reported, delving into many aspects of econometric estimation and inference. Still, several important aspects have not yet been explored. Unfortunately, the accumulated evidence, applied to the basic question of choosing among 2SLS, LIML, 3SLS, and FIML, is incomplete and often contradictory; the same is true of experiments concerned with identification testing. The reason that this is the case is stated in the last sentence of the previous paragraph: our evidence is conditional upon the particular model used in the investigation. Let us expand upon this.

When an analytical exploration of the distribution of an estimator is undertaken, its properties are first elucidated under some convenient "classical" assumptions. Subsequently, complicating factors—violations of the classical assumptions—are introduced and their separate effects deduced. Finally, the joint effects of two or more violations might be analyzed. The evolution of sampling experiment design has not been so orderly. Many experimenters strive for "realism" by using actual economic data and models with the attendant data problems, potential misspecifications, computational difficulties, and so on; inconclusive and contradictory results are "explained" by reference to those problems. Add this to the fact that interpretation of results across experimental models is difficult and it is transparent why systematic evidence for evaluating the merits of four simultaneous equations estimators or three identifiability tests has not been established. Nowhere do we find an experiment that serves as a classical reference point.

The analytical and experimental approaches should be complementary. It is surprising to find that they have not been combined more frequently, with sampling experiments designed to take full advantage of known analytical results. The sampling experiment described here has been carefully designed with this consideration in mind. It should provide a "classical" reference point for subsequent studies.

In particular, the analytical results cited in Section II reveal that the properties of the exact finite-sample density functions of the 2SLS coefficient estimators and GCL identifiability test statistic are determined by the elements of a means-sigma matrix (Section II,C) in both the correctly specified and misspecified cases. Thus, reporting these parameters for various sampling experiments should lead to more fruitful cross-experiment comparisons. They also provide a clear basis for experimental design. Although it has not been demonstrated that the elements of the means-sigma matrix are fundamental determinants of the finite-sample behaviors of the 3SLS, LIML, and FIML estimators, we conjecture in Section II that this is the case.

The plan of this article is as follows: in Section II we draw upon the known analytical exact finite-sample results to form conjectures about the behavior of the estimators and test statistics of interest. We also turn to those analytical results for inspiration in creating a sampling experiment designed to test those conjectures and to illuminate other open questions. The experimental design is presented in Section III. We present the sampling experiment results for estimators of the fundamental parameters of the 2SLS estimators, the identifiability test statistics, and the endogenous variable coefficient estimators in Sections IV, V, and VI, respectively. We conclude with some remarks on future work in Section VII.

II. INSPIRATION AND CONJECTURES

Analytical results concerning the exact finite-sample distribution of the 2SLS endogenous-variable-coefficient estimator serve as our primary source of inspiration for the experimental design. Exact results on the existence of moments of the alternative estimators lead to specific conjectures concerning their behavior relative to 2SLS. In addition, exact results on some of the identifiability test statistics help us generate conjectures about their range of behavior. The experimental design incorporates features that make tests of the conjectures possible.

A. The Equation Systems

The equation systems used in this experiment are particular examples of systems of the following general form.

Let

$$\boldsymbol{\beta}_{\Delta}\mathbf{y}_{\Delta t} + \boldsymbol{\beta}_{\Delta\Delta}\mathbf{y}_{\Delta\Delta t} + \boldsymbol{\gamma}_{*}\mathbf{z}_{*t} + \boldsymbol{\gamma}_{**}\mathbf{z}_{**t} = \mathbf{u}_{1t} \qquad t = 1, \ldots, T \tag{1}$$

be the first equation in a system of G (≥ 2) structural equations, where the following definitions obtain:

$\mathbf{y}_{\Delta t}(G_{\Delta} \times 1)$ and $\mathbf{y}_{\Delta\Delta t}(G_{\Delta\Delta} \times 1)$ are vectors of observations on endogenous variables

$\mathbf{z}_{*t}(K_{*} \times 1)$ and $\mathbf{z}_{**t}(K_{**} \times 1)$ are vectors of observations on exogenous variables

$\boldsymbol{\beta}'_{\Delta}(G_{\Delta} \times 1)$ and $\boldsymbol{\beta}'_{\Delta\Delta}(G_{\Delta\Delta} \times 1)$ are coefficient vectors

$\boldsymbol{\gamma}'_{*}(K_{*} \times 1)$ and $\boldsymbol{\gamma}'_{**}(K_{**} \times 1)$ are coefficient vectors

$$G = G_{\Delta} + G_{\Delta\Delta}$$
$$K = K_{*} + K_{**}.$$

We define $\mathbf{u}_{1t}$ as an unobservable random deviate assumed to have a $\mathrm{N}(\mathbf{0}, \sigma^2)$ distribution.

The reduced form corresponding to (1) is

$$\underset{}{\mathbf{y}'_{\Delta t}} = \underset{(K_{*} \times G_{\Delta})}{\mathbf{z}'_{*t}\boldsymbol{\Pi}'_{\Delta *}} + \underset{(K_{**} \times G_{\Delta})}{\mathbf{z}'_{**t}\boldsymbol{\Pi}'_{\Delta **}} + \mathbf{V}_{\Delta t} \qquad t = 1, \ldots, T \tag{2a}$$

$$\mathbf{y}'_{\Delta\Delta t} = \underset{(K_{*} \times G_{\Delta\Delta})}{\mathbf{z}'_{*t}\boldsymbol{\Pi}'_{\Delta\Delta *}} + \underset{(K_{**} \times G_{\Delta\Delta})}{\mathbf{z}'_{**t}\boldsymbol{\Pi}'_{\Delta\Delta **}} + \mathbf{V}_{\Delta\Delta t} \tag{2b}$$

where

$$\mathbf{V}_{\Delta t} \sim \mathrm{N}_{G_{\Delta}}(\mathbf{0}, \boldsymbol{\Sigma}), \tag{3}$$

and dimensions of reduced form coefficient matrices are shown in parentheses.

Because questions of functional form are logically prior to questions of estimation, we discuss identifiability tests next; the discussion of the endogenous-variable-coefficient estimators follows in Section II,C.

B. The Identifiability Test Statistics

We are interested in testing the overidentifying restrictions

$$H_0\colon \boldsymbol{\gamma}_{**} = \mathbf{0} \tag{4}$$

against the complement of H_0. The restrictions (4) are called the identifiability hypothesis. If $K_{**} \leqslant G_\Delta - 1$, then Equation (1) is either under- or just-identified and no test of (4) is known. On the other hand, (4) together with $K_{**} > G_\Delta - 1$ suggests that (1) is overidentified.

Strategies for testing the identifiability hypothesis may be dichotomized according to whether they proceed from the structure directly or from the reduced form. Testing may be done in either context because the structure and reduced form are logically equivalent: restrictions placed upon the structural parameters impose restrictions upon the elements of the matrices of reduced form parameters. Identifiability tests (ID tests) also differ, as they apply to the entire structural system or engage but single equations. Note that we must confine our attention to tests of the overidentifying restrictions: the just-identifying restrictions are preserved as part of the maintained hypothesis.

Basmann (1965, 1966) exemplified a procedure for constructing exact tests of the individual deduced restrictions on the reduced form parameters. His procedure is rigorous and elegant and has the advantage of focusing on individual identifiability relations, which may be useful for diagnostic purposes. Furthermore, because Basmann's tests are exact, we conjecture that they will be powerful for detecting false null hypotheses. However, Basmann's procedure has not found much application, apparently because deduction of the appropriate identifiability relations and exact test statistics is quite challenging, even for small models. Byron (1974) takes a different approach to testing via the reduced form and has constructed a Wald test that may be applied to individual equations or to the entire system. This test is asymptotically equivalent to the corresponding likelihood ratio test under the null hypothesis (cf. Anderson and Rubin, 1949), and the approximate critical region is asymptotically justified. Sampling experiments conducted by Byron show that this test does not perform well under H_0 for small samples but that it does display evidence of more power for rejecting incorrect restrictions than alternative tests. Furthermore, Byron's system tests seem to detect incorrect restrictions, even in a single equation, better than the single-equation tests. Rhodes (1981a) presents exact distributions and approximate critical regions for yet a third approach: testing the normalizing restrictions imposed to assure that the joint collection of identifying and normalizing restrictions are valid.

Tests proceeding directly from the structural form are based on likelihood ratio tests or on tests whether the exclusion restrictions impose significant costs in terms of increased sums of squared residuals. The structural form ID test statistics that have been proposed developed concomitantly with simultaneous equations estimation techniques. The first was proposed by Anderson and Rubin (1949) in conjunction with their derivation of the LIML estimation technique. A second test, proposed by Basmann (1960), is based on the 2SLS estimators.

Although considerable effort has been applied to the development of single-equation tests of overidentifying restrictions, two considerations argue for application of system-wide tests. First, system-wide estimation techniques seem to be sensitive to incorrect identifiability restrictions (cf. Cragg, 1968). We therefore expect that a test statistic based on FIML will be powerful for distinguishing between correct and incorrect identifiability hypotheses. A more fundamental consideration is presented by Byron (1974) and deals with the inherent disadvantage of testing complex hypotheses via separate tests on subset hypotheses. He argues that separate tests of subset hypotheses may conclude a poor test of the joint hypothesis unless the subset hypotheses are independent. We do not normally expect our identifying restrictions to be independent across equations. The full-system test statistic that we plan to evaluate is one based on FIML that was suggested by Hendry (1971).

Despite their importance, implementation of the ID tests has not been widely undertaken because the properties of the sampling distributions of the test statistics remain largely unknown. A paper by George Rhodes (1981b) has established the functional form of the LIML ID test statistic for the most general case (any number of included endogenous variables), but the distribution of the GCL ID test statistic has been derived only for the two included endogenous variables case by Richardson (1968a). The exact distribution function of the FIML ID test has not been derived. Even where the distribution functions are known, they have not been tabulated because the functional forms are quite complicated. In view of these difficulties, approximate critical regions have been proposed based upon the asymptotic properties of the test statistics.

The reliability of the approximations and relative reliability of the alternative tests has been evaluated only in very limited circumstances. As noted earlier, Byron (1974) conducted sampling experiments to assess the performances of his test statistic with mixed results: his statistic did not perform uniformly well for small samples and it was not powerful for detecting a false null hypothesis. The GCL and LIML ID test statistics have been compared against each other in limited respects by Basmann (1960), using approximate critical regions based on asymptotic distributions, and the GCL ID test statistic seems to be the more reliable statistic in the cases investigated. Basmann (this volume, page 197) also compared experimentally the exact finite-sample distribution functions of the GCL and LIML ID test statistics against the same approximate distribution function (Snedecor's F) that we use, and he found good agreement in both cases, though the GCL statistic did better. We find that the close approximations are not entirely general and are apparently due to "a subtle specialization inherent in the choice of the parameters . . . and in the selection of the fixed variates'' (Basmann, this volume; cf. Section V,A, this article). The performance of the FIML ID test statistic has never been assessed. The analytical aspects of the three identifiability test statistics considered here are presented in Appendix A.

The exact finite-sample results for the identifiability test statistics that have been extracted by Rhodes (1981a, b) and Richardson (1968a) record the number of moments defined by the ID test statistics based on LIML and 2SLS, respectively. The LIML statistic defines $G_\Delta(T - K)/2$ moments whereas the 2SLS statistic defines moments up to $(T - K)/2$. We therefore proffer

CONJECTURE 1: *Because the LIML ID test statistic defines G_Δ as many moments as the 2SLS ID test statistic defines, we expect the distribution of the LIML ID test statistic to be the more concentrated of the two and to therefore be more closely approximated by its asymptotic distribution under the null hypothesis.*

Preliminary work has indicated that the 2SLS and LIML ID test statistics are not very powerful for rejecting the identification hypothesis when it is false. However, in Cragg's (1968) experiment, FIML estimation was not robust under incorrect identifiability restrictions. This leads us to form

CONJECTURE 2: *The ID test statistic based on FIML will be powerful for distinguishing between correct and incorrect identifiability hypotheses.*

C. The Endogenous-Variable Coefficient Estimators

It is well-known that 3SLS and FIML have asymptotically normal distributions with smaller asymptotic covariance matrices than the asymptotic normal distributions of 2SLS and LIML, respectively, under classical assumptions. Furthermore, on the basis of their asymptotic distributions, 2SLS is not distinguished from LIML, and 3SLS is equivalent to FIML. However, it is a different story with the respective *exact finite-sample distributions.*

Derivation of the exact finite-sample distribution function of the 2SLS estimator of endogenous-variable coefficients, hereafter called β-coefficients, in an equation containing arbitrary numbers of both endogenous and exogenous variables has been accomplished by Phillips (1980). This work continues generalization of the previous results reported by Basmann (1961, 1963), Richardson (1968b), and others. Derivation of the exact finite-sample distribution function has also been accomplished for the LIML estimator of the endogenous variable coefficient in a simple simultaneous equation model by Mariano and Sawa (1972). These distribution functions are very complex, and the elucidation of the actual behavior of the distributions is difficult. Furthermore, such derivations have not been accomplished at all for the full-system estimators, though some results have been deduced concerning the existence of their moments. Phillips (1980) has confirmed Basmann's (1961, 1963) conjecture that the exact finite-sample distributions for the 2SLS estimators of the β-coefficients define moments only up to the number of overidentifying restrictions on the equation of interest, whereas Mariano and Sawa (1972) showed that the exact finite-sample distribution function for the LIML estimator of the β-coefficient in an equation containing two endogenous variables has no moments of any integer order. These results suggest that the distributional properties of LIML and 2SLS are distinct in the finite-sample context: they suggest that 2SLS will be more "efficient" than LIML in the sense of being less dispersed.

No expressions for the exact distributions of 3SLS or FIML have yet been adduced; the mathematics involved present formidable difficulties. Sargan (1970) has, however, been able to demonstrate that FIML has no moments of integer order where LIML has none, which is to say that FIML has no moments at all. Sargan (1978) has also shown that, as with the 2SLS estimator, the moments of the 3SLS structural β-coefficient estimator exist only up to the degree of overidentification of the equation of interest. We thus find that 3SLS and FIML are distinct in respect of their finite-sample distributions, and we conjecture that 3SLS will be the more "efficient" of the two because it has more moments in any overidentified equation. But none of these results suggests anything about the relative "efficiencies" of 2SLS versus 3SLS or LIML versus FIML.

Note that we have enclosed the words *efficient* and *efficiencies* in quotation marks. This is to remind the reader that care must be exercised in applying the notions of asymptotic expectation, variance, and efficiency of simultaneous equations estimators in a finite-sample context. These terms are defined by moments of the distributions, and as we have just seen, the moments often do not exist for finite samples.

The standardized density functions of the 2SLS estimator presented by Richardson (1978b) for the correct equation specification and by Rhodes and Westbrook (1981) for the misspecified case in an equation containing only two endogenous variables show most perspicuously the dependence of the finite-sample behavior of reduced form and structural estimates on the population parameters that characterize the location, dispersion, and shapes of their exact finite-sample distributions. Although these derivations pertain directly to the case of equations containing only two endogenous variables, the work by Phillips (1980), Richardson and Rohr (this volume), and Sargan (1976, 1978) suggests that the results for the simple case do generalize to the more complex cases.

In the simple case, the degrees of freedom (ν) are equal to the number of excluded exogenous variables; once a model is specified, this takes on a particular value and the density function is determined by location ($\boldsymbol{\beta}$) and dispersion ($\boldsymbol{\Omega}$) matrices. The elements of $\boldsymbol{\Omega}$ embody the effects of misspecification where that is the case, but in the correctly specified case the elements of $\boldsymbol{\Omega}$ are simple functions of $\boldsymbol{\beta}$ and the multivariate generalization of the coefficient of variation, often called the concentration parameter (μ^2 in Richardson's notation). We will adopt Richardson's notation in discussing the correctly specified case and will refer explicitly to Ω when referring to misspecification.

Though we do not discuss the multicollinearity problem in this article, we would like to point out that Mariano, McDonald, and Tishler (1981) have shown the manner in which the effects of multicollinearity on the sampling distribution of the β-coefficient estimator are transmitted—solely through the concentration parameter, which may either be increased or decreased by multicollinearity. These authors cite a conjecture made by Klein and Nakamura (1962) that the order of increasing sensitivity to multicollinearity is OLS, 2SLS, and LIML. We are able to provide some mixed evidence bearing on that conjecture (cf. Section VI,A).

Similar parameters determine the LIML estimator density function given by Mariano and Sawa (1972). We note that the *concentration parameter* is so named because the exact finite-sample distributions of the 2SLS and LIML β-estimators share the property that as the concentration parameter becomes indefinitely large their distributions tend toward the normal distribution.

Since the finite-sample densities of the coefficient estimators that are known depend only on three fundamental parameters in the correctly specified case, we have focused our design on those three factors: the true parameter value, the concentration parameter, and the degree of overidentification. The roles of the three parameters in the known exact finite-sample density functions inspire some specific conjectures about the behavior of the estimators; presentation of the conjectures at this point adumbrates several features of the experimental design detailed in the following section.

The nature of the concentration parameter leads us to

CONJECTURE 3: *The performance of all estimators should be better for equations associated with large concentration parameters, all other things equal, where the equation system is correctly specified.*

Conventional wisdom suggests that the full-system estimators will have smaller dispersions than the single-equation estimators because the former have smaller asymptotic variances. As an alternative we present

CONJECTURE 4: *Because the GCL estimators always define at least as many moments as the ML estimators, we expect the GCL estimators to be less dispersed than the ML estimators.*

Exact results show that the maximum number of integer moments defined by the 2SLS and 3SLS estimators are one less than the number of exclusion restrictions. This yields

CONJECTURE 5: *All other things equal, the finite-sample distributions of the GCL coefficient estimators become more concentrated as the number of degrees of freedom increases. This effect is less pronounced for the ML estimators because they define no integer moments.*

We offer no conjectures concerning the influences of $\boldsymbol{\beta}$; we hope to determine whether variations in this parameter distinguish the alternative estimators in any way, thereby laying the foundation for further conjectures and research.

Having presented our five conjectures, we now describe the experimental design that allows us to accomplish tests of the conjectures.

III. DESIGN OF THE SAMPLING EXPERIMENT

This experiment was designed as a "baseline" investigation in which the data and equation systems accord with the classical assumptions. Under the classical assumptions, the test statistics should exhibit their "best" behavior and we should be able to study the intrinsic differences among them, unencumbered by common data and specification problems. Furthermore, some special design features were imposed to ensure a high degree of computational accuracy.

Two separate systems of experimental equations, with different exclusion restrictions imposed on the exogenous variables, were used to generate results under a variety of identifiability configurations. In addition, a variant of the experiment was conducted in which both systems were deliberately misspecified by the imposition of false identifying restrictions, so that we might assess the power of the identifiability tests for detecting a false null hypothesis. Equation systems A and B, their reduced forms, and design parameters are presented in Table 1.

Throughout the article we refer to equation systems A and B and to their component equations: A1, A2, B1, and B2, respectively. Assumptions defining the data matrices and disturbances are common to both systems:

1. The random elements of $\mathbf{v}_1$ and $\mathbf{v}_2$ are normally distributed with covariance structure shown in Table 1.
2. Variables are measured in deviation form.
3. $\mathbf{Z}'\mathbf{Z} = \mathbf{I}_4$, where $\mathbf{Z} = [\mathbf{z}_1\mathbf{z}_2\mathbf{z}_3\mathbf{z}_4]$. The values used in Z were selected to facilitate construction of $\mathbf{Z}'\mathbf{Z} = \mathbf{I}$. This feature enhances the computational accuracy of the estimation routines.
4. $T = 24$.
5. 1000 independent replications were performed for each system under each specification.

The parameter spaces defined in Table 1 were selected to provide standardized concentration parameters and identifiability configurations with certain characteristics. Two of the μ^2 values are small and two are large. For the small values of μ^2 we expect the asymptotic approximations to be least accurate and the differences among the estimators to be most pronounced. Equation system A, with both equations overidentified by one, should isolate the effect of differences in concentration parameters, whereas system B, by comparison with system A, should serve to indicate the effect of the order of identification.

The exogenous variables of both systems of equations are given in accordance with the third assumption above. The sample matrix $\mathbf{Z}$ is:

$$\mathbf{Z} = \left(1/\sqrt{24}\right)\begin{bmatrix}1\\1\\1\end{bmatrix} \otimes \begin{bmatrix} 1 & 1 & \sqrt{2} & 0 \\ -1 & 1 & 0 & \sqrt{2} \\ 1 & 1 & -\sqrt{2} & 0 \\ -1 & 1 & 0 & -\sqrt{2} \\ 1 & -1 & \sqrt{2} & 0 \\ -1 & -1 & 0 & \sqrt{2} \\ 1 & -1 & -\sqrt{2} & 0 \\ -1 & -1 & 0 & -\sqrt{2} \end{bmatrix} \tag{5}$$

The samples of endogenous variables for systems A and B were generated in two steps:

Table 1. Sampling Experiment Design: Correct Specification.

System A		System B
	STRUCTURAL FORM	
$-\mathbf{y}_{1t} + 0.5\mathbf{y}_{2t} - 0.5\mathbf{z}_{1t} + 0.75\mathbf{z}_{2t} = \mathbf{u}_{1t}$		$-\mathbf{y}_{1t} + 0.5\mathbf{y}_{2t} - 0.5\mathbf{z}_{1t} + 0.75\mathbf{z}_{2t} - 4.0\mathbf{z}_{3t} = \mathbf{u}_{1t}$
$4.0\mathbf{y}_{1t} - \mathbf{y}_{2t} - 4.0\mathbf{z}_{3t} + 1.6\mathbf{z}_{4t} = \mathbf{u}_{2t}$		$4.0\mathbf{y}_{1t} - \mathbf{y}_{2t} + 1.6\mathbf{z}_{4t} = \mathbf{u}_{2t}$
	REDUCED FORM	
$\mathbf{y}_{1t} + 0.5\mathbf{z}_{1t} - 0.75\mathbf{z}_{2t} + 2.0\mathbf{z}_{3t} - 0.8\mathbf{z}_{4t} = \mathbf{v}_{1t}$		$\mathbf{y}_{1t} + 0.5\mathbf{z}_{1t} - 0.75\mathbf{z}_{2t} + 4.0\mathbf{z}_{3t} - 0.8\mathbf{z}_{4t} = \mathbf{v}_{1t}$
$\mathbf{y}_{2t} + 2.0\mathbf{z}_{1t} - 3.0\mathbf{z}_{2t} + 4.0\mathbf{z}_{3t} - 1.6\mathbf{z}_{4t} = \mathbf{v}_{2t}$		$\mathbf{y}_{2t} + 2.0\mathbf{z}_{1t} - 3.0\mathbf{z}_{2t} + 16\mathbf{z}_{3t} - 1.6\mathbf{z}_{4t} = \mathbf{v}_{2t}$
	COVARIANCE STRUCTURE	
$E[\mathbf{v}_{1t}\mathbf{v}'_{2t}] = \boldsymbol{\Sigma} = \begin{bmatrix} 1.0 & 0.5 \\ 0.5 & 1.0 \end{bmatrix}$		$E[\mathbf{u}_{1t}\mathbf{u}'_{2t}] = \boldsymbol{\beta\Sigma\beta}' = \begin{bmatrix} 0.75 & -3.0 \\ -3.0 & 13.0 \end{bmatrix}$
	IDENTIFICATION STATUS	
Equation 1: overidentified by one		Equation 1: just-identified
Equation 2: overidentified by one		Equation 2: overidentified by two
	STANDARDIZED CONCENTRATION PARAMETERS	
$\mu_1^2 = \pi_{23}^2 + \pi_{24}^2 = 18.56$		$\mu_1^2 = \pi_{24}^2 = 2.56$
$\mu_2^2 = \pi_{11}^2 + \pi_{12}^2 = 0.8125$		$\mu_2^2 = \pi_{11}^2 + \pi_{12}^2 + \pi_{13}^2 = 16.8125$

1. For each system, a standard random number generator was used to generate a sample of 48,000 uniform random variables, which were transformed to bivariate normal random variates η_1 and η_2 satisfying Assumption (1).
2. The sample endogenous variables were then obtained by computing

$$\begin{bmatrix} \mathbf{Y}_{1t} \\ \mathbf{Y}_{2t} \end{bmatrix} = \mathbf{Z}'\mathbf{\Pi} + \eta_{it} \qquad i = 1, 2 \tag{6}$$

for each of the 24,000 sample points in each system of equations.

The Kolmogorov-Smirnov test was conducted on each sample to test their supposed normality: in both cases the null hypothesis was confirmed.

As a check on the accuracy of the computational routines and the experimental design, all programs were executed on the ''pure'' or non-randomized data. The results were good: all routines estimated the ''true'' parameters correctly to at least five decimal places.

The particular misspecification introduced into our models is of special interest to the practicing econometrician and is related to the identifiability hypothesis. We studied the wrongful inclusion in an equation of an exogenous variable that should be excluded from that equation, and the converse, the wrongful exclusion from an equation of an exogenous variable that should be included in the equation. This was accomplished by performing the estimation of equation system A using the data for system B, and vice versa. Thus, system A (misspecified) has variable $\mathbf{z}_3$ wrongly excluded from Equation A1 and wrongly included in Equation A2. Similarly, for system B (misspecified) variable $\mathbf{z}_3$ is wrongly included in Equation B1 but wrongly excluded from equation B2. Because the appearance of the variable $\mathbf{z}_3$ in the two-equation model is known to be correct, the questionable aspect concerns which of the two equations properly includes $\mathbf{z}_3$. Thus, our concern is closely linked with the identifiability hypothesis. The experimental design under misspecification is shown in Table 2.

Interpretation of the population parameters and degrees of overidentification in the context of misspecification may at first seem confounding. The *forms* of the population parameters are established by the specification under the (incorrect) null hypothesis; the *values* are obtained by insertion of the values of the reduced form parameters from the maintained hypothesis. Similarly, the degree of overidentification is established by the specification under the null hypothesis.

Reports of sampling experiments usually display only the structural equations and their covariance structures. Often the reduced form is neglected, and discussion of the degrees of freedom and concentration parameters is almost always neglected. We have already noted, however,

Table 2. Sampling Experiment Design: Misspecification.

System A	*System B*
STRUCTURAL FORM	
$-\mathbf{y}_{1t} + 0.5\mathbf{y}_{2t} - 0.5\mathbf{z}_{1t} + 0.75\mathbf{z}_{2t} = \mathbf{u}_{1t}$	$-\mathbf{y}_{1t} + 0.5\mathbf{y}_{2t} - 0.5\mathbf{z}_{1t} + 0.75\mathbf{z}_{2t} - 4.0\mathbf{z}_{3t} = \mathbf{u}_{1t}$
$4.0\mathbf{y}_{1t} - \mathbf{y}_{2t} - 4.0\mathbf{z}_{3t} + 1.6\mathbf{z}_{4t} = \mathbf{u}_{2t}$	$4.0\mathbf{y}_{1t} - \mathbf{y}_{2t} + 1.6\mathbf{z}_{4t} = \mathbf{u}_{2t}$
REDUCED FORM (from system B)	REDUCED FORM (from system A)
$\mathbf{y}_{1t} + 0.5\mathbf{z}_{1t} - 0.75\mathbf{z}_{2t} + 4.0\mathbf{z}_{3t} - 0.8\mathbf{z}_{4t} = \mathbf{v}_{1t}$	$\mathbf{y}_{1t} + 0.5\mathbf{z}_{1t} - 0.75\mathbf{z}_{2t} + 2.0\mathbf{z}_{3t} - 0.8\mathbf{z}_{4t} = \mathbf{v}_{1t}$
$\mathbf{y}_{2t} + 2.0\mathbf{z}_{1t} - 3.0\mathbf{z}_{2t} + 16\mathbf{z}_{3t} - 1.6\mathbf{z}_{4t} = \mathbf{v}_{2t}$	$\mathbf{y}_{2t} + 2.0\mathbf{z}_{1t} - 3.0\mathbf{z}_{2t} + 4.0\mathbf{z}_{3t} - 1.6\mathbf{z}_{4t} = \mathbf{v}_{2t}$
COVARIANCE STRUCTURE	
$\mathrm{E}[\mathbf{v}_{1t}\mathbf{v}_{2t}'] = \mathbf{\Sigma} = \begin{bmatrix} 1.0 & 0.5 \\ 0.5 & 1.0 \end{bmatrix}$	$\mathrm{E}[\mathbf{u}_{1t}\mathbf{u}_{2t}'] = \boldsymbol{\beta\Sigma\beta}' = \begin{bmatrix} 0.75 & -3.0 \\ -3.0 & 0.75 \end{bmatrix}$
PUTATIVE IDENTIFICATION STATUS	
Equation 1: Overidentified by one (improper exclusion)	Equation 1: Just-identified
Equation 2: Overidentified by one	Equation 2: Overidentified by two (improper exclusion)
STANDARDIZED CONCENTRATION PARAMETERS	
$\mu_1^2 = \pi_{23}^2 + \pi_{24}^2 = 258.56$	$\mu_1^2 = \pi_{24}^2 = 2.56$
$\mu_2^2 = \pi_{11}^2 + \pi_{12}^2 = 0.8125$	$\mu_2^2 = \pi_{11}^2 + \pi_{12}^2 + \pi_{13}^2 = 4.8125$

Table 3. Sampling Experiment Design: Population Means-Sigma Matrices.*

System A	*System B*
EQUATION A1 CORRECT SPECIFICATION	EQUATION B1 CORRECT SPECIFICATION
$\mathbf{\Omega} = \mu^2\begin{bmatrix}\beta_{12}^2 & \beta_{12}\\ \beta_{12} & 1\end{bmatrix} = \begin{bmatrix}4.64 & 9.28\\ 9.28 & 18.56\end{bmatrix}$	$\mathbf{\Omega} = \mu^2\begin{bmatrix}\beta_{12}^2 & \beta_{12}\\ \beta_{12} & 1\end{bmatrix} = \begin{bmatrix}0.64 & 1.28\\ 1.28 & 2.56\end{bmatrix}$
EQUATION A1 MISSPECIFICATION (Wrongful Exclusion)	EQUATION B1 MISSPECIFICATION (Wrongful Inclusion)
$\mathbf{\Omega} = \begin{bmatrix}16.64 & 65.28\\ 65.28 & 258.56\end{bmatrix}$	$\mathbf{\Omega} = \begin{bmatrix}0.64 & 1.28\\ 1.28 & 2.56\end{bmatrix}$
EQUATION A2 CORRECT SPECIFICATION	EQUATION B2 CORRECT SPECIFICATION
$\mathbf{\Omega} = \mu^2\begin{bmatrix}\beta_{21}^2 & \beta_{21}\\ \beta_{21} & 1\end{bmatrix} = \begin{bmatrix}13.0 & 3.25\\ 3.25 & 0.8125\end{bmatrix}$	$\mathbf{\Omega} = \mu^2\begin{bmatrix}\beta_{21}^2 & \beta_{21}\\ \beta_{21} & 1\end{bmatrix} = \begin{bmatrix}269.0 & 67.25\\ 67.25 & 16.8125\end{bmatrix}$
EQUATION A2 MISSPECIFICATION (Wrongful Inclusion)	EQUATION B2 MISSPECIFICATION (Wrongful Exclusion)
$\mathbf{\Omega} = \begin{bmatrix}13.0 & 3.25\\ 3.25 & 0.8125\end{bmatrix}$	$\mathbf{\Omega} = \begin{bmatrix}29.0 & 11.25\\ 11.25 & 4.8125\end{bmatrix}$

* Details of the construction of these matrices are presented in Appendix B.

that the exact sampling behavior of the β-coefficient estimators is determined by the true $\boldsymbol{\beta}$ and degrees of overidentification *and* by the elements of the means-sigma matrix $\mathbf{\Omega}$. Thus, to complete our presentation of the experimental design, we show the standardized means-sigma matrices for the experiment in Table 3. Details of the construction of these matrices have been removed to Appendix B.

Note that the design matrices satisfy the conditions mentioned by Rhodes and Westbrook (1981), namely, in the correctly specified cases $\mathbf{\Omega}$ has rank one, but under misspecification $\mathbf{\Omega}$ is of full rank. Testing the rank condition for identification in the two-equation case is equivalent to testing whether the rank of $\mathbf{\Omega}$ is one. The ramifications of the behavior of $\mathbf{\Omega}$ on the exact finite-sample distributions of the β-coefficient estimators is discussed in some detail by Rhodes and Westbrook (1981).

IV. DISTRIBUTIONS OF ESTIMATES OF FUNDAMENTAL PARAMETERS

The fundamental parameters of the exact finite-sample distribution functions contain information about both the characteristics of those distributions and about the identification status of the equation system. In practice the values of the fundamental parameters are not known, but they may be estimated as functions of the estimated reduced form parameters. If estimates of the fundamental parameters are shown to be reliable, then we may use them to make inferences about the characteristics of the exact distributions. For example, if an estimator of the concentration parameter is found to be reliable in some sense and a large estimate is produced, then we would expect the 2SLS estimator to be highly concentrated. Similarly, if the estimated smallest root of the means-sigma matrix is large, then we infer that misspecification is a serious possibility. Of course, this presupposes that "large" has been defined in a manner suitable to our purpose. Some of our previous work (Rhodes and Westbrook, 1979, 1981) indicates that standardized concentration parameters exceeding 25 may be considered large in many practical situations.

The population values of concentration parameters, elements of means-sigma matrices, and roots of means-sigma matrices were given in Tables 1 through 3. Estimates of the parameters were calculated for each of the replications in systems A and B under both specification regimes. The design values of the parameters, the experimental sample means of the parameter estimates, their sample standard deviations, and the 5% and 95% fractiles of the empirical cumulative distribution functions (empirical CDFs) are given in Tables 4–11. In Tables 4–11, m_{11}, m_{12}, and μ^2 are the elements of the (symmetric) standardized means-sigma matrix. Details of the standardizing transformation and construction of the means-sigma matrices are provided in Appendix B. Finally, R_1 and R_2 are the smallest and largest roots, respectively, of $\mathbf{\Omega}$.

In these models, according to the experimental sample means, the magnitudes of the elements of the standardized means-sigma matrices

Table 4. Distributions of Fundamental Parameters for Equation A1, Correct Specification: $\nu = 1$. Maintained Hypothesis: A

				Fractiles	
Parameter	*Design Value*	*Sample Mean*	*Sample SD*	*5%*	*95%*
m_{11}	4.64	7.41	6.21	0.79	18.79
m_{12}	9.28	11.37	7.67	2.07	24.72
μ^2	18.56	22.46	12.48	7.11	46.19
R_1	0.00	0.63	1.18	0.0021	2.16
R_2	23.20	29.24	16.52	9.36	60.20

Table 5. Distributions of Fundamental Parameters for Equation A2, Correct Specification: $\nu = 1$. Maintained Hypothesis: A

Parameter	*Design Value*	*Sample Mean*	*Sample SD*	*Fractiles* 5%	95%
m_{11}	13.00	16.51	10.55	4.28	36.56
m_{12}	3.25	4.67	5.66	−2.13	15.29
μ^2	0.81	3.24	3.38	0.12	10.01
R_1	0.00	0.83	1.18	0.0026	3.35
R_2	13.81	18.91	12.40	4.95	43.77

Table 6. Distributions of Fundamental Parameters for Equation A1, Misspecified: $\nu = 1$.* Maintained Hypothesis: B

Parameter	*Design Value*	*Sample Mean*	*Sample SD*	*Fractiles* 5%	95%
m_{11}	16.64	20.85	11.97	6.48	42.16
m_{12}	65.28	73.94	73.94	33.70	133.94
μ^2	258.56	289.83	109.26	159.83	477.56
R_1	0.15	1.04	2.01	0.005	4.21
R_2	275.05	309.64	119.11	169.73	515.64

* One wrongful exclusion.

Table 7. Distributions of Fundamental Parameters for Equation A2, Misspecified: $\nu = 1$.* Maintained Hypothesis: B

Parameter	*Design Value*	*Sample Mean*	*Sample SD*	*Fractiles* 5%	95%
m_{11}	13.00	16.51	10.55	4.28	36.56
m_{12}	3.25	4.67	5.66	−2.13	15.29
μ^2	0.81	3.24	3.38	0.12	10.01
R_1	0.00	0.83	1.18	0.0036	3.35
R_2	13.81	18.91	12.40	4.95	43.77

* One wrongful inclusion.

Table 8. Distributions of Fundamental Parameters for Equation B1, Correct Specification: $\nu = 0$. Maintained Hypothesis: B

Parameter	*Design Value*	*Sample Mean*	*Sample SD*	*Fractiles* 5%	*Fractiles* 95%
m_{11}	0.64	1.87	3.11	0.007	7.39
m_{12}	1.28	1.97	2.98	−0.71	7.74
μ^2	2.56	3.84	4.33	0.06	12.40
R_1	0.00	0.00	0.00	0.00	0.00
R_2	3.20	5.71	6.29	0.24	17.76

are consistently overestimated; reliance on estimated concentration parameters would tend to make us overconfident with respect to the degree of concentration of distributions of the parameter estimators. In addition, the 5% and 95% fractiles of the empirical CDFs seem to be rather far apart, sometimes admitting estimates of the wrong sign to the 90% interval between the fractiles. The diagonal elements of the standardized means-sigma matrices have noncentral F distributions with noncentrality parameters equal to the true values of those elements; these distributions could be used for statistical inference about the magnitudes of the diagonal elements. However, the distributions of the off-diagonal elements of the standardized means-sigma matrix are linear functions of products of different normally distributed variates, and their distributions are not so easily inferred.

In tracing the effects of misspecification on the means-sigma matrices and the estimates of their elements, it is proper to focus on a *given maintained hypothesis* (reduced form A or B) and to observe its conjunction with two alternative structures. Thus, we associate the correctly specified

Table 9. Distributions of Fundamental Parameters for Equation B2, Correct Specification: $\nu = 2$. Maintained Hypothesis: B

Parameter	*Design Value*	*Sample Mean*	*Sample SD*	*Fractiles* 5%	*Fractiles* 95%
m_{11}	269.00	302.57	114.53	168.63	513.93
m_{12}	67.25	76.54	33.51	36.03	139.07
μ^2	16.81	22.13	11.74	7.66	45.95
R_1	0.00	1.81	1.85	0.08	5.43
R_2	285.81	322.89	122.43	177.88	551.21

Table 10. Distributions of Fundamental Parameters for Equation B1, Misspecified: $\nu = 0$.* Maintained Hypothesis: A

Parameter	*Design Value*	*Sample Mean*	*Sample SD*	*Fractiles*	
				5%	*95%*
m_{11}	0.64	1.87	3.11	0.007	7.39
m_{12}	1.28	1.97	2.98	−0.71	7.74
μ^2	2.56	3.84	4.33	0.06	12.40
R_1	0.00	0.00	0.00	0.00	0.00
R_2	3.20	5.71	6.29	0.24	17.76

* One wrongful inclusion.

structural system A (Tables 4 and 5) as well as the misspecified structural system B (Tables 10 and 11), with the reduced form designed for A. Reduced form B is similarly associated with correctly specified structural system B (Tables 8 and 9) and misspecified structural system A (Tables 6 and 7).

Comparing correctly specified Equation A1 with Equation B1 misspecified, which has variable $\mathbf{z}_3$ improperly included, we find that the design values of all of the elements of the standardized means-sigma matrix have decreased. This is reflected in the sample statistics for the parameter estimates: all sample means and sample standard deviations for the elements of $\mathbf{\Omega}$ are smaller for equation B2 misspecified. Comparing the second equations in these systems, however, reveals the converse result: the improper *exclusion* of variable $\mathbf{z}_3$ in moving from A2 correct to B2 misspecified leads to increases in all of the elements of the standardized design means-sigma matrices, as well as in their respective estimates.

Table 11. Distributions of Fundamental Parameters for Equation B2, Misspecified: $\nu = 2$.* Maintained Hypothesis: A

Parameter	*Design Value*	*Sample Mean*	*Sample SD*	*Fractiles*	
				5%	*95%*
m_{11}	29.00	35.15	17.85	14.33	70.90
m_{12}	11.25	14.05	9.30	2.75	32.29
μ^2	4.81	8.73	6.12	1.67	21.13
R_1	0.39	1.92	1.97	0.10	5.72
R_2	33.42	41.96	21.62	16.86	84.36

* One wrongful exclusion.

Moving now to the structures associated with the maintained hypothesis B, we find the same pattern: wrongful exclusion indicates an increase in the design values and estimates of the elements of the standardized means-sigma matrix; wrongful inclusion produces decreases in those parameters and sample statistics.

Examination of the design values and sample statistics of the elements of the means-sigma matrices does not appear to reveal the presence or absence of misspecification. However, the two roots of the means-sigma matrix summarize the information contained in the complete means-sigma matrix. It is therefore reasonable to look to them for information regarding the specification status of each equation. Under proper specification, the rank of the means-sigma matrix is zero, hence the small root R_1 is zero. This condition fails upon introduction of misspecification by wrongful exclusion of relevant explanatory variables; the LIML identifiability test is based on testing whether R_1 is indeed zero. We observe that an improper exclusion restriction does indeed increase the magnitudes of sample means of R_1. Wrongful inclusion of a variable reduces the magnitudes of those statistics. Note, however, that for just-identified equations, whether correctly or incorrectly specified, the values of R_1 are always identically zero.

The larger root does not seem to convey any unique information concerning misspecification; the advent of misspecification increases the design values and estimated values of R_2 in much the same manner as it affects R_1.

Although the means-sigma matrices do not appear to disclose the advent of misspecification—cross-system comparisons are not helpful if one does not already know which equation incorrectly includes a variable or which incorrectly omits a variable—it is apparent that misspecification may have a profound effect upon the sampling distributions of the estimators. The effects operate through the means-sigma matrices and through the degrees of freedom ν. These effects of misspecification are displayed for this experiment in Section VI. The information about misspecification conveyed by the smallest root R_1 of $\mathbf{\Omega}$ and formalized in the LIML ID test is examined more thoroughly in Section V.

V. IDENTIFIABILITY TEST STATISTICS

Examination of the performance of the three identifiability tests included in this section consists of comparing the empirical cumulative frequency distributions generated by the experiment with the approximate distribution functions suggested by the asymptotic properties of the test statistics. The comparison involves three aspects. First, we examine the "goodness-of-fit'' of the empirical CDFs to their asymptotic distributions by viewing graphs of the pairs of distributions and by conducting the Kolgomorov-Smirnov test on each pair. Second, we calculate the proportion of Type I errors for each test statistic, given the critical values generated by the asymptotic distributions. Finally, we repeat the first and second steps given the type of misspecification that we have defined in this experiment, in order to learn whether the test statistics exhibit power to detect and reject null hypotheses that are false. Again, refer to Appendix A for the technical details associated with the three ID tests.

A. Results under Correct Specification

The correct identification status of each equation was built into the data; the only deviations from zero that 2SLS $\hat{F}$, LIML $\tilde{F}$, and FIML $-2\ln(\lambda)$ ID test statistics should exhibit are those introduced by the normal randomization of the observations on the endogenous variables. Recall that the test statistics do not apply for just-identified equations.

Summary results for all three ID test statistics under *correct specification* are compactly contained in Tables 12 and 13; detailed results are graphically presented in Figures 1 through 8. The figures display the empirical cumulative frequency functions of the test statistics along with a plot of the $F(\nu, m)$ appropriate to each case.

Table 12 gives a tabulation of the summary statistics associated with the empirical distributions of 2SLS $\hat{F}$ and LIML $\tilde{F}$, and records their proportion of Type I errors at the $\alpha = 1\%$ and 5% critical points given by $F(\nu, m)$. In this context we take ''proportion of Type I errors'' to be the proportion of sample values of 2SLS $\hat{F}$ and LIML $\tilde{F}$ that fall in the approximate critical region given by $F(\nu, m)$.

Figures 1, 3, and 5 provide some interesting information about the LIML $\tilde{F}$ ID test statistic. The empirical CDF of LIML $\tilde{F}$ for Equation A1 is very closely approximated by the F-distribution with numerator and denominator degrees of freedom of 1 and 20, respectively. Here the degree of overidentification is one and the value of the concentration parameter is large (18.56). Reducing the concentration parameter to 0.8125, as in Equation A2, and keeping $\nu = 1$ causes the approximation by the F-distribution to deteriorate slightly, but the Kolmogorov-Smirnov test is passed for both Equations A1 and A2 at the 1% significance level (cf. Table 12). However, restoring a fairly large value to the concentration parameter (16.8125) and increasing the degree of overidentification to 2, as in Equation B2, we note a more substantial deterioration in the approximation: the Kolmogorov-Smirnov test *rejects* the hypothesis that the empirical CDF is not significantly different from the F-distribution

Table 12. Summary Statistics for Single-Equation Identifiability Test Statistics.*

				Fractiles		*Proportion of Type I Errors*		*Kolmogorov-Smirnov D Statistics*	
Eq	*Statistic*	*Sample Mean*	*Sample SD*	*5%*	*95%*	$\alpha = 0.01$	$\alpha = 0.05$	*D*	*Critical Values for* $\alpha = 0.01$
A1	LIML $\bar{F}$	1.19	1.87	0.004	4.68	0.013	0.055	0.025	0.052
A1	2SLS $\hat{F}$	1.01	1.61	0.003	3.98	0.005	0.042	0.041	0.052
A2	LIML $\bar{F}$	1.23	1.66	0.004	4.79	0.006	0.060	0.051	0.052
A2	2SLS $\hat{F}$	2.98	5.22	0.004	13.68	0.115	0.200	0.177	0.052
B2	LIML $\bar{F}$	1.43	2.97	0.063	4.23	0.017	0.090	0.120	0.052
B2	2SLS $\hat{F}$	1.57	2.30	0.053	4.69	0.030	0.104	0.095	0.052

* $F(1, 20, \alpha = 0.01) = 8.10$.
$F(1, 20, \alpha = 0.05) = 4.35$.
$F(2, 20, \alpha = 0.01) = 5.85$.
$F(2, 20, \alpha = 0.05) = 3.49$.

Table 13. Summary Statistics for Full-System Identifiability Test Statistics.*

				Fractiles		*Proportion of Type I Errors*		*Kolmogorov-Smirnov D Statistics*	
Eq	*Statistic*	*Sample Mean*	*Sample SD*	*5%*	*95%*	$\alpha = 0.01$	$\alpha = 0.05$	*D*	*Critical Values for* $\alpha = 0.01$
A†	$-2\ln(\lambda)$	2.39	3.18	0.089	7.76	0.036	0.076	0.041	0.055
B†	$-2\ln(\lambda)$	2.98	5.01	0.122	7.99	0.043	0.097	0.115	0.054

* $\chi^2(2, \alpha = 0.01) = 9.21$.
$\chi^2(2, \alpha = 0.05) = 5.99$.
† The FIML ID statistics were computed for 864 replications in system A and 925 replications in system B. FIML failed to converge for the remaining replications. The empirical CDFs, proportions, and Kolmogorov-Smirnov critical values are based on the number of FIML replications actually completed.

with numerator and denominator degrees of freedom of 2 and 20, respectively.

Conducting a similar analysis of Figures 2, 4, and 6 for the 2SLS $\hat{F}$ ID test statistic, we note that the F-distribution again provides a good approximation of the empirical CDF associated with Equation A1; and again the Kolmogorov-Smirnov test does not reject the null hypothesis. Moving to Equation A2, however, we note a dramatic rightward shift of the empirical CDF: the approximation by the F-distribution is quite poor. For Equation B2, the behavior of the 2SLS $\hat{F}$ is similar to that of the LIML $\tilde{F}$ ID test statistic. Adding one degree of overidentification diminishes the closeness of the approximation in spite of restoration of the magnitude of the concentration parameter.

Comparing 2SLS $\hat{F}$ and LIML $\tilde{F}$ equation by equation, we see that the LIML $\tilde{F}$ is always more closely approximated by $F(\nu, m)$ than the 2SLS $\hat{F}$; thus, we find support for Conjecture 1. Note that the vertical

Figure 1. Empirical Distribution of LIML $\tilde{F}$ for System A, Equation 1.*

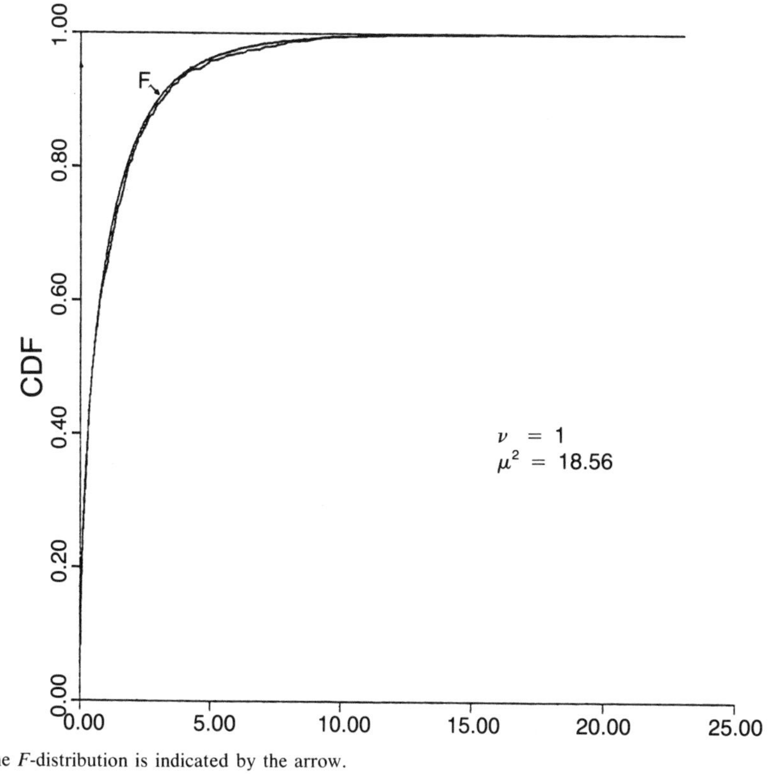

* The F-distribution is indicated by the arrow.

distance between the empirical CDF and $F(\nu, m)$ may appear to be greater in Figure 6 than in Figure 5. That this is not the case is indicated by the relevant Kolmogorov-Smirnov statistics. The largest vertical distance is in Figure 5 at a value of approximately 2 on the horizontal axis. For all cases except 2SLS $\hat{F}$ in equation A1, the statistics tend to reject the true null hypothesis more frequently than would be indicated by the significance level set for $F(\nu, m)$; hence, these tests are generally biased against the identifiability hypothesis. Two-stage least squares $\hat{F}$ is generally worse in this respect than LIML $\tilde{F}$. These results are in contradiction with Basmann's (this volume) experimental results, which show that the GCL (2SLS) ID test statistic performs somewhat better than the LIML statistic. We note, however, that the concentration parameter associated with the equation for which Basmann reports results is 1119. Our results suggest that the distribution of the 2SLS ID test statistic is more responsive

Figure 2. Empirical Distribution of 2SLS ID Test Statistic for System A, Equation 1.*

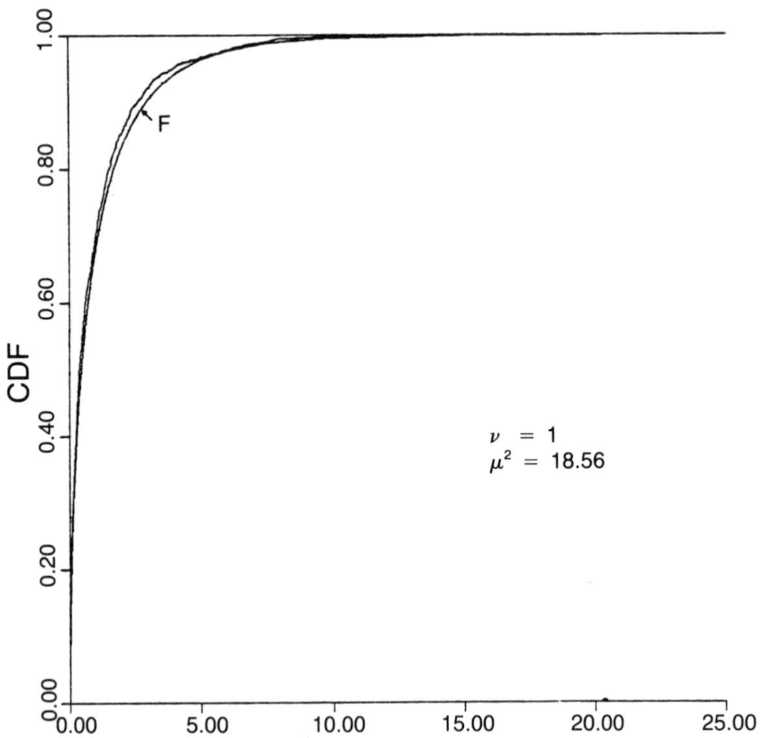

* The *F*-distribution is indicated by the arrow.

to variations in the concentration parameter than is the LIML ID test statistic; with a concentration parameter of 1119, it is not surprising that the 2SLS statistic is superior to LIML $\tilde{F}$—or that both experimental distributions follow quite closely their asymptotic approximations.

Table 13 presents results for the asymptotic FIML ID test statistic $-2\ln(\lambda)$, the empirical distributions of which appear as Figures 7 and 8. The performances of the FIML ID test statistic for systems A and B are similar, which is not surprising, since both systems are specified with the same number of prior restrictions, and have similar pairs of concentration parameters. The overidentifying restrictions are, however, distributed differently across the pair of equations in each system. For neither system is the approximation by the χ^2 very close. For system A, the Kolmogorov-Smirnov test fails to reject the null hypothesis at the 1% significance level; for system B, the rejection is decisive. For

Figure 3. Empirical Distribution of LIML $\tilde{F}$ for System A, Equation 2.*

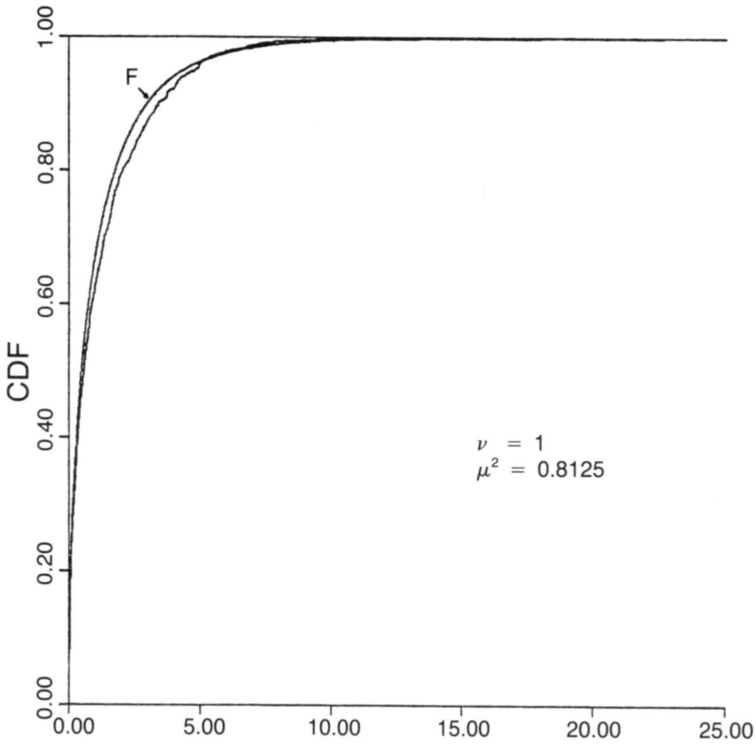

* The *F*-distribution is indicated by the arrow.

both systems the probability of Type I error, given the approximate critical region, exceeds the significance level, so the FIML ID test statistic is also biased against the identifiability hypothesis. On the basis of our results, it appears that the LIML ID test statistic with approximate critical region given by $\tilde{F} \geqslant F(\nu, m)$ should be the single-equation identifiability test of choice, when the equation system is properly specified. However, a problem arises here. Though LIML $\tilde{F}$ may do better for ID testing, most estimation uses 2SLS: the need for a better approximation to the distribution of 2SLS $\hat{F}$ is apparent.

B. Results under Misspecification

The type of misspecification imposed on equation systems A and B is closely related to the identifiability hypothesis and provides a vehicle

Figure 4. Empirical Distribution of 2SLS ID Test Statistic for System A, Equation 2.*

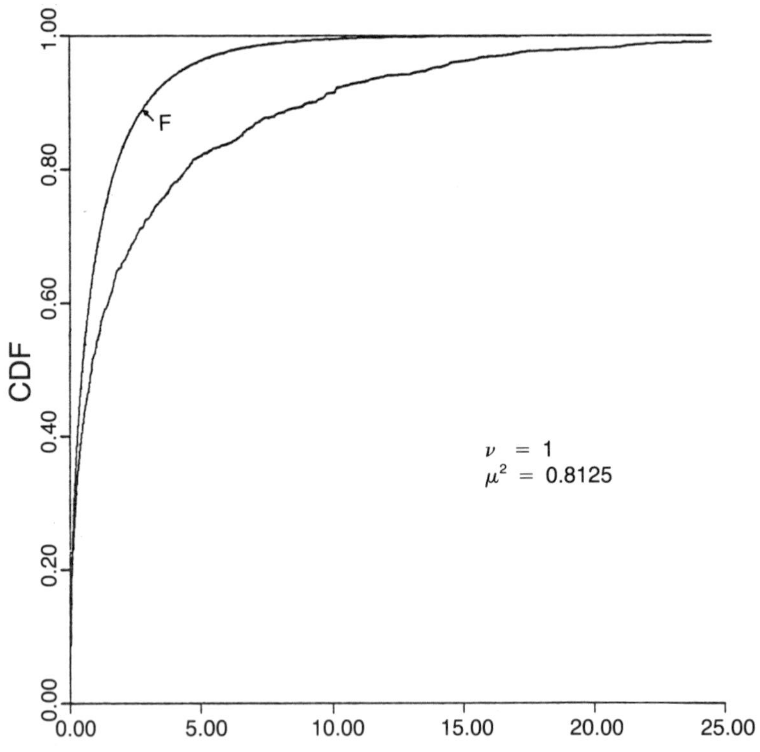

* The *F*-distribution is indicated by the arrow. Nine extreme values have been omitted from the upper tail of the empirical distribution.

for assessing the powers of the alternative tests for rejecting the null hypothesis when it is in fact false.

To observe the powers of the tests for properly rejecting the false null hypothesis, it seems reasonable to proceed by tracing the behavior of the various test statistics calculated under alternative null hypotheses for a *given* maintained hypothesis. This need not preclude examination of the test statistics from misspecified structures vis-à-vis the *same* structure applied to a different maintained hypothesis. We follow the first mode of presentation for the general results and discussion, but, in fact, the latter strategy seems to be more natural and is more convenient for the detailed exposition presented later.

Under the maintained hypothesis A, and taking the single-equation tests first, we compare correctly specified structural equations A1 and A2 with misspecified structural equations B1 and B2, respectively (cf.

Figure 5. Empirical Distribution of LIML $\tilde{F}$ for System B, Equation 2.*

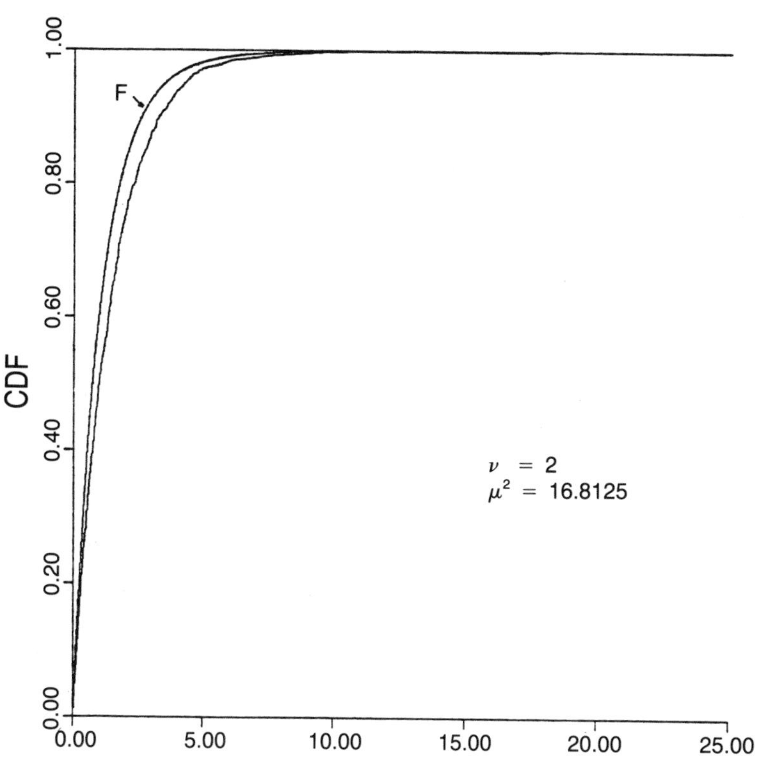

* The F-distribution is indicated by the arrow.

Figure 6. Empirical Distribution of 2SLS ID Test Statistic for System B, Equation 2.*

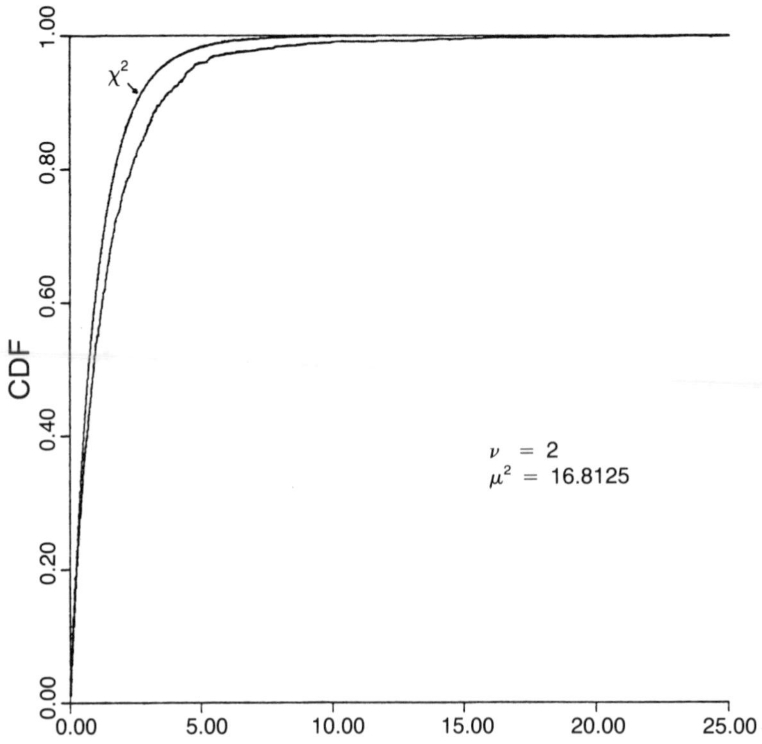

* The F-distribution is indicated by the arrow. Two extreme values have been omitted from the upper tail of the empirical distribution.

Table 14). Misspecified equation B1 is just-identified and the identifiability test statistics do not apply; hence, we have no comparison for correctly specified equation A1. For misspecified equation B2, which has $\mathbf{z}_3$ wrongly *excluded,* both test statistics fall in the critical region substantially more often than they do for correctly specified equation A2. Still, the power of rejection is not large. For a significance level set at 5%, the rate of rejection is 13% by LIML $\tilde{F}$ and 25.5% for 2SLS $\hat{F}$. Following maintained hypothesis B through both systems, we compare correctly specified equations B1 and B2 with misspecified equations A1 and A2, respectively. Because correctly specified equation B1 is just-identified again, the test statistics are not defined; we have no comparison for misspecified equation A1, from which $\mathbf{z}_3$ is improperly excluded. We only note that for misspecified equation A1 both LIML $\tilde{F}$ and 2SLS $\hat{F}$ reject the false null hypothesis slightly more frequently than specified by $F(\nu, m)$, but their

Figure 7. Empirical Distribution of FIML ID Test Statistic for System A.*

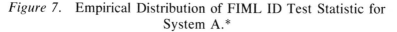

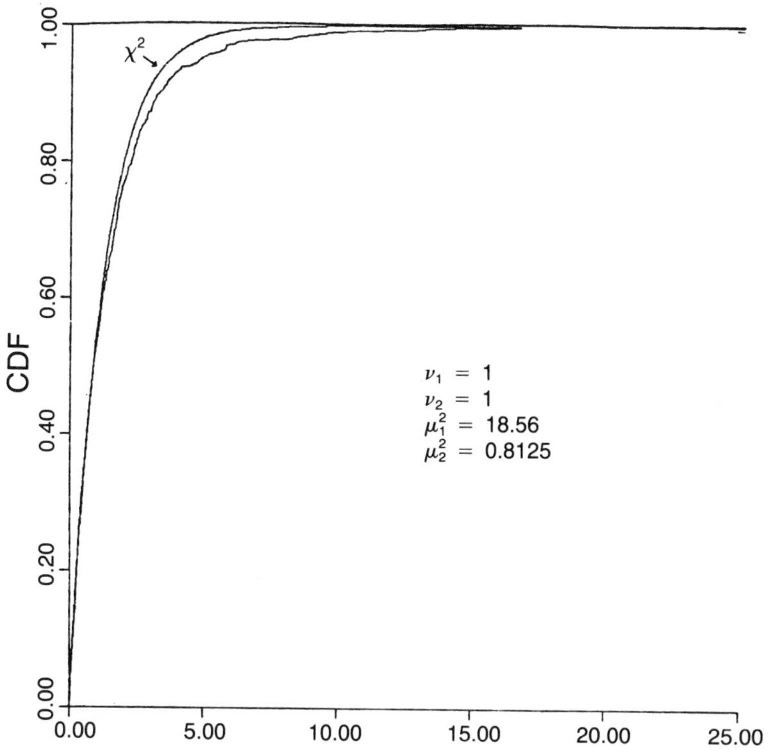

* The χ^2 distribution is indicated by the arrow. Two extreme points were omitted from the upper tail of the empirical distribution.

behavior is not markedly different from correctly specified cases. Finally, comparing correctly specified equation B2 with misspecified equation A2, we find no change; *inclusion* of the irrelevant variable $\mathbf{z}_3$ in misspecified equation A2 is not recorded by the identifiability test statistics.

Proceeding as above for the FIML ID test statistics, we compare a 7.6% rejection rate for correctly specified system A to an 11.6% power of rejection for misspecified system B, both calculated for the critical region specified by the distribution at a 5% significance level. In the other pairwise comparison—correctly specified system A *versus* misspecified system B—we find a *smaller* power of rejection in the misspecified case: 8.5% *versus* 9.7% for the proper specification. The FIML ID test statistic does not seem to be powerful for rejecting a false null hypothesis.

We now describe in detail the performances of the ID test statistics under the false null hypothesis with the help of Tables 14 and 15 and

Table 14. Summary Statistics for Single-Equation Identifiability Test Statistics under Misspecification.*

				Fractiles		Proportion of Type I Errors		Kolmogorov-Smirnov D Statistics	
Eq	Statistic	Sample Mean	Sample SD	5%	95%	$\alpha = 0.01$	$\alpha = 0.05$	D	Critical Values for $\alpha = 0.01$
A1	LIML $\tilde{F}$	1.60	2.71	0.009	6.10	0.032	0.092	0.088	0.052
A1	2SLS $\hat{F}$	1.34	2.26	0.008	5.10	0.024	0.067	0.048	0.052
A2	LIML $\tilde{F}$	1.23	1.66	0.004	4.79	0.006	0.060	0.051	0.052
A2	2SLS $\hat{F}$	2.98	5.22	0.004	13.68	0.115	0.200	0.177	0.052
B2	LIML $\tilde{F}$	1.71	1.75	0.083	4.70	0.033	0.130	0.175	0.052
B2	2SLS $\hat{F}$	2.93	4.11	0.074	11.05	0.129	0.255	0.251	0.052

* $F(1, 20, \alpha = 0.01) = 8.10$.
$F(1, 20, \alpha = 0.05) = 4.35$.
$F(2, 20, \alpha = 0.01) = 5.85$.
$F(2, 20, \alpha = 0.05) = 3.49$.

Table 15. Summary Statistics for Full-System Identifiability Test Statistics under Misspecification.*

				Fractiles		Proportion of Type I Errors		Kolmogorov-Smirnov D Statistics	
Eq	Statistic	Sample Mean	Sample SD	5%	95%	$\alpha = 0.01$	$\alpha = 0.05$	D	Critical Values for $\alpha = 0.01$
A†	$-2\ln(\lambda)$	2.55	3.18	0.100	7.75	0.032	0.085	0.074	0.056
B†	$-2\ln(\lambda)$	3.07	3.79	0.153	8.93	0.049	0.116	0.135	0.056

* $\chi^2(2, \alpha = 0.01) = 9.21$.
$\chi^2(2, \alpha = 0.05) = 5.99$.
† The FIML ID test statistics were computed for 839 replications in system A and 836 replications in system B. FIML failed to converge for the remaining replications. The empirical CDFs, proportions, and Kolmogorov-Smirnov critical values were based on the number of FIML replications actually completed.

Figure 8. Empirical Distribution of FIML ID Test Statistic for System B.*

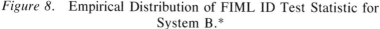

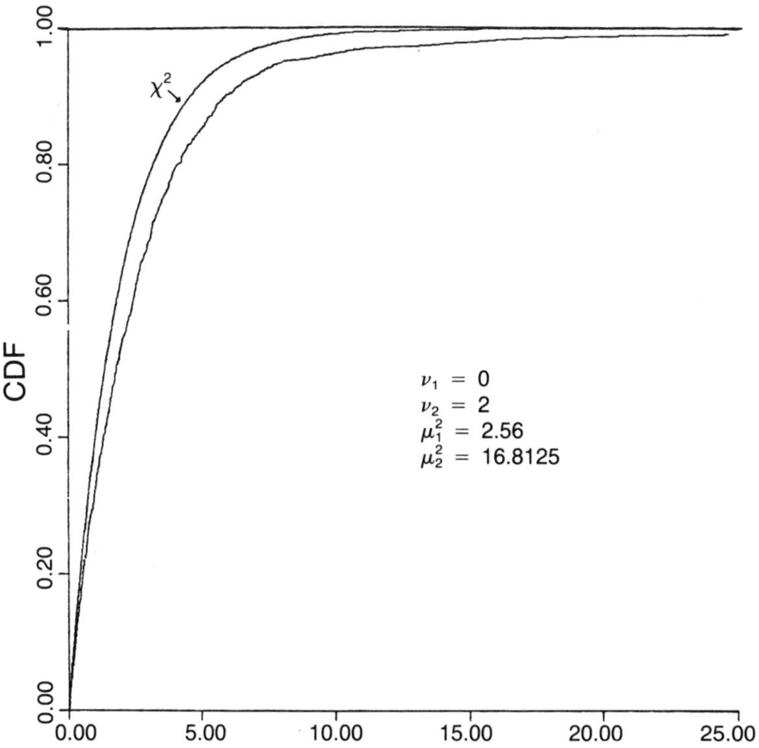

* The χ^2 distribution is indicated by the arrow. Six extreme points were omitted from the upper tail of the empirical distribution.

Figures 9 through 16. The *comparative* results for LIML $\tilde{F}$ and 2SLS $\hat{F}$ are analogous to the results under the correct specification: the LIML $\tilde{F}$ approximations to $F(\nu, m)$ are closer than the corresponding 2SLS $\hat{F}$ approximations, except for equation A1, and the 2SLS $\hat{F}$ are generally much more likely to reject the hypothesis of identification. The misspecification results are, however, distinct in one respect: for the equations in which the variable $\mathbf{z}_3$ is wrongly excluded, the empirical cumulative frequency functions of both $\hat{F}$ and $\tilde{F}$ shift to the right, most appreciably for the 2SLS $\hat{F}$ in equation B2 (Figure 14). No change appears for equation A2, which wrongly includes variable $\mathbf{z}_3$, nor for that matter for equation B1, which is just-identified. The computational routines still report both the LIML and 2SLS statistics as identically zero in the just-identified case.

Figure 9. Empirical Distribution of LIML $\tilde{F}$ for System A, Equation 1: Misspecified Case.*

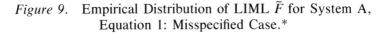

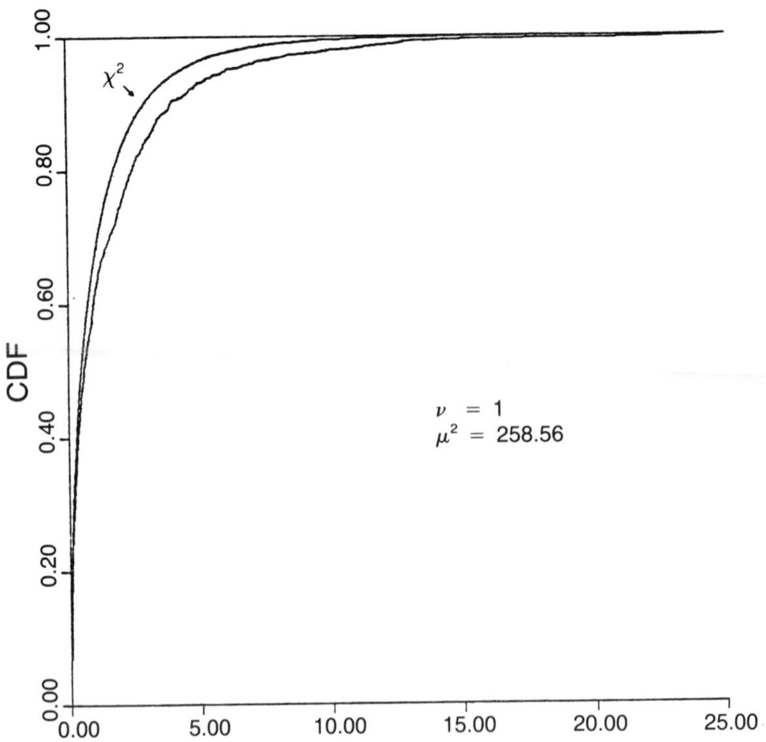

* The F-distribution is indicated by the arrow. One extreme value has been omitted from the upper tail of the empirical distribution.

Figures 9, 11, and 13 and the associated Kolmogorov-Smirnov statistics relate the behavior of the LIML $\tilde{F}$ ID test statistic under misspecification. The wrongful inclusion of variable $\mathbf{z}_3$ in equation A2 produces no change in the empirical CDF of LIML $\tilde{F}$, so we will not dwell on Figure 11. In Figure 9, however, reflecting the wrongful exclusion of variable $\mathbf{z}_3$ from equation A1, we find a rightward displacement of the empirical CDF in spite of the fact that equation A1 now has a much larger concentration parameter (258.56). For equation B2 we also observe a rightward shift, shown by Figure 13, but the shift is not large. Much of the shift may probably be attributed to the small value of the concentration parameter (4.8125) and to the presence of two degrees of overidentification (cf. Figures 1, 3, and 5). This suggests that as the degree of overidentification

Figure 10. Empirical Distribution of 2SLS ID Test Statistic for System A, Equation 1: Misspecified Case.*

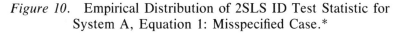

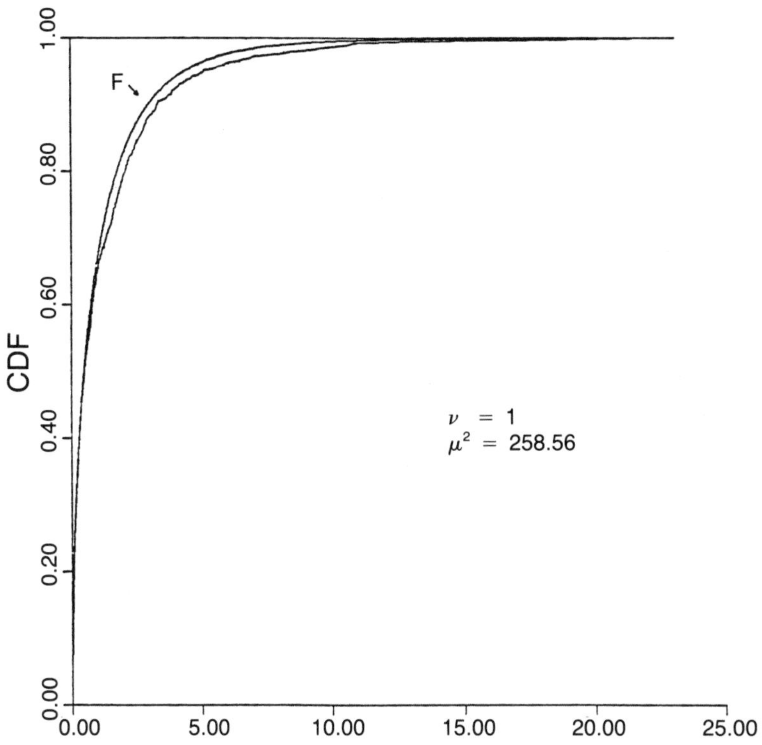

* The *F*-distribution is indicated by the arrow.

increases, the impact upon LIML $\tilde{F}$ of one false overidentifying restriction declines.

For the 2SLS $\hat{F}$ ID test statistic, Figures 10, 12, and 14 and their Kolmogorov-Smirnov statistics are relevant. Here, we find much the same situation as for the LIML $\tilde{F}$ described above: there has been no change for equation A2, and the empirical CDF for 2SLS $\hat{F}$ has been displaced for equations A1 and B2. However, the displacement has been substantial only in the case of equation B2. By comparison with Figures 2, 4, and 6, it appears possible that this displacement is more a result of incrementing the degrees of overidentification by one and decreasing the concentration parameter than it is of the one false overidentifying restriction.

Figure 11. Empirical Distribution of LIML $\tilde{F}$ for System A, Equation 2: Misspecified Case.*

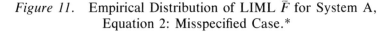

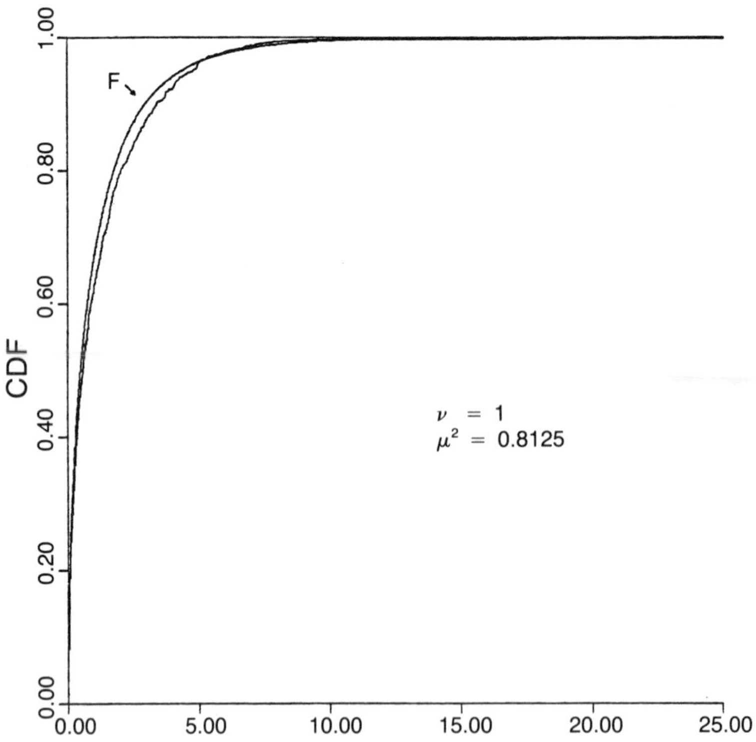

* The F-distribution is indicated by the arrow.

Naturally, where the empirical distributions of 2SLS $\hat{F}$ and LIML $\tilde{F}$ have shifted rightward, the approximations by $F(\nu, m)$ (under the null hypothesis) are invalidated to varying degrees. This is reflected, in all cases except those connected with equation A2, by increases in the Kolmogorov-Smirnov test statistics, indicating greater divergences between the empirical CDFs and their F-distribution approximations. The hypothesis that the empirical CDFs and approximations are not distinct is now rejected at the 1% significance level in all cases except 2SLS $\hat{F}$ for equation A2. Despite the shift, though, the powers of the identifiability tests to reject the false identifiability hypothesis are not very large. The FIML ID test statistics do not reflect the advent of misspecification very strongly. The powers of rejection have increased only slightly, comparing the proper specification to the misspecified cases by system (cf. Tables

Figure 12. Empirical Distribution of 2SLS ID Test Statistic for System A, Equation 2: Misspecified Case.*

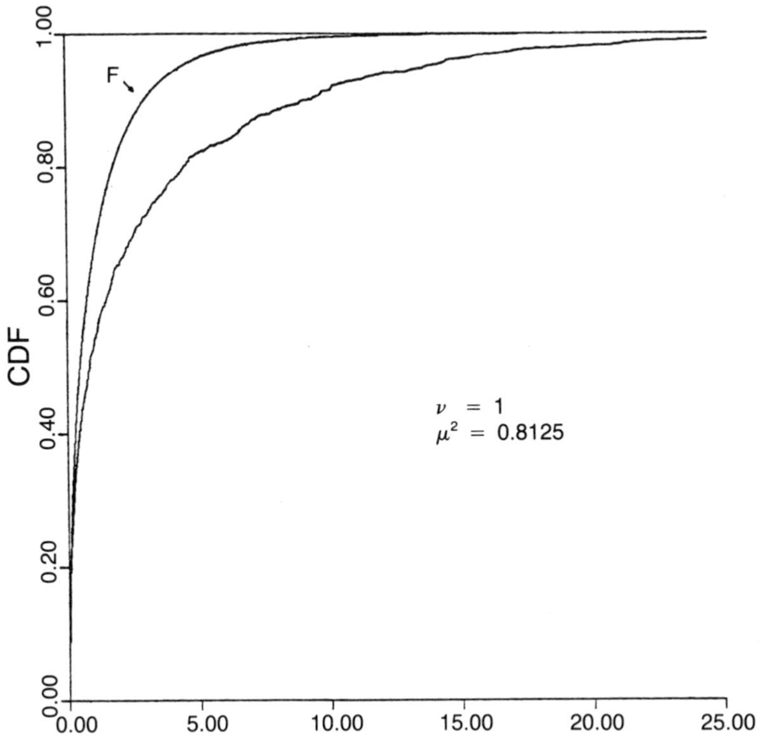

* The *F*-distribution is indicated by the arrow. Nine extreme values have been omitted from the upper tail of the empirical distribution.

12–15). In addition, the empirical CDFs have shifted only slightly under misspecification, as indicated by Figures 15 and 16 and the Kolmogorov-Smirnov test statistics. It is possible, of course, that these results could change if all 1000 replications for FIML had been completed. But even if all noncompleted replications had resulted in rejection of the false null hypothesis, the power would not be impressive. Thus, we hold our Conjecture 2 in disrepute.

It is troublesome to find that the ID test statistics investigated in this study are not powerful for detecting a false identifiability hypothesis. Perhaps tests based on the rank condition for identifiability (Rhodes, 1981b) will prove to be more reliable.

Figure 13. Empirical Distribution of LIML $\tilde{F}$ for System B, Equation 2: Misspecified Case.*

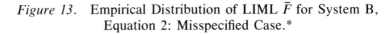

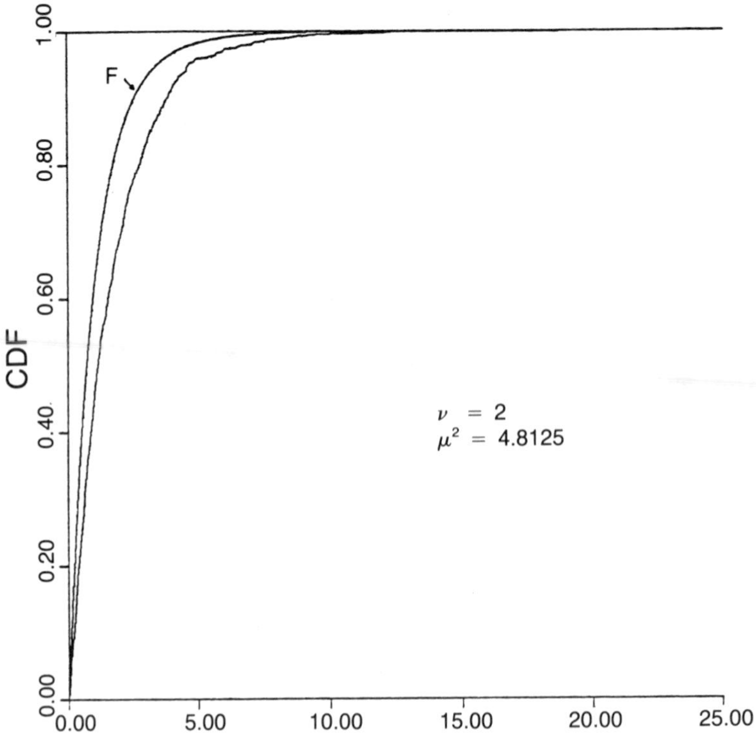

* The *F*-distribution is indicated by the arrow. One extreme value has been omitted from the upper tail of the empirical distribution.

In the following section, we have the opportunity to examine the behavior of our β-coefficient estimators under all of the experimental conditions, including misspecification.

VI. ESTIMATOR PERFORMANCE

A. Correct Specification

In this section we present a series of tables and figures that elucidate the behavior of the estimators studied in the experiment. Our focus is on the β-coefficient estimators. In the discussion, the particular estimators are identified according to five-character names. For example,

Beta (B) or Gamma (G)
The customary coefficient subscript
System A or B
Estimation technique:
LIML (L)
2SLS (2)
3SLS (3)
FIML (F)

B 12 A L

Thus, B12AL is the LIML estimator of β_{12} in system A, and B21BF is the FIML estimator of β_{21} in system B.

Our primary result in this section is that the important dichotomy among simultaneous equations estimators is the GCL/ML demarcation,

Figure 14. Empirical Distribution of 2SLS ID Test Statistic for System B, Equation 2: Misspecified Case.*

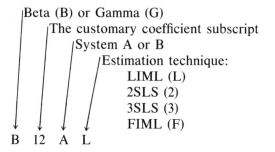

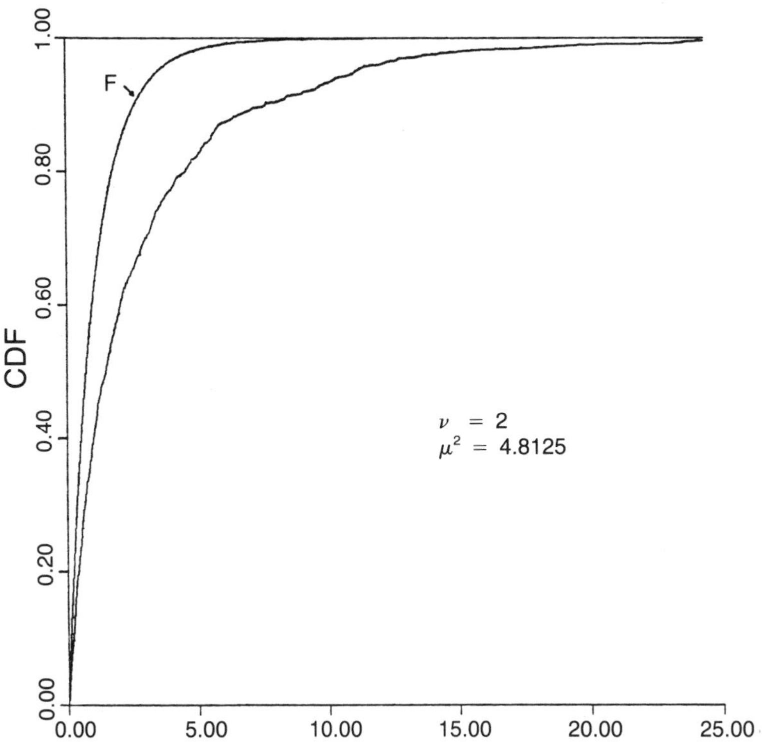

* The *F*-distribution is indicated by the arrow. Four extreme values have been omitted from the upper tail of the empirical distribution.

Figure 15. Empirical Distribution of FIML ID Test Statistic Under Misspecification, System A.*

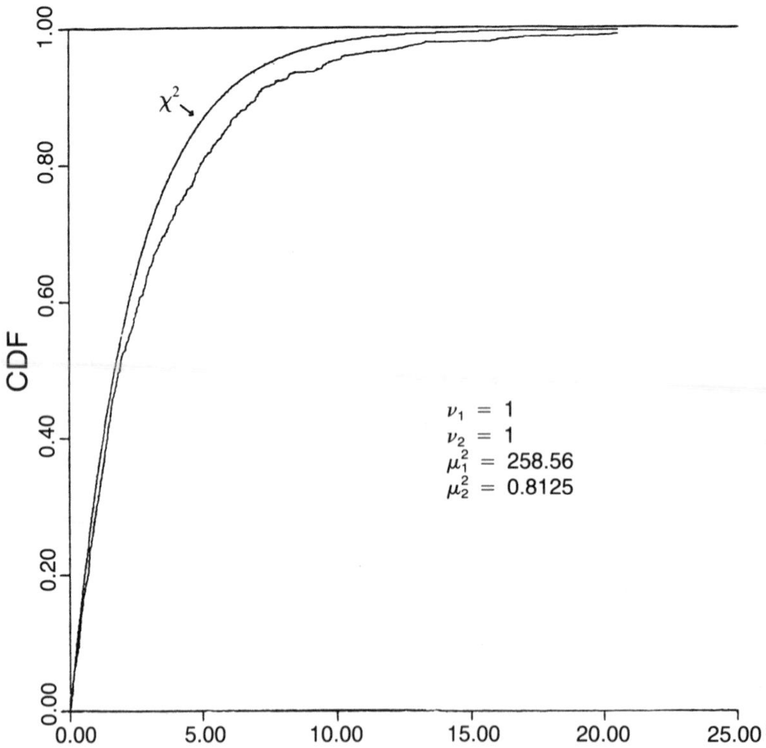

* The χ^2 distribution is indicated by the arrow. Five extreme points were omitted from the upper tail of the empirical distribution.

not the full-system/single-equation classification. The evidence strongly confirms our Conjecture 4 that the general classical linear methods perform substantially better than the maximum-likelihood methods as regards their concentration.

Figures 17 through 30 show the empirical cumulative frequency functions of the estimators of the β-coefficients for both equation systems. Each distribution is accompanied by the primary descriptive statistics for the sample represented by the distribution. In addition, all of the summary statistics are collected in Table 16. The empirical statistics included are descriptive of the experimental distribution functions only; they *may not* be used in place of the corresponding parameters in the exact finite-sample distributions. We recall that certain of the exact moments do not even exist.

Figure 16. Empirical Distribution of FIML ID Test Statistic Under Misspecification, System B.*

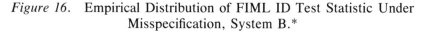

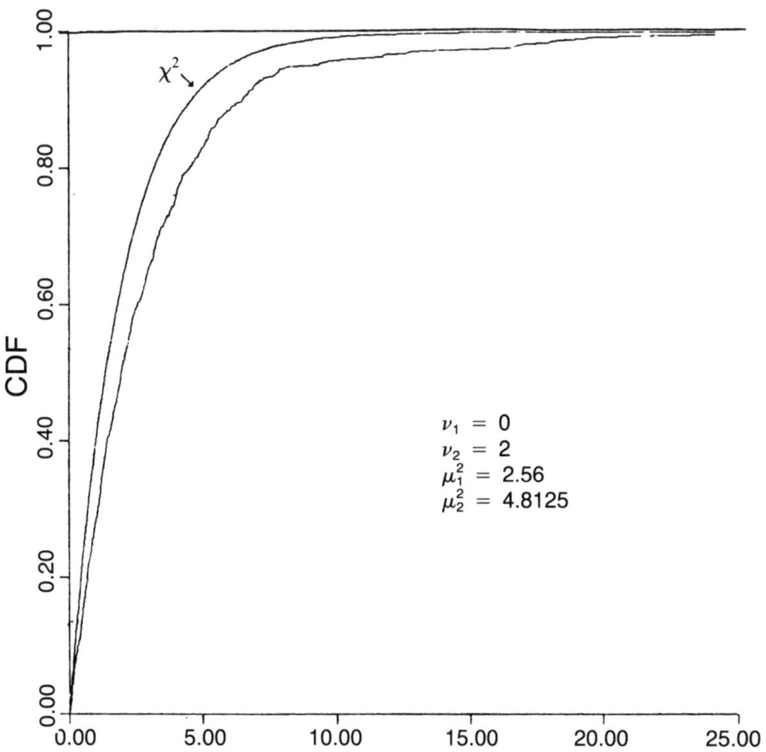

* The χ^2 distribution is indicated by the arrow. Three extreme points were omitted from the upper tail of the empirical distribution.

Examination of Figures 17 through 30 reveals a curious result: all the statistics for 2SLS and 3SLS estimators of β are identical, and those of LIML and FIML are frequently quite similar to each other. This is to be expected for equation B1, which is just-identified; and, in fact, all four estimators yield identical results there. But we expected differences to arise among the estimators for the remaining equations. Detailed examination of the individual coefficients confirms that the estimates are always identical for 2SLS and 3SLS and are identical in many cases for LIML and FIML, with differences such as there are probably due to computational differences only. Apparently this result is due to our particular experimental design. We have demonstrated analytically (ex post) that under our experimental design the 2SLS and 3SLS estimators of the β-coefficients are identical. And although we have not demonstrated

Figure 17. Empirical Distribution of B12AL.*

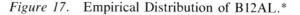

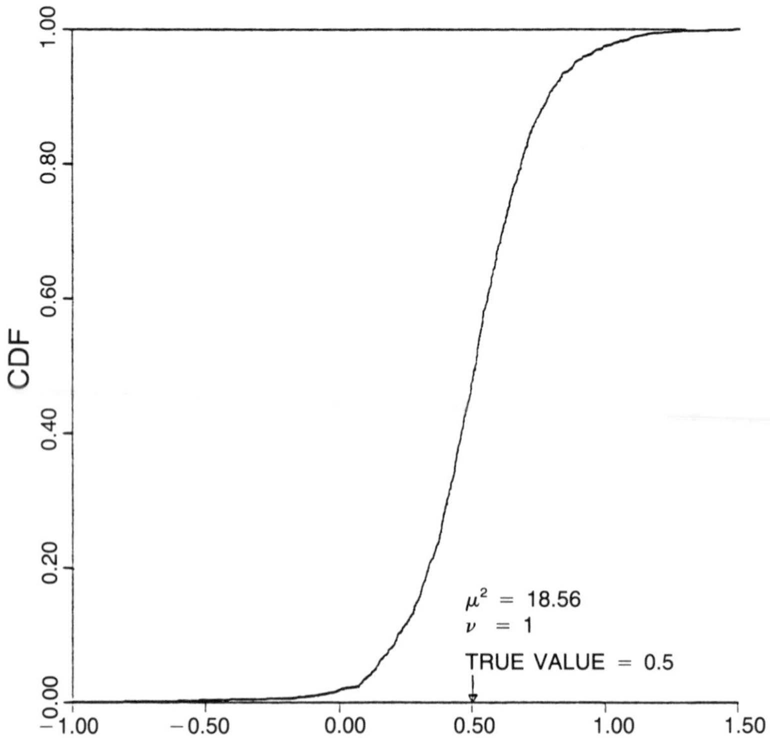

* Sample statistics: minimum = −1.1805; maximum = 1.5445; mean = 0.5090; SD = 0.2403. One extreme value has been omitted from each tail.

that this is the case for the LIML and FIML estimators, we *conjecture* that it is. Computation of the differences between the LIML and FIML estimates of the β-coefficients on an individual basis yielded the information that the mean differences were on the order of 0.0005 to 0.003 when compared with the true parameter values; these differences we attribute to computation error in the iterative FIML algorithm. Although the summary statistics for the FIML and LIML estimators exhibit greater differences than could be accounted for by the small differences between the individual coefficient estimates, we recall that 135 members of data set A and 75 members of data set B were not completed by FIML. It is possible that the absence of these members caused the empirical FIML frequency functions to be artificially skewed. Some evidence for this assertion emerges from a comparison of the LIML and FIML results for equation B1, which is just-identified. Here, we expect the LIML and

Figure 18. Empirical Distribution of B12A2.*

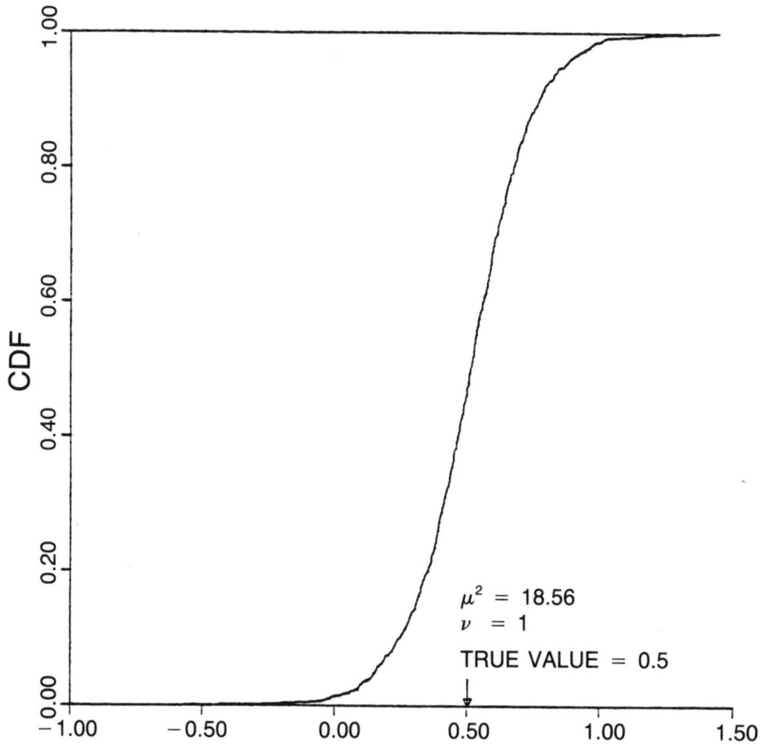

* Sample statistics: minimum = −0.5711; maximum = 1.4365; mean = 0.5084; SD = 0.2147.

FIML estimates to be identical. They are not. For this reason, the summary statistics presented for FIML estimation are held to be misleading. Perhaps the LIML statistics would be a good approximation in this experiment.

Generation of identical estimates by competing techniques provides little ground for comparison of those techniques. But we have not yet considered all of the information generated by the four estimators, and the results outlined above lead to some interesting conjectures about the nature of the FIML and 3SLS estimators and their relationships to LIML and 2SLS, respectively. Furthermore, as regards estimator performance with respect to equation-system parameters, the apparent collapse of the full-system estimators is not as restrictive as it may appear; we are still able to record the influence of ν or μ^2 on the empirical cumulative frequency functions.

We consider the difference between the mean of the estimated β-coefficients and the true value of β to estimate the bias of each estimation

Table 16. Summary Statistics for Empirical Distribution Functions of $\hat{\beta}$.

Estimator	Design Value	Sample Mean	Sample SD	Fractiles 5%	Fractiles 95%	Conc Param	Degree of Overid
B12A2	0.5	0.5084	0.215	0.150	0.863	18.56	1
B12A3	0.5	0.5084	0.215	0.150	0.863	18.56	1
B12AL	0.5	0.5090	0.240	0.132	0.884	18.56	1
B12AF*	0.5	0.5061	0.246	0.134	0.888	18.56	1
B21A2	4.0	1.4263	5.62	−3.044	5.255	0.8125	1
B21A3	4.0	1.4263	5.62	−3.044	5.255	0.8125	1
B21AL	4.0	4.5195	64.29	−14.443	21.273	0.8125	1
B21AF*	4.0	0.9005	34.78	−14.443	11.342	0.8125	1
B12B2	0.5	0.4149	7.82	−1.032	2.241	2.56	0
B12B3	0.5	0.4149	7.82	−1.032	2.241	2.56	0
B12BL	0.5	0.4149	7.82	−1.032	2.241	2.56	0
B12BF*	0.5	0.4180	8.13	−1.191	2.404	2.56	0
B21B2	4.0	3.7118	0.814	2.712	5.259	16.8125	2
B21B3	4.0	3.7118	0.814	2.712	5.259	16.8125	2
B21BL	4.0	4.2480	1.452	2.952	6.379	16.8125	2
B21BF*	4.0	4.1862	1.122	2.939	6.191	16.8125	2

* Recall that the FIML sample statistics are based only on the number of replications actually completed.

technique. For equations A1 and B1, the biases generated by all estimation techniques are similar. Of course, this is expected to be identically true for just-identified equation B1. In equation A2, LIML yields a bias much smaller and opposite in sign from those of 2SLS and 3SLS; FIML fares badly. Finally, in equation B2, the two- and three-stage biases are nearly the same magnitude as that of LIML, but still of the opposite sign. FIML has improved considerably here. In terms of the design parameters of the experiment, we echo some analytical results that are known for 2SLS and LIML. In equations A1 and B1, the magnitude of the bias is small, as is expected when the true parameter value is small. That it is much smaller in equation B1 than in equation A1 reflects the effect of the concentration parameter (larger in system A) and the degrees of overidentification of the equation (1 in equation A1; 0 in B1). Increasing each of those parameters tends to diminish the bias {Rhodes and Westbrook (1979)}. For both equations A2 and B2, the same argument applies. The magnitudes of the biases are larger because the true parameter value is larger, but the effects of the concentration parameter and the degrees of overidentification parallel those outlined above for equations A1 and B1. We note that the sign of the bias for 2SLS in equation A1 is inconsistent with results presented by Richardson and Wu (1971); they show that

Figure 19. Empirical Distribution of B12A3.*

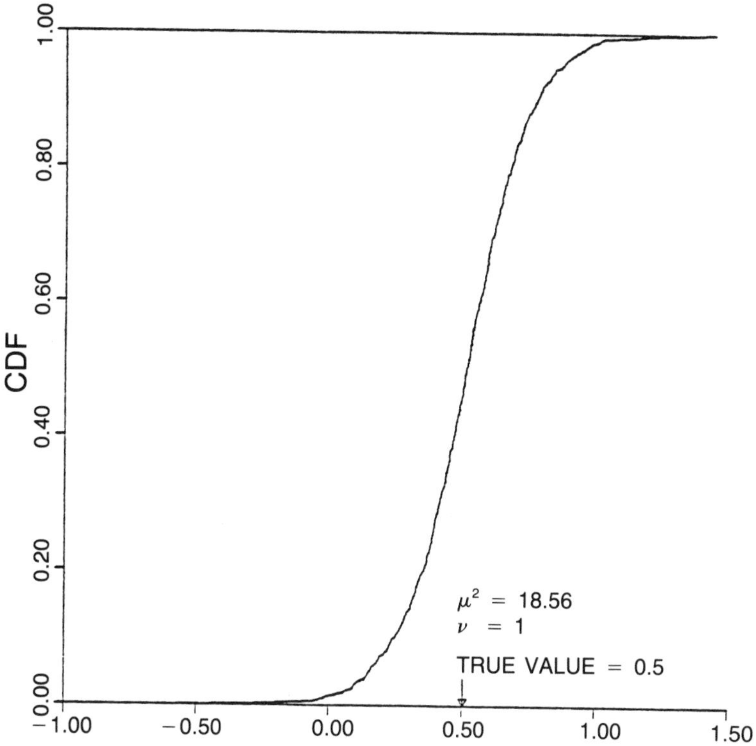

* Sample statistics: minimum = −0.5711; maximum = 1.4365; mean = 0.5084; SD = 0.2147.

when an equation is correctly specified, the bias is opposite in sign from the true parameter value. However, because the magnitude of the bias for the 2SLS estimator in equation A1 is so small, we attribute the inconsistency to sampling variation. This underscores the desirability of conducting large numbers of replications in sampling experiments.

It appears that the maximum-likelihood methods are generally somewhat less biased than 2SLS and 3SLS and that the increasing concentration parameter and degrees of overidentification exert stronger influences on 2SLS and 3SLS than on LIML and FIML, thus closing the bias gap between the classical methods and the maximum-likelihood methods as μ^2 increases. In examining the biases as proportions of the true parameter values, the same conclusion obtains.

The classical methods of estimation perform uniformly and substantially better than the maximum-likelihood estimators in terms of the concentrations of the empirical distribution functions, according to information

Figure 20. Empirical Distribution of B12AF.*

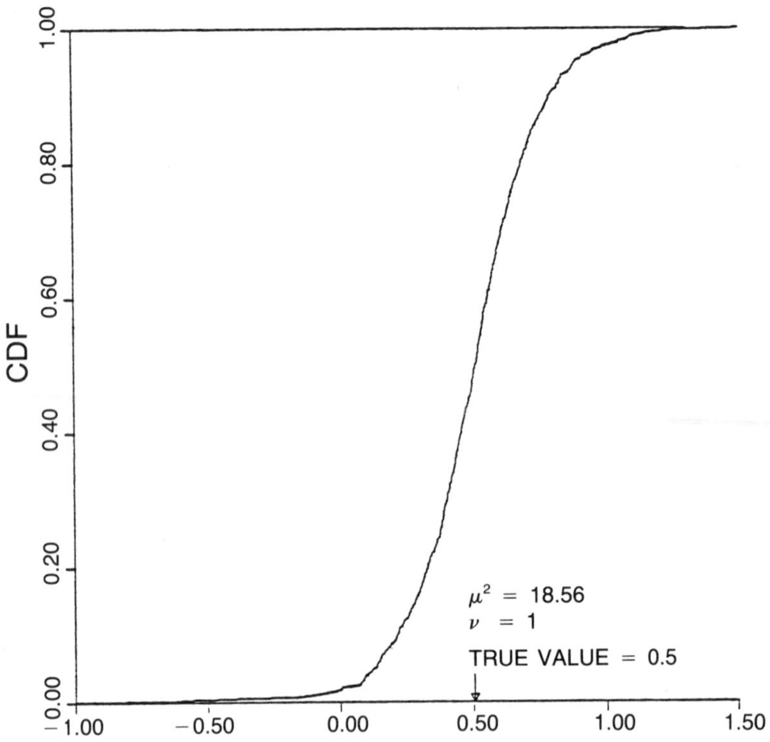

* Sample statistics: minimum = −1.1804; maximum = 1.5443; mean = 0.5061; SD = 0.2458. One extreme value has been omitted from each tail.

conveyed by the Sample SD columns in Table 16 and by the lengths of the 90% intervals between the 5% and 95% fractiles. Apparently, the most dramatic effect upon the concentration of any particular estimator is provided by the concentration parameter.

It is also interesting to note that as the degree of overidentification increases from just-identified to overidentified by 1 in moving from equation B1 to A2, even though the concentration parameter is slightly smaller, and the true parameter value is larger, the effect is for the 2SLS and 3SLS distributions to increase in concentration. Both LIML and FIML, on the other hand, lose concentration dramatically, indicating that a large concentration parameter is essential in reducing the dispersion of the ML methods even where the equations are overidentified. Aside from the conclusions drawn above, we are unable to invoke ceteris paribus broadly enough to strictly isolate the individual impacts of the degree

Figure 21. Empirical Distribution of B21AL.*

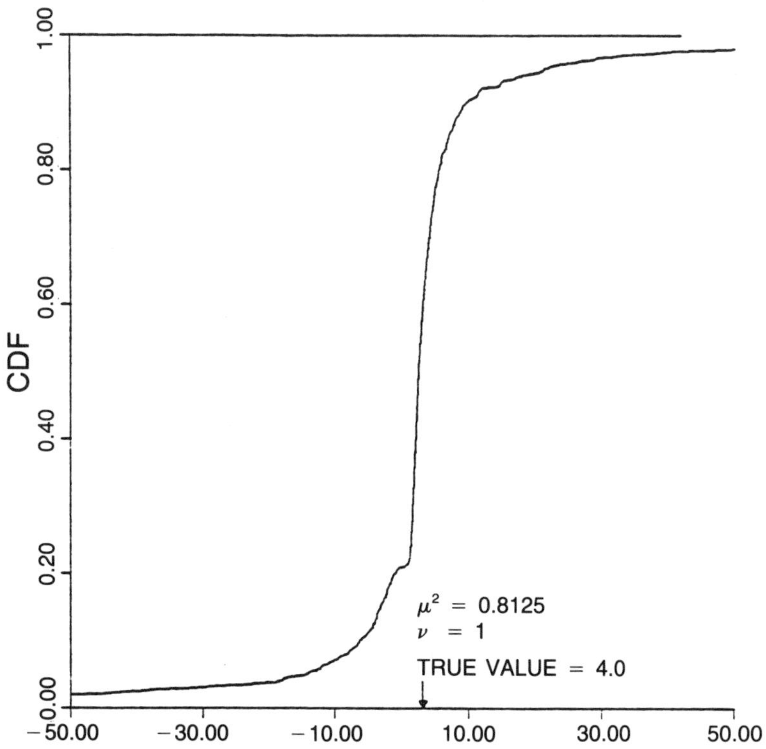

* Sample statistics: minimum = −946.43; maximum = 1056.3; mean = 4.5195; SD = 64.290. Twenty extreme values have been omitted from the lower tail; twenty-one from the upper tail.

of overidentification and the concentration parameter size upon each estimator. Nonetheless these results tend to support Conjecture 5 that increasing the degree of overidentification improves the behaviors of all the estimators but has a stronger impact on the GCL estimators than on the ML estimators.

Table 17 presents the concentrations of the estimators' empirical cumulative frequency functions in an alternative fashion. The value shown is the proportion of the experimental points that lie within an interval of given length, centered on the true parameter value. Again, the classical estimators exhibit performance superior to that of the maximum-likelihood techniques, except for short probability intervals, where the smaller biases of LIML and FIML give them the advantage. Throughout our analysis of Tables 16 and 17, we find strong evidence in support of Conjecture 3: as the magnitude of the concentration parameter increases, the per-

Table 17. Experimental Precision of the Estimation of β.

		Proportion of Estimates Within $\pm c$ of β			
Equation	*c*	*LIML*	*2SLS*	*3SLS*	*FIML*
A1	0	0	0	0	0
$\mu^2 = 18.56$	0.10	0.392	0.406	0.406	0.387
$\beta = 0.5$	0.20	0.669	0.695	0.695	0.654
	0.30	0.830	0.850	0.850	0.818
	0.40	0.919	0.933	0.933	0.914
	0.50	0.958	0.973	0.973	0.956
A2	0	0	0	0	0
$\mu^2 = 0.8125$	1.0	0.187	0.123	0.123	0.172
$\beta = 4.0$	2.0	0.431	0.356	0.356	0.414
	3.0	0.635	0.684	0.684	0.628
	4.0	0.664	0.815	0.815	0.679
	5.0	0.690	0.868	0.868	0.703
	10.0	0.821	0.971	0.971	0.845
B1	0	0	0	0	0
$\mu^2 = 2.56$	0.10	0.154	0.154	0.154	0.141
$\beta = 0.5$	0.20	0.283	0.293	0.293	0.275
	0.30	0.418	0.418	0.418	0.388
	0.40	0.519	0.519	0.519	0.489
	0.50	0.598	0.598	0.598	0.571
	1.0	0.801	0.801	0.801	0.805
	2.0	0.923	0.923	0.923	0.918
B2	0	0	0	0	0
$\mu^2 = 16.8125$	0.25	0.263	0.209	0.207	0.266
$\beta = 4.0$	0.50	0.458	0.430	0.430	0.466
	1.0	0.769	0.765	0.765	0.769
	1.5	0.899	0.947	0.947	0.907
	2.0	0.939	0.981	0.981	0.945
	2.5	0.954	0.989	0.989	0.960
	3.0	0.969	0.995	0.995	0.974

formances of *all* of the estimators *improve*, both in terms of reduced bias and reduced dispersion. The GCL estimators seem to be more sensitive to the bias reduction effect of increasing μ^2: they have larger biases to start with. On the other hand, the ML estimators seem to be more sensitive to the concentration effect of μ^2: they are more dispersed to begin with. This bears on the Klein–Nakamura conjecture, mentioned in Section II,C, of the order of sensitivity of estimators to the effects of multicollinearity. The sensitivity rankings seem to be a matter of judgment that depends upon whether the focus is on location or dispersion of the simultaneous equations estimators. Regarding ordinary least squares

Figure 22. Empirical Distribution of B21A2.*

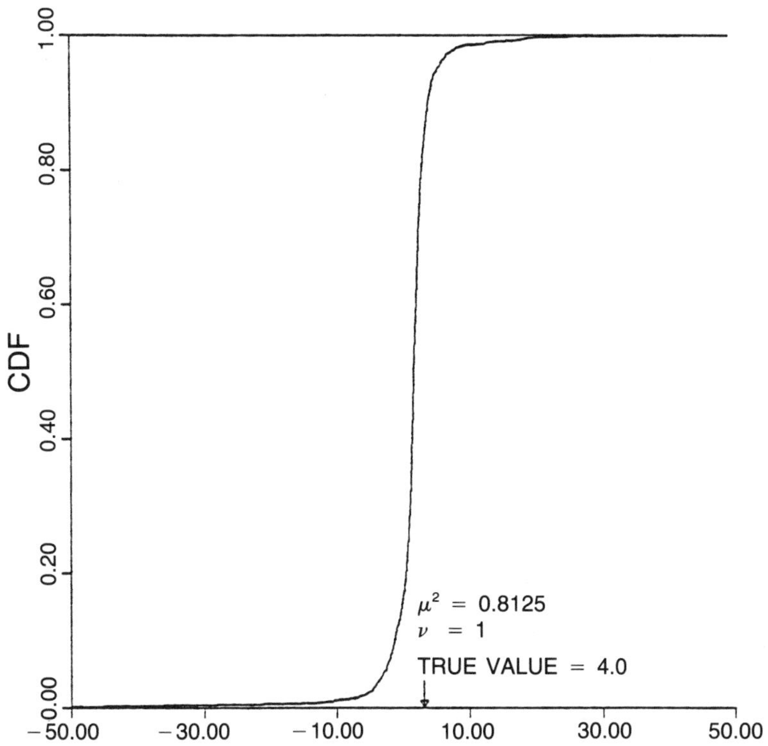

* Sample statistics: minimum = −108.67; maximum = 48.783; mean = 1.4263; SD = 5.6197. Two extreme values have been omitted from the lower tail.

(OLS), our earlier work (Rhodes and Westbrook, 1979, 1981) suggests that OLS will be more sensitive than 2SLS to the effect of μ^2 upon the bias but less sensitive than 2SLS to the effect of μ^2 upon the dispersion. We thus preserve the Klein–Nakamura rankings for sensitivity to multicollinearity, as far as dispersion is concerned, but we *invert* the order when considering location.

We have lamented the fact that taking $(\mathbf{Z}'\mathbf{Z}) = \mathbf{I}$ prevents us from contrasting the full-system estimators with the single-equation estimators. That is so, but it ought not to obscure the important results that do emerge from the experiment. Indeed, although the exact finite-sample distribution functions for the full-system estimators have not been derived, we have established the manner in which the distribution functions of the full-system estimators behave as the system-specified parameters vary. The parameters are those that are well known in the finite-sample

Figure 23. Empirical Distribution of B21A3.*

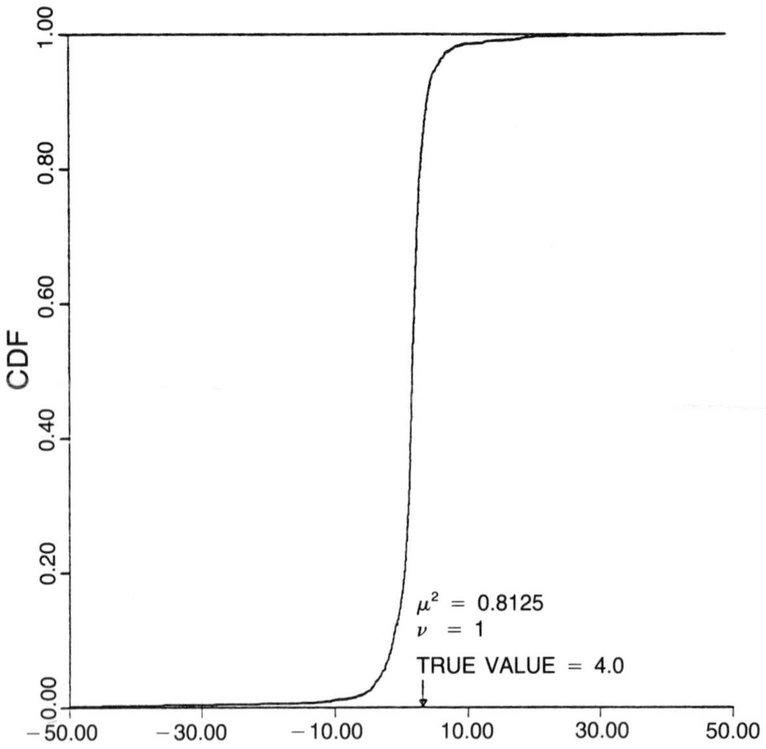

* Sample statistics: minimum = −108.67; maximum = 48.783; mean = 1.4263; SD = 5.6197. Two extreme values have been omitted from the lower tail.

distribution theory for 2SLS and LIML: the concentration parameter, the degree of overidentification, and the true coefficient value. The patterns of behavior of 3SLS and FIML are qualitatively identical to those exhibited by 2SLS and LIML, for example, as the concentration parameter or degree of overidentification increases, the concentration of the density function also increases and the magnitude of the bias decreases. Clearly, a natural followup is the investigation of the quantitative aspects of the distributions' behaviors with emphasis on the robustness of our results as $(\mathbf{Z}'\mathbf{Z})$ assumes various configurations. It is still an important open question how significant the differences are between full-system estimators and single-equation estimators in general applications.

We have elucidated, albeit in a very special case, the behavior of the distribution functions of the full-system estimators. In this experiment

Figure 24. Empirical Distribution of B21AF.*

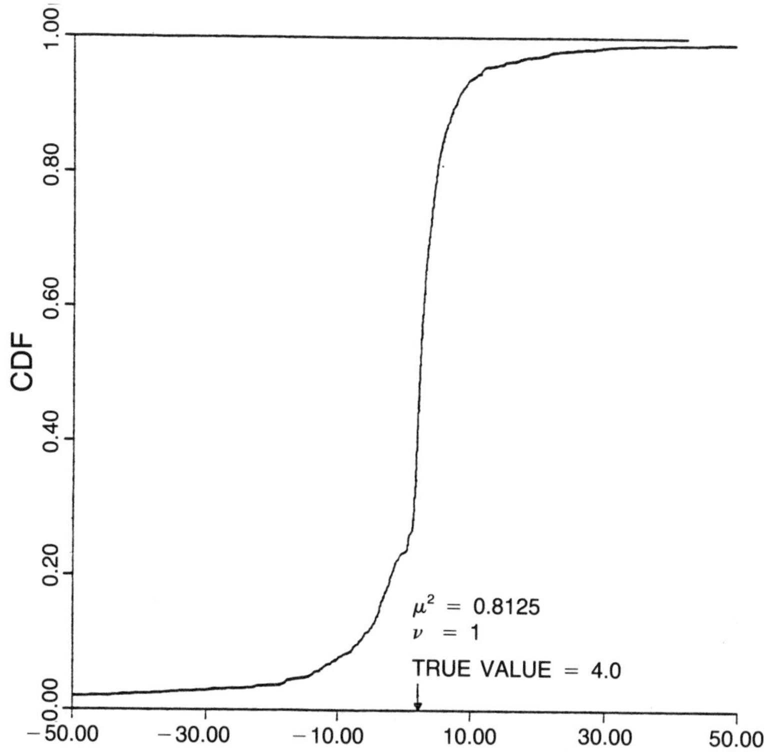

* Sample statistics: minimum = −324.87; maximum = 727.04; mean = 0.9005; SD = 34.782. Seventeen extreme values have been omitted from the lower tail; eight from the upper tail.

improvement in the estimation of simultaneous equations systems is not achieved *via* supplanting the single-equation techniques with the more intricate full-information techniques. Rather, the important dichotomy lies between the GCL methods and the ML methods. The former are uniformly and substantially superior to the latter as regards the concentration of the estimators' (empirical) finite-sample frequency functions, but the latter exhibit smaller biases. However, as the concentration parameter becomes even moderately large, the divergence between the biases becomes less consequential, although the differences in concentration remain substantial. It seems that important contributions remain to be made in the design of experiments to determine just how special—or general—the results of this experiment are.

Figure 25. Empirical Distribution of B12BX.*,†

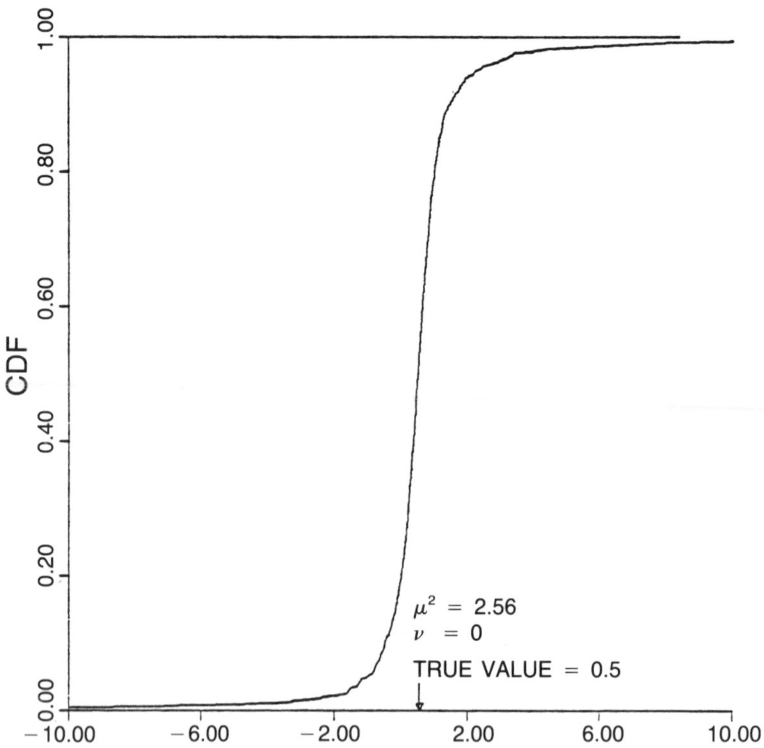

* X: LIML, 2SLS, and 3SLS.

† Sample statistics: minimum = −179.73; maximum = 106.3; mean = 0.4149; SD = 7.8192. Five extreme values have been omitted from the lower tail; seven from the upper tail.

B. Estimator Performance under Misspecification

The effects of misspecification are manifested in changes in the estimator performances reflected in their empirical cumulative frequency functions. These changes are readily observed by comparing the results under misspecification, given in Table 18, with the results presented in Table 16.

Apparent in Table 18 is the fact that misspecification does not alter the rankings of the estimators with respect to bias and concentration. In addition, the patterns of behavior of the estimators for different concentration parameter and identifiability configurations that were discerned from Tables 16 and 17 and Figures 17 through 30 are evident under misspecification. Thus, the apparent confirmation of Conjectures 3 through 5 remains unchanged by the introduction of misspecification; misspeci-

Table 18. Summary Statistics for Empirical Distribution Functions of $\tilde{\beta}$ under Misspecification.

Estimator	Design Value	Sample Mean	Sample SD	Fractiles 5%	Fractiles 95%	Conc Param	Degree of Overid
B12A2	0.5	0.2543	0.056	0.157	0.342	258.56	1
B12A3	0.5	0.2543	0.056	0.157	0.342	258.56	1
B12AL	0.5	0.2533	0.056	0.155	0.341	258.56	1
B12AF*	0.5	0.2501	0.056	0.154	0.336	258.56	1
B21A2	4.0	1.4263	5.62	−3.04	5.26	0.8125	1
B21A3	4.0	1.4263	5.62	−3.04	5.26	0.8125	1
B21AL	4.0	4.5037	64.91	−14.44	21.27	0.8125	1
B21AF*	4.0	1.0271	35.36	−14.19	11.95	0.8125	1
B12B2	0.5	0.4149	7.82	−1.030	2.241	2.56	0
B12B3	0.5	0.4149	7.82	−1.030	2.241	2.56	0
B12BL	0.5	0.4149	7.82	−1.030	2.241	2.56	0
B12BF*	0.5	0.3924	4.12	−1.194	2.439	2.56	0
B21B2	4.0	1.7811	0.90	0.715	3.132	4.8125	2
B21B3	4.0	1.7811	0.90	0.715	3.132	4.8125	2
B21BL	4.0	3.2003	14.25	1.250	8.053	4.8125	2
B21BF*	4.0	2.7640	3.73	0.769	6.540	4.8125	2

* Recall that the FIML sample statistics are based only on the number of replications actually completed.

fication apparently does not alter the *influences* of the fundamental parameters of the exact finite-sample distribution functions, though it may, of course, change the *values* of those parameters. To conserve space, we have foregone production of a series of figures that would display the cumulative frequency functions of the estimators under misspecification; they would look very much like their counterparts in Figures 17 through 30.

Juxtaposition of Tables 16 and 18 makes clear that a crucial aspect of misspecification is whether the variable in question is wrongly excluded from or wrongly included in an equation. In both equations A2 and B1, where now variable $\mathbf{z}_3$ is wrongly included, the estimators are identical with the properly specified case, aside from insignificant computational differences in the LIML case. This is not surprising in view of the fact that the concentration parameters for these equations did not change with the advent of misspecification. On the other hand, $\mathbf{z}_3$ is wrongly excluded from equations A1 and B2, with the result that the estimators of β become substantially more biased in the downward direction. Furthermore, the concentrations of the estimators for equation A1 have increased markedly, and those for equation B2 have decreased somewhat.

Figure 26. Empirical Distribution of B12BF.*

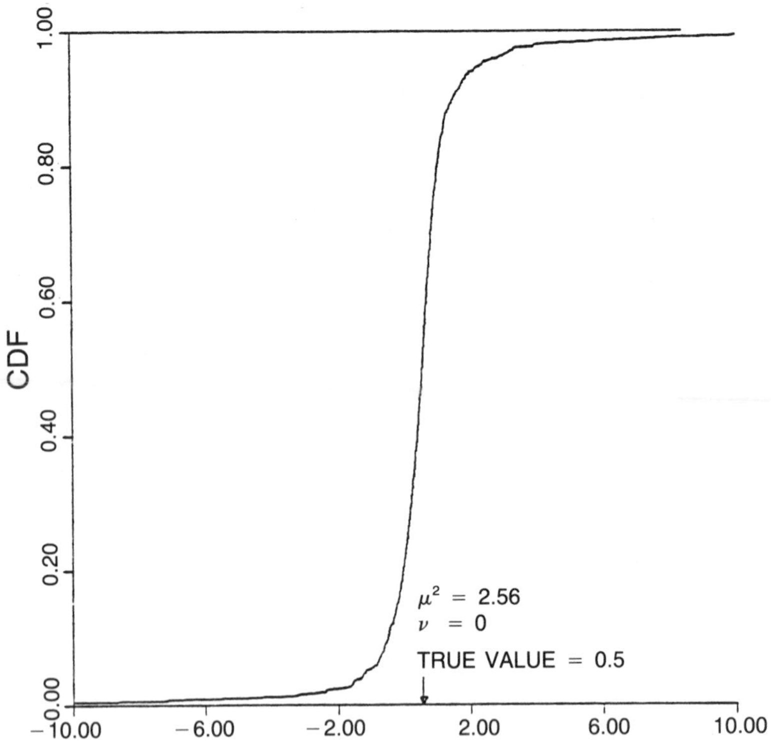

* Sample statistics: minimum = −179.73; maximum = 106.3; mean = 0.4180; SD = 8.1290. Five extreme values have been omitted from the lower tail; seven from the upper tail.

These results, too, are consistent with predictions based on the changes in the concentration parameters. Note also that for equation A1 all three estimators yield identical results, an indication, perhaps, that equation A1 is just-identified *according to the data.* As odd as it may seem that wrongful exclusion of a variable could improve estimator performance as measured by concentration, such a result is fully expected, according to Hale, Mariano, and Ramage (1980) and Rhodes and Westbrook (1981).

VII. CONCLUSIONS AND REMARKS ON FURTHER WORK

This article has addressed several of the leading open questions provided by simultaneous equation estimation and inference. In the course of exploring those questions, we intended to provide an example of the

Figure 27. Empirical Distribution of B21BL.*

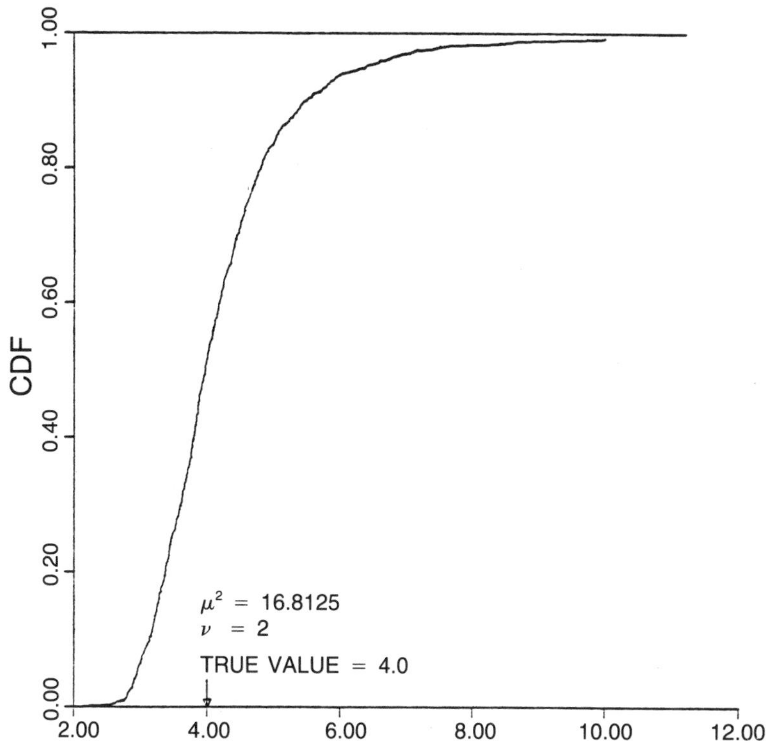

* Sample statistics: minimum = 2.1513; maximum = 30.917; mean = 4.2480; SD = 1.4522. Eight extreme values have been omitted from the upper tail.

manner in which known analytical results could be used to design sampling experiments that focus directly on the issues at hand.

Our experimental design revolves around the selection of the "fundamental parameters" that determine the exact finite-sample density functions of the 2SLS estimators. Thus, not only are we able to compare the empirical sampling distributions of the alternative estimators, but we may also ascertain whether the fundamental parameters play similar roles in all of the distributions and perhaps we can identify the magnitudes of their various effects. Similar considerations guided our investigation of the identifiability test statistics.

If the fundamental parameters do determine the natures of the exact finite-sample distribution functions of the estimators and test statistics and if we can detect the manner of this determination, then we ought also to examine *estimates* of the fundamental parameters themselves,

Figure 28. Empirical Distribution of B21B2.*

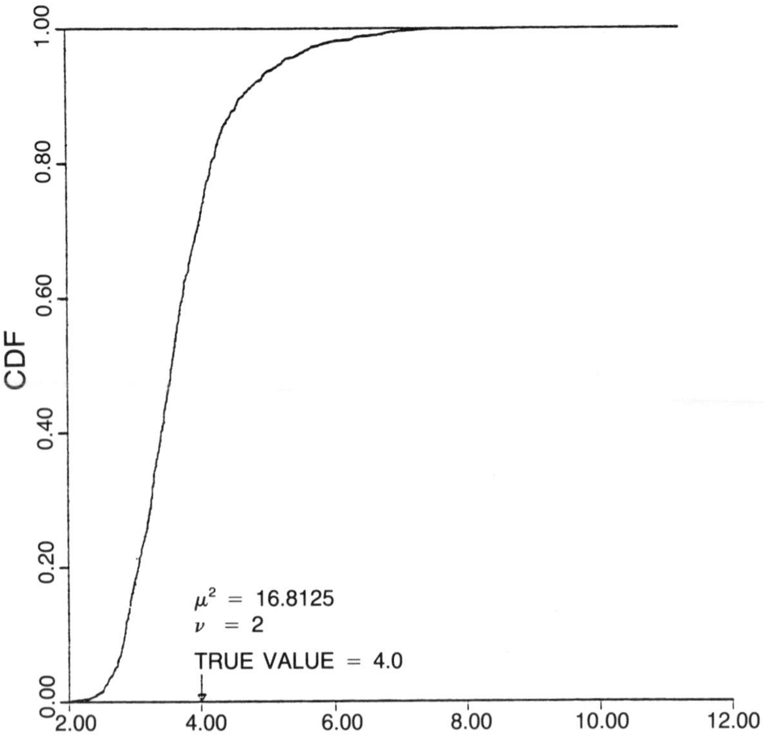

* Sample statistics: minimum = 2.0262; maximum = 9.4592; mean = 3.7118; SD = 0.8136.

which may not be known in practice. If reliable estimates can be found, then we can reliably infer the behavior of the estimators and test statistics in practice. The distributions of estimates of fundamental parameters were examined in Section IV. There, we found that the elements of the standardized means-sigma matrices were consistently overestimated. As the standardized concentration parameter is the lower diagonal element of the standardized means-sigma matrix, reliance on estimated values of μ^2 would tend to induce overconfident inferences concerning the degree of concentration of the simultaneous equation estimators. Furthermore, the distributions of estimates of fundamental parameters seem to exhibit rather large dispersions.

Given that the elements of the means-sigma matrix contain information about the identification status of the equations as well as about the exact finite-sample distributions of the estimators, we examined the distributions

Figure 29. Empirical Distribution of B21B3.*

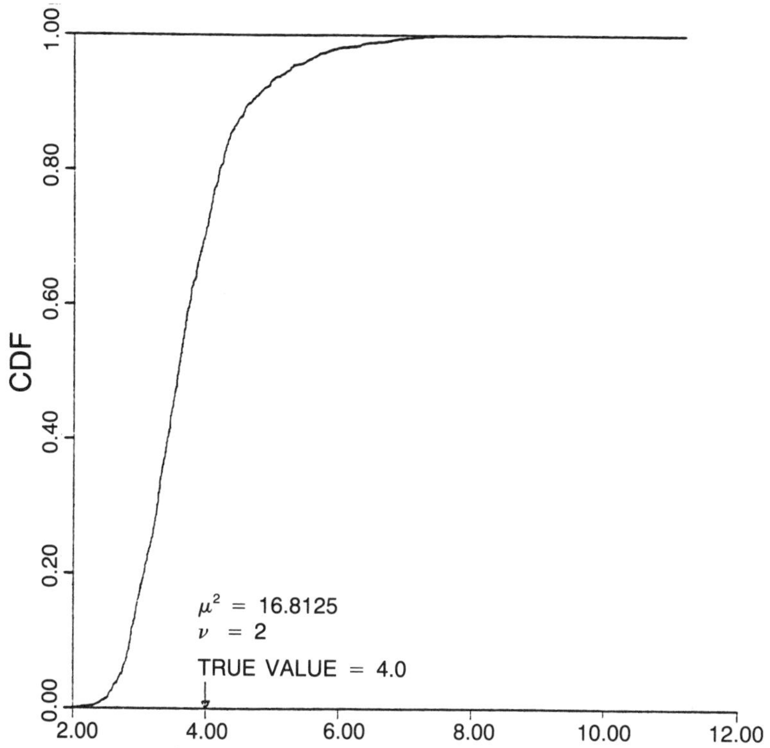

* Sample statistics: minimum = 2.0262; maximum = 9.4592; mean = 3.7118; SD = 0.8136.

of the estimates of fundamental parameters under two specification regimes: a correct specification and a misspecification. Under misspecification the design values of the elements of the means-sigma matrices changed, sometimes profoundly. Increases in the values of the elements were noted for equations from which a variable was wrongly excluded, and decreases were noted for the other equations, which contained an extraneous variable. The estimates of the fundamental parameters reflected these changes; their impacts upon the simultaneous equation coefficient estimators were presented in Section VI. Although the impacts of misspecification on the simultaneous equations estimators were directly traced, examination of the elements of the means-sigma matrices themselves does not reveal the presence of misspecification. The smallest root of the standardized means-sigma matrix does, however, convey information about misspecification: examination of that smallest root is equivalent to examination of the LIML $\tilde{F}$ ID test statistic and was treated in Section V.

Figure 30. Empirical Distribution of B21BF.*

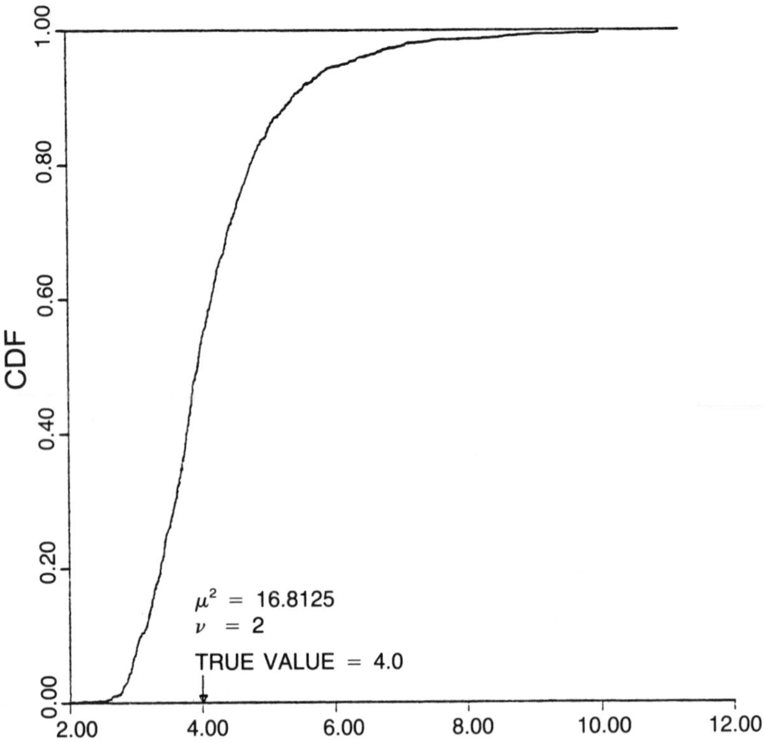

* Sample statistics: minimum = 2.0306; maximum = 13.429; mean = 4.1862; SD = 1.1218. Four extreme values have been omitted from the upper tail.

In Section V we presented a comparison of three identifiability test statistics and evaluated their behaviors under correct and incorrect specifications. We found support for Conjecture 1, namely, that the distribution of the LIML $\tilde{F}$ statistic is more closely approximated by the F-distribution than is the 2SLS $\hat{F}$. We also recorded the variations in behavior of the empirical cumulative distribution functions of LIML $\tilde{F}$ and 2SLS $\hat{F}$ as the concentration parameter and degree of overidentification changed: increasing concentration with increasing concentration parameter; decreasing concentration with increasing degree of overidentification. Under the null hypothesis, both test statistics produce "conservative" results in the sense of being somewhat biased against the null hypothesis. The full-system test, based on FIML, yielded results similar to the single-equation tests. In particular, the approximation by its asymptotic distribution, the χ^2, was not good and the FIML test is also somewhat biased against the true null hypothesis. The results under misspecification were somewhat "disappointing." While the 2SLS $\hat{F}$ statistic was relatively more powerful than the LIML $\tilde{F}$ for rejecting the false null hypothesis, neither it nor the LIML $\tilde{F}$ was very powerful for doing so. Furthermore, we were required to falsify our second conjecture: the full-system test based on FIML was not powerful at all for rejecting the false null hypothesis. In fact, where the maintained hypothesis was "B" and the structure "A" was employed in estimation, the proportion of FIML ID test statistics falling in the acceptance region actually *increased*. We note again the caveat with which all of our FIML results are presented: not all of the FIML replications converged; if they had, it is possible that the results we report could be marginally altered.

Finally, we summarize our findings concerning the alternative estimation techniques themselves: FIML, LIML, 3SLS, and 2SLS. Our primary result regarding the alternative simultaneous equation estimators was adumbrated by the known analytical results concerning the existence of the integer moments of the exact finite-sample distribution functions associated with the estimators. Specifically, it is known that the GCL estimators possess a certain number of integer moments; the ML estimators do not. This is reflected in the behavior of the empirical cumulative frequency functions of estimates generated by our experiment: the GCL methods perform substantially better than the ML methods as regards their concentration. Thus, we find evidence in support of Conjecture 4.

Evidence in support of Conjecture 3 is apparent throughout Section VI, and tends to underscore the GCL/ML dichotomy. As the magnitude of the concentration parameter increases, the performances of all of the estimators improve, both in terms of reduced bias and reduced dispersion. These effects are most pronounced upon the estimators having the larger bias or dispersion to start with, the GCL or ML, respectively. Finally, when we examine the effect of changing the degree of overidentification, we find supporting evidence for Conjecture 5: increasing the degree of overidentification (which is equivalent to the degrees of freedom for the 2SLS estimator) improves the behaviors of all of the estimators but has a stronger impact on the GCL estimators.

Under misspecification we find that the rankings of the estimators with respect to bias and dispersion remain unaltered, as do the patterns of behavior of the estimators for various combinations of concentration parameters and identification. The apparent confirmation of Conjectures 3 through 5 is upheld under misspecification.

Throughout this article we have stressed the importance of conducting tests of identification. The results of our experiment indicate at least two aspects in which current tests of identification are inadequate. First, while most simultaneous equation estimation uses the 2SLS estimator, we have found that the identifiability test based on 2SLS is sometimes not accurately approximated by its asymptotic distribution, Snedecor's F. The need for a better approximation to the distribution of the 2SLS $\hat{F}$ is therefore apparent. Second, none of the test statistics examined proved very powerful for rejecting the identification hypothesis when it was false. Some research should be directed toward ascertaining the powers of alternative tests: perhaps the test of the rank condition considered by Rhodes (1981b) will prove to be more reliable. Finally, we recall Byron's (1974) arguments in favor of full-system tests of identification and note that Hendry's (1971) test based on FIML was neither very well approximated by the chi-squared distribution nor powerful for rejecting the false null hypothesis. Research in the area of system-wide tests of overidentifying restrictions therefore seems to be called for.

Regarding estimation techniques, the areas of extension are also fairly obvious. Naturally, it will be of interest to relax the condition $\mathbf{Z}'\mathbf{Z} = \mathbf{I}$ and to observe the manner in which the estimates diverge and the degree to which the GCL/ML dichotomy is then maintained. Similarly, extensions may be made to systems of three or more equations, where our five conjectures may be reexamined, and some new conjectures formed. For example, we have determined that taking $\mathbf{Z}'\mathbf{Z} = \mathbf{I}$ for a three-equation system does not generate the equivalence of 2SLS and 3SLS or LIML and FIML; thus, three-equation systems will permit us to ascertain and evaluate the differences among all four estimation techniques while enjoying the computational advantages afforded by $\mathbf{Z}'\mathbf{Z} = \mathbf{I}$.

APPENDIX A

The Identifiability Test Statistics

Consider the first equation in a system of $G \geqslant 2$ linear structural equations

$$\boldsymbol{\beta}_{\Delta}\mathbf{y}_{\Delta t} + \boldsymbol{\beta}_{\Delta\Delta}\mathbf{y}_{\Delta\Delta t} + \boldsymbol{\gamma}_{*}\mathbf{z}_{*t} + \boldsymbol{\gamma}_{**}\mathbf{z}_{**t} = \mathbf{u}_{1t} \tag{A.1}$$

where the notation is defined in the text (see equation 1, Section II,A). The variables $\mathbf{y}_{\Delta\Delta}$ and $\mathbf{z}_{**}$ are hypothetically absent from equation (A.1). This constitutes an identifiability hypothesis by way of exclusion restrictions. We confine our attention to overidentifying restrictions on exogenous variables and write the null hypothesis

$$H_0\colon \boldsymbol{\gamma}_{**} = \mathbf{0} \tag{A.2}$$

We may define certain sums of squared residuals (cf. Basmann, 1960):

$$G_1(\boldsymbol{\beta}_{1\Delta}) = (\mathbf{y}_1 - \boldsymbol{\beta}_{1\Delta}\mathbf{y}_{1\Delta})'(\mathbf{I} - \mathbf{z}_*(\mathbf{z}_*'\mathbf{z}_*)^{-1}\mathbf{z}_*')(\mathbf{y}_1 - \boldsymbol{\beta}_{1\Delta}\mathbf{y}_{1\Delta}) \tag{A.3}$$

and

$$G_2(\boldsymbol{\beta}_{1\Delta}) = (\mathbf{y}_1 - \boldsymbol{\beta}_{1\Delta}\mathbf{y}_{1\Delta})'(\mathbf{I} - \mathbf{z}(\mathbf{z}'\mathbf{z})^{-1}\mathbf{z}')(\mathbf{y}_1 - \boldsymbol{\beta}_{1\Delta}\mathbf{y}_{1\Delta}) \qquad \text{(A.4)}$$

Here, $\mathbf{y}_1$ is the normalized endogenous variable and $\mathbf{y}_{1\Delta}$ represents the remaining included endogenous variables. $\boldsymbol{\beta}_{1\Delta}$ is the coefficient vector associated with $\mathbf{y}_{1\Delta}$. The observation index t has been dropped for notational clarity. From $G_1(\boldsymbol{\beta}_{1\Delta})$ and $G_2(\boldsymbol{\beta}_{1\Delta})$ we construct

$$Q(\boldsymbol{\beta}_{1\Delta}) = G_1(\boldsymbol{\beta}_{1\Delta}) - G_2(\boldsymbol{\beta}_{1\Delta}) \qquad \text{(A.5)}$$

and

$$\phi = [G_1(\boldsymbol{\beta}_{1\Delta}) - G_2(\boldsymbol{\beta}_{1\Delta})]/G_2(\boldsymbol{\beta}_{1\Delta}) \qquad \text{(A.6)}$$

The 2SLS estimates of $\boldsymbol{\beta}_{1\Delta}$ denoted $\hat{\boldsymbol{\beta}}_{1\Delta}$, are obtained by minimizing (A.5) with respect to $\boldsymbol{\beta}_{1\Delta}$ (cf. Basmann, 1957). The LIML estimates of $\boldsymbol{\beta}_{1\Delta}$ are obtained by minimizing the ratio (A.6) with respect to $\boldsymbol{\beta}_{1\Delta}$: denote the LIML estimates $\tilde{\boldsymbol{\beta}}_{1\Delta}$. Insertion of $\hat{\boldsymbol{\beta}}_{1\Delta}$ and $\tilde{\boldsymbol{\beta}}_{1\Delta}$ into the expression for ϕ yields, respectively,

$$\hat{\phi} = [G_1(\hat{\boldsymbol{\beta}}_{1\Delta}) - G_2(\hat{\boldsymbol{\beta}}_{1\Delta})]/G_2(\hat{\boldsymbol{\beta}}_{1\Delta}) \qquad \text{(A.7)}$$

and

$$\tilde{\phi} = [G_1(\tilde{\boldsymbol{\beta}}_{1\Delta}) - G_2(\tilde{\boldsymbol{\beta}}_{1\Delta})]/G_2(\tilde{\boldsymbol{\beta}}_{1\Delta}) \qquad \text{(A.8)}$$

Several functions of $\hat{\phi}$ and $\tilde{\phi}$ have been proposed as identifiability test statistics with approximate critical regions based on the χ^2 and F-distributions with various degrees of freedom. Basmann's (1960) study indicated that the test

$$\hat{F} = (m/\nu)\hat{\phi} \geqslant F(\nu, m) \qquad \text{(A.9)}$$

where $m = N - K$ and $\nu = K_{**} - G + 1$ was most promising. Consequently, in this article we examine the single-equation identifiability test statistics $\hat{F}$ and the analogous statistic based on LIML estimation:

$$\tilde{F} = (m/\nu)\tilde{\phi} \qquad \text{(A.10)}$$

The FIML ID test statistic suggested by Hendry (1971), our full-system identifiability test statistic, is based on a likelihood ratio. If the system is just-identified, the unrestricted reduced-form parameters may be solved for unique values of the structural parameters. The system likelihood value associated with this solution is proportional to

$$L_{\text{rf}} = |\hat{\mathbf{v}}'\hat{\mathbf{v}}|^{-T/2} \qquad \text{(A.11)}$$

where $\hat{\mathbf{v}}'\hat{\mathbf{v}}$ is the covariance matrix of reduced-form residuals. When any of the equations are overidentified, the likelihood value associated with estimates of the structural parameters is proportional to

$$L_{\text{fiml}} = |\hat{\boldsymbol{\beta}}^{-1}\hat{\mathbf{u}}'\hat{\mathbf{u}}\hat{\boldsymbol{\beta}}'^{-1}|^{-T/2} \tag{A.12}$$

where $\mathbf{u}'\mathbf{u}$ is the covariance matrix of structural residuals. The likelihood ratio

$$\lambda = L_{\text{rf}}/L_{\text{fiml}} \tag{A.13}$$

is bounded on (0, 1), and $-2\ln(\lambda)$ is asymptotically distributed as χ^2 with $k - G^2$ degrees of freedom. The parameter k is the total number of prior restrictions on all G equations in the system, including the normalization restriction for each equation. If $-2\ln(\lambda)$ is significant at some predetermined level, we may conclude that the overidentifying restrictions are inconsistent with the information contained in the sample.

APPENDIX B

The Means-Sigma Matrices

The exact finite-sample density functions of the 2SLS estimators of β in an equation containing one endogenous variable on the right-hand side has its particular behavior determined by its degrees of freedom (ν), the true parameter value (β), and the elements of a means-sigma matrix ($\boldsymbol{\Omega}$). For correctly specified equations, the standardized means-sigma matrix may be expressed in terms of β and the concentration parameter (μ^2) alone. Details of the role of $\boldsymbol{\Omega}$ can be found in Rhodes and Westbrook (1981).

To find $\boldsymbol{\Omega}$ for the experiment, we write

$$\boldsymbol{\Omega} = \boldsymbol{\Sigma}_{22}^{-1}\boldsymbol{\Pi}\mathbf{z}'[\mathbf{z}(\mathbf{z}'\mathbf{z})^{-1}\mathbf{z}' - \mathbf{z}_*(\mathbf{z}_*'\mathbf{z}_*)^{-1}\mathbf{z}_*']\mathbf{z}\boldsymbol{\Pi}' \tag{B.1}$$

where $\boldsymbol{\Sigma}_{22}$ is a submatrix of the reduced form covariance matrix corresponding to right hand side endogenous variables, and $\mathbf{z}_*$ represents exogenous variables excluded from the equation being estimated. With $\mathbf{z}'\mathbf{z} = \mathbf{I}$, as in the experiment, the expression in (B.1) collapses to

$$\boldsymbol{\Omega} = \boldsymbol{\Sigma}^{-1}\boldsymbol{\Pi}_*\boldsymbol{\Pi}_*' \tag{B.2}$$

where $\boldsymbol{\Pi}_*$ represents the partition of the reduced form coefficient matrix associated with the exogenous variables of interest. In the experiment,

$\boldsymbol{\Sigma}$ is $\left[\begin{smallmatrix}1 & 0.5\\ 0.5 & 1\end{smallmatrix}\right]$ so $\boldsymbol{\Sigma}_{22}$ is 1.0 for each equation, and for the first equation in system A, $\boldsymbol{\Pi}_*$ is $\left[\begin{smallmatrix}2.0 & -0.8\\ 4.0 & -1.6\end{smallmatrix}\right]$. This yields

$$\boldsymbol{\Omega} = \begin{bmatrix} 2.0 & -0.8 \\ 4.0 & -1.6 \end{bmatrix}\begin{bmatrix} 2.0 & 4.0 \\ -0.8 & -1.6 \end{bmatrix} = \begin{bmatrix} 4.64 & 9.28 \\ 9.28 & 18.56 \end{bmatrix}. \tag{B.3}$$

Under a standardizing transformation that carries $\boldsymbol{\Sigma}$ to $\mathbf{I}_2$, the means-sigma matrix would be simply $\boldsymbol{\Pi}_*\boldsymbol{\Pi}_*'$, or

$$\boldsymbol{\Pi}_*\boldsymbol{\Pi}_*' = \begin{bmatrix} 2.0 & -0.8 \\ 4.0 & -1.6 \end{bmatrix}\begin{bmatrix} 2.0 & 4.0 \\ -0.8 & -0.6 \end{bmatrix} = \begin{bmatrix} 4.64 & 9.28 \\ 9.28 & 18.56 \end{bmatrix} \tag{B.4}$$

Thus, we see that for this experiment, the standardized and nonstandardized $\boldsymbol{\Omega}$ matrices are identical.

The standardized means-sigma matrix may also be written as

$$\boldsymbol{\Omega} = \mu^2\begin{bmatrix} \beta^2 & \beta \\ \beta & 1 \end{bmatrix} \tag{B.5}$$

where μ^2 is the standardized concentration parameter; in this case $\mu^2 = 18.56$ and $\beta = 0.5$. It is apparent from (B.5) that for correctly specified equations, the determinant of $\boldsymbol{\Omega}$ is zero.

Conducting similar exercises for the four equations in systems A and B under correct specification, we enter the results in Table B.1.

When the equation in question is misspecified, the construction of $\boldsymbol{\Omega}$ is the same; we just have to remember to substitute $\boldsymbol{\Pi}_*$ values from the appropriate maintained hypothesis. Thus, when we specify equation A1 when we should have done B1, the appropriate partition to use for $\boldsymbol{\Pi}_*$

Table B.1. Means-Sigma Matrices for the Experimental Design.

	$\boldsymbol{\Omega} = \boldsymbol{\Sigma}_{22}^{-1}\boldsymbol{\Pi}_*\boldsymbol{\Pi}_*' = \boldsymbol{\Pi}_*\boldsymbol{\Pi}_*' = \mu^2\begin{bmatrix} \beta^2 & \beta \\ \beta & 1 \end{bmatrix}$	Det($\boldsymbol{\Omega}$)
A1	$\begin{bmatrix} 4.64 & 9.28 \\ 9.28 & 18.56 \end{bmatrix}$	0
A2	$\begin{bmatrix} 13.0 & 3.25 \\ 3.25 & 0.8125 \end{bmatrix}$	0
B1	$\begin{bmatrix} 0.64 & 1.28 \\ 1.28 & 2.56 \end{bmatrix}$	0
B2	$\begin{bmatrix} 269.0 & 67.25 \\ 67.25 & 16.8125 \end{bmatrix}$	0

Table B.2. Means-Sigma Matrices for the Experimental Design Misspecified Cases.

	$\Omega = \Sigma_{22}^{-1}\Pi_*\Pi_*' = \Pi_*\Pi_*'$	Det(Ω)
A1	$\begin{bmatrix} 16.64 & 65.28 \\ 65.28 & 258.56 \end{bmatrix}$	40.96
A2	$\begin{bmatrix} 13.0 & 3.25 \\ 1.28 & 0.8125 \end{bmatrix}$	0
B1	$\begin{bmatrix} 0.64 & 1.28 \\ 1.28 & 2.56 \end{bmatrix}$	0
B2	$\begin{bmatrix} 29.0 & 11.25 \\ 11.25 & 4.8125 \end{bmatrix}$	13.00

is

$$\Pi_* = \begin{bmatrix} 4.0 & -0.8 \\ 16.0 & -1.6 \end{bmatrix}. \tag{B.6}$$

Under misspecification, Ω can no longer be expressed as equation (B.5) and the determinant of Ω is no longer zero. Carrying out this new exercise for the four misspecified equations, we tabulate the results in Table B.2.

Note that the means-sigma matrices do not change for equations A2 and B1 that have exogenous variables incorrectly *included*. Because the values of the elements of Ω are determined by the partition of Π related to *excluded* variables, wrongful inclusion has no effect.

ACKNOWLEDGMENTS

Rhodes' partial support by Colorado State University Experiment Station and Westbrook's partial support by the Georgetown University Summer Grant program is appreciatively acknowledged. The authors are also grateful to Michael Fidler and Hugh Geary of the Instructional and Research Computer Center at the Ohio State University and to Jan Larsen of the Academic Computation Center at Georgetown University for programming assistance.

NOTE

1. Schumpeter, J., *History of Economic Analysis,* Chapter 4, Oxford University Press, Boston, 1954.

REFERENCES

Anderson, T. W. and H. Rubin (1949). Estimation of the parameters of a single equation in a complete system of stochastic equations, *Ann. Math. Statis. 20,* 46–63.

Basmann, R. L. (1957). A generalized classical method of linear estimationn of coefficients in a structural equation, *Econometrica 25,* 77–83.

Basmann, R. L. (1960). On finite-sample distributions of generalized classical linear identifiability test statistics, *JASA 55,* 650–659.

Basmann, R. L. (1961). A note on the exact finite-sample frequency functions of generalized classical linear estimators in two leading overidentified cases, *JASA 56,* 619–636.

Basmann, R. L. (1963). A note on the exact finite-sample frequency functions of generalized classical linear estimators in a leading three equation case, *JASA 58,* 161–171.

Basmann, R. L. (1965). On the application of the identifiability test statistic in predictive testing of explanatory economic models: Part 1, *Econometric Annual of the Indian Economic Journal 23,* 387–423.

Basmann, R. L. (1966). On the application of the identifiability test statistic in predictive testing of explanatory economic models: Part 2, *Econometric Annual of the Indian Economic Journal 24,* 233–252.

Byron, R. P. (1974). Testing structural specification using the unrestricted reduced form, *Econometrica 42,* 869–883.

Cragg, J. G. (1968). Some effects of incorrect specification on the small sample properties of several simultaneous equations estimators, *Int. Econ. Rev. 9,* 63–86.

Dent, W. and J. Geweke (1980). On specification in simultaneous equation models, *In* J. Kmenta and J. B. Ramsey (eds.), *Evaluation of Econometric Models,* New York: Academic Press.

Farebrother, R. W. and N. E. Savin (1974). The graph of a *k*-class estimator, *Rev. Econ. Studies 41,* 533–538.

Haavelmo, T. (1947). Methods of measuring the marginal propensity to consume, *JASA 42,* 105–122.

Hale, C., R. S. Mariano and J. G. Ramage (1980). Finite sample analysis of misspecification in simultaneous equation models, *JASA 75,* 418–427.

Hendry, D. F. (1971). Maximum-likelihood estimation of systems of simultaneous regression equations with errors generated by a vector autoregressive process, *Int. Econ. Rev. 12,* 257–272.

Klein, L. R. and M. Nakamura (1962). Singularity in the equation systems of econometrics: Some aspects of the problem of multicollinearity, *Int. Econ. Rev. 3,* 274–299.

Liu, T. C. (1960). Underidentification, structural estimation, and forecasting, *Econometrica 28,* 855–865.

Mariano, R. S., J. B. McDonald and A. Tishler (1981). On the effects of multicollinearity upon the properties of structural coefficient estimators, Brigham Young University.

Mariano, R. S. and T. Sawa (1972). Exact finite-sample distribution of the limited-information maximum-likelihood estimator in the case of two included endogenous variables, *JASA 67,* 159–163.

Phillips, P. C. B. (1980). The exact distribution of instrumental variable estimators in an equation containing $n + 1$ endogenous variables, *Econometrica 48,* 861–878.

Rhodes, G. F. (1981a). A study of the likelihood ratio test for normalizing restrictions, Colorado State University.

Rhodes, G. F. (1981b). Exact density functions and approximate critical regions for likelihood ratio identifiability test statistics, *Econometrica 49,* 1035–1056.

Rhodes, G. F. and M. D. Westbrook (1979). Power and confidence interval comparisons for OLS and 2SLS estimators in structural equations with two endogenous variables, Presented at the Econometric Society Meetings, Atlanta, Georgia.

Rhodes, G. F. and M. D. Westbrook (1981). A study of estimator densities and performance under misspecification, *J. Econometrics 16,* 311–337.

Richardson, D. H. (1968a). On the distribution of the identifiability test statistic, *In* J. P. Quirk and A. M. Zarley (eds.), *Quantitative Economics,* pp 203–216. University of Kansas Press.

Richardson, D. H. (1968b). The exact distribution of a structural coefficient estimator, *JASA 63,* 1214–1226.

Richardson, D. H. and D. M. Wu (1971). A note on the comparison of ordinary and two-stage least squares estimators, *Econometrica 39,* 973–981.

Sargan, J. D. (1970). The finite sample distribution of FIML estimators, Presented at the Cambridge World Congress of the Econometric Society, 1970.

Sargan, J. D. (1976). Econometric estimators and the Edgeworth approximation, *Econometrica 44,* 421–448.

Sargan, J. D. (1978). On the existence of the moments of the 3SLS estimators, *Econometrica 46,* 1329–1350.

Sims, C. (1980). Macroeconomics and reality, *Econometrica 48,* 1–48.

Zellner, A. (1979). Statistical analysis of econometric models, *JASA 74,* 628–651.

AN EXPERIMENTAL INVESTIGATION OF SOME APPROXIMATE FINITE SAMPLE TESTS OF LINEAR RESTRICTIONS ON MATRICES OF REGRESSION COEFFICIENTS

R. L. Basmann

I. INTRODUCTION

Let $\mathbf{x}_t$ denote a column vector with p components and expectation

$$\mathrm{E}\mathbf{x}_t = \overline{\mathbf{\Pi}}\mathbf{z}_t \tag{1}$$

where $\overline{\mathbf{\Pi}}$ is a $(p \times q)$ matrix of regression coefficients, and $\mathbf{z}_t$ is a column

Advances in Econometrics, Volume 2, pages 197–208

ISBN: 0-89232-183-0

vector of q components. Let

$$E(\mathbf{x}_t - \overline{\mathbf{\Pi}}\mathbf{z}_t)(\mathbf{x}_t - \overline{\mathbf{\Pi}}\mathbf{z}_t)' = \mathbf{\Sigma} \tag{2}$$

where $\mathbf{\Sigma}$ is a $(p \times p)$ positive definite matrix. Let $\mathbf{x}_t$ be uncorrelated with $\mathbf{x}_s$ for every $t \neq s$. Define the $(p \times q)$ matrix $\mathbf{\Pi}$ by

$$\mathbf{\Pi} = \left(\sum_{t=1}^{N} \mathbf{x}_t\mathbf{z}_t'\right)\left(\sum_{t=1}^{N} \mathbf{z}_t\mathbf{z}_t'\right)^{-1} \tag{3}$$

$\mathbf{\Pi}$ is an estimate of $\overline{\mathbf{\Pi}}$. The estimate $\mathbf{S}$ of $\mathbf{\Sigma}$ is obtained from

$$(N - q)\mathbf{S} = \sum_{t=1}^{N} (\mathbf{x}_t - \mathbf{\Pi}\mathbf{z}_t)(\mathbf{x}_t - \mathbf{\Pi}\mathbf{z}_t)' \tag{4}$$

Let the hypothetical distribution of $\mathbf{x}_t$ be normal with mean (1) and variance–covariance matrix (2).

Suppose that $p \times q_2$ ($q_2 \geqslant p$) submatrix $\overline{\mathbf{\Pi}}_2$ of regression coefficients is of rank $r < p$. If this hypothesis is true, then there exist $p - r$ linearly independent column vectors $\boldsymbol{\gamma}$ of p components that satisfy

$$\boldsymbol{\gamma}'\overline{\mathbf{\Pi}}_2 = \mathbf{0} \tag{5}$$

Without consequent loss of generality we shall in this article confine our attention to the case where $r = p - 1$. Let $[\overline{\mathbf{\Pi}}_1 : \overline{\mathbf{\Pi}}_2]$ denote the partition of $\overline{\mathbf{\Pi}}$, and let $(\mathbf{z}_{1t}; \mathbf{z}_{2t})$ denote the corresponding partition of $\mathbf{z}_t$. We make the transformation

$$\mathbf{v}_t = \mathbf{z}_{2t} - \left(\sum_{s=1}^{N} \mathbf{z}_{2s}\,\mathbf{z}_{1s}'\right)\left(\sum_{s=1}^{N} \mathbf{z}_{1s}\,\mathbf{z}_{1s}'\right)^{-1} \mathbf{z}_{1t} \tag{6}$$

and define $\mathbf{Q}$ by

$$\mathbf{Q} = \sum_{t=1}^{N} \mathbf{v}_t\,\mathbf{v}_t' \tag{7}$$

Notice that the submatrix $\mathbf{\Pi}_2$ of $\mathbf{\Pi}$ (3) is

$$\mathbf{\Pi}_2 = \left(\sum_{t=1}^{N} \mathbf{x}_t\,\mathbf{v}_t'\right)\mathbf{Q}^{-1} \tag{8}$$

Anderson obtains maximum-likelihood estimates of $\overline{\mathbf{\Pi}}_2$ and $\mathbf{\Sigma}$ under the assumption that $\mathbf{x}_t$ is normally distributed and *under the restriction* (5) by choosing as an estimate of $\boldsymbol{\gamma}$ that vector $\mathbf{c}$ for which the ratio

$$l = \frac{\mathbf{c}'\,\mathbf{\Pi}_2\mathbf{Q}\mathbf{\Pi}_2'\mathbf{c}}{\mathbf{c}'\,(N - q)\mathbf{S}\mathbf{c}} \tag{9}$$

is a minimum; that is, **c** is the characteristic vector corresponding to the smallest root (say) ϕ_p of

$$|\mathbf{\Pi}_2\mathbf{Q}\mathbf{\Pi}_2' - \phi(N - q)\mathbf{S}| = 0 \tag{10}$$

If $\mathbf{x}_t$ and $\mathbf{z}_t$ be interpreted as the endogenous and exogenous vectors of a system of simultaneous structural equations, as in econometrics, then $\overline{\mathbf{\Pi}}$ is the matrix of reduced-form coefficients and (5) represents a set of identifying restrictions on the coefficients in $\overline{\mathbf{\Pi}}_2$. The statistic ϕ_p is then essentially the so-called *limited-information* identifiability test statistic.

The likelihood ratio criterion for testing the hypothesis that the rank of $\overline{\mathbf{\Pi}}_2$ is $p - 1$ is

$$\lambda = (1 + \phi_p)^{-N/2} \tag{11}$$

If the rank of $\overline{\mathbf{\Pi}}_2$ is $p - 1$, $-2\ln \lambda$ is asymptotically distributed like χ^2 with $[p - (p - 1)] \times [q_2 - (p - 1)]$ degrees of freedom.Thus,

$$N \ln (1 + \phi_p) \sim \chi^2 \qquad \text{with } q_2 - p + 1 \text{ d.f.} \tag{12}$$

as $N \to \infty$. In large samples $N\ln(1 + \phi_p)$ is approximately equal to $N\phi_p$, and thus,

$$N\phi_p \sim \chi^2 \qquad \text{with } q_2 - p + 1 \text{ d.f.} \tag{13}$$

It has been shown that the exact finite sample density function of ϕ_p is very complicated; see the exact expressions for it in McDonald (1972) and Rhodes (1981). Corresponding exact expressions for GCL test statistics are in Basmann (1965, 1966) and Richardson (1968). It is expected that tables of the exact distribution of ϕ_p will be difficult to compute and unwieldy in practical use. This expectation motivates the search for good approximations of the exact distribution of ϕ_p by much simpler distribution functions. T. W. Anderson (1951) has suggested an approximate finite sample test of the hypothesis that the rank of $\overline{\mathbf{\Pi}}_2$ is $p - 1$ against the hypothesis that it is p. For Anderson's test, the critical region (of rejection) corresponding to the level of significance α is

$$[(N - q)/q_2]\, \phi_p \geqslant F_{q_2, N-q}(\varepsilon) \tag{14}$$

where $F_{q_2,N-q}$ denotes Snedecor's F with q_2 and $N - q$ degrees of freedom. Anderson mentions that this test is "conservative" in the sense that the probability is less than $1 - \varepsilon$ of rejecting the foregoing null hypothesis when it is true. Here $\varepsilon = 1 - \alpha$ where α is the level of significance of the test.

Recalling that the limiting distribution of $F_{q_2,N-q}$ as $N \to \infty$ is that of χ^2 with q_2 degrees of freedom, we notice the lack of consistency between the finite sample test (14) and the asymptotic distribution (12) and (13) of $-2\ln\lambda$. The approximate finite sample test based on the critical region

$$[(N - q)/(q_2 - p + 1)]\,\phi_p \geqslant F_{q_2-p+1,N-q}(\varepsilon) \tag{15}$$

is consistent with (12) and (13) and is less biased in favor of the null hypothesis than is Anderson's test (14).

II. EXPERIMENTAL RESULTS

A. Description of the Sampling Experiment

In order to compare the reliabilities of tests of significance based on the critical regions (12), (14), and (15), I have used the results of a sampling experiment with 200 independent samples $[\mathbf{x}_t']$, $t = 1, 2, \ldots, N$, generated from a multivariate normal population with expectations (1) and (2), where

$$[\bar{\mathbf{\Pi}}_1 : \bar{\mathbf{\Pi}}_2] = \begin{bmatrix} -7.2763 & 0.7315 & 0 & -1.3424 & -1.2451 & 1.6965 \\ 1.0856 & 0.5973 & 0 & -0.5136 & 0.1323 & 0.0447 \\ -10.0700 & -0.7160 & 0.4000 & -1.5800 & -0.6540 & 1.1910 \end{bmatrix} \tag{16}$$

$$\bar{\mathbf{\Sigma}} = \begin{bmatrix} 448.2882 & -63.2987 & 121.4734 \\ & 21.2150 & -20.7019 \\ & & 303.0165 \end{bmatrix} \tag{17}$$

and sample size $N = 16$, $p = 3$, $q = 6$, $q_2 = 3$. The fixed variables are shown in Table 1. $\bar{\mathbf{\Sigma}} = \mathbf{AA}'$ where

$$\mathbf{A} = \begin{bmatrix} 14.71815 & -11.99752 & -9.36609 \\ 0 & 2.05985 & 4.11971 \\ 10.05015 & 10.05015 & -10.05015 \end{bmatrix}$$

The matrix $\bar{\mathbf{\Pi}}_2$ satisfies the restriction

$$\boldsymbol{\gamma}'\bar{\mathbf{\Pi}}_2 = \mathbf{0} \qquad \text{where } \boldsymbol{\gamma} = \begin{bmatrix} \gamma_1 \\ \gamma_2 \\ \gamma_3 \end{bmatrix} \text{ and}$$

$$\gamma_2/\gamma_1 = 2.000 \tag{18}$$

$$\gamma_3/\gamma_1 = -1.5000. \tag{19}$$

The sampling experiment was conducted in 1958 at Hanford Laboratories

Table 1. Fixed Sample of Independent Variates.

z_1	z_2	z_3	z_4	z_5	z_6
1.0	157	95	64	12	79
1.0	170	72	90	25	68
1.0	162	89	67	45	67
1.0	166	81	68	24	74
1.0	155	100	56	37	70
1.0	159	98	68	12	23
1.0	164	80	61	38	51
1.0	147	72	90	10	60
1.0	149	85	54	14	23
1.0	163	79	83	15	35
1.0	152	76	50	49	87
1.0	170	86	50	14	89
1.0	144	97	88	18	21
1.0	141	97	99	32	55
1.0	148	87	97	16	47
1.0	141	103	72	25	48

Operation, General Electric Company (Richland, WA). Numerical analysis and programming were done by Clee L. Childress. Computations were performed on the IBM 702 EDPM (Electronic Data Processing Machine). The employment of a professional numerical analyst and programmer and the choice of machine were dictated by the need to keep accumulated round-off error negligible.

B. Tables and Figures

Table 2 presents 200 independent observations of ϕ_p arranged in order of increasing magnitude. Table 3 presents 200 independent observations of $\ln(1 + \phi_p)$ arranged in order of increasing magnitude. The values shown in Tables 2 and 3 are precise to the fifth decimal place. The experimental mean $\bar{x}$ and standard deviation s are shown in the footnote of each table. The *empirical probability function*

$$P_{200}\{\phi_p < x\} = \nu(x)/200 \tag{20}$$

where $\nu(x)$ is the number of experimental values of ϕ_p that are less than x, is exhibited in Figure 1; with $x = 0, 0.01, 0.02, \ldots, 2.0$. Superimposed on Figure 1 are several points of the distribution function of the beta variate $(1/10)\,F_{1,10}$, the conjectured approximate distribution function of $\chi_1^2/16$.

Table 2. Experimental Values of ϕ_p.

0.00000	0.00910	0.04636	0.13905
0.00003	0.00939	0.04834	0.14059
0.00007	0.01017	0.05274	0.14296
0.00009	0.01067	0.05301	0.14307
0.00009	0.01074	0.05317	0.14557
0.00009	0.01091	0.05438	0.14860
0.00010	0.01105	0.05521	0.14947
0.00010	0.01135	0.05604	0.14958
0.00014	0.01176	0.05632	0.14959
0.00016	0.01304	0.05645	0.15252
0.00024	0.01311	0.05649	0.15276
0.00030	0.01367	0.05783	0.15598
0.00036	0.01373	0.05935	0.15703
0.00044	0.01379	0.06132	0.17578
0.00047	0.01517	0.06519	0.17677
0.00052	0.01663	0.06809	0.19371
0.00057	0.01770	0.06852	0.19407
0.00057	0.01775	0.06892	0.19575
0.00062	0.01782	0.07083	0.19625
0.00066	0.01813	0.07194	0.20513
0.00078	0.01905	0.07321	0.20916
0.00101	0.01921	0.07711	0.22137
0.00142	0.01937	0.07835	0.22267
0.00150	0.02009	0.07897	0.22483
0.00196	0.02124	0.08010	0.22581
0.00208	0.02223	0.08242	0.24798
0.00213	0.02225	0.08576	0.24855
0.00214	0.02403	0.08609	0.25001
0.00239	0.02439	0.08800	0.25447
0.00245	0.02458	0.09208	0.26670
0.00259	0.02612	0.09284	0.27139
0.00304	0.02716	0.09381	0.28041
0.00321	0.03131	0.09545	0.28889
0.00344	0.03352	0.09844	0.30620
0.00388	0.03435	0.10136	0.30992
0.00410	0.03511	0.10177	0.31918
0.00454	0.03538	0.10245	0.33578
0.00516	0.03586	0.10399	0.33855
0.00531	0.03619	0.10791	0.34605
0.00552	0.03781	0.11210	0.38033
0.00653	0.03782	0.11343	0.39672
0.00682	0.03849	0.11480	0.39762
0.00685	0.03944	0.11830	0.41792
0.00691	0.04079	0.11879	0.41840
0.00693	0.04098	0.12550	0.43208
0.00735	0.04129	0.12805	0.44108
0.00814	0.04148	0.12830	0.46882
0.00885	0.04266	0.13475	0.61953
0.00887	0.04376	0.13732	0.66730
0.00901	0.04508	0.13834	1.92404

$\bar{x} = 0.10317$; $s = 0.17698$; median = 0.04572.

Table 3. Experimental Values of ln (1 + ϕ_p).

0.00000	0.00906	0.04532	0.13020
0.00003	0.00934	0.04721	0.13154
0.00007	0.01012	0.05140	0.13362
0.00009	0.01061	0.05166	0.13372
0.00009	0.01068	0.05181	0.13590
0.00009	0.01085	0.05295	0.13854
0.00010	0.01099	0.05374	0.13930
0.00010	0.01128	0.05453	0.13940
0.00014	0.01169	0.05479	0.13940
0.00016	0.01295	0.05491	0.14195
0.00024	0.01303	0.05495	0.14216
0.00030	0.01357	0.05622	0.14495
0.00036	0.01364	0.05765	0.14586
0.00044	0.01370	0.05951	0.16193
0.00047	0.01505	0.06316	0.16277
0.00052	0.01649	0.06587	0.17707
0.00057	0.01755	0.06628	0.17736
0.00057	0.01760	0.06665	0.17878
0.00062	0.01766	0.06843	0.17920
0.00066	0.01800	0.06947	0.18659
0.00078	0.01887	0.07066	0.18993
0.00101	0.01902	0.07428	0.19997
0.00142	0.01919	0.07543	0.20104
0.00150	0.01990	0.07601	0.20281
0.00196	0.02102	0.07705	0.20360
0.00208	0.02198	0.07920	0.22153
0.00213	0.02201	0.08228	0.22198
0.00214	0.02374	0.08259	0.22315
0.00239	0.02410	0.08434	0.22672
0.00245	0.02428	0.08809	0.23642
0.00259	0.02578	0.08878	0.24011
0.00303	0.02680	0.08967	0.24718
0.00320	0.03083	0.09117	0.25378
0.00343	0.03297	0.09389	0.26712
0.00387	0.03377	0.09655	0.26997
0.00409	0.03451	0.09692	0.27701
0.00453	0.03477	0.09753	0.28952
0.00514	0.03524	0.09893	0.29159
0.00530	0.03555	0.10247	0.29718
0.00550	0.03711	0.10625	0.32232
0.00651	0.03712	0.10744	0.33413
0.00679	0.03777	0.10868	0.33477
0.00682	0.03868	0.11181	0.34919
0.00689	0.03998	0.11225	0.34953
0.00690	0.04016	0.11822	0.35913
0.00732	0.04046	0.12049	0.36539
0.00810	0.04064	0.12071	0.38446
0.00881	0.04177	0.12641	0.48214
0.00883	0.04283	0.12868	0.51121
0.00897	0.04409	0.12957	1.07297

$\bar{x}$ = 0.08939; s = 0.12293; median = 0.04570.

Figure 1. Empirical Distribution of ϕ_p, $P(\phi_p < x$ (---) and Distribution of $(1/10)F_{1,10}$ •••.

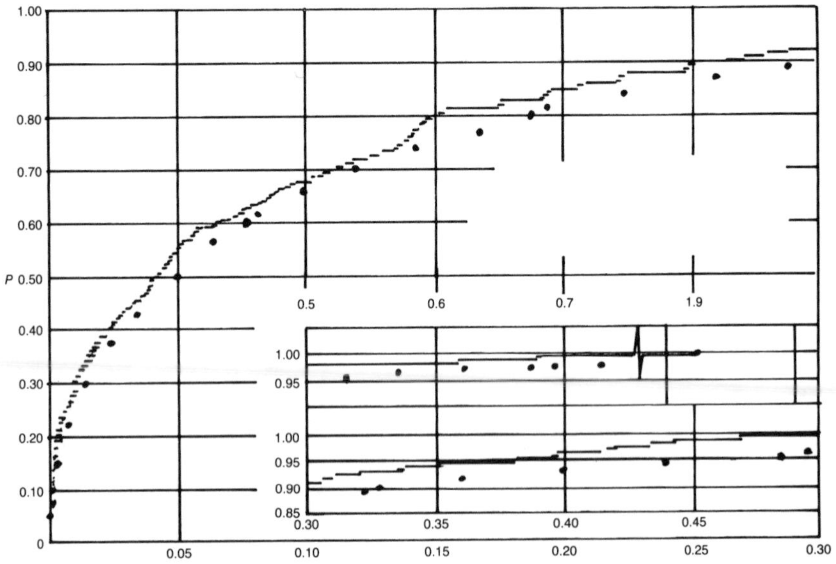

Figure 2. Empirical Distribution of $\ln(1 + \phi_p)$, $P\{\ln(1 + \phi_p) < x\}$ and Distribution of $\chi_1^2/16$ •••.

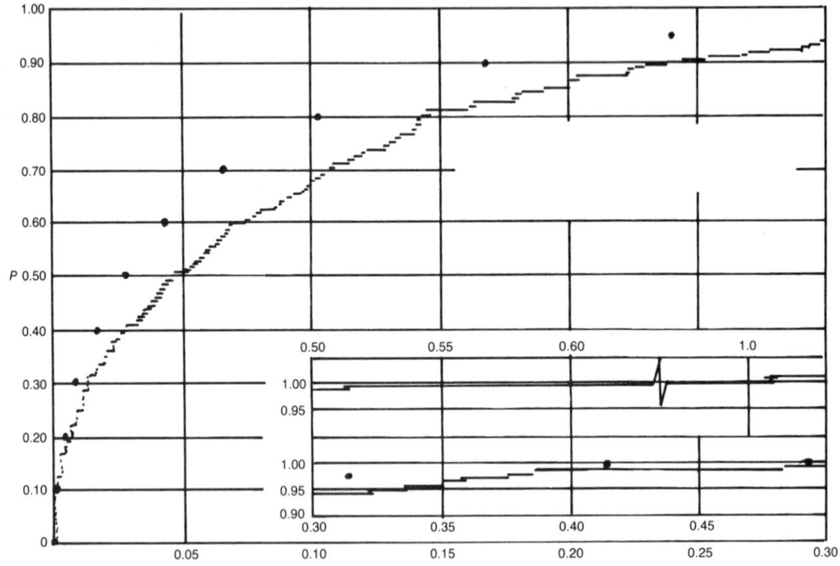

III. RESULTS

A. χ^2 Goodness-of-Fit Test of H_0: $\phi_p \sim (3/10)F_{3,10}$

The approximation of the distribution function of ϕ_p by the distribution function of $(3/10)F_{3,10}$ must be close if tests of significance based on the critical region (14) are to be reliable. Using six intervals, closed on the right, with suprema equal to the 10%, 30%, 50%, 70%, 90%, and 100% points of $(3/10)F_{3,10}$, one obtains from Table 1 the value of the goodness-of-fit criterion (with 5 degrees of freedom)

$$\begin{aligned} u &= \frac{(91 - 20)^2}{20} + \dots + \frac{(1 - 20)^2}{20} \\ &= 496.287 \end{aligned} \tag{21}$$

The experimental data disconfirm H_0, for

$$P\{\chi_5^2 \geqslant 496.287\} = 0 \text{ essentially}. \tag{22}$$

At the commonly used levels of significance $\alpha = 0.10$ and $\alpha = 0.05$, we have $F_{3,10}\ (0.90) = 2.73$ and $F_{3,10}\ (0.95) = 3.71$. Under H_0, the expected number of experimental values of $\phi_p > (3/10)F_{3,10}\ (0.90) = 0.819$ is 20. Inspection of Table 2 reveals that only one experimental value of ϕ_p exceeds 0.819 in contrast to the expected 20.

Unless there is a subtle specialization inherent in the choice of the parameters specified by (16) and (17) and in the selection of fixed variates (Table 1), it is reasonable to disbelieve the conjecture that $[q_2/(N - g)]\ \phi_{q_2,N-q}$ is in general approximately distributed as Snedecor's F with q_2 and $N - q$ degrees of freedom and, consequently, to conclude that the test based on the critical region (14) is too "conservative" and, therefore, too unreliable to be of practical use. Some additional comments about this appear in Section IV.

B. Test of the Hypothesis H_0: $\phi_p \sim (1/10)F_{1,10}$

The approximation of the exact distribution function of ϕ_p by the distribution function of $(1/10)F_{1,10}$ must be close if tests of significance based on the critical region (15) are to be reliable. Visual inspection of Figure 1 reveals that the empirical probability function (20) is approximated closely by the distribution function of $(1/10)F_{1,10}$. The maximum absolute deviation D_{200} between the empirical and theoretical distributions is located (by visual inspection) at $x = 0.156$ and is approximately $d_{200} = 0.05$. Because the probability function (20) in Figure 1 is a close approximation to the *empirical distribution function* $F_n(x)$, we shall make use of the limiting form of the Kolmogorov distribution (Kolmogorov, 1941), (Birnbaum, 1952) as a partial test of H_0. Let $D_n = \sup_x |F(x) - F_n(x)|$ where $F(x)$ is the distribution function of $(1/10)F_{1,10}$; then

$$\lim \mathrm{P}\{D_n \geqslant 0.05\} = 2 \sum_{k=1}^{\infty} (-1)^{k+1} \exp[-2\, k^2(0.05)^2] > 0.50. \quad (23)$$

That is, for large samples, the probability of observing an absolute deviation at least as large as $d_{200} = 0.05$ is greater than 0.50, given that ϕ_p is distributed as $(1/10)F_{1,10}$.

We also apply the χ^2 goodness-of-fit test. Using six intervals with suprema equal to the 10%, 30%, 50%, 70%, 90%, and 100% points of $(1/10)F_{1,10}$, we obtain from Table 1, the value

$$\begin{aligned} u &= \frac{(24 - 20)^2}{20} + \ldots + \frac{(14 - 20)^2}{20} \\ &= 30.0375. \end{aligned} \quad (24)$$

There is a fairly large probability of u exceeding this value if H_0 is true, for

$$P\{\chi_5^2 \geqslant 3.0375\} = 0.70 \qquad \text{(approximately)}. \quad (25)$$

At the commonly used levels of significance $\alpha = 0.10$ and $\alpha = 0.05$, we have $F_{1,10}\,(0.90) = 3.29$ and $F_{1,10}\,(0.95) = 4.96$. Under H_0 the expected number of experimental values of $\phi_p > (1/10)F_{1,10}\,(0.90) = 0.329$ is 20. Inspection of Table 2 reveals that only 14 experimental values exceed 0.329, in contrast to the expected 20. Under H_0 the expected number of experimental values of $\phi_p > 0.496$ is 10; inspection of Table 2 reveals that only 3 experimental values of ϕ_p exceed 0.496, in contrast to the expected 10. Although the distribution of $(1/10)F_{1,10}$ appears to afford a good approximation to the distribution of ϕ_p generally, the approximation appears to be poor in the "tails"; in particular the approximation is poor at the commonly used percentage points $F_{1,10}\,(0.90)$ and $F_{1,10}\,(0.95)$. Some additional remarks about this appear in Section IV.

C. Test of the Hypothesis H_0: $16\ln(1 + \phi_p) \sim \chi^2$ with 1 Degree of Freedom

Visual inspection of Figure 3 reveals a considerable deviation of the empirical probability function of $\ln(1 + \phi_p)$ from the theoretical distribution $\chi_1^2/16$. The maximum absolute deviation is located (by visual inspection) at $x = 0.067$ and is approximately $d_{200} = 0.11$. Because the empirical probability function in Table 3 is a very close approximation to the empirical distribution function, we again make use of the limiting distribution of the Kolmogorov statistic D_n (see Section III,B). According to Birnbaum's asymptotic formulas (1952, p. 427).

$$P(D_n < 1.3581n^{-1/2}) = 0.95. \tag{26}$$

Because $n = 200$ in this experiment, it follows from (26) that the probability of a deviation as large as $d_{200} = 0.11$ or larger is somewhat less than 0.05, if $16 \ln(1 + \phi_p)$ is distributed like χ^2 with one degree of freedom.

We also apply the χ^2 goodness-of-fit test. Using 10 intervals with suprema equal to the 10%, 20%, ..., 100% points of χ^2, 1 d.f., we obtain from Table 2, the value

$$\begin{aligned} u &= \frac{(21 - 20)^2}{20} + \dots + \frac{(35 - 20)^2}{20} \\ &= 18.6000. \end{aligned} \tag{27}$$

The experimental data contradict the hypothesis H_0; for if $16 \ln(1 + \phi_p) \sim \chi^2$ with one degree of freedom, then

$$P\{\chi_9^2 \geqslant 18.6000\} = 0.03 \qquad \text{(approximately)}. \tag{28}$$

At the commonly used levels of significance $\alpha = 0.10$ and $\alpha = 0.05$, we have $\chi_1^2\ (0.90) = 2.71$ and $\chi_1^2\ (0.95) = 3.84$. Under H_0 the expected number of experimental values of $\ln(1 + \phi_p) > 2.71$ is 20. Inspection of Table 3 reveals that no experimental value of ϕ_p exceeds 3.84.

IV. CONCLUSION

The evidence provided by the sampling experiment described here favors the use of critical regions based on the distribution of $F_{q_2 - p + 1, N - q}$ as a finite sample test of the hypothesis that the rank of $\overline{\mathbf{\Pi}}_2$ is $p - 1$ against the alternative hypothesis that it is p.

Although the exact statistical distribution functions of ϕ_p and $\ln(1 + \phi_p)$ do not change form as the parameters $\overline{\mathbf{\Pi}}$, $\overline{\mathbf{\Sigma}}$, and $\mathbf{Z'Z}$ are varied from experiment to experiment, the probability distributions determined do vary. Consequently, the reliabilities of tests of significance based on the critical regions (14) and (15) vary with the parameters $\overline{\mathbf{\Pi}}$, $\overline{\mathbf{\Sigma}}$, and $\mathbf{Z'Z}$.

EDITORIAL NOTE

This article was originally written and accepted for publication in *Annals of Mathematical Statistics* in 1959. The editors of *Annals of Mathematical Statistics* accepted the article subject to some stylistic revisions. Preoccupied with other studies, Professor Basmann neglected to make the revisions and resubmit the article; consequently, the article was not published in *Annals of Mathematical Statistics*. The research results reported in this article fill an important gap in the literature on identifiability test statistics. That gap is made evident by several of the articles included in this volume. At my suggestion, Professor Basmann agreed to publish the article in *Advances in Econometrics*. It is a pleasure to include this article in *Advances in Econometrics,* where the results may be used and appreciated by those interested in identifiability testing.—G.F.R.

REFERENCES

Anderson, T. W. (1951). Estimating linear restrictions on regression coefficients for multivariate distributions, *Ann. Math. Statist. 22,* 327–351.

Basmann, R. L. (1958). An experimental investigation of some small-sample properties of (GCL) estimators of structural equations: Some preliminary results, Richland, WA: General Electric Company, Hanford Laboratories Operation, Mimeo.

Basmann, R. L. (1965). On the Application of the Identifiability Test Statistic in Predictive Testing of Explanatory Economic Models: Part 1, *Econometric Annual of the Indian Economic Journal 13,* 387–423.

Basmann, R. L. (1966). On the application of the identifiability test statistic in predictive testing of explanatory economic models: Part 2, *Econometric Annual of the Indian Economic Journal 14,* 233–252.

Birnbaum, Z. W. (1952). Numerical tabulation of the distribution of Kolmogorov's statistic for finite sample size, *JASA 47,* 425–441.

Kolmogorov, A. N. (1941). Confidence limits for an unknown distribution function, *Ann. Math. Statist. 12,* 461–463.

McDonald, J. B. (1972). The exact finite sample distribution function of the limited information maximum likelihood identifiability test statistic, *Econometrica 40,* 1109–1119.

Rhodes, G. F. (1981). Exact density functions and approximate critical regions for likelihood ratio identifiability test statistics, *Econometrica 49,* 1035–1055.

Richardson, D. H. (1968). On the distribution of the identifiability test statistic, *Research Papers in Theoretical and Applied Economics,* University of Kansas, Paper No. 8. Reprinted in J. R. Quirk and A. M. Zarley (eds.), *Papers in Quantitative Economics,* Lawrence, KA: University Press of Kansas (1968).

MISCLASSIFICATION OF VARIABLES AND THE TWO-STAGE LEAST SQUARES ESTIMATION

Parthasaradhi Mallela and Anil K. Bhargava

I. INTRODUCTION

It is not uncommon that in empirical work an investigator deals with incomplete models. A case in point is the ordinary least squares (OLS) applied to a single equation when some of the explanatory variables are in fact jointly dependent. It is well known that in such an event, in general, the OLS produces inconsistency not only in the parameters of the misclassified variables but in all the parameters of the equation.[1] Such misclassification occurs more frequently in the context of more than one equation when, say, two-stage least squares (2SLS) is applied to an equation of a system when some of the variables treated as independent are actually jointly dependent. This misclassification of some

Advances in Econometrics, Volume 2, pages 209–217

ISBN: 0-89232-183-0

of the dependent variables as independent ones renders the system incomplete and results in the inconsistency of the 2SLS estimator. It is of great interest to know if there are conditions under which the 2SLS estimator is consistent despite the misclassification. It is the purpose of this exercise, inter alia, to show that, with the data available on the incomplete model, the 2SLS cannot produce consistent estimates of *all* the parameters of the equation. However, there are conditions under which the 2SLS yields consistent estimates of the coefficients of the independent variables of the equation. We derive necessary and sufficient conditions for this "partial consistency" in incomplete models.

Section II deals with notation and assumptions. The main results of the paper are derived in Section III. These results bring out the need and importance of block triangular systems. Section IV is devoted to concluding remarks. It also mentions the further conditions under which 2SLS yields "partial consistency" in block triangular systems.

II. NOTATION AND ASSUMPTIONS

The equations are considered in their observational form; the one estimated by the 2SLS is the first one, normalized with respect to the first dependent variable $\mathbf{y}_{.1}$ and is given by

$$\underset{T\times 1}{\mathbf{y}_{.1}} = \underset{T\times m_1}{\mathbf{Y}_2}\boldsymbol{\beta}_{21} + \underset{T\times l}{\mathbf{Y}_3}\boldsymbol{\beta}_{31} + \underset{T\times k_1}{\mathbf{X}_1}\boldsymbol{\gamma}_{11} + \underset{T\times 1}{\mathbf{u}_{.1}} \tag{1}$$

where the l jointly dependent variables corresponding to the columns of $\mathbf{Y}_3$ are misclassified as independent variables.[2] Because only the variables present in the first equation are given in (1), every component of each of $\boldsymbol{\beta}_{21}$, $\boldsymbol{\beta}_{31}$, and $\boldsymbol{\gamma}_{11}$ is different from zero. We assume that the equation (1) is identified even when the variables in $\mathbf{Y}_3$ are treated as dependent.[3] Without loss of generality, we assume that the only dependent variables in the true complete model are those in $\mathbf{y}_{.1}$, $\mathbf{Y}_2$, and $\mathbf{Y}_3$[4] and that the true model (in partitioned form) is given by

$$[\mathbf{y}_{.1}\ \mathbf{Y}_2\ \mathbf{Y}_3]\begin{bmatrix} \mathbf{1} & \boldsymbol{\beta}_{12} & \boldsymbol{\beta}_{13} \\ -\boldsymbol{\beta}_{21} & \mathbf{B}_{22} & \mathbf{B}_{23} \\ -\boldsymbol{\beta}_{31} & \mathbf{B}_{32} & \mathbf{B}_{33} \end{bmatrix} + [\mathbf{X}_1\ \mathbf{X}_2]\begin{bmatrix} -\boldsymbol{\gamma}_{11} & \boldsymbol{\Gamma}_{12} & \boldsymbol{\Gamma}_{13} \\ \mathbf{0} & \boldsymbol{\Gamma}_{22} & \boldsymbol{\Gamma}_{23} \end{bmatrix} = [\mathbf{u}_{.1}\ \mathbf{U}_2\ \mathbf{U}_3]. \tag{2}$$

More compactly, the true complete system is given by

$$\mathbf{YB} + \mathbf{X\Gamma} = \mathbf{U} \tag{3}$$

where $\mathbf{Y} = [\mathbf{y}_{.1}\ \mathbf{Y}_2\ \mathbf{Y}_3]$; $\mathbf{X} = [\mathbf{X}_1\ \mathbf{X}_2]$; and $\mathbf{U} = [\mathbf{u}_{.1}\ \mathbf{U}_2\ \mathbf{U}_3]$. However, the investigator mistakenly considers the incomplete model[5]

$$[\mathbf{y}_{.1}\ \mathbf{Y}_2]\begin{bmatrix} 1 & \boldsymbol{\beta}_{12} \\ -\boldsymbol{\beta}_{21} & \mathbf{B}_{22} \end{bmatrix} + [\mathbf{Y}_3\ \mathbf{X}_1\ \mathbf{X}_2]\begin{bmatrix} -\boldsymbol{\beta}_{31} & \mathbf{B}_{32} \\ -\boldsymbol{\gamma}_{11} & \boldsymbol{\Gamma}_{12} \\ \mathbf{0} & \boldsymbol{\Gamma}_{22} \end{bmatrix} = [\mathbf{u}_{.1}\ \mathbf{U}_2]. \tag{4}$$

The following observations are in order. The super row corresponding to the coefficients of $\mathbf{Y}_3$ in (4) appears as part of the third super row of $\mathbf{B}$ in (2). Data are available to the investigator only on the dependent variables in $\mathbf{y}_{.1}$, $\mathbf{Y}_2$, $\mathbf{Y}_3$, and the independent variables in $\mathbf{X}_1$ and $\mathbf{X}_2$. We thus assume that the only independent variables in the true complete model are those in $\mathbf{X}_1$ and $\mathbf{X}_2$. The equation (2) reflects the above observation. Furthermore, the third equation of (2) corresponding to the misclassified variables $\mathbf{Y}_3$ is not available to the investigator. Hence, we may as well assume the knowledge of only the corresponding part of the true reduced form; that is, we assume

$$\boldsymbol{\beta}_{13} = \mathbf{0}; \quad \mathbf{B}_{23} = \mathbf{0}; \quad \mathbf{B}_{33} = \mathbf{I}_l. \tag{5}$$

The true reduced form is given by

$$\mathbf{Y} = \mathbf{X\Pi} + \mathbf{V} \tag{6}$$

(where $\mathbf{\Pi} = -\mathbf{\Gamma B}^{-1}$ and $\mathbf{V} = \mathbf{UB}^{-1}$), which in partitioned form is given by (with obvious notation)

$$[\mathbf{y}_{.1}\ \mathbf{Y}_2\ \mathbf{Y}_3] = \mathbf{X}[\boldsymbol{\pi}_{.1}\ \mathbf{\Pi}_{.2}\ \mathbf{\Pi}_{.3}] + [\mathbf{v}_{.1}\ \mathbf{V}_2\ \mathbf{V}_3]. \tag{7}$$

The error term $\mathbf{u}_{.1}$ of the estimated equation (1) and those of the reduced form are related by

$$\mathbf{u}_{.1} = \mathbf{v}_{.1} + \mathbf{V}_2\boldsymbol{\beta}_{21} + \mathbf{V}_3\boldsymbol{\beta}_{31} \qquad (= \mathbf{V}\boldsymbol{\beta}_{.1}, \text{ say}), \tag{8}$$

where $\boldsymbol{\beta}'_{.1} = [1, \boldsymbol{\beta}'_{21}, \boldsymbol{\beta}'_{31}]$. We make the following classical assumptions of only the contemporaneous correlations for the errors and

$$\text{plim}\ T^{-1}\,\mathbf{U}'\mathbf{U} = \underset{m \times m}{\mathbf{\Omega}} \qquad m = 1 + m_1 + l \tag{9}$$

$$\textit{plim}\ T^{-1}\,\mathbf{V}'\mathbf{V} = \underset{m \times m}{\mathbf{\Sigma}} \tag{10}$$

$$\mathbf{lim}\ \boldsymbol{T}^{-1}\,\mathbf{X}'\mathbf{X} = \underset{k \times k}{\mathbf{M}} \qquad k = k_1 + k_2; k_2 \geq m_1 + l \tag{11}$$

The matrices $\mathbf{\Omega}$, $\mathbf{\Sigma}$, and $\mathbf{M}$ are positive definite, with

$$\mathbf{\Omega} = \mathbf{B}'\mathbf{\Sigma}\mathbf{B}. \tag{12}$$

Let the covariance matrix $\mathbf{\Sigma}$ be partitioned corresponding to that of the dependent variables:

$$\boldsymbol{\Sigma} = \begin{bmatrix} \sigma_{11} & \sigma_{12} & \sigma_{13} \\ \sigma_{21} & \boldsymbol{\Sigma}_{22} & \boldsymbol{\Sigma}_{23} \\ \sigma_{31} & \boldsymbol{\Sigma}_{32} & \boldsymbol{\Sigma}_{33} \end{bmatrix}. \tag{13}$$

We finally assume that the only restrictions on the (incomplete) model (4) are coefficient restrictions of the exclusion type.

We are now in a position to present the main results.

III. MAIN RESULTS

THEOREM 1: *If the variables in* $\mathbf{Y}_3$ *in the incomplete system (4) are misclassified as independent, then all that the 2SLS estimator of (1) can achieve is the consistency of the subset of parameters relating to the truly independent variables in it, a set of necessary and sufficient conditions for which is given by*

$$\boldsymbol{\beta}_{12} = \mathbf{0}; \qquad \boldsymbol{\Gamma}_{12} = \mathbf{0}; \qquad \boldsymbol{\Gamma}_{13} = \mathbf{0}; \qquad \mathbf{M}_{12} = \mathbf{0}.$$

REMARK 1: The conditions of Theorem 1 specify that the model reduces, to

$$\mathbf{y}_{.1} - \mathbf{Y}_2\boldsymbol{\beta}_{21} - \mathbf{Y}_3\boldsymbol{\beta}_{31} - \mathbf{X}_1\boldsymbol{\gamma}_{11} = \mathbf{u}_{.1} \tag{14}$$

$$\mathbf{Y}_2\mathbf{B}_{22} + \mathbf{Y}_3\mathbf{B}_{23} + \mathbf{X}_2\boldsymbol{\Gamma}_{22} = \mathbf{U}_2 \tag{15}$$

$$\mathbf{Y}_3\mathbf{B}_{33} + \mathbf{X}_2\boldsymbol{\Gamma}_{23} = \mathbf{U}_3. \tag{16}$$

This means that the RHS dependent variables in the equation estimated depend only on the independent variables excluded from that equation. Further, $\mathbf{M}_{12} = \mathbf{0}$ implies that such independent variables excluded from the estimated equation are orthogonal (in the limit) to those that are included. Then and only then the 2SLS estimator of (1), when $\mathbf{Y}_3$ is misclassified as independent, yields partial consistency—consistency of the parameters of the truly independent variables $\mathbf{X}_1$ in the estimated equation.

PROOF OF THEOREM 1: *Let* $\mathbf{X}^*$ be defined by

$$\mathbf{X}^* = [\mathbf{Y}_3, \mathbf{X}_1, \mathbf{X}_2] \tag{17}$$

Then the 2SLS estimator $\hat{\boldsymbol{\delta}}' = [\hat{\boldsymbol{\beta}}'_{21}, \hat{\boldsymbol{\beta}}'_{31}, \hat{\boldsymbol{\gamma}}'_{11}]$ of the coefficient parameters

$\boldsymbol{\delta}'_{.1} = [\boldsymbol{\beta}'_{21}, \boldsymbol{\beta}'_{31}, \boldsymbol{\gamma}'_{11}]$ satisfies:

$$\begin{bmatrix} \mathbf{Y}'_2\mathbf{X}^*(\mathbf{X}^{*\prime}\mathbf{X}^*)^{-1}\mathbf{X}^{*\prime}\mathbf{Y}_2 & \mathbf{Y}'_2\mathbf{Y}_3 & \mathbf{Y}'_2\mathbf{X}_1 \\ \mathbf{Y}'_3\mathbf{Y}_2 & \mathbf{Y}'_3\mathbf{Y}_3 & \mathbf{Y}'_3\mathbf{X}_1 \\ \mathbf{X}'_1\mathbf{Y}_2 & \mathbf{X}'_1\mathbf{Y}_3 & \mathbf{X}'_1\mathbf{X}_1 \end{bmatrix} \begin{bmatrix} \hat{\boldsymbol{\beta}}_{21} - \boldsymbol{\beta}_{21} \\ \hat{\boldsymbol{\beta}}_{31} - \boldsymbol{\beta}_{31} \\ \hat{\boldsymbol{\gamma}}_{11} - \boldsymbol{\gamma}_{11} \end{bmatrix} = \begin{bmatrix} \mathbf{Y}'_2\mathbf{X}^*(\mathbf{X}^{*\prime}\mathbf{X}^*)^{-1}\mathbf{X}^{*\prime}\mathbf{u}_{.1} \\ \mathbf{Y}'_3\mathbf{u}_{.1} \\ \mathbf{X}'_1\mathbf{u}_{.1} \end{bmatrix} \tag{18}$$

The following results are easily established using (7)–(11) and (13):

$$\operatorname{plim} T^{-1}\mathbf{Y}'_2\mathbf{X}^* = [\boldsymbol{\Pi}'_{.2}\mathbf{M}\boldsymbol{\Pi}_{.3} + \boldsymbol{\Sigma}_{23}, \boldsymbol{\Pi}'_{.2}\mathbf{M}] \tag{19}$$

$$\operatorname{plim} T^{-1}\mathbf{X}^{*\prime}\mathbf{X}^* = \begin{bmatrix} \boldsymbol{\Pi}'_{.3}\mathbf{M}\boldsymbol{\Pi}_{.3} + \boldsymbol{\Sigma}_{33} & \boldsymbol{\Pi}'_{.3}\mathbf{M} \\ \mathbf{M}\boldsymbol{\Pi}'_{.3} & \mathbf{M} \end{bmatrix} \tag{20}$$

$$\operatorname{plim} T^{-1}\mathbf{X}^{*\prime}\mathbf{u}_{.1} = \operatorname{plim} T^{-1} \begin{bmatrix} \mathbf{Y}'_3\mathbf{u}_{.1} \\ \mathbf{X}'_1\mathbf{u}_{.1} \\ \mathbf{X}'_2\mathbf{u}_{.1} \end{bmatrix} = \begin{bmatrix} \boldsymbol{\sigma}_{31} - \boldsymbol{\Sigma}_{32}\boldsymbol{\beta}_{21} - \boldsymbol{\Sigma}_{33}\boldsymbol{\beta}_{31} \\ \mathbf{0} \\ \mathbf{0} \end{bmatrix} \tag{21}$$

The argument involved in the following two statements will be employed in further discussion:

STATEMENT A: *If under additional assumptions,*[6] $\hat{\boldsymbol{\delta}}_{.1}$ *is not consistent for* $\boldsymbol{\delta}_{.1}$, *then without the additional assumptions also* $\hat{\boldsymbol{\delta}}_{.1}$ *is not consistent for* $\boldsymbol{\delta}_{.1}$.

STATEMENT B: *If the conditions given in the statement of the Theorem 1 are necessary under additional assumptions, they would be necessary without the additional assumptions as well.*

For convenience of further argument, impose the additional restrictions $\mathbf{M} = \mathbf{I}_k$ and $\boldsymbol{\Sigma}_{23} = \mathbf{0}$. Dividing both sides of (18) by T and taking plims under the additional assumptions, we obtain[7] (in equivalent form)

$$\begin{bmatrix} \boldsymbol{\Pi}'_{22}\boldsymbol{\Pi}_{22} & \boldsymbol{\Pi}'_{22}\boldsymbol{\Pi}_{23} & \mathbf{0} \\ \boldsymbol{\Pi}'_{23}\boldsymbol{\Pi}_{22} & \boldsymbol{\Pi}'_{23}\boldsymbol{\Pi}_{23} & \mathbf{0} \\ \boldsymbol{\Pi}_{12} & \boldsymbol{\Pi}_{13} & \mathbf{I} \end{bmatrix} \begin{bmatrix} \operatorname{plim}(\hat{\boldsymbol{\beta}}_{21} - \boldsymbol{\beta}_{21}) \\ \operatorname{plim}(\hat{\boldsymbol{\beta}}_{31} - \boldsymbol{\beta}_{31}) \\ \operatorname{plim}(\hat{\boldsymbol{\gamma}}_{11} - \boldsymbol{\gamma}_{11}) \end{bmatrix} = \begin{bmatrix} \mathbf{0} \\ \boldsymbol{\sigma}_{31} - \boldsymbol{\Sigma}_{33}\boldsymbol{\beta}_{31} \\ \mathbf{0} \end{bmatrix}. \tag{22}$$

Now consider the first two equations of (22). These equations involve only the variables $\operatorname{plim}(\hat{\boldsymbol{\beta}}_{21} - \boldsymbol{\beta}_{21})$ and $\operatorname{plim}(\hat{\boldsymbol{\beta}}_{31} - \boldsymbol{\beta}_{31})$. Observing that no component of $\boldsymbol{\sigma}_{31} - \boldsymbol{\Sigma}_{33}\boldsymbol{\beta}_{31}$ is equal to zero, it is easy to see that $\operatorname{plim}(\hat{\boldsymbol{\beta}}_{31} - \boldsymbol{\beta}_{31}) \neq \mathbf{0}$ and that $\operatorname{plim}(\hat{\boldsymbol{\beta}}_{21} - \boldsymbol{\beta}_{21}) = \mathbf{0}$ if and only if $\boldsymbol{\Pi}'_{22}\boldsymbol{\Pi}_{23} = \mathbf{0}$. But the rank of $\boldsymbol{\Pi}'_{22}\boldsymbol{\Pi}_{23}$ is equal to $\min\{m_1, l\}$ almost everywhere (a.e.) in the parameter space.[8] Thus, *no component* of $\boldsymbol{\beta}_{21}$ and of $\boldsymbol{\beta}_{31}$ is consistently estimated by the 2SLS (see Statement A above) and if at all, only $\boldsymbol{\gamma}_{11}$ can consistently be estimated. It is now clear from the third equation of (22) that the estimator of $\boldsymbol{\gamma}_{11}$ is consistent for $\boldsymbol{\gamma}_{11}$ only if $\boldsymbol{\Pi}_{12} = \mathbf{0}$ and $\boldsymbol{\Pi}_{13} = \mathbf{0}$.

We will now prove that $\mathbf{M}_{12} = \mathbf{0}$ is also necessary for the same purpose. As mentioned earlier, under the additional assumption of $\boldsymbol{\Sigma}_{23} = \mathbf{0}$, the equation to be considered for checking the consistency of 2SLS is equation (N1) of Note 7. Now, imposing further additional assumption $\mathbf{M}_{22} = \mathbf{I}$ and the necessary conditions $\boldsymbol{\Pi}_{12} = \mathbf{0}$ and $\boldsymbol{\Pi}_{13} = \mathbf{0}$, equation (N1) will reduce to

$$\begin{bmatrix} \boldsymbol{\Pi}'_{22}\boldsymbol{\Pi}_{22} & \boldsymbol{\Pi}'_{22}\boldsymbol{\Pi}_{23} & \boldsymbol{\Pi}'_{22}\mathbf{M}_{21} \\ \boldsymbol{\Pi}'_{23}\boldsymbol{\Pi}_{22} & \boldsymbol{\Pi}'_{23}\boldsymbol{\Pi}_{23} & \boldsymbol{\Pi}'_{23}\mathbf{M}_{21} \\ \mathbf{M}_{12}\boldsymbol{\Pi}_{22} & \mathbf{M}_{12}\boldsymbol{\Pi}_{23} & \mathbf{M}_{11} \end{bmatrix} \begin{bmatrix} \text{plim}(\hat{\boldsymbol{\beta}}_{21} - \boldsymbol{\beta}_{21}) \\ \text{plim}(\hat{\boldsymbol{\beta}}_{31} - \boldsymbol{\beta}_{31}) \\ \text{plim}(\hat{\boldsymbol{\gamma}}_{11} - \boldsymbol{\gamma}_{11}) \end{bmatrix} = \begin{bmatrix} \mathbf{0} \\ \boldsymbol{\sigma}_{31} - \boldsymbol{\Sigma}_{33}\boldsymbol{\beta}_{31} \\ \mathbf{0} \end{bmatrix} \qquad (23)$$

Once again resorting to the argument similar to that in the earlier case, one can easily see that $\mathbf{M}_{12} = \mathbf{0}$ is necessary for consistent estimability of $\boldsymbol{\gamma}_{11}$. Thus, the conditions $\boldsymbol{\Pi}_{12} = \mathbf{0}$, $\boldsymbol{\Pi}_{13} = \mathbf{0}$, and $\mathbf{M}_{12} = \mathbf{0}$ are necessary for consistent estimation of $\boldsymbol{\gamma}_{11}$.

It is easy to show that the above conditions are sufficient for the same purpose; this is done by considering the plim version of the third equation of (18) and observing the $\text{plim}(T^{-1}\mathbf{X}'_1\mathbf{Y}_2) = \mathbf{0}$ and $\text{plim}(T^{-1}\mathbf{X}'_1\mathbf{Y}_3) = \mathbf{0}$ when $\boldsymbol{\Pi}_{12} = \mathbf{0}$, $\boldsymbol{\Pi}_{13} = \mathbf{0}$, and $\mathbf{M}_{12} = \mathbf{0}$.

It remains to show that the conditions $\boldsymbol{\Pi}_{12} = \mathbf{0}$, $\boldsymbol{\Pi}_{13} = \mathbf{0}$ are equivalent to $\boldsymbol{\beta}_{12} = \mathbf{0}$, $\boldsymbol{\Gamma}_{12} = \mathbf{0}$, and $\boldsymbol{\Gamma}_{13} = \mathbf{0}$ a.e. It is clear from the structure of the matrix $\mathbf{B}$ in (3)—$\boldsymbol{\beta}_{13} = \mathbf{0}$ and $\mathbf{B}_{23} = \mathbf{0}$ (and $\mathbf{B}_{33} = \mathbf{I}$)—that $\boldsymbol{\Gamma}_{13} = \boldsymbol{\Pi}_{13}$ $(= \mathbf{0})$ using which $\boldsymbol{\Pi}_{12} = \mathbf{0}$ is equivalent to[9]

$$-\boldsymbol{\gamma}_{11}\boldsymbol{\beta}^{12} + \boldsymbol{\Gamma}_{12}\mathbf{B}^{22} = \mathbf{0} \qquad (24)$$

Observing that no component of $\boldsymbol{\gamma}_{11}$ is equal to zero and that $|\mathbf{B}^{22}| \neq 0$, and that the matrices involved are parameter matrices, it is clear that (24) implies that $\boldsymbol{\beta}^{12} = \mathbf{0}$ and $\boldsymbol{\Gamma}_{12} = \mathbf{0}$. Further, $\boldsymbol{\beta}^{12} = \mathbf{0}$ (and $\boldsymbol{\beta}^{13} = \mathbf{0}$ and $\mathbf{B}^{23} = \mathbf{0}$) implies that $\mathbf{B}^{-1}$ is lower (block) triangular and hence $\boldsymbol{\beta}_{12} = \mathbf{0}$. This completes the proof of the theorem.

IV. CONCLUDING REMARKS

Several points of incidental interest arise in the context of the main results of this article. The theorem of Section III shows that if the true complete system (2) contains no independent variables other than those in the incomplete system (4), then there are no circumstances under which the 2SLS results in consistent estimates of a subset of parameters that includes some relating to the RHS dependent variables of the equation estimated. In other words, unless the misclassified variables depend on independent variables other than those in the incomplete system, there is no hope for consistent estimability of the parameters of the RHS dependent variables. Assuming that the misclassified variables $\mathbf{Y}_3$ depend on some variables $\mathbf{X}_3$ not appearing in the incomplete model, it appears that the consistent estimability of (some of) the parameters of the RHS dependent variables crucially depends on the orthogonality (in the limit) of $\mathbf{X}_3$ with those independent variables in $\mathbf{X}_1$ and $\mathbf{X}_2$ appearing in the incomplete model. For example, consider the block triangular system given by

$$\mathbf{y}_{.1} - \mathbf{Y}_2\boldsymbol{\beta}_{21} - \mathbf{Y}_3\boldsymbol{\beta}_{31} - \mathbf{X}_1\boldsymbol{\gamma}_{11} = \mathbf{u}_{.1} \tag{25}$$

$$\mathbf{Y}_2\mathbf{B}_{22} + \mathbf{Y}_3\mathbf{B}_{23} + \mathbf{X}_2\boldsymbol{\Gamma}_{22} = \mathbf{U}_2 \tag{26}$$

$$\mathbf{Y}_3\mathbf{B}_{33} + \mathbf{X}_3\boldsymbol{\Gamma}_{33} = \mathbf{U}_3 \tag{27}$$

where the $\mathbf{Y}_3$ in (27) depends only on variables in $\mathbf{X}_3$ that do not appear in the incomplete system given by (25) and (26). It can easily be proved that when $\mathbf{Y}_3$ is misclassified as independent variables, the 2SLS of (25) yields consistent estimates of, for example,

(i) $\boldsymbol{\beta}_{21}$ if $\lim T^{-1}\mathbf{X}_1'\mathbf{X}_2 = 0$ and $\lim T^{-1}\mathbf{X}_2'\mathbf{X}_3 = 0$ and

(ii) $\boldsymbol{\beta}_{21}$ and of $\boldsymbol{\gamma}_{11}$ if $\lim T^{-1}\mathbf{X}_1'\mathbf{X}_3 = 0$ and $\lim T^{-1}\mathbf{X}_2'\mathbf{X}_3 = 0$.

But the orthogonality conditions like $\lim T^{-1}\mathbf{X}_i'\mathbf{X}_3 = 0$, $i = 1, 2$, cannot be verified for want of data on the independent variables in $\mathbf{X}_3$. That is why the true model (2) is assumed to contain only the independent variables $\mathbf{X}_1$ and $\mathbf{X}_2$ appearing in the incomplete model (4). Under these conditions, it is demonstrated that, if at all, only the parameters $\boldsymbol{\gamma}_{11}$ can be consistently estimated by the 2SLS. Furthermore, it is almost obvious that the conditions given in Theorem 1 are sufficient for such "partial consistency." However, Theorem 1 demonstrates that the "obviously sufficient" conditions are also necessary.

Another point of interest is when one or more of the equations of the incomplete model (4) have constant terms in them. In this case, in general, the orthogonality condition $\lim T^{-1}\mathbf{X}_1'\mathbf{X}_2 = 0$ does not hold. However, the constant terms can be eliminated by considering the variables measured from their means. This does not affect the conditions of Theorem 1 relating to the block triangularity of the model (2).

If now the orthogonality condition $\lim T^{-1}\mathbf{X}_1'\mathbf{X}_2 = 0$, when $\mathbf{X}_1$ and $\mathbf{X}_2$ are measured from their means, also holds, then all the components of $\boldsymbol{\gamma}_{11}$, except the one relating to the constant term, can be consistently estimated. The problem, however, gets complicated if some lagged dependent variables appear as explanatory variables in $\mathbf{X}_1$ and $\mathbf{X}_2$. In this event, though the sufficiency of some farfetched conditions can be demonstrated, obtaining conditions that are also necessary becomes virtually intractable.

ACKNOWLEDGMENT

We are grateful to Robert A. Pollak, Editor of the *International Economic Review* for suggesting the topic of discussion of this paper.

NOTES

1. See Dhrymes (1970, 176–177) for a thorough discussion of the statement. An exception, for example, is a recursive system (Dhrymes, 1970, 303–311) Identification in recursive and block recursive systems is discussed by Fisher (1966, 118–126).
2. The order of the parameter vectors $\boldsymbol{\beta}_{21}$, $\boldsymbol{\beta}_{31}$, and $\boldsymbol{\gamma}_{11}$ is understood by inference; for example, $\boldsymbol{\beta}_{21}$ is $m_1 \times 1$.
3. This implies that when $\mathbf{Y}_3$ is misclassified as independent, the degree of overidentification of (1) is at least equal to l. If there are k_2 independent variables elsewhere in the system, in addition to the k_1 in (1), then the needed order condition is given by $k_2 \geq m_1 + l$. The implications of the corresponding rank condition will be used while outlining the proof of the results of this exercise.
4. If there exist dependent variables in the system other than those in $\mathbf{y}_{.1}$, $\mathbf{Y}_2$, and $\mathbf{Y}_3$, they are not relevant for the purposes of 2SLS estimation.
5. The coefficients of $\mathbf{Y}_3$ in (4) and in (1) are in the notation of β's to emphasize the fact that variables in $\mathbf{Y}_3$ are indeed dependent variables. The lowercase letters signify vectors and the uppercase letters stand for matrices. The matrix $\mathbf{B}_{22}$ in (4) is nonsingular so that the incomplete model of (4) can mistakenly be treated as complete. Further, the $\mathbf{B}_{33}$ in (4) is also nonsingular.
6. The additional assumptions should not disturb the identifiability of equation (1).
7. For example, using only $\boldsymbol{\Sigma}_{23} = \mathbf{0}$ in (19)–(21), we have

$$\operatorname{plim} T^{-1}\mathbf{Y}_2'\mathbf{X}^* (\mathbf{X}^{*\prime}\mathbf{X}^*)^{-1}\mathbf{X}^{*\prime}\mathbf{u}_{.1} = \boldsymbol{\Pi}_{.2}'(\mathbf{M}\boldsymbol{\Pi}_{.3}, \mathbf{M}) \begin{bmatrix} \boldsymbol{\Pi}_{.3}'\mathbf{M}\boldsymbol{\Pi}_{.3} + \boldsymbol{\Sigma}_{33} & \boldsymbol{\Pi}_{.3}'\mathbf{M} \\ \mathbf{M}\boldsymbol{\Pi}_{.3} & \mathbf{M} \end{bmatrix}^{-1} \begin{bmatrix} \boldsymbol{\Sigma}_{3.}\boldsymbol{\beta}_{.1} \\ \mathbf{0} \end{bmatrix}$$

$$= \boldsymbol{\Pi}_{.2}'(\mathbf{0}, \mathbf{I}) \begin{bmatrix} \boldsymbol{\Sigma}_{3.}\boldsymbol{\beta}_{.1} \\ \mathbf{0} \end{bmatrix} = 0.$$

Similarly, $\operatorname{plim} T^{-1}\mathbf{Y}_2'\mathbf{X}^* (\mathbf{X}^{*\prime}\mathbf{X}^*)^{-1}\mathbf{X}^{*\prime}\mathbf{Y}_2 = \boldsymbol{\Pi}_{.2}'\mathbf{M}\boldsymbol{\Pi}_{.2}$, etc., so that the equation under consideration becomes

$$\begin{bmatrix} \boldsymbol{\Pi}_{.2}'\mathbf{M}\boldsymbol{\Pi}_{.2} & \boldsymbol{\Pi}_{.2}'\mathbf{M}\boldsymbol{\Pi}_{.3} & \boldsymbol{\Pi}_{.2}' \begin{bmatrix} \mathbf{M}_{11} \\ \mathbf{M}_{21} \end{bmatrix} \\ \boldsymbol{\Pi}_{.3}'\mathbf{M}\boldsymbol{\Pi}_{.2} & \boldsymbol{\Pi}_{.3}'\mathbf{M}\boldsymbol{\Pi}_{.3} & \boldsymbol{\Pi}_{.3}' \\ [\mathbf{M}_{11}, \mathbf{M}_{12}]\boldsymbol{\Pi}_{.2} & [\mathbf{M}_{11}, \mathbf{M}_{12}]\boldsymbol{\Pi}_{.3} & \mathbf{M}_{11} \end{bmatrix}; \begin{bmatrix} \operatorname{plim}(\hat{\boldsymbol{\beta}}_{21} - \boldsymbol{\beta}_{21}) \\ \operatorname{plim}(\hat{\boldsymbol{\beta}}_{31} - \boldsymbol{\beta}_{31}) \\ \operatorname{plim}(\hat{\boldsymbol{\gamma}}_{11} - \boldsymbol{\gamma}_{11}) \end{bmatrix} = \begin{bmatrix} \mathbf{0} \\ \boldsymbol{\sigma}_{31} - \boldsymbol{\Sigma}_{33}\boldsymbol{\beta}_{31} \\ \mathbf{0} \end{bmatrix}. \quad \text{(N1)}$$

Putting $\mathbf{M} = \begin{bmatrix} \mathbf{M}_{11} & \mathbf{M}_{12} \\ \mathbf{M}_{21} & \mathbf{M}_{22} \end{bmatrix} = \begin{bmatrix} \mathbf{I} & \mathbf{0} \\ \mathbf{0} & \mathbf{I} \end{bmatrix}$, $\boldsymbol{\Pi}_{.2} = \begin{bmatrix} \boldsymbol{\Pi}_{12} \\ \boldsymbol{\Pi}_{22} \end{bmatrix}$, and $\boldsymbol{\Pi}_{.3} = \begin{bmatrix} \boldsymbol{\Pi}_{13} \\ \boldsymbol{\Pi}_{23} \end{bmatrix}$ in (11) and premultiplying the third super row of the result by $\boldsymbol{\Pi}_{12}'$ and $\boldsymbol{\Pi}_{13}'$ and subtracting from its second and third super rows, respectively, yields the equation (22).

8. It is easy to prove that the rank of the $k_2 \times m_1$ matrix $\boldsymbol{\Pi}_{22}$ is equal to m_1 ($m_1 \leq k_2 - l$, see Note 4) a.e.; that $\mathbf{Y}_3$ should depend on at least l columns of $\mathbf{X}_2$ [otherwise, equation (1) is not identified] so that rank of $\boldsymbol{\Pi}_{23}$ is equal to l a.e. Though, in general, one can only

conclude that the rank of the product $\mathbf{\Pi}_{22}'\mathbf{\Pi}_{23}$ *does not exceed* min $\{m_1, l\}$, in the case under consideration, one can assert that rank of $\mathbf{\Pi}_{22}'\mathbf{\Pi}_{23} = \min\{m_1, l\}$. The statements of this footnote can be proved rigorously by using the methods developed in Mallela and Rao (1979; see especially the appendix therein).

9. $\mathbf{B}^{ij}$ denotes the (i, j)th super element of $\mathbf{B}^{-1}$, partitioned corresponding to that of $\mathbf{B}$.

REFERENCES

Dhrymes, P. J. (1970). *Econometrics: Statistical Foundations and Applications*, New York: Harper & Row.

Fisher, F. M. (1966). *The Identification Problem in Econometrics*, New York: McGraw-Hill.

Mallela, P. and A. S. Rao (1979). Necessary and sufficient conditions for inadmissibility of transformations in time, *Int. Econ. Rev. 20,* 157–167.

ERRATUM AND ADDENDUM TO VOLUME 1:

MODELS FOR THE ANALYSIS OF LABOR FORCE DYNAMICS

C. Flinn, University of Wisconsin and

J. J. Heckman, University of Chicago

Appendix A of our paper "Models For The Analysis of Labor Force Dynamics" (Flinn and Heckman, 1982) published in Volume 1 of *Advances in Econometrics* contains an important error which we correct in this erratum. The likelihood function and associated derivatives reported in that Appendix are correct only for a two state model ($N = 2$ in our notation) or for other restricted versions of a multistate model.[1] A completely corrected and revised Appendix A follows this note.

All of the expressions before equation (A9) in the Appendix are correct. Equation (A9) is the cumulative distribution function of the latent times t_{ij} (*i.e.* the cdf corresponding to the density (A1)). Equation (A10) is the density associated with the cdf given in (A9). However, except in the case $N = 2$, or in the case of a generalized birth process (see footnote 1) equation (A10) is not the required density of observed durations corresponding to i to j transitions for the mth spell.

Advances in Econometrics, Volume 2, pages 219–223

ISBN: 0-89232-183-0

In the general case ($N > 2$), the density of observed i to j exit times is obtained as the product of the probability of an i to j transition (P_{ij}, see equation (A3) in the Appendix) times the conditional density of exit time from i to j given that exit from i occurs in this fashion (see (A4) in the Appendix). Note that $P_{ij} = 1$ when $N = 2$ and that (A1) and (A4) are identical when $j = j'$.

Thus for $N > 2$, equation (A10) should be replaced by[2]

$$f_{i_m j_m}(t_{rm}) = h_{i_m j_m}(t_{rm})\exp\left\{-\int_0^{t_{rm}} \sum_{\substack{k=1 \\ k \neq i_m}}^{N} h_{i_m k}(u)du\right\}. \tag{A10)'$$

With this change equations (A11)–(A13) are correct. Note that the term in braces in (A11),

$$\prod_{\substack{k=1 \\ k \neq i_M}}^{N} [1 - F_{i_M k}(t_M)],$$

is just the probability that the Mth spell is not completed (see equation A6). This term is called the survivor function in the duration analysis literature.

For $N > 2$, the expressions after (A13) must be modified in an obvious way.[3] For notational convenience define the set

$$S_i = \{m \mid i_m = i\}$$

which indexes all spells that begin in i. Then in place of (A14) we write

$$\frac{\partial L_r(\beta, V)}{\partial \beta_{gij}} = \left\{\sum_{m \varepsilon S_i}\left[\left(\left.\frac{\partial f_{i_m k_m}}{\partial \beta_{gij}}\right|_{t_m}\right)\prod_{b \neq m} f_{i_b j_b}(t_b)\right]\right\}\prod_{\substack{h \neq i_M \\ h=1}}^{N} [1 - F_{i_M h}(t_M)]$$

$$+\left[\prod_{m=1}^{M-1} f_{i_m j_m}(t_m)\right]\left[-\left.\frac{\partial F_{i_M j}}{\partial \beta_{gij}}\right|_{t_M}\right]\left\{\prod_{\substack{h \neq i_m, j \\ h=1}}^{N} [1 - F_{i_m h}(t_M)]\right\}. \tag{A14)'$$

In place of (A15) should be written

$$\frac{\partial f_{i_m k_m}}{\partial \beta_{gij}} = \left[\left(\frac{\partial h_{i_m k_m}(t_m)}{\partial \beta_{gij}}\right) - h_{i_m k_m}(t_m)\int_0^{t_m} \frac{\partial h_{i_m j}(u)}{\partial \beta_{gij}} du\right] \tag{A15)'$$

$$\exp\left\{-\int_0^{t_m}\left[\sum_{\substack{k=1 \\ k \neq i_m}}^{N} h_{i_m k}(u)\right]du\right\}$$

for $m \varepsilon S_i$. Note that

$$\frac{\partial h_{i_m k_m}(u)}{\partial \beta_{gij}} = Z_g(u + \tau_m)h_{i_m k_m}(u) \quad \text{for } i_m = i \text{ and } k_m = j$$
$$= 0 \qquad \text{otherwise.}$$

Define $d_{i_m k_m} = 1$ if $i_m = i$ and $k_m = j$. $d_{i_m k_m} = 0$ otherwise. Then (A16) becomes

$$\frac{\partial f_{i_m k_m}}{\partial \beta_{gij}} = \left[Z_g(t_m + \tau_m)d_{i_m k_m} - \int_0^{t_m} Z_g(u + \tau_m)h_{i_m j}(u)du \right] \cdot f_{i_m k_m}(t_m) \qquad \text{(A16)}'$$

for $m \varepsilon S_i$ and (A17) is as reported in the Appendix except $i = i_M$ (not $i = i_m$).

Upon making a last round of substitutions and defining $d_{i_m} = 1$ if $i_m = i$, $d_{i_m} = 0$ otherwise, we conclude that (A18) should be replaced by

$$\frac{\partial L_r(\beta, V)}{\partial \beta_{gij}} = \Bigg(\Bigg\{ \sum_{\substack{m \varepsilon S_i \\ m<M}} \Bigg[Z_g(t_m + \tau_m)\mathrm{d}_{i_m k_m} - \int_0^{t_m} Z_g(u + \tau_m)h_{i_m j}(u)du \Bigg] \Bigg\} - d_{i_M} \int_0^{t_m} Z_g(u + \tau_M)\, h_{i_M j}(u)du \Bigg) \cdot L_r(\beta, V) \qquad \text{(A18)}'$$

for $m \varepsilon S_i$. Equations (A19) and (A20) are correct. For the sake of brevity, the required modification to (A21) is not given because in the corrected likelihood as in the original likelihood the second partials are approximated by the method of Anderson (as cited in the original Appendix). The complete corrected Appendix A follows this erratum.

Contrary to what we report in the Appendix, heterogeneity distributions other than the normal are available in our corrected program. The multistate-multiepisode model may also be fit with lognormal and general gamma heterogeneity.

The error in the likelihood for the case $N > 2$ for the non birth process model does not affect any of the empirical results reported in our paper except our test of the two versus three state model (Tables 6 and 7). Corrected versions of these Tables are labeled "Table 6" and "Table 7" in this erratum.

Table 6. Parameter Estimates for the Three State Unrestricted Model[1]

	From Employment To		*To Employment From*	
	Unemployment	*OLF*	*Unemployment*	*OLF*
Constant	−3.654	−6.509	− .800	−2.824
	(9.442)	(3.311)	(4.396)	(3.131)
Tenure/10	0.247	0.589	−1.454	1.338
	(.428)	(.302)	(1.795)	(.293)
$Tenure^2/100$	−0.200	−0.052	0.513	(0.193
	(.847)	(0.077)	(.970)	(.075)
MSP	−0.428	0.044	0.181	0.462
	(1.073)	(.053)	(.528)	(.197)
C_{ij}	1.149	1.503	− .316	−1.738
	(3.908)	(.822)	(1.477)	(.750)
£ = −760.83				

Note:
[1] Absolute Value of Asymptotic Normal Statistics in Parentheses.

Performing the likelihood ratio test to compare restricted and unrestricted models using the revised estimates, the value of the test statistic is 28.20 (twice log likelihood). The critical value of the $\chi^2(5)$ test statistic (for five restrictions) at a 5 percent significance level is 11.07. Thus, with the revised numbers, as with the numbers reported in our original paper, we reject the null hypothesis of equality of the parameters governing the

Table 7. Parameter Estimates for the Three State Restricted Model[1]

	From Employment to		*Nonemployment to Employment*
	Unemployment	*OLF*	
Constant	−3.544	−6.654	−1.012
	(9.872)	(3.337)	(5.918)
Tenure/10	0.156	0.639	−1.635
	(.270)	(.392)	(2.163)
$Tenure^2/100$	−0.180	−0.058	.684
	(.763)	(.097)	(1.293)
MSP	−0.480	0.010	.292
	(1.234)	(.012)	(.825)
C_{ij}	1.056	1.608	−0.313
	(3.718)	(.831)	(1.449)
£ = −774.93			

Note:
[1] Absolute Value of Asymptotic Normal Statistics in Parentheses

two nonemployment states. Thus "out of the labor force" and "unemployment" are not artificial distinctions for our sample of young men.

Copies of the corrected program (called CTM for Continuous Time Models) are available at cost from Professor V. Joseph Hotz, Economics Research Center, NORC, 6030 S. Ellis, Chicago, Ill. 60637.

ACKNOWLEDGMENT

We are indebted to Stephen R. Cosslett for bringing the error in Appendix A to our attention.

NOTES

1. The likelihood as written is correct for a generalized birth process. Thus if there are N states, all individuals start in 1 and can only leave 1 via 2, 2 via 3 and so forth until the final state N is achieved.
2. This term is sometimes called a subdensity. See Kalbfleisch and Prentice (1980, p. 167).
3. Note that in the Appendix and in this erratum we assume that the β vectors are not restricted across different i to j transitions. Our program allows the user to impose such restrictions.

REFERENCES

Flinn, C. J. and J. J. Heckman (1982). "Models for the Analysis of Labor Force Dynamics." In R. Basmann and G. Rhodes, Jr. (eds), *Advances in Econometrics,* Vol. 1, JAI Press, Greenwich, CT: pp. 35–95.

Kalbfleisch, J. D. and R. Prentice (1980). *The Statistical Analysis of Failure Time Data.* New York: Wiley.

THE LIKELIHOOD FUNCTION FOR THE MULTISTATE-MULTIEPISODE MODEL IN "MODELS FOR THE ANALYSIS OF LABOR FORCE DYNAMICS"

C. Flinn, University of Wisconsin and

J. J. Heckman, University of Chicago

In this paper we discuss general issues in the estimation of continuous time probability models and the formulation of multiepisode-multievent likelihoods. The results reported here correct and simplify results reported in Appendix A in our earlier paper (Flinn and Heckman, 1982). We do not explicitly discuss the initial conditions problem (but see our previous paper). For another treatment of multistate models, see Kalbfleisch and Prentice (1980, Chapter 7).

Advances in Econometrics, Volume 2, pages 225–231

ISBN: 0-89232-183-0

Let there be N states the individual can occupy at any moment of time. If the individual begins "life" in state i there are $N-1$ "latent times" with densities

$$f_{ij}(t_{ij}) = h_{ij}(t_{ij}) \exp\left[-\int_0^{t_{ij}} h_{ij}(u)du\right] \qquad (j = 1, \ldots, N; j \neq i) \quad \text{(A1)}$$

where $f_{ij}(\cdot)$ is the density function of exit times from state i into state j, and $h_{ij}(\cdot)$ is the associated hazard function. The joint density of the $N-1$ latent exit times is given by

$$\prod_{\substack{j=1 \\ j\neq i}}^{N} h_{ij}(t_{ij}) \exp\left[-\int_0^{t_{ij}} h_{ij}(u)du\right]. \quad \text{(A2)}$$

An individual exits from state i to state j' if the j' th first passage time is the smallest of the $N-1$ potential first passage times, i.e., if

$$t_{ij'} < t_{ij} \qquad (j = 1, \ldots, N; j \neq j'; j,j' \neq i).$$

Let the probability that the individual leaves state i and then directly enters state j' be denoted by $\boldsymbol{P}_{ij'}$. Then

$$\boldsymbol{P}_{ij'} = \int_0^\infty \left[\int_{t_{ij'}}^\infty \cdots \int_{t_{ij'}}^\infty \left\{\prod_{\substack{j=1 \\ j\neq i \\ j\neq j'}}^{N} h_{ij}(t_{ij}) \exp\left[-\int_0^{t_{ij}} h_{ij}(u)du\right]dt_{ij}\right\}\right.$$

$$\left. \times \left\{h_{ij'}(t_{ij'}) \exp\left[-\int_0^{t_{ij'}} h_{ij'}(u)du\right]\right\}\right]dt_{ij'}$$

$$= \int_0^\infty h_{ij'}(t_{ij'}) \exp\left\{-\int_0^{t_{ij'}} \left[\sum_{\substack{k=1 \\ k\neq i}}^{N} h_{ik}(u)\right]du\right\}dt_{ij'}. \quad \text{(A3)}$$

The conditional density of exit times from state i into state j' given that $t_{ij'} < t_{ij}$, $(\forall j\colon j \neq j'; j,j' \neq i)$ is

$$g(t_{ij'} \mid t_{ij'} < t_{ij})(\forall j\colon j \neq j'; j,j' \neq i) \quad \text{(A4)}$$

$$= \frac{h_{ij'}(t_{ij'}) \exp\left\{-\int_0^{t_{ij'}} \left[\sum_{\substack{k=1 \\ k\neq i}}^{N} h_{ik}(u)\right]du\right\}}{\boldsymbol{P}_{ij'}}.$$

It follows that the density of exit times from state i into all other states combined can be written

$$f_{i\cdot}(t_{i\cdot}) = \sum_{\substack{j'=1 \\ j' \neq i}}^{N} \boldsymbol{P}_{ij'} g(t_{ij'} | t_{ij'} < t_{ij})(\forall j: j \neq j'; j,j' \neq i)$$

$$= \left[\sum_{\substack{k=1 \\ k \neq i}}^{N} h_{ik}(t_{i\cdot})\right] \exp\left\{-\int_0^{t_{i\cdot}} \left[\sum_{\substack{k=1 \\ k \neq i}}^{N} h_{ik}(u)\right] du\right\}. \tag{A5}$$

The probability that the spell is not complete by time C is simply

$$\text{Prob}(T > C) = \int_C^{\infty} f_{i\cdot}(t)dt$$

$$= exp\left\{-\int_0^{C} \left[\sum_{\substack{k=1 \\ k \neq i}}^{N} h_{ik}(u)\right] du\right\}. \tag{A6}$$

This term enters the likelihood function for incomplete spells of at least C in length. In this manner all spells, not only completed ones, are used in the estimation of the parameters of the hazard function. This is not the case in regression analyses of durations in a state (or some transformation of duration) on exogenous variables, where only completed spells can be used in a straightforward fashion. (Obviously a nonlinear regression procedure can account for censoring).

We now describe in some detail the specific form of the likelihood function used in our analysis. Let $Z_{rm}(u + \tau_{rm})$ be a $K \times 1$ vector of explanatory variables of the rth individual in his mth spell at time $(u + \tau_{rm})$, where u is the duration of time spent in the current spell and τ_{rm} is the date in calendar time at which the individual has entered his mth spell. Included among the explanatory variables are functions of the spell duration variables. In particular, the form of $Z'_{rm}(u + \tau_{rm})$ is

$$[1\ Z_{1rm}(u + \tau_{rm}) \ldots Z_{(K-2)rm}(u + \tau_{rm})\ V_r].$$

The last element is an unobserved heterogeneity term, invariant over time for the individual, which is permitted to have a standard normal distribution, i.e.,

$$V_r \sim N(0,1)\ \forall r.$$

In our general program we also permit $V^* = e^V$ to be log normal or gamma distributed (with general gamma distribution). (See the CTM manual, Hotz, 1983).

Parameter vectors are indexed by transition. β_{ij} is $K \times 1$ vector of coefficients of explanatory variables in the hazard function. To be specific

$$\beta_{ij} = [\beta_{0ij}\, \beta_{1ij} \ldots \beta_{(K-2)ij}\, C_{ij}]. \tag{A7}$$

As discussed in our paper (Flinn and Heckman, 1982) we impose a one factor specification, so that C_{ij} is the factor loading associated with the i to j transition. The usual normalizations required in factor analysis in discrete data models are imposed. (See Heckman, 1981, pp. 167–174).

We write the hazard function for the mth spell and rth individual as

$$\begin{aligned} h_{i_m j_m}(t_{rm}) &= \exp\left[Z'_{rm}(t_{rm} + \tau_{rm})\beta_{i_m j_m} \right] \\ &= \frac{f_{i_m j_m}(t_{rm})}{1 - F_{i_m j_m}(t_{rm})} \end{aligned} \tag{A8}$$

where $f_{i_m j_m}$ is the *cdf* associated with (A1).

The probability that an observation for the mth spell leaves state i_m via state j_m is $P_{i_m j_m}$ (see equation A3). The conditional density of exit time from state i_m into state j_m is given by expression (A4). The density of a duration in the mth spell that begins in i_m and terminates in state j_m is the product of these two terms and is written as

$$g_{i_m j_m}(t_{rm}) = h_{i_m j_m}(t_{rm}) \exp\left\{ -\int_0^{t_{rm}} \sum_{\substack{k=1 \\ k \neq i_m}}^{N} h_{i_m k}(u)du \right\}. \tag{A9}$$

Densities of this type are called subdensities in the duration analysis literature (see Kalbfleisch and Prentice, 1980, p. 167). It is notationally convenient to write the exp term in (A9) as

$$S_{i_m}(t_{rm}) = \exp\left\{ -\int_0^{t_{rm}} \sum_{\substack{k=1 \\ k \neq i_m}}^{N} h_{i_m k}(u)du \right\} \tag{A10}$$

so

$$g_{i_m j_m}(t_{rm}) = h_{i_m j_m} S_{i_m}(t_{rm}).$$

Note that from (A6) the probability that the mth spell lasts more than t_{rm} is

$$P(T_{rm} > t_{rm}) = S_{i_m}(t_{rm}) \tag{A11}$$

so S has a substantive probabilistic interpretation. It is called the survivor function in the duration analysis literature.

Consider an individual's contribution to the likelihood function (suppressing the individual's subscript for notational convenience)

$$L(\beta, V) = \left[\prod_{i=1}^{M-1} g_{i_m j_m}(t_m) \right] S_{i_M}(t_M) \tag{A12}$$

where the Mth (and final) censored spell is assumed to last longer than t_M.

Treating V as a random effect, the integrated likelihood is

$$L(\beta) = \int_{-\infty}^{\infty} L(\beta, V) du(V) \tag{A13}$$

where $du(V)$ is the density of V. Now define

$$£(\beta) = \ell n[\overline{L}(\beta)].$$

Note that

$$\frac{\partial £(\beta)}{\partial \beta_{gij}} = \frac{1}{\overline{L}(\beta)} \frac{\partial \overline{L}(\beta)}{\partial \beta_{gij}}$$

$$= \frac{1}{\overline{L}(\beta)} \int_{-\infty}^{\infty} \frac{\partial \overline{L}(\beta, V)}{\partial \beta_{gij}} du(V) \tag{A14}$$

where g denotes the gth element of the β vector for i to j transitions. To simplify the analysis we assume a common β for each i to j transition independent of the serial order of the spell although this is not required in the general CTM program (Hotz, 1983). To further simplify the notation define the set

$$J_i = \{m \mid i_m = i\}$$

which consists of the index set of spells that begin in state i. Then

$$\frac{\partial L(\beta, V)}{\partial \beta_{gij}} = \left\{ \sum_{m \varepsilon J_i} \left[\left(\frac{\partial g_{i_m k_m}}{\partial \beta_{gij}} \bigg|_{t_m} \right) \prod_{b \neq m} g_{i_b j_b} \right] \right\} S_{i_M}(t_m)$$
$$+ \left[\prod_{m=1}^{M-1} g_{i_m j_m}(t_m) \right] \frac{\partial S_{i_M}}{\partial \beta_{gij}}. \tag{A15}$$

Note that

$$\frac{\partial S_{i_M}(t_M)}{\partial \beta_{gij}} = \left(- \int_0^{t_M} \frac{\partial h_{i_M j}(u)}{\partial \beta_{gij}} du \right) S_{i_M}(t_M) \text{ for } i_M = i$$
$$= 0 \qquad \text{otherwise} \tag{A16}$$

and

$$\frac{\partial g_{i_m k_m}}{\partial \beta_{gij}} = \left[\frac{\partial h_{i_m k_m}}{\partial \beta_{gij}} - h_{i_m k_m}(t_m) \int_0^{t_m} \frac{\partial h_{i_m j}(u)}{\partial \beta_{gij}} \, du \right] S_{i_m}(t_m). \tag{A17}$$

Note further using (A8)

$$\begin{aligned} \frac{\partial h_{i_m k_m}(u)}{\partial \beta_{gij}} &= Z_g(t_m + \tau_m) h_{i_m j_m}(u) \quad \text{for } i_m = i \text{ and } j_m = j \\ &= 0 \quad \text{otherwise.} \end{aligned} \tag{A18}$$

Defining $d_{i_m k_m} = 1$ if $i_m = i$ and $k_m = j$; $d_{i_m k_m} = 0$ otherwise, and $d_{i_m} = 1$ if $i_m = i$, $d_{i_m} = 0$ otherwise, we use (A16), (A17) and (A18) to write (A15) as

$$\begin{aligned} \frac{\partial L(\beta, V)}{\partial \beta_{gij}} = \Bigg(\Bigg\{ & \sum_{\substack{m \in J_i \\ m < M}} \Bigg[Z_g(t_m + \tau_m) d_{i_m k_m} \\ & - \int_0^{t_m} Z_g(u + \tau_m) h_{i_m j}(u) du \Bigg] \\ & - d_{i_M} \int_0^{t_M} Z_g(u + \tau_m) h_{i_m j}(u) du \Bigg\} L(\beta, V) \Bigg). \end{aligned} \tag{A19}$$

The computation of the second partials is uninformative and so is not presented here. In the likelihood function, we employ the well known approximation due to T. W. Anderson (1959) based on the summed outer product of the vector of first partials. (This approximation is often called BHHH in econometrics but a better name would be TWA.)

Copies of the computer program which enables the user to impose cross transition restrictions and select among alternative heterogeneity specifications and which exploits the computational simplifications possible in many models are available from V. Joseph Hotz, Economics Research Center, NORC, 6030 S. Ellis, Chicago, ILL. 60637.

REFERENCES

Anderson, T. W. (1959). "Some Scaling Models and Estimation Procedures in the Latent Class Model" in U. Grenander (ed.), *Probability and Statistics*, Uppsala.

Flinn, C. and J. Heckman. (1982). "Models for the Analysis of Labor Force Dynamics." In R. Basmann and G. Rhodes (eds.), *Advances in Econometrics*, Volume 1, JAI Press, Greenwich, CT: pp. 35–95.

Heckman, J. J. (1981). "Statistical Models for Discrete Panel Data." In C. Manski and D. McFadden (eds.), *Structural Analysis of Discrete Data with Econometric Applications*, Cambridge, Mass.: MIT Press.

Hotz, V. Joseph (1983). *Continuous Time Models (CTM): A Manual*, GSIA, Pittsburgh, Pennsylvania: Carnegie-Mellon.
Kalbfleisch, J. and R. Prentice (1980). *The Statistical Analysis of Failure Time Data*, New York: Wiley.

ACKNOWLEDGMENT

This research was supported by NSF Grant SES-8107963 and NIH Grant NIH-1-RO1-HD16846-01.